F
M
T

D0620826

MHCC WITHDRAWN

MHCC WITHDRAWN

WEYERHAEUSER ENVIRONMENTAL BOOKS

William Cronon, Editor

Weyerhaeuser Environmental Books explore human relationships with natural environments in all their variety and complexity. They seek to cast new light on the ways that natural systems affect human communities, the ways that people affect the environments of which they are a part, and the ways that different cultural conceptions of nature profoundly shape our sense of the world around us.

GOLD HILL

THE NATURE *of* GOLD

An Environmental History of

the Klondike Gold Rush

KATHRYN MORSE

Foreword by William Cronon

UNIVERSITY OF WASHINGTON PRESS

Seattle and London

For M & D

The Nature of Gold is published with the assistance of a grant
from the Weyerhaeuser Environmental Books Endowment,
established by the Weyerhaeuser Company Foundation,
members of the Weyerhaeuser family,
and Janet and John Creighton.

Copyright © 2003 by the University of Washington Press
Printed in the United States of America
Designed by Pamela Canell
10 09 08 07 06 05 04 03   6 5 4 3 2 1

All rights reserved. No part of this publication may be reproduced or transmitted
in any form or by any means, electronic or mechanical, including photocopy,
recording, or any information storage or retrieval system,
without permission in writing from the publisher.

University of Washington Press
PO Box 50096, Seattle, WA 98145
www.washington.edu/uwpress

Library of Congress Cataloging-in-Publication Data
can be found at the back of the book.

The paper used in this publication is acid-free and recycled from 10 percent
post-consumer and at least 50 percent pre-consumer waste. It meets the
minimum requirements of American National Standard for Information
Sciences—Permanence of Paper for Printed Library Materials,
ANSI Z39.48–1984. ♾ ♲

CONTENTS

MAPS

FOREWORD: ALL THAT GLITTERS

William Cronon

THE GREAT GOLD RUSHES of the nineteenth century are certainly among the most dramatic episodes of American western history. Their story typically begins with John Marshall's finding of a nugget in John Sutter's millrace near Sacramento, California, on January 24, 1848. Although Sutter tried desperately to prevent word of the discovery from leaking out, the news spread rapidly to San Francisco and proved so electrifying that an astonishing portion of the male population headed for the hills. In the harbor, sailors decided almost instantly to trade their maritime work for mining, with the result that abandoned, rotting ships would clog the city's wharves for years to come. When the news finally reached the East Coast a few months later, the phenomenon repeated itself constantly: with remarkable speed, an amazing number of people abandoned their former jobs and homes to head west in search of fortune. Prospectors fanned out across the Sierra Nevada, intent on striking it rich by finding a telltale streak of yellow in the gray gravel of a river bed, or perhaps even by locating the fabled mother lode itself. Camps and towns sprang up almost overnight, launching the cycles of boom and bust that would so characterize the mining West for the rest of the century and beyond.

This is the stuff of which legends are made, and western history has been marked by romantic narratives of gold and glory ever since. What happened in California in 1848–49 would happen at places whose names are famous today mainly because of the "rushes" that once swept over them: Pike's Peak, the Comstock, Cripple Creek, Leadville, Tombstone, and—the final chapter that closes out the nineteenth-century story with the most flamboyant episode of all—the Klondike. There, George Washington Carmack found gold in the Klondike River in 1896, prompting tens of thousands of would-be prospectors from all across the United States and Canada to race into the wilds of the Yukon, woefully unprepared for one of the most hostile environments one could ever imagine for such a migration. We know their stories today not just because their hardships were so severe, but because their tales were told by writers skilled enough to leave a permanent literary mark on our collective consciousness: Rex Beach, Robert Service, and Jack London. Although it should by rights be more a Canadian story than an American one—the Klondike is, after all, in Yukon Territory—the movement of U.S. citizens into the Canadian Far North was so enormous that history books usually commit a temporary act of narrative imperialism by annexing the Yukon to the United States just long enough to tell this story.

These gold rushes are so familiar that it's easy to take them for granted. On the one hand, they can seem like colorful happenings from a long-ago time when gullible people proved surprisingly susceptible to dreams that in most cases never came true. From such a perspective, they look simultaneously quaint and exotic. On the other hand, the motives that led people to dash off in search of easy wealth can seem so transparently obvious that they don't require much thought or analysis. Who *wouldn't* head off to the gold fields if there was a reasonable chance to become a millionaire and permanently change one's life by doing so? What could be more natural?

The trouble with both such reactions is their either/or quality, discouraging us from seeing that the most valuable historical lessons come when we juxtapose these perspectives and hold them in our minds simultaneously. Only then can we see both how truly strange the mining gold rushes were, and also how much they tell us about the cultural values and political-economic institutions that made them possible—values and institutions that are still very much a part of our own day-to-day lives. The challenge is to experience both the weirdness and ordinariness of a gold rush at the same time.

The special virtue of Kathryn Morse's *The Nature of Gold* is that it meets this challenge head-on, thereby yielding rich insights not just into the Klondike Gold Rush, but into the history of much larger ideas about wealth and risk and opportunity, to say nothing of the human place in nature. Morse's chief goal is to explore the different contexts—historical, economic, cultural, natural—that made a nineteenth-century gold rush possible. Her starting point is the assumption that the desire for gold is not quite so self-evident as our histories and myths would tempt us to believe. Sure, gold has certain attractive features that set it apart from other elements of the periodic table. It is the most malleable and ductile of metals, capable of being beaten into virtually any shape or form that the human imagination might care to impose on it. It combines with so few other elements that it can often be found in relatively pure form. Because it does not oxidize or react with other gases in the atmosphere, it displays none of the rust or tarnish that bedevil other metals. And then there is that rich, seductive color. Surely the human attraction for this magical stuff was ordained by nature and maybe even hard-wired into our very genes?

Perhaps. But Kathy Morse wants us to remember that even a material like gold, whose appeal to human beings can seem so natural, always exists within a web of cultural relationships that change over time to reflect the historical epoch in which they occur. She therefore asks us to look at the Klondike Gold Rush through a series of different lenses that quite drastically change our understanding of what those miners were doing up there in the Far North at the very end of the nineteenth century. She reminds us, for instance, that the 1890s were arguably the most volatile decade in American history for post–Civil War debates about a contracting money supply. Republicans, Democrats, and Populists were vehement in their claims about gold vs. silver as the proper foundation for the dollar, and the Klondike occurred just as silver was losing out as an alternative to gold. Despite William Jennings Bryan's eloquence in declaring in 1896—the year of George Washington Carmack's discovery on the Klondike—that "you shall not crucify mankind upon a cross of gold," it was William McKinley who won the White House that fall. The market for gold had never been better, providing all the more incentive for those who thought they might follow in Carmack's footsteps.

But monetary policy is only one of the contexts in which Morse places this gold rush. Another is the complex network of transport and mercantile relationships that carried the miners north and supplied them once they arrived. Here we learn that what looks like the most remote and forlorn of all mining frontiers was in fact a highly urban outpost. Its supply lines stretched halfway across the continent from Dawson City, up and down the Yukon River or across the Chilkoot Pass, to the entrepôt city of Seattle, which experienced an explosion of growth as the miners arrived to prepare for their journey. Virtually everything that made the Klondike possible—food, clothing, shelter, tools, horses, mining supplies—passed through that city or some other. And quite apart from these supply lines, without a metropolitan economy to provide a market for the district's gold production the rush would never have occurred in the first place. The magical appeal of gold could not by itself have prompted such an enterprise. Although rarely given much of a role in the tales of Jack London or the poems of Robert Service, the hard-nosed decisions of merchants and corporations were at least as important as the romantic siren song of gold itself.

Finally, since Kathy Morse is first and foremost an environmental historian, there is the all-encompassing context of the natural systems in which the Klondike Gold Rush took place. Here she offers a fine-grained analysis of the many ways in which prospectors and miners came to know nature through labor and through direct personal experience: the extreme climate that made travel and work so hazardous; the permafrost that created unique challenges and dangers in underground tunnels; the scarce water supplies that made it so difficult to process gold-bearing gravel; the draught animals that endured such hardships on the Chilkoot and Dyea trails; the native vegetation and wildlife that sustained massive disruption with the influx of human immigrants; and so on and on. Morse demonstrates the dramatic environmental damage created by the gold rush, but she also helps us understand the very real accommodations that miners had to make if they hoped to survive in these far northern landscapes. The result is a much more nuanced interpretation of the environmental and human impacts that accompanied the gold rush.

Why should anyone wish to read about the Klondike Gold Rush more than a century after its heyday has passed? For one thing, it remains among the most compelling tales in all of North American frontier history. Kathy Morse is a superb storyteller with a wry sense of humor, a flair for the quirky detail and the revealing anecdote, and a keen appreciation for the tragicomic underside of this famous event. More importantly, her book is a powerful reminder of the immense human capacity to alter the natural systems of which we are part. That capacity derives in equal measure from individual human dreams and from the collective systems that embody those dreams in our material lives.

Tens of thousands of people made the long trek up the Chilkoot Trail. They did so for personal reasons unique to themselves, and this gives their individual stories a poignant, heroic, tragic edge. But they did so as well because of a national currency that was backed by one metal and not another, transport networks that could move them and their gear as never before, industrial technologies that gave them the capacity to process immense volumes of frozen gravel . . . and, not least, values that taught them to see nature as the raw material for extractive wealth, waiting to be seized by those with the vision and strength of will to make it their own. Wealth beyond the dreams of avarice: such, we often seem to think, is the glittering nature of gold. The Klondike shows what a potent force this way of understanding the wealth of nature can be not just for human beings, but for the environments we view through this peculiar lens. Only time will tell what this golden vision may mean for earth's future—and our own.

ACKNOWLEDGMENTS

THIS BOOK BEGAN as a doctoral dissertation at the University of Washington, directed by Richard White. Richard read and commented on every draft with extraordinary energy and care, and those familiar with Richard's work in *The Organic Machine, Land Use, Environment, and Social Change* and other books will recognize the ways in which his ideas shape my interpretations of the history of gold mining in Alaska and the Yukon. Although Richard may not recognize the final product, and bears no responsibility for its flaws, his guidance made it possible. I could not have gotten a better start as an historian, a teacher, or a writer, and I am grateful to him for that. I am grateful as well to the University of Washington Department of History for supporting my work during graduate school, and for financial assistance which included the John Calhoun Smith Memorial Scholarship, a three-year teaching assistantship, a Rondeau Evans Travel Fellowship, the John Calhoun Smith Dissertation Fellowship, the University Dissertation Fellowship, several quarters of pre-doctoral lectureships, and several more quarters of funding from the Center for the Study of the Pacific Northwest. John Findlay was instrumental in shepherding my way through graduate school. I thank him for his support and for his unswerving devotion to excellence in the careful crafting of historical arguments.

In the fall of 1995 I was fortunate to do archival research in the Yukon Territory and Alaska. Mac Swackhammer at the Dawson City Museum allowed me free access to rich materials in the museum archive, unlimited reign over his xerox machine, and even kindly lent me his truck for up-close exploration of the Klondike mining sites. The staffs of the Yukon Archive in Whitehorse and the Manuscripts and Archives Division of the University of Alaska, Fairbanks, library provided invaluable assistance in finding sources, making xeroxes, and shipping materials to me in Seattle. Prof. Terrence Cole and the staff of the University of Alaska, Fairbanks, Department of History graciously helped with the logistics of life in Fairbanks.

Despite the wealth of historical materials in the Yukon and Alaska, I could not have completed this book without the University of Washington libraries, in particular the Manuscripts, Special Collections, and University Archives Division. Staff members there, over the years, have patiently put up with countless requests and questions. I thank Karyl Winn, Richard Engeman, Carla Rickerson, and others for their kind tolerance and assistance. Kris Kinsey provided invaluable help with the photograph collection, which not only enriches this book, but is an unparalleled resource for research on Alaska and the Yukon. No small amount of thanks is due, as well, to the men and women whose diaries and letters, carefully collected and preserved in these archives, opened the world of the gold rush to me. Historical research and writing are solitary pursuits, but for much of the time devoted to this work, I was in the company of brave and funny people who spoke to me through their writings and kept me laughing. I'm sure Nora Crane, Hunter Fitzhugh, Bill Ballou, Mac McMichael, Lynn Smith, Asahel Curtis, John Callbreath, Jonas Houck, and James McCrae never suspected that their letters and journals would become fodder for a book such as this one. I could not have asked for finer companions, and I hope that I have served their memories well.

Since I arrived in 1997, the Middlebury College Department of History and the Program in Environmental Studies have provided not only new intellectual homes, but also ongoing support for the completion of this book. Both the Abernethy Lecture Series at Starr Library and the Environmental Studies Program Howard E. Woodin Colloquium provided opportunities to work through the ideas in this book with the help of enthusiastic colleagues and students. I am fortunate to have landed amongst so many fine scholars and teachers for whom the writing of books remains the best and highest of human endeavors.

At the University of Washington Press, Julidta Tarver has exhibited patience, wisdom, and enthusiasm far beyond the editor's call of duty. I am grateful for all of that, and for her keen eye for words and images. Bill Cronon has championed my journey through academic life since the moment I walked into his undergraduate classroom in 1986. His editorial guidance in the writing of this book is only the latest example of that support. Bill's own work, particularly *Nature's Metropolis* and his 1992 essay "Kennecott Journey," literally defined the paths that led to my interest in the environmental history of gold mining in Alaska and the Yukon. That I have found my own path through the writing of *The Nature of Gold* is in great part due to Bill's thoughtful advice.

Like all books, this one got written both despite and because of the small and not-so-small distractions of daily life, which for me included my first few years as a professor at Middlebury College, and my first few years building a life in rural Vermont. Middlebury College made this book possible through its generous support of faculty research and writing, and by funding some of the maps and images. My thanks go to all the many friends and colleagues who helped with both the writing and the distractions. Around the country, these included my brother Peter Morse and sister-in-law Cris Morse, Clyde A. Milner II, Carol O'Connor, Helen Bronk, Lori Sherman, Marcie Sidman, Brian Norris, Maggie Miller, Bonnie Christensen, Robert Self, Matt Klingle, Linda Nash, Ellen Stroud, Annie Gilbert Coleman, Cristal Weber, Mary Cunningham, Lisa Maki, and Mary Sullivan. Closer to home in Vermont, I am grateful to my colleagues in History and Environmental Studies, and to Lisa Landino, Rebecca Kneale Gould, Holly Allen, Michael Newbury, Jan Albers, Paul Monod, all of the Amigos, and all of the Doughboys, Doughwomen, and Doughkids. Thanks as well to the exemplary women of Ultimate Harmony. My dear and extraordinary friends Amy Briggs, Daniel Scharstein, and Anna Briggs Scharstein welcomed me into their family and in so many ways made it both possible and joyful for me to complete this work. While Daniel kept me singing, Amy commented on drafts and provided endless encouragement. Together they showed me that if you get up every morning and put your shoes on, your time will come. Anna shows me every day that her parents were right.

This book is for my parents, Deanne and Stephen Morse, with thanks for their love and faith, not to mention their encouragement, humor, grace, and astounding generosity. They supported the research and writing of this book in countless ways. Although a book seems an inadequate token of thanks, my parents always gave me books, even before I developed the expensive habit of asking for them. Sometime around 1974 they gave me Laura Ingalls Wilder's *Little House in the Big Woods*, which in all likelihood began the journey which made me a western and environmental historian. I offer a book in return, with gratitude for the journey.

K.M.

March 2003

THE NATURE *of* GOLD

INTRODUCTION

On the Chilkoot

C hances are good that even if you picked up this book knowing absolutely nothing about the Klondike gold rush, you have probably seen the photographs before. They are the most famous images that this gold rush produced. They show, from one angle or another, up close or from a distance, a long, apparently endless line of determined gold seekers, burdened with packs, heads cast downward, marching lockstep in single file up a precipitous snow-covered slope to the summit of the Chilkoot Pass, in southeast Alaska.

The Chilkoot photographs captured in a stark black-and-white moment a dramatic story of heartbreaking physical and emotional effort. Reproduced hundreds of times in newspapers, magazines, films, and histories since 1897 and 1898, the Chilkoot images have not lost their power to evoke a visceral sense of awe and historical pride. In 1997, for the Klondike gold rush centennial, the state of Alaska chose this image for its new automobile license plates to express the very core of Alaskan identity. In another automobile-related connection, the Nissan Corporation, in advertising its 2002 "Chilkoot Edition" Pathfinder sports utility vehicle, described the mountain trail for which the car was named as "the ultimate test of physical endurance and human will."[1]

The late-nineteenth-century gold seekers who actually crossed the Chilkoot Trail would have agreed. Unaccustomed as they were to the grueling physical labor necessary to cross the pass, they found the Chilkoot Trail almost indescribable in its intensity. In diaries and letters home, men and women struggled for the words to convey the physical and mental experience of hauling their bodies and their heavy packs and sleds over the coastal mountains to the headwaters of the Yukon River. James Hamil wrote home to Iowa from the Chilkoot in October 1897:

> It would be an utter impossibility for me to attempt to describe the hardships one must endure on this trail[;] it is about 30 miles long and every lb. of Grub or any thing to be taken over this trail must be carried on ones back. . . . To go over this trail [one] must wade [a] stream running at the rate of 10 miles per hour and ice cold that runs out from the snow and over Glaciers. . . . One must climb high peaks over jagged rocks down through deep canyons and over mountains of ice which never disappear. So the summit of Chillicoth mountains is 4,500 above sea level and one mile of the climb to the top is almost perpendicular and a portion of this one must crawl on his hands and knees.[2]

Even in the face of such challenges, however, the adrenaline flowed. As Herman Ferree wrote from the Chilkoot summit in 1898, "This is the most excitement the world ever knew."[3]

In 1897 and 1898, thousands of gold rushers, filled with hopes for sudden wealth, traveled from the west coast of the United States and Canada over the Chilkoot Pass to the confluence of the Klondike and Yukon Rivers where, in 1896, a small group of prospectors had happened upon a stunningly rich pocket of gold. Although most western mining by the 1890s was heavily industrialized, dependent on capital investments in machinery and processing plants, mining in the broad basin carved by the Yukon River remained surface, streamside, placer mining. A miner needed very little initial wealth to seek and mine placer gold. With a few hand tools and a willingness to labor in the earth, gold could be his. Spurred by this golden promise, some rushers traveled by steamer from Seattle, San Francisco, or Vancouver, British Columbia, to St. Michael at the mouth of the Yukon, and then upriver by sternwheeler to Dawson City, the town that sprang up at the mouth of the Klondike. Others steamed up the protected coastal corridor of the Inside Passage to the Lynn Canal, and disembarked at the foot of the two mountain passes, the White Pass and the Chilkoot Pass. Those landing at Skagway, Alaska, chose the Skagway or White Pass Trail, a longer, muddier, somewhat flatter route to the lower-elevation White Pass. Those

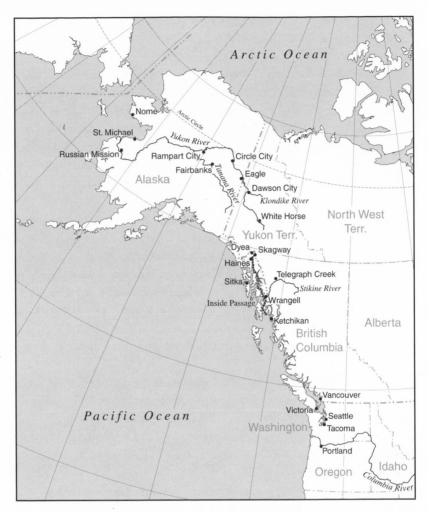

MAP 1. Geography of the Alaska-Yukon gold rush

landing at nearby Dyea headed up the Dyea or Chilkoot Trail, the shorter of the two trails at 28 miles, which ended in the truly precipitous summit climb captured in the Chilkoot images. Well above tree line, the steep icy slopes of the Chilkoot led to a wind- and snow-swept summit, higher than the White Pass and, due to weather and avalanches, far more treacherous. From both summits, gold seekers descended with their thousands of pounds of supplies to the lakes which formed the headwaters of the Yukon River, and headed downstream toward Dawson City and the promise of gold scattered in the small creeks that ran down gulches to join the Klondike River (maps 2, 4, 5, and 6).

The fear and excitement of these journeys overwhelmed the gold seekers with exhaustion and wonder. In the days and weeks they spent on the Chilkoot and White Pass Trails, they experienced things they had never imagined, and recorded them with excitement, awe, surprise, and dread. They saw men and animals hauling every imaginable load, from boats and canoes to iron stoves, raw lumber, wire cables, and iron rails for narrow-gauge railroads. They saw pack animals, dogs, and mules, cruelly beaten and starving, and they walked the White Pass Trail on the rotting carcasses of dead horses. They saw women dressed in pants and bloomers; they saw men immobilized by exhaustion, despair, and grief.[4] They saw human beings dead and dying from accidents, meningitis, and from suffocation in the tragic Chilkoot avalanche of April 1898. They saw women headed home, their husbands dead on the trail. They saw huge caches of supplies buried at the summit in thirty feet of snow. And their bodies suffered. They endured the burning pain of snow blindness, as well as sore muscles, bruised legs, and freezing hands and feet. They spent days in sweat-soaked clothing, chilled by blizzard winds.

More than anything else, however, gold seekers on the mountain trails saw crowds, masses of human beings, all of them pushing, pulling, and hauling themselves and their burdens in a desperate rush to move through snow, ice, and shoe-sucking, horse-drowning mud. "I can see down the canyon for five miles," Herman Ferree wrote from the Chilkoot summit, "and every morning it is actually black with people."[5] Mac McMichael wrote of the climbers as "a big black snake crawling up the hill." "They are so close that when a man lifts his foot another puts his in the same place."[6] The "motley throng" swarmed so tightly below the Chilkoot summit that they transformed the trail into what became known as the golden staircase, which McMichael described as "nitches [sic] cut into the hard snow which makes it about like up a flight of stairs 1,600 feet high and just about as steep." A few days later he wrote of the crowded staircase, "I had to wait twenty minutes to get into line and then about forty-five or fifty more to get up the 1600 feet." At the top, he wrote, "The jam of men, sleds, dogs, etc. was awful and the snow so thick we could scarcely see."[7]

It was this jam of people, this swarm of determined humanity, unified in its dogged quest for gold, that the Chilkoot photographs captured for posterity and transformed into the icon of the Klondike, or Alaska-Yukon, gold rush, and of Alaska as a whole. An image of a lone miner, after all, would convey a different power. This was a mass rush, a collective journey toward a shared destination, and as such it suggests stories not about individual miners' desires and dreams, but about the whole nation's—indeed the world's—shared dreams of success, wealth, and liberation through gold. In the Chilkoot images are seen any number of possible stories: mass madness for gold; grim, collective effort against insurmountable obstacles; a journey into savage or primitive nature; an escape from modern civilization; the battle of humankind against nature; a profound humility in the face of nature's scale and power; a journey through hope or defeat, promise or betrayal, human strength or human folly.

Why were they there? All of the possible tales start from the same point: gold. They were there because gold had great value and meaning. They were there because gold's value could be transformed into so many other valuable things: food, clothing, shelter, farms, homes, and businesses. They were there because gold was capital. Its value could be turned into more value as it was put to work to create even more wealth. Beyond value and capital, however, gold, particularly in the United States in the 1890s, sat at the center of a political and economic maelstrom, a contest over the nation's social and economic future. These particular debates and meanings intertwined with human beings' long history of valuing, worshipping, and mining gold to grant Yukon and Alaska gold a brief but powerful place in that longer history.

Gold held great promise for all Americans in the 1890s, but those promises spoke most directly to the thousands who risked the Chilkoot, who set out to press the natural world to fulfill that promise in their individual lives. Why and how did gold hold such value and promise? The question of why human beings value gold or any other part of the earth is crucial to understanding their connections to nature. What we choose to value in the earth shapes what we do with the earth, what we take from it to sustain ourselves, and what we leave behind. What we choose to value in the earth has consequences, both for the physical environment and for us as material and social beings. Gold's great economic and cultural value in the 1890s is just a starting point, therefore, for understanding the images of gold miners trudging up the Chilkoot Pass. Gold's value started them on their journeys to the icy, avalanche-prone slopes near the summit. As those journeys unfolded over the passes, down the Yukon to the gold creeks, through the labor of mining and the struggle to feed and shelter and supply themselves, they revealed the many human connections to nature forged as a result of gold's value.

Value, after all, can be an intangible, cultural, human creation. It takes concrete, material form only when human beings act on it, when they turn to the earth with their hands and their bodies and use those bodies to put value in motion. The miners on the Chilkoot Pass put gold's value in motion in a real, physical, compelling way. They risked their safety on Alaska trails and on the Yukon River in order to reach the gold creeks flowing into the Klondike River. On those journeys, their physical efforts to move their bodies and supplies brought intense connections with snow, ice, mud, and water. Along the gold creeks, grueling labor brought new contact with gravel, muck, permafrost, water, wood, smoke, and fire. Hunting and fishing ventures connected miners to the salmon, moose, and caribou they harvested for their dinner tables. These labors created direct, tangible, visible ties to the earth, to animals, trees, soils, creeks, and mountains, to local places and ecosystems, and to the burnished yellow dust and nuggets of gold itself. Through all of those connections to nature, miners transformed both the landscape of the gold creeks and the lives and livelihoods of Alaska and Yukon Native peoples. Through their labor they made Alaska and the Yukon part of the modern, industrial world, with very real consequences for nature and for human beings.

The miners who risked the Chilkoot forged connections to nature far beyond the pass itself, and beyond the creeks which held the gold. Gold's value, while powerful, was not enough alone to transport crowds of miners thousands of miles over the Chilkoot to the Klondike and Alaska. To make the journey, to mine gold, and to survive northern winters, gold miners needed railroads, steamships, and industrial cities, as well as plenty of other human help. Gold seekers on the Chilkoot hired Native Alaskan and Native Yukon packers to haul their supplies up the trail. Aboard sternwheel steamships on the Yukon, other gold rushers consumed not only the cordwood which fueled the boats, but the labor of the woodcutters, deckhands, and pilots who kept the boats running. And all gold seekers, no matter how they got to Alaska and the Yukon, ate industrially processed, mass-produced food shipped north from distant farms and cities. Their production of gold forged connections to nature close at hand, but their broad consumption of food, clothing, and supplies and of the labor and knowledge of other workers forged connections—often through other human beings—to other, far distant natures.

When a hungry gold miner paused on the Chilkoot Trail to open a can of Van Camp's pork and beans for lunch, for example, he connected himself first to the nature that had produced its ingredients, perhaps a hog farm in Iowa and a bean field in California. Those were complex natural systems in their own right, transformed by human labor to produce pork and beans and tomatoes for a market in prepared foods. That particular lunch brought connections to laborers across the continent: hog and bean farmers in Iowa and California, pork packers, railroad workers, canners, label makers, wholesale warehouse shippers, advertisers, and retail salespeople. All of those workers, in order to produce and move a can of pork and beans, in turn consumed their share of food, clothing, and shelter, all of it produced by yet *other* workers in other places. Slaughterhouse workers in Cincinnati, field hands in California, and warehouse clerks in Seattle in turn ate lunch to fuel the labor that fed the Klondike miners, who produced gold because it had great value. All of their lunches came from yet *other* producers, whose own further connections to nature and to human labor became part of the increasingly vast network linking miners on the Chilkoot Trail to places and natures far and wide. Balanced on the icy Chilkoot slopes, each miner formed the center of a rapidly proliferating network of linkages to nature, forged through his own labor in the gold rush economy, but also through the labor of many others who worked to supply and sustain him. Follow those linkages outward from the Chilkoot, and you find connections to a worldwide industrial economy.

This network in some ways resembled an ever-expanding railroad system, much like the one which transformed North American transportation in the nineteenth century and made the Alaska-Yukon gold rush possible. The individual miner himself formed a Grand Central Station, with lines radiating outward in multiple directions, 360 degrees around. Some of those radiating lines linked the miner directly to the natural environment around him, to the mud and snow of the White Pass and Chilkoot Trails, to the permafrost soil from which the miners dug gold, or to the salmon and moose steaks that fueled their bodies. Other rail lines led, however, to other, secondary stations: Seattle retail shops, Chicago wholesale warehouses, Cincinnati packing plants, and California bean fields (mimicking the *actual* rail stations in such places). Those secondary hubs had rail lines radiating out in every direction as well, to all the people and the natures which connected *them* to all the many natures that fueled their human labors of production and consumption. Spreading infinitely outward, these clusters of stations and lines came to encompass producers and consumers and ecosystems around the world. For each miner, the entire network, with all its connections to all those natures, led back to a common starting point: the value of gold.

As they hauled their sacks of pork and beans and flour over the Chilkoot Pass, miners carried this industrial economy north to the Yukon and Alaska in order to produce a single valuable commodity, gold, for that economy. Their ability to do so depended not only on railroads, steamships, and Native packers, but also on the previous several decades of North American industrialization. For over sixty years prior to the gold rush, managers, workers, capitalists, and inventors had mechanized and rationalized the production of consumer goods. As a result, nineteenth-century American workers slowly shifted from an older, preindustrial household production of their own pork and beans, flour and beef, and clothing and shelter to eating factory-canned pork and beans while producing a single product or service, such as winter wheat, bicycle spokes, or sewing machine parts. This shift changed human beings' relationships to the world around them. In a preindustrial economy, where work often meant the primary production of a range of necessary items, including food, each of those productive labors connected humans directly to their environment. Production meant direct bodily engagement with soil and water, with pigs, beans, rain, and mud. With industrialization, productive labor narrowed to a single task, such as gold mining or meat-packing. Workers' direct engagement with the physical world was thus narrowed to the tools and resources needed to do any one thing, whether hog farming or gold mining.

At the same time, industrial technologies and production techniques allowed fewer and fewer workers to produce the food, clothing, shelter, and services needed to sustain more and more consumers. Industrial workers became consumers par excellence, purchasing food, clothing, shelter, tools, transportation, and entertainment, all available in a market economy. When compared with preindustrial production, this wider consumption constituted a very different sort of engagement with nature. Removed from the day-to-day ecological realities of producing their own pork and beans, industrial Americans found it easier and easier to lose sight of where their food came from. At the same time, steam-driven railroads revolutionized transportation speed in ways that transformed older ideas of space, time, and distance. Pork and beans produced in Iowa and California, and given market value in Chicago, could travel to New York or Seattle, almost, it seemed, instantaneously, as if the distance and travel time between urban centers no longer existed. Technology eliminated the space between the places where pork and beans were produced, and where they were consumed. For consumers, that space and that nature no longer mattered in daily life. That made it very easy to forget that pork and beans came from anywhere specific at all.[8]

Such transformations did not go unnoticed. From the moment the first factories and railroads appeared on the horizon, Americans debated the meaning and import of industrialization, and the ways in which it transformed the place and importance of nature in daily life. Over the last 150 years or so, stories about industrialization and nature told by writers, scholars, and journalists have fallen into two rough categories. In one view, industrialization allowed human beings to conquer or control nature, and to claim victory in the long battle to free themselves from material restrictions on production, wealth, and prosperity. After all, railroads, steam engines, rationalized management, mechanization, and specialized mass production all granted new levels of command over the material products of the earth. Although the victory was never absolute, industrial capitalism allowed human beings to gain unprecedented control over water, weather, seasons, time, and disease, and out of that control to build the strongest economies and nations in history. Industrial consumers with a steady supply of canned pork and beans could turn their energies to other work. In that view, freedom from nature, nature's absence from daily life, constituted one of humankind's highest achievements.

In the other view, however, this control over nature meant not victory, but defeat, an alienation of human beings from nature and a widespread degradation and destruction of the earth itself.[9] In not knowing where their pork and beans came from, in losing that direct connection to and knowledge of nature and production within nature, industrial consumers lost an older, preindustrial intimacy with the ecosystems that sustained them.[10] Environmental historians researching the ecological consequences of industrial capitalism have shown how market capitalism brought not just prosperity, but also a revolutionary and problematic cultural change in the human relationship to nature. Capitalism turned all of the earth's resources into commodities, given value by markets, separate from any broader considerations of human subsistence or of the earth's own limits of production. Capitalist culture treated nature, the nature which produced pork, beans, gold, and every other thing that humans valued, as an instrument to be harvested and exploited to the point of destruction for maximum profit.[11] In the nineteenth century, that culture moved westward to exploit the abundant resources beyond the Mississippi. Capitalist production degraded diverse and delicate ecosystems in the name of production and profit. It led, in the words of William Cronon, to "large-scale deforestation, threats of species extinction, unsustainable exploitation of natural resources, widespread destruction of habitat."[12] It left behind a transformed world.

Control of nature or destruction of nature: these are very different histories of industrialization. They share, however, an overarching picture of an industrial capitalism in which, one way or another, nature disappeared from human beings' daily lives. Both stories imply nature's dwindling presence and power, either through conquest or destruction. Both suggest that with nature drastically altered, distanced, conquered, or destroyed, industrial human beings were fundamentally alienated from their environment.

The Alaska-Yukon gold rush, however, suggests a more complicated view of industrial capitalism and human relationships with nature. The 1890s gold rush recapitulated in a very short time period many of the economic changes associated with industrialization, with shifts from subsistence production to mass production and industrial consumption. In the gold rush's early stages, miners left behind the familiar world of railroads, steamships, and telegraphs, a world in which they had been thoroughgoing industrial consumers. When they stepped off the Seattle steamer at Skagway, Dyea, or Dawson City en route to the goldfields, they entered a world of far broader production in which they became, in part, subsistence producers, directly engaged with nature in securing their own survival. They produced their own transportation, moving themselves over the Chilkoot Pass into and through the Yukon interior with their own bodily labor. They produced some of their food by hunting, fishing, and gathering. They cut wood for shelter, fuel, and mining. And they dug for gold. As producers, their connections to nature led directly into local ecosystems. In this intimacy with local places, the miners' labors sometimes seemed preindustrial, harking backward in time to the era of subsistence production, in which human beings survived through their knowledge of nature, on the fruits of the earth and the fruits of their own labor. At times, the miners' labors brought primitive, elemental, physical struggle with nature. Visions of such preindustrial physical labor attracted many miners to the gold rush, as they sought escape from the boredom of industrial labor in the 1890s, a decade of rapid urbanization, industrialization, and economic turmoil.

Although miners certainly experienced intimacy with the earth, their relationships with nature were never straightforward and could never be fully preindustrial. After all, they ate plenty of canned pork and beans. One moment might bring profound physical immersion in a dangerous environment. In the next moment, however, or in the next week or month, the minute a wage-labor job or a railroad car or a can of pork and beans came into view, miners found themselves in a familiar world defined more by consumption than production. They created a specialized world of work in which they produced only gold, and purchased and consumed just about everything else. In carrying industrial capitalism, and cans of pork and beans, over the passes to the Yukon and Alaska, miners carried all of its parts as well: markets, commodification, mass-produced consumer goods, and shifts from subsistence production to widespread consumption.

Miners' day-to-day labors, therefore, allow a particularly close look at the ways in which shifts between production and consumption changed human relations with the natural world. The miners' connections to nature certainly changed as those shifts unfolded, and those changes often included elements of alienation and distancing from nature and the control and conquest of nature which historians have associated with the industrial era. The labor of gold mining also reveals shifts in human relations to nature, however, that are more complicated than *just* conquest, alienation, or destruction. As often as gold miners experienced a distancing from the earth, their own letters and journals showed that in their labors as industrial producers and consumers, they were never fully separated from nature. Everything they produced and everything they consumed connected them to nature.

From the moment that miners departed for the Yukon, those connections, rather than getting simpler or *less* industrial, expanded outward into the industrial economy, belying the gold seekers' hopes for simple production and intimacy with the land. As consumers, in shifting the labor of transportation to other human beings and animals, gold rushers created a market that commodified space, distance, and the labor and bodies of those humans and animals. In shifting the labor and expertise of transportation to packers and, on rivers, to steamboat pilots, they shifted to others the intimate experience with and knowledge of nature that accompanied such physical movement through nature. In shifting much of the burden of producing food and supplies back to other hunters, fishers, farmers, gardeners, and food processors, they replaced their own direct connections to nature with more elaborate, mediated ties.

What complicated these networks of relationships to nature even further, however, was the miners' constant shifting back and forth between production and consumption. Yukon gold rushers did not simply cross over from a modern, industrial world to a preindustrial world of hunting and foot travel, and then cross back to an industrial consumer economy of railroads and canned pork and beans, to stay there permanently. As workers and travelers in a distant corner of the North American continent, always in need of food, supplies, shelter, and transportation, the miners crisscrossed the border between a local subsistence economy and the decidedly nonlocal industrial mining economy they brought to the Yukon. They shifted back and forth so often that they demonstrated the border itself to be illusory. Klondike gold miners thus reveal that the shift from production to consumption that might have defined the arrival of an industrial economy was not a single, clear, irreversible change in economic life or in human connections to nature. It was a fuzzier but also more complex sort of change, a widening of economic activities to embrace both older preindustrial forms of production and a range of industrial forms of production and consumption.

Moving back and forth, simultaneously within and without the industrial world, gold miners demonstrated the ways in which both worlds connected them to nature, albeit in different ways. The contrasts between a dinner of local moose steaks and a can of pork and beans, between transport by dogsled and by sternwheeler, between individual prospecting and wage labor in an underground mining drift delineated the different connections to nature inherent in an industrial world. In the end, to the miners, it was all just work, a jumble of muscle and machine, market values and intangible values, local and nonlocal linkages, production and consumption. Their work erased the difference between preindustrial and industrial and revealed them as one: an industrial economy and an industrial relationship with nature.

Gold miners did not set out on the Chilkoot Trail in 1897 and 1898 to explore their connections to the physical environment, or to elucidate the industrial relationship to nature. They set out because gold held great value, and if they gave any thought to their industrial capitalist world, they sought, through gold, either to escape it or to harness gold's power to return to it on better terms. Gold's value seemed a simple and straightforward starting point for their journeys north toward wealth and freedom. Even something as unquestionable as the value of gold, however, contained a complicated human relationship with nature. Even in granting gold value, human beings were connected to nature.

In the most famous Klondike gold rush story, Jack London's *The Call of the Wild*, Buck, "an unduly civilized dog," is kidnapped from his California home to be sold in Seattle to Yukon gold rushers. Standing on the beach at Dyea, at the foot of the Chilkoot Trail, Buck "had been suddenly jerked from the heart of civilization and flung into the heart of things primordial."[13] Like Buck, Alaska-Yukon miners sometimes saw themselves on a journey away from culture and into primitive nature. On one level, especially at trying moments on the Chilkoot Pass, those perceptions were accurate. They did journey into nature, through nature, and with nature. But rather than journey out of culture or away from it, they journeyed into and through their own industrial culture, and into and through the relationships with nature at the heart of that culture. Their journeys through the nature of gold, including their journeys over the Chilkoot Pass, revealed that no matter how far they traveled, they remained within a culture which rapidly transformed human relations with the environment. And no matter how thoroughly industrial culture transformed nature, human beings remained connected to their environment. The nature of gold was a nature from which they could never be fully separated.

1

THE CULTURE
OF GOLD

I t was the natural thing to do. There could be few more powerful arguments about any human endeavor than this one, that it was the natural thing to do. The gold seekers on the Chilkoot Pass and on the other trails and rivers that led to the Yukon and Alaska risked their lives in pursuit of gold. Why? The answer perhaps seems simple: gold would make them rich. But the answer goes further. Late-nineteenth-century Americans naturalized gold's value and gold rushes. They removed gold and everything gold-related from the realm of human culture, and called them nature, called them natural. According to those naturalizations, the men and women struggling up the Chilkoot acted out of fundamental human nature, in response to the powerful nature of gold and to natural economic laws. Culture had nothing to do with it. These understandings of nature, however, were profoundly cultural. They were rooted in human culture, history, and belief, and in Euro-American political, economic, and social traditions. It took a fair amount of culture, after all, to make the Chilkoot crossing seem the natural thing to do.

Of course, Americans had been calling gold rushes natural for a long time. All the way back to the first inklings of New World riches, Euro-Americans believed humans to have a natural, universal attraction to and desire for gold. In *Gold Seeking*, a recent cultural history of the 1850s gold rushes in California and Australia, David Goodman notes that most mining histories depict gold rushes "as though it were the most natural thing that men

16

should leave all that was valuable to them in one part of the world, to seek for precious minerals in remote regions."[1] The familiar explanations for gold seeking, greed, lust, and madness naturalized events by ascribing them to elemental human passions. The human drive to rush out and wrest gold from the earth occurred by nature, like an epidemic disease, "gold fever," or in the 1890s, "Klondike fever." Gold's value and allure worked on the nature of the human body and the human soul, beyond the realm of reason, history, and culture. Even through the twentieth century, historians continued to portray gold rushes as quasi-natural events. They unfolded far from "civilization," close to "nature." They remained, according to historian Paula Mitchell Marks, "essentially the same from year to year and place to place . . . outside history."[2] In setting the context for the Alaska-Yukon gold rush, historians mention the depression of the 1890s, and little else. The economy was stagnant; people were desperate. That is all it took.[3] Given the attractions of real and instant wealth, rushing off to the Yukon seemed, well, the natural thing to do. In the late 1890s, however, Americans' naturalization of gold moved beyond these general ideas about gold fever and gold rushes. During one of the most hotly contested presidential elections of the century, the culture of gold reached its highest summit.

On July 9, 1896, a little over a month before Yukon prospectors stumbled onto a rich pocket of gold along Bonanza Creek, William Jennings Bryan took the podium at the Democratic Convention in Chicago and transfixed his audience with one of the most famous political speeches in American history. With great energy, style, pacing, and poetry, Bryan railed against the gold standard for the nation's money supply, his Republican opponents' favored policy. Bryan fervently believed that the gold standard would unjustly limit the amount of currency in national circulation and bring economic oppression to the nation's workers. "Having behind us the producing masses of this nation and the world," he declared, bringing his speech to a crowd-rousing finale, "we will answer their demand for the gold standard by saying to them: You shall not press down upon the brow of labor this crown of thorns, you shall not crucify mankind upon a cross of gold."[4] Never had gold suffered such hatred and condemnation. The speech electrified the audience, which exploded in response, the sound likened by one reporter to "one great burst of artillery." "'Bryan, Bryan, Bryan!'" they shouted, twenty thousand strong, ripping off their coats and throwing them in the air, "on their chairs wildly waving hats, canes, umbrellas, anything that came to hand." They responded next with their votes, nominating Bryan for president.[5] Bryan's bold images, the crown of thorns and the cross of gold, appeared in political cartoons in periodicals across the nation. Those images brought the gold standard debate home to the American people. They brought clarity to an almost incomprehensible topic, and became the most powerful salvo in a long political battle over the nature of gold.

Growing in part out of the severe economic depression of the early 1890s, the gold standard debate, or "Battle of the Standards," was at root about far broader issues: the economic dominance of the eastern region of the country and the subjugation of the West; the role of producers in an industrial economy; the power of cities in an age of rapid urbanization; and the future of the Democratic party. The fight also concerned whether the solutions to the boom-and-bust vagaries of industrialization should come from the unfettered play of natural law or from the social powers of political action. By the summer of 1896, however, those many complicated issues had boiled down to the choice between monetary standards, between a bimetallist standard (gold and silver together), or simply gold.

Advocates of the gold standard, led by Bryan's opponent in the presidential election, William McKinley, wanted every dollar in the nation's money supply backed by real, physical gold, held in the United States Treasury. They wanted any American holding a paper dollar to be able to present it at the Treasury and receive a dollar's worth of gold in return. As a commodity, a raw material used by jewelers, dentists, metallurgists, and others, gold had a market value, which determined just how much made up "a dollar's worth." This was most confusing when the U.S. government actually coined gold. As the market value of gold shifted, a gold dollar coin might contain more or less than a dollar's worth of gold according to the current market value of gold as a commodity. This was one reason why it was easier to issue paper dollars, backed by physical gold safely stored in the nation's vaults.

Dollars backed by gold, however, meant that the amount of physical gold in the nation's vaults determined—and limited—the amount of paper money in circulation. That policy meant a stronger, more valuable dollar, but it also meant fewer dollars and lower prices. Bimetallists, on the other hand, including William Jennings Bryan, wanted the amount of money in circulation to be determined by—and each paper dollar backed by—two metals: gold and silver. They wanted any American holding a paper dollar to be able to present it at the Treasury for a dollar's worth of gold *or* silver, or a combination of both. This would increase the supply of money in national circulation, because the Treasury's gold and silver supplies, when combined, made up a much larger amount of precious metal than just gold alone. Although the feverish debate proved somewhat technical and confusing, at its core it boiled down to one simple question: Where did gold's value come from?

Just days after Bryan condemned the nation's crucifixion on the cross of gold, prospectors in the Yukon Territory stumbled up Bonanza Creek above the Klondike Valley and found a rich pocket of gold. The Alaska-Yukon gold rush thus began with the same simple question: Where did gold's value come from? This gold rush—any gold rush—was predicated on gold's economic value, and, based on that value, unfolded in a predictable sequence of events. In this gold rush, prospectors discovered gold in the gravels of a distant Yukon creek in the summer of 1896. The following summer, news of their discoveries reached telegraph and newspaper offices around the world and, as Mac McMichael wrote in June 1898, "set a continent on fire with greed for gold."[6] Millions of individual men and women heard the news, and some of them—relatively few—mulled over the possibilities of setting off in search of gold.

Within that simple chain of events, however, lay the far fuzzier process by which human beings granted gold value. The decision to grant value to any physical element of the natural world is an important but complicated one. In choosing which earthly elements to value, harvest, and use, humans powerfully shape the earth itself. Such "choices," however, are rarely identifiable as particular historical moments; they are buried in cultural and economic processes, and, as in the case of gold (and silver), buried in the past. Gold's value, as commodity, currency, capital, and as a sacred container of pure value, was centuries old by the 1890s, unquestioned and unquestionable. Yukon and Alaska gold, however, was a recent discovery. Along Bonanza Creek in 1896, a long-standing cultural value collided with a New World nature, relatively untouched by Euro-American ideas about what was valuable and what was not.

Hence the gold miners' first connection to the natural world was a connection not to the particular, physical nature of actual gold, or to the earth which contained that gold, but rather to gold's intangible economic value. No one on the Chilkoot Trail could see gold's value, or reach out to touch it, yet no one gave that value a second thought. Gold was valuable, and gold would make the miners rich. This first and necessary connection to gold, this complicated process called value, set in motion everything that followed.

But where did gold's value come from? It came from innumerable sources, most of them shrouded by time. In the 1890s, however, those sources came into public discussion, filtered through the American political debate over the gold standard. That debate turned on further questions: Did gold's value come from nature, or from culture? Was it a natural thing, or a cultural thing? What was natural? Gold money or other forms of money? As geographer David Harvey explains, political arguments about nature, and about what is natural, are always also about conflicts over social power, as opposing sides struggle "to gain command of institutions, social relations, and material practices for particular purposes."[7] Thus the battle of the standards, a battle over the nature of gold, was at heart also a battle over the future of American social and economic institutions, and over the material practices of mining, making, and using gold and silver money.

By 1896, that battle had been building for thirty years. It grew out of the federal government's attempts to reduce the amount of paper money in circulation in the United States and return to the gold standard, with each paper dollar backed by gold. Prior to the Civil War, all U.S. money had been backed by silver and gold together, although due to dwindling silver supplies, gold predominated. During the Civil War, however, manufacturers of everything from guns to clothing drew heavily on existing gold reserves to finance rapid wartime production. The gold supply dwindled, and with it, the amount of money in circulation.[8] Under pressure to finance the Union Army, Congress issued paper dollars, called greenbacks, their value determined by international exchange. Greenbacks were backed only by government guarantee, not by gold or silver. If you took a greenback dollar to the bank, you would get less than a dollar's worth of gold, if you got any gold at all; there was no direct tie between the U.S. dollar and precious metal.[9]

By 1865, when greenbacks had seen the Union Army to victory, these paper dollars, due to inflation, exchanged for less than fifty cents' worth of gold.[10] A greenback was a much "cheaper" dollar than a gold dollar, worth far less, with far less purchasing power both at home and internationally. Fiscal conservatives in Congress, led by Treasury Secretary Hugh McCulloch, wanted every paper dollar to be worth a dollar in gold. He wanted the nation on a gold standard. There were half a billion greenbacks out there, and the government had to figure out a way to take them out of circulation and make the dollar once again "as good as gold."[11] Through the 1870s, the treasury held the amount of paper money in circulation stable, while the economy, the population, and the nation's gold reserves all grew; this slowly increased the value of each dollar until it matched a dollar's worth of gold. Despite falling prices, high interest rates, and increased economic hardship, particularly for western farmers, the plan succeeded, and the nation resumed the gold standard on January 2, 1879. "Soft money," backed only by government promise, had been banished in favor of "hard money," backed by gold.[12]

Resumption of the gold standard did not go uncontested, however. Political groups and writers calling themselves Greenbackers fought from the start to keep soft money in circulation. The Greenback Party organized to argue that paper money, and the inflation that went with it, maintained high prices and helped the "producing classes," farmers and industrial workers. When financial disaster struck in the Panic of 1873, falling prices, bankruptcy, and business failures further galvanized farmers and other producers in opposition to hard money and the gold standard.[13] At the same time, Nevada silver miners struck rich lodes in the Comstock, ending a decades-long scarcity of silver. As silver prices plummeted, silver became more plentiful than gold, and silver dollars the more plentiful dollars. Anyone with gold coin or gold bullion profited by selling it on the open market as raw material for a greater number of silver dollars.[14] Thus, if silver dollars were allowed into circulation in any amount, they would quickly replace and even eliminate the nation's gold currency supply. This would bring inflation, but also pose a significant threat to resumption of the gold standard.[15]

That was exactly what Greenbackers and other soft money advocates wanted. By the mid-1870s, in the midst of these economic troubles, Greenbackers became silverites, or rather, bimetallists. They adopted silver as a second panacea after paper greenbacks, hoping to use the new silver supplies to back new silver dollars, expand the currency supply, and resurrect the economy. The soft money ideology became a silver ideology and a growing political force.[16] Only when the 1893 depression sank the nation into severe economic crisis, however, did the money debate gain real momentum, exploding full force into the political spotlight in the 1896 contest between McKinley and Bryan.[17]

The arguments, accusations, and economic theories in this contest ranged far and wide, but they continued to circle around the question of where gold's value came from. Gold standard advocates—or goldbugs—argued that gold's value came from nature, and that gold-backed dollars were naturally valuable. Greenbackers, silverites, and bimetallists, demanding paper dollars, silver dollars, and gold dollars, argued that *all* value came from culture, that all dollars and all monetary standards were given value by human societies and governments. In speeches, articles, and pamphlets, both sides distorted the economics of the question, advocating theories that were, according to historian Lawrence Goodwyn "conceptually flawed."[18] Despite their simplifications, however, both goldbugs and silverites clung to their positions, firm in the belief that their respective causes were moral and just. In the midst of economic chaos, poverty, and despair, the question of gold's value became a question of the nation's economic morality.

INTRINSIC VALUE

Goldbugs staked the nation's future on their belief that gold's value came from nature, from the intrinsic, natural qualities of gold itself. As a result of this inner natural value, gold's use as currency was also natural, decreed by God or nature as law, rather than created by human beings as part of economic culture. Gold was thus *naturally* suited to serve the United States' social and economic interests as the *natural* basis of a civilized monetary system. Drawing on a long tradition of economic thought, gold standard supporters naturalized gold. They did not give gold's value a second thought, because gold's value was not the product of thought; it was the product of nature.[19]

Separate from the question of its value, gold, of course, *was* the product of nature. It did and does have a nature, a set of chemical, physical, tangible attributes. Gold is bright yellow, the color of the sun. It is heavy, extraordinarily malleable, and profoundly enduring; it never decays. As some human societies discovered centuries ago, those natural characteristics made gold useful in particular ways. Gold was well suited to be forged into jewelry and other ornaments as a symbol of enduring power and wealth. It also worked well as a representative and store of value. But the nature of gold, its bundle of physical characteristics, did not determine how human beings would use it. That nature alone also did not explain the wide-ranging, complicated, and powerful meanings that different groups of human beings ascribed to gold over time. To argue that gold was well suited to represent value and to be money was a shade apart from the goldbugs' claims that gold was, by nature, valuable and, by nature, money.

For goldbugs in the 1870s, as historian Michael O'Malley writes, "money's value was intrinsic, governed like the value of gold by the laws of nature rather than society."[20] Intrinsic value is a powerful but slippery idea, as such value is difficult to see and measure; it just *is*.[21] Even in the 1870s and 1890s, despite new economic theories which placed the source of all value in human labor, economists and politicians continued to argue that gold's value rested literally in its physical nature, and hence that *that* intrinsic value gave gold coins their true value as money. Such claims drew from a long tradition. From Thomas Aquinas to John Locke to 1890s goldbugs, economic thinkers argued that the value of a coin was determined by the intrinsic value of the metal from which it was made rather than by its state-designated face value.[22] As historian James Barnes wrote of the American goldbugs in the 1890s, they believed that a dollar, "regardless of any official markings of a state would because of its intrinsic value be the same anywhere in the world; to them it was an instrument (created by nature and directed by natural laws) for use in buying and selling."[23]

Gold standard economists who wrote more systematically about gold's value retained the idea of intrinsic value, but rooted it not in gold's vague "nature," but in the stability of its value, and in the labor required to extract it from the earth. Karl Marx, for one, denied that value could be an inherent quality, the physical property of a thing itself. "So far," he wrote, "no chemist has ever discovered exchange value either in a pearl or a diamond."[24] A century earlier, Adam Smith had clearly stated a labor theory of value, writing in 1776 that "Labour is the real measure of the exchangeable value of all commodities. . . . Labour alone . . . never varying in its own value, is alone the ultimate and real standard by which the value of all commodities can at all times and places be estimated and compared."[25] The labor theory of value thus argued that gold's value came from the work required to extract it from the earth. Classical economist David Ricardo wrote that "gold and silver, like other commodities, have an intrinsic value, which is not arbitrary, but is dependent on their scarcity, the quantity of labour bestowed in procuring them, and the value of the capital employed in the mines which produce them."[26]

But could labor value still be natural value? Did the labor theory of value negate the idea that gold's value came from nature? In the 1890s, goldbug economists and pamphlet writers acknowledged the labor of gold miners as part of gold's value, but they then naturalized that labor, moving miners themselves into the realm of nature, as part of gold's nature and the natural laws of supply and demand. According to David Wells's popular gold standard tracts of the 1870s and 1890s, *Robinson Crusoe's Money* and *The Silver Question*, gold's natural scarcity, beauty, and permanence meant that it was always in demand. Due to its random distribution in places difficult to access, it required a lot of work, "vast labor," to extract it from the earth.[27] For the miners themselves, that work was worth doing only when demand for gold and the market value of gold were both high. When gold was scarce, workers found it worth their while to leave other tasks and turn to the vast labor of gold mining, even though few miners found great wealth. When miners produced enough gold to increase the supply and lower demand, the value fell, sending miners back to other jobs, which, with more gold in circulation, were once again productive. If the economy again outgrew the money supply, and demand for gold again rose, workers would go back again to find more gold.[28] This natural seesaw of supply and demand, Wells explained, kept gold's value remarkably stable, and this natural stability made gold the best commodity on which to base currency. In the 1890s, Senator John Sherman argued that the value of gold was "as immutable as the law of gravitation."[29] Hence nature controlled the quantity of wealth and money through its meting out of gold in the earth, and nature controlled the rate at which humans sought it out.[30] A bimetallic currency standard, however, with dollars backed by both silver and gold, would be, Wells wrote, "a violation of the natural laws of supply and demand."[31]

Wells thus naturalized gold miners as well as gold money: in the detailed heart of intrinsic value, there were gold miners hard at work, but not as agents of their own destiny. Miners sought gold not as individuals, and not because it paid them well to do so; they sought gold, the argument went, when the natural laws of supply and demand dictated that the labor of gold mining was necessary for the economy. Gold miners acted as part of the economic system, responding to its demand for gold and to the market price that rewarded some miners for the labor of all. For such economic theorists, the miners ascending the Chilkoot Pass were not simply journeying into nature, they *were* nature. They were doing the natural thing. As cogs in the natural economic machine, gold miners were part of nature, and their labor gave gold its natural value.[32]

However the theorists defined gold's intrinsic value, McKinley's goldbug supporters seized on the idea for their 1896 political campaign against Bryan and bimetallism. In addition to intrinsic value, McKinley supporters also marshaled other arguments, building a case not only for gold's natural value, but for its divine power as well. Gold standard supporters argued that God had created and guaranteed the value of gold, gold money, and the gold standard itself so that all might serve as the basis of a sound economy for His people. Put simply, the gold standard was divinely ordained. God had intended gold for use as money. Its value stood as a divinely fixed point against which all other value could be measured. Gold stood not only for sound economic practice, but for proper religious values as well. Historian Irwin Unger quotes a source that declared the gold standard to be "God's will and the nature of things."[33] Protestant preachers and writers led the attack against the heresy of paper money, inflation, and silver in Christian newspapers and at the pulpit.[34] To refute the gold standard with an "artificial" bimetallic standard was, according to David Wells, "warfare against the beneficence of the Almighty."[35] The New York *Christian Advocate* claimed that "atheism is not worse in religion than an unstable or irredeemable currency."[36] A Protestant moral and religious fervor pervaded the nation, and, Lawrence Goodwyn writes of the fall of 1896, the "autumn air bristled with apocalyptic moral terminology."[37]

In stark contrast, gold standard supporters also drew from recent scientific theories in building their case for gold. David Wells declared both the gold standard and gold money to be the triumphant product of Darwin's laws of evolution, applied to the economic realm. Over time, he explained, human societies progressed from the primitive stages of barter to the use of shells or other simple commodities as money. As they experimented with different monetary policies, wrote Wells,

> people, as it were by instinct, found out that a given quantity of gold represented more permanently a given amount of . . . human labor . . . than any other substance. And . . . gold . . . had further acquired two other attributes, which fitted, above all things else, to serve as money; namely . . . that it had become a measure or standard of value . . . and second, that its value or purchasing power was so constant and continuously inherent in itself.[38]

The gold standard thus emerged atop the pyramid of evolution through the survival of the fittest (fig. 1.1). Gold's nature made it money.[39]

In the less rigorous goldbug literature, gold's stable value promised far more than mere adherence to natural law. It also promised honesty, morality, and soundness. Among the most popular and effective gold standard images were those that linked the gold dollar to moral values and honesty while decrying the silver dollar as immoral and dishonest.[40] A U.S. senator from Nevada, speaking in 1894, declared of gold that "So exact a measure is it to human effort, that when it is exclusively used as money it teaches the very habit of honesty. It neither deals in, nor tolerates false pretenses. It can-

THE SURVIVAL OF THE FITTEST.

FIG. 1.1. "The Survival of the Fittest." This Thomas Nast cartoon naturalizes the gold standard through ideas and images of Darwinian evolution. The gold standard has risen to the top of the heap through natural processes of evolution and emerges as the true and natural currency standard, bathed in the dawning light of truth. (David A. Wells, *Robinson Crusoe's Money*, 1896) not lie, it keeps its promises to rich and poor alike."[41] Americans in the Gilded Age pursued "progress, stability, and materialism," and they associated gold with that broader spectrum of cultural meanings.[42] Gold standard supporters linked gold money's stable and sound value to social stability and soundness as well, to the nation's prosperity and to the progress of civilization. In one campaign poster, William McKinley stands atop a giant gold coin as it is held aloft by a diverse group of workers representing the American people. In the background, merchant ships crowd the docks of a prosperous city, while above the scene floats the slogan "Prosperity at Home, Prestige Abroad." In another, McKinley uses a golden key to unlock the "Temple of Prosperity," barred by "Financial Mistrust," and bearing a sign that reads "This Door Will Be Opened November 3rd, 1896," election day. Other cartoons and posters identified gold as the currency of superior, Western, white, civilized nations, and linked silver to Japan, Mexico, China, and other supposedly inferior, unstable, non-white, uncivilized nations.[43] In one such image from the San Francisco *Wasp,* two well-dressed Victorian-era voters stand outside Democratic Campaign Headquarters gazing at posters of poverty-stricken peasants, one of which reads: "Vote for Free Silver and Be Prosperous like South America," where wages were low, 20 cents a day (fig. 1.2).[44]

Pushing these arguments even further, Wells and other goldbug writers ridiculed the idea that paper money could represent value, having no intrinsic value itself. Wells called this notion ideal or imaginary value, and used Thomas Nast's cartoon, showing paper milk ("This is milk by act of Congress") offered to a rag doll ("This is a baby by act of Congress") to illustrate his outrage at the idea of money, and thus of value, as a socially created token standing in for something not present in the money itself. The paper dollar in the cartoon reads "This is money by act of Congress."[45] Value could not be created out of thin air, by governments printing paper money or minting an overabundance of silver. As Lawrence Goodwyn explains, paper money, with no intrinsic value, "transgressed both economic and moral laws." This "essentially corrupt" money constituted "a morally corrupt method of running a society."[46]

Goldbugs also flat-out ridiculed the opposition. The silver dollar, worth only 53 cents in gold, appeared in cartoon form with Bryan's caricature and words on one side that read "In God We Trust," and on the other side "For the other 47 cents." Another mock 53–cent coin reads "In God We Trust, With Bryan We Bust." A popular magazine, *Judge,* featured a similar cartoon a few years later during the 1900 election debates. One dollar, featur-

FIG. 1.2. "Dubious." A pro–gold standard campaign cartoon shows two Americans standing outside Democratic headquarters before the 1896 presidential election. Campaign posters urge them to vote for William Jennings Bryan and free silver with tongue-in-cheek claims that free silver will make the United States "prosperous" like the other clearly poor countries pictured in the posters. Goldbugs claimed that bimetallism would impoverish the nation and lower Americans to the economic level of poor, non-white peoples around the world. (*North American Review of Reviews,* November 1896)

ing McKinley's head, reads "Worth 100 cents." The other, with Bryan's head, reads "Worth 53 cents." To subvert the laws of nature with such valueless money was to threaten the very basis of civilization. It would, according to William McKinley, "derange all existing values."[47] In opposition to that threat, gold became a symbol of stable social values, a check on discord, a force for order and reason in turbulent economic times. The argument about values, both monetary and moral, was rooted in the symbol of gold, and in nature, a nature created with certain purposes by a Protestant God.

CULTURAL VALUE AND PRODUCER IDEOLOGY

Greenbackers, silverites, and bimetallists countered these naturalizations of gold's value, the gold standard, and gold money with the relatively simple argument that the true value of gold—the value of anything— came not from nature, but from the labor and culture of human beings. Hence gold money did not have any special, natural, or intrinsic value, or a natural role to play as money. Bimetallists took a righteous stand for the long-held view that societies, rather than nature or God, created money and granted it value in order to measure, store, represent, and exchange other products of human labor. Money thus had no natural need to be made of a specific, valuable material. A gold nugget was no more naturally money than were silver or paper or seashells. Gold money, the product of tradition, superstition, and custom, had no intrinsic value; its value came from government decree, from the collective act of the American people, who set the value of gold and silver coins and paper dollars out of common economic interest.[48] In one of the more successful bimetallist pamphlets, Ignatius Donnelly called gold a "yellow accident," "a mere conventional symbol, with no value save what the common consent of society gives it."[49] In his story, two men, a farmer and a banker, argue the issue while journeying by train from Chicago to Seattle. They are joined by a young woman, whose naïveté on the monetary question makes her a sounding board for their arguments. The innocent woman declares, "I thought gold was the real wealth." Donnelly's farmer denounces this as "poisonous nonsense."[50]

Real wealth, Donnelly and others believed, lay not in some ridiculously small amount of one random yellow metal, but in the many abundant products created by the nation's workers and producers. Value came from the soil, from the labor of people who worked with nature to produce goods for market, goods that fulfilled real human needs for sustenance. Real wealth came from labor and nature together, from the producers who brought forth abundance from the limitless resources of the land. As Donnelly put it, it came from "the farmer who makes twenty bushels of wheat grow where one is sown . . . or the workman who converts the growing forest trees into houses . . . for they produce those things without which civilization could not endure. But the man who brings money into the country simply makes slaves."[51]

Soft money advocates and bimetallists thus celebrated the virtue of producers and the true source of wealth, the products of the soil. This "producer ideology" formed the core of the bimetallist currency movement and of the Populist agrarian political movement of which bimetallism was part. Producer ideology drew from the Greenbackers of the 1870s and from the influence, far earlier, of French thinkers, called physiocrats, who located the source of all value in the soil. It grew as well out of Jeffersonian agrarianism, which ascribed a "supreme economic function" to rural workers who produced for the good of society.[52] An August 1897 cover of the humor magazine *Puck* showed a farmer carrying a huge sheaf of wheat which bore the label "Enormous Wheat Crop of 1897." The caption reads, "The *True* Agent of Prosperity."[53] Such images and others denounced the "money power," those who manipulated wealth but did nothing to produce it; such ideas constituted, in the words of historian Daniel Rodgers, a "stubborn moral affirmation of the indispensability of those who toiled and produced."[54]

Populists and silverites thus denied the natural value of gold money and its moral superiority as money because a shrunken money supply, based on gold, could never represent the true wealth produced by the nation's workers. Much of the fervor behind this producerism grew out of the steady fall in prices from the 1870s through the 1890s which accompanied resumption of the gold standard.[55] On a simplified, hypothetical level, one can see the power of the reasoning that fueled discontent among western farmers and other commodity producers. If an American farmer produced 100 bushels of wheat worth one dollar each in an economy which had 100 dollars in circulation, then each bushel sold for one dollar. If gold standard supporters reduced circulation to 60 dollars, then each bushel sold for 60 cents. At the same time, if production increased and farmers produced 200 bushels in an economy with 60 dollars in circulation, then each bushel sold for 30 cents. A farmer who borrowed cash to buy land and equipment in an economy with 100 dollars in circulation had to pay back that debt in an economy with 60 dollars in circulation. He had to pay debts with an income of 30 cents a bushel that he had incurred while making one dollar a bushel. Producers, in growing debt, felt squeezed by monopolies, banks, corporations, money, resumption policy, and the gold standard. They staked their political and economic power on combating those forces because they believed that their futures depended on the battle.[56]

Of course, the Treasury Departments of the 1870s reduced currency circulation from 100 dollars to 60 dollars because the U.S. Treasury held only 60 dollars' worth of gold. Farmers, silver producers, and other soft money advocates believed that if the Treasury would open its doors and allow 40 dollars' worth of silver in, then the nation would be back to having 100 dollars in circulation again, backed by gold and silver together. Prices would then rise. Pure Greenbackers, on the other hand, advocated a straightforward issue of 100 dollars of paper money, guaranteed by the government and not backed by metal at all.

In Ignatius Donnelly's view, and that of other bimetallist writers, the resumption of the gold standard, in limiting the amount of money available to represent the nation's abundance of commodities, constricted the supply of money available to those who created true value: the producers. The real, natural source of wealth was stymied by the gold standard, the money power's unnatural and ultimately immoral limit on true wealth. Donnelly described it as "an artificial interference with natural conditions."[57] He invented a metaphor of a child who, when small, was fitted with an iron band around his waist. As the child grew, the iron band, like a money supply based on gold alone, failed to grow with him, and squeezed him to death.[58] If hard work and a fertile earth created real wealth, then it was the government's moral duty to institute a money supply that justly reflected that wealth through an expanded circulation based on gold and silver, not through a dwindling supply based on gold alone. The most famous pro-silver pamphlet, William H. ("Coin") Harvey's *Coin's Financial School,* included a famous illustration of "all of the gold in the world," one unimpressive cube sitting on the floor of the Chicago wheat exchange pit. Harvey and his readers questioned whether such a paltry chunk could possibly fuel the fastest growing economy in the world.[59] The gold standard stopped the creation of real wealth; the gold standard, Donnelly wrote, "crie[d] out to the earth, 'stop multiplying thy seed,' to . . . man 'stop thy toil,' to the wild beasts 'you are safe in your fastnesses, for man shall advance no more.'"[60]

The silverites' and bimetallists' refutation of gold's natural value, combined with their naturalization of productive labor, together constituted a strong statement for the social creation of money. Money, they argued, was a social tool rather than a natural entity. It did not matter what form it took, paper or metal, so long as it allowed all elements of society to benefit and be productive. Through a plentiful supply of gold and silver dollars, labor and capital could share in the wealth produced rather than allow eastern bankers to hoard a scarce supply of metallic money at the expense of the masses.[61] Of course, some silverites echoed the goldbugs' claim to divine authority when they invoked silver's own natural value. Silver, like gold, came from nature, and some silverites argued that, like gold, it had a divine purpose as money. Charles D. Lane, a California gold mine owner who favored silver coinage, asserted in 1896 that "I believe the Almighty made no mistake when he placed silver in the hills."[62]

Economic theories were difficult to explain on the campaign trail, so silverites and bimetallists followed their goldbug opponents in using news-

FIG. 1.3. "Take Your Choice." An illustration from the popular anti-gold pamphlet *Coin's Financial School* shows a stark contrast between two worlds. The figure of "Silver" presents a choice between the prosperous industrial economy of 1872, under bimetallism, and the impoverished world brought on by the gold standard. (William H. Harvey, *Coin's Financial School*, 1894)

paper and magazine cartoons to present simplified images that evoked the bimetallist position. Several cartoons contrasted the state of the economy under the gold standard with its likely state under a bimetallist standard. They depicted life under a gold standard with images of impoverished farmers and workers, unable to feed their children, standing gaunt and wide-eyed in raggedy clothing in front of foreclosed farms and factories. Life with silver and gold coinage, in contrast, featured happy, prosperous, well-clothed working families in front of well-kept homes and busy factories (fig. 1.3).

Other images simplified the issue even further, portraying gold as evil and goldbugs as wealthy oppressors. Such images made it clear that gold did not come from nature, or from God. It came from banks, and was controlled by bankers who did no productive labor.[63] Cartoons in Harvey's *Coin's Financial School* showed "one of the men who owns the gold," a fat eastern banker with top hat and cane, contrasted with "one of the men who owns the silver," a starving farmer. Another image showed the top-hatted figure of England (a gold standard nation) strangling the helpless female image of "Prosperity" while the young handsome figure of "Silver," chained to

FIG. 1.4. In the popular bimetallist pamphlet *Coin's Financial School*, William Harvey portrayed the life-and-death struggle of "Prosperity" against the figure of "England" (a gold standard country), while the manly and able-bodied but chained "Silver," unable to rescue her, looks on in vain. (William H. Harvey, *Coin's Financial School*, 1894)

the column of a government building, helplessly looks on (fig. 1.4). An anti-gold poster depicts the well-dressed figure of "Monopoly" with the tiny head of William McKinley tucked into his jacket pocket, ready to place an enormous weight labeled "Gold Standard" on an already burdened farmer and mechanic. The helpless figures hang on by their fingertips to a scaffold marked "Life" and "Existence." They are already weighed down by low wages, hunger, debt, taxes, low wheat prices, and high transportation charges. The great heft of the gold standard will surely send them plunging down into the gulf of poverty (fig. 1.5). In another image, a stone doorway bears the

FIG. 1.5. "Popular Silver Poster." A pro-silver, anti-gold poster in which two ordinary Americans cling to life, weighed down by hunger, low wages, debts, taxes, and other burdens. A wealthy goldbug figure named "Monopoly," with William McKinley in his pocket, approaches with yet an additional burden, the gold standard, which will surely send them plunging into the gulf of poverty. (*North American Review of Reviews,* November 1896)

FIG. 1.6. "Leave Hope Behind." Anti-gold writer William "Coin" Harvey's succinct portrayal of the nation's hopeless future under the gold standard. (William H. Harvey, *Coin's Financial School,* 1894)

carved words "Gold Standard," and the slogan "All Ye Who Enter Here Leave Hope Behind" (fig. 1.6). Yet for many western producers, Klondike gold would a few months later offer not the end of hope, but entrance to a new promised land.

Bimetallists and silverites thus denaturalized gold and gold money. They removed them from the realm of nature and called them cultural creations. They made it clear that gold's value did not come from nature. In place of gold, however, Populists and bimetallists naturalized productive labor as the true and natural source of economic value. Their naturalizations, in combination with the goldbugs' naturalizations of gold itself, came together in the campaign rhetoric of 1896 to create a powerful context for the possibility of gold mining, the natural productive labor that produced natural wealth in the form of gold.

The goldbugs and their gold standard won, of course. Following the election of William McKinley and the worldwide increase in the gold supply from South Africa, the Yukon, Alaska, and elsewhere, the United States in 1900 officially adopted a gold standard currency system, tying the money supply directly to gold. In doing so, Americans joined many European nation-

states in bringing the naturalization of gold and gold money to its most powerful point in history. In the United States between 1900 and 1914, gold and
money were identical. As one historian of the gold standard wrote, "to say
an ounce of gold was worth $20.67 was like saying a foot was twelve inches
long; $20.67 was, in reality, an ounce of pure gold put up in the form of
money."[64] An American magazine, in 1898, expressed this ultimate naturalization in an apt simile. In advising silverites and bimetallists to abandon their lost causes, the article declared of the gold standard that "For all
practical purposes the existing monetary standard might well be accepted
as if it were a fundamental physical factor in the position of the country,
like the Mississippi River or the Rocky Mountains."[65]

ON TO ALASKA AND THE YUKON

When news of the Klondike gold strikes spread across the nation and the
world in 1897, goldbugs and bimetallists alike found themselves in an interesting political quandary. Just days after the reports hit the papers, a political cartoon in the *San Francisco Examiner* captured the fluidity of the
moment (fig. 1.7). It depicted Uncle Sam, hightailing it to Alaska at a dead
run, shovel in hand. The caption read "The New National Gold Party."[66]
What were the opposing sides to think in the face of what appeared to be
an unexpected flood of gold into the economy? On the goldbug side, the
Klondike gold strike appeared to vindicate all of the goldbugs' arguments,
to vindicate gold, the gold standard, and the natural powers of both. Gold
was good, more gold was better, and nature had seen fit to provide for the
American people and their faith in the nature of gold.[67] A writer for *The
Nation* quipped as much in July 1897, as news of the Yukon strike arrived:
"The great gold finds on the Klondike come at a most awkward time for
international or any other kind of bimetallism," he wrote. "When vast new
quantities of gold are found, to go into that terrible vacuum in the currency
which nothing but silver was available to fill, it begins to look as if not only
bankers and creditor-nations and the powers of darkness, but Providence
also, were on the side of the gold-bugs."[68] On the other hand, goldbugs feared
that this new abundance of gold threatened the essential scarcity upon which
gold standard advocates based their confidence in gold as a natural measure of value. Would too much gold flood the economy, increase the currency in circulation, and bring back the wartime inflation goldbugs had
fought so long to banish?

FIG. 1.7. "The New National Gold Party." The nation, in the form of Uncle Sam, hightails it for Alaska days after news of the Klondike gold strike. The "old" gold party supported the gold standard, while the "new" gold party thought only of the great riches to be gained in Alaska and the Yukon. Suddenly, no matter what political stand Americans took in the battle of the gold standard, everyone was for gold. (*San Francisco Examiner,* July 25, 1897)

On the bimetallist side, questions arose as well. Many of the men and women who sought gold in Alaska and the Yukon were workers in financial straits. It would be easy to conclude that the gold rushers of 1897 to 1900, whatever their Populist or silverite leanings during the 1896 election, simply abandoned those political beliefs to embrace Yukon gold. In 1897, a pro-Bryan machinist from Tacoma, Washington, captured the paradox of the situation. He wrote home to his wife from the Klondike, overwhelmed by the abundance of gold, and convinced of a sure profit of $100,000. "Tell Henry that we will have to change our politics," Lewis Anderson crowed, "because the Klondike will kill Bryan and the silver question and the money power of Wall Street will try to demonetize gold."[69]

It was a complicated situation. Here they were, these Bryan men and women, united in their distrust of eastern bankers and corporate bigwigs, all of a sudden off in search of gold, the very symbol of the reviled eastern banking power, the very heart of the devil. After Bryan lost the election and the gold rush began, Bryan supporters suddenly found themselves celebrating the discovery of a metal they had spent months denouncing. Yet they did not abandon Bryan. Even four years later, in 1900, plenty of miners in Alaska supported Bryan's second, futile bid for the presidency. Hunter Fitzhugh reported from an Alaska gold camp in 1900 that "Bryan is the man. . . . Most of my friends here are western men, and they are all Bryan men."[70] Instead of embracing the goldbug cause, they transformed gold itself from a symbol of economic oppression into a symbol of their producer ideology.

Thus for the men and women ascending the Chilkoot Pass, gold was more complicated than simply wealth, or simply good and evil. The gold standard debates provided them with a broad spectrum of beliefs about gold and nature that allowed them to think about gold mining in many possible ways. On the goldbug side, after all, economists such as David A. Wells naturalized the labor of gold miners as well as the value of gold. The natural laws governing the economy dictated that when gold became scarce and even more valuable than usual, miners would naturally do the intense labor necessary to find and mine it. Silverites and bimetallists, on the other side, celebrated labor in the earth, and thus made it possible to celebrate gold mining as mining, rather than strictly as gold. This made gold mining, as productive labor, a natural source of goodness and wealth as well as a source of the oft-vilified gold money. Within the culture of gold, gold miners could oppose the gold standard while staking their lives and futures on a dangerous quest for gold itself. A Seattle cartoon showed the female figure of wheat—the symbol of farming and producerism—abandoning her former flame, silver, to be squired happily into the future by a new suitor, gold. As fuzzy and self-contradictory as this appeared, the culture of gold connected miners to gold and gold mining in powerful ways that hinged both on gold's natural value and on gold mining as productive labor. Those often contradictory naturalizations of gold and gold mining made it quite possible, and even consistent, for bimetallist, silverite, and pro-Bryan western producers to turn to Yukon gold mining as a personal and even political solution to economic crisis. Despite their clear-cut difference on the topic of gold money and the gold standard, both goldbugs and silverites found something in gold mining that was natural. No matter which side you were on, therefore, gold mining made sense as the natural thing to do.

Despite these powerful ideas, however, the Alaska-Yukon gold rush was not a natural thing to do; it was a profoundly cultural thing to do. Gold's value came from culture. The decisions to value gold and gold mining in these particular ways, at this particular historical moment, were cultural decisions, and such decisions brought consequences. Through their journeys north to the gold creeks, through mining labor, through the supplies they consumed, that gold mining connected Klondike miners to the earth and to other human beings. Those industrial connections to nature transformed the passes, the trails, and the gold creeks as well as lives of the Native peoples who had long called the Yukon River basin home. From the values bestowed by culture flowed a new set of human connections to nature, as an industrial economy transformed the Yukon basin into the Land of Gold.

2

THE NATURE
OF THE JOURNEY

In the spring of 1898, Kentucky-born gold seeker Hunter Fitzhugh spent
a soul-wrenching fifty-seven days on foot traversing the Teslin Trail from
Telegraph Creek on the Stikine River to the Yukon headwaters at Lake
Teslin. Although far less famous than the Chilkoot Pass route into the Yukon,
Fitzhugh's 197–mile journey more than captured the ordeal of gold rush
transportation (map 2). Fitzhugh's was a largely industrialized journey, but
for long stretches of that journey he could not escape the labor of moving
his body through nature, or the direct connection to nature that such labor
brought. He and his partner hauled 1,400 pounds of food and 400 pounds
of other supplies on sleds and in packs, with the help of one dog. Each man
took 200 to 400 pounds at a time on his sled, with the dog pulling a third
sled of 300 pounds. A day's work meant two or three trips each to move the
gear to the next camp, doubling back each time with empty sleds. Much of
the trail was covered with snow at the start, which made hauling easier,
and the men also followed frozen rivers and streams and crossed lakes wherever they could. Meandering streams took them out of their way, however,
so the men took shortcuts overland to shorten the distance. These were
"man-killers," Fitzhugh explained in a letter home to his father, "bare of
snow, and nothing but swamp, the very hardest sort of country through
which to pull a sled."

Still short of their destination in April, the men faced melting snow and
ice, which left the trails bare, and previously solid streams and ponds dan-

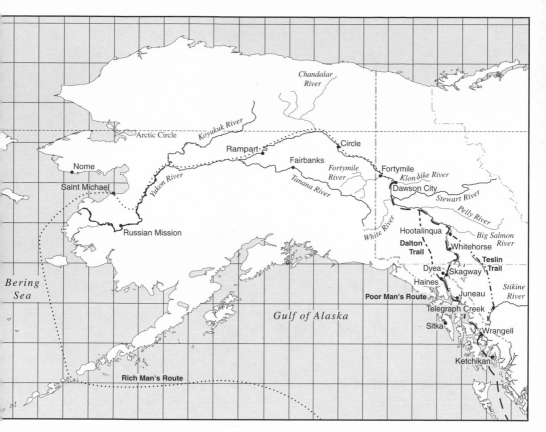

MAP 2. Selected transportation routes to goldfields in the Yukon and Alaska, including the "Rich Man's Route," the "Poor Man's Route," and the Teslin Trail

gerously rotten. One day they slogged over seven miles of dry land: "We pulled and jerked and swore and sweat over that 1,800 lbs. until sometimes I thought I would go actually crazy with weariness and aggravation." "You see," he explained to his father, "we were too late in the season, and the Spring being warmer than usual, the trail was perfectly bare in spots from a few feet to several miles in length. Nothing that a man could write or say could give you the faintest idea of the *awful* work that we had to do on that long, long trail." He called it "pulling my life out."

As the ice melted, men and sleds fell again and again into icy water, nearly fifty times by the end. Fitzhugh had to dive in more than once to fish both dog and sled out of the freezing slush. They all ended up permanently in the water by the end, wading down a stream while struggling to keep the gear dry. "The strain on our minds and bodies during the five days it took to get through that water was maddening. Our lives and possessions were both in the greatest danger, and the work was fearful." They were saved in another spot by a turn in the weather. "Next night a merciful providence sent us a pretty good freeze," he explained, "and we took our entire outfit to the last portage over ice as hard and smooth as glass."

That final portage challenged Fitzhugh's powers of description. For his father he painted the picture of hardship in terms of familiar landscapes at home in Lexington, Kentucky: "Just think of pulling 400 pounds from Lexington to Castleton, up a hill steeper than the South Broadway Hill. Think of that hill being crossed in every direction by thousands of burnt logs and the space between the logs soft and boggy, with from a few inches to a foot or more of ice water standing on it. Then add a mile of winding, pitching, snowless down-hill trail crossed here and there with torrents of water, and you have the tail of the Teslin Trail." In closing his letter, Fitzhugh provided further insight into his mental state. "A man is so utterly, absolutely prostrated with weariness on the trail that his mind is almost effected by it, and then the displays of temper are something terrible. My temper was never very sweet, but now it is fiendish. I have had to use every bit of self-possession I could raise time and again to keep me from killing the poor dog when he had pitched head over heels down a hill with the sled." Shifting back into Victorian rectitude, Fitzhugh concluded, "Oh, it is no use to write about these things. . . . I am . . . safe, and in splendid shape, so let it drop."[1]

Miners like Fitzhugh forged a whole new level of connection to nature on these journeys north toward gold. The American culture of gold connected them to ideas about gold's nature and gold's value, but journeys over the Teslin, the Chilkoot, and the White Pass Trails forged their first physical connections to the natural world of the Yukon and Alaska. These thousands of miles traveled by foot, horse, mule, dogsled, scow, canoe, raft, and steamboat revealed that the industrial relationship with nature, no matter how dependent on modern technologies, did not preclude an extraordinary intimacy with the natural world. Fitzhugh's intense immersion in nature stood at one end of a broad spectrum of the gold seekers' modes of transportation. That spectrum ran from this intense and direct experience of nature, through a whole other set of more complicated, mediated, and distanced relations to the physical environment, to the ease of railroad travel on the far end of the spectrum. The miners' shifting along that transportation spectrum captured some of what it meant to move through nature in a rapidly industrializing world.

In 1897 and 1898, prior to their journeys north, miners still safe at home consulted an instant glut of Klondike and Alaska guidebooks, special newspaper editions, and magazine articles. Here they found a font of information on just how to get themselves to the Klondike River and to certain wealth. In an attempt to simplify the situation, reporters and guidebook writers divided the many possible pathways to gold into two basic categories: the "Rich Man's Route" and the "Poor Man's Route" (map 2). Rich men, it seemed, could travel in ease and comfort all the way to the goldfields: by train to Seattle, by steamer to St. Michael at the mouth of the Yukon River, and then by sternwheeler up the Yukon to Dawson City. Anyone with enough money for the tickets, usually between $300 and $500, could travel all the way to the Klondike, in the words of historian Pierre Berton, "without lifting a finger."[2]

The "Poor Man's Route," on the other hand, offered a less expensive but more difficult option: first railroads to the West Coast, and steamers to Wrangell, Skagway, or Dyea; then an overland trek across either the Chilkoot or the White Pass, or on the Teslin Trail, to the headwaters of the Yukon; and finally, a journey down the Yukon to Dawson City on handmade rafts and boats. For the gold rushers themselves, the choice was simple. Either they had the money for the easier journey or they did not, and most did not. Rich men could buy their way to the goldfields; poor men had to do the work themselves. Over half took the difficult, physically demanding poor men's route through Skagway and Dyea, over the passes on foot, and then down the Yukon. Their labors immersed them in the natural world in ways often beyond their powers to describe, and connected them to their environment in ways that some, before they actually experienced it, would have deemed impossible in such a technologically advanced age.

Below the surface, the dichotomy between rich men's travel and poor men's travel represented the difference between two modes of transportation: transportation as production, and transportation as consumption. Transportation as production meant the bodily production of movement through walking, hauling, and rowing. Transportation as consumption meant the purchase of movement within a market economy. Production and consumption, in turn, constituted two very different relations to nature. The miners' physical production of bodily movement expanded their connections to nature in one direction, through intense contact with the nature through which they slogged in attempts to reach the Klondike and other gold camps. Transportation as consumption expanded the miners' connections to nature in another direction, through the capital invested in railroads and steamers, and through the labor of other workers who provided transport services and were themselves connected to nature through their labor in a market economy.

Production and consumption, as such different ways of moving through nature, in some ways upheld the sharp distinction between the poor men's route and the rich men's route. But from the start, individual miners ranged far and wide on that spectrum, producing their own transport one moment only to buy and sell movement as a commodity the next moment. Furthermore, over the course of a very few years, from 1897 to 1900, journeys such as those over the Chilkoot and White Passes, which had required miners' intense labor in the production of their own transportation, were quickly transformed into journeys quite easily consumed. By 1899, with the completion of the White Pass & Yukon Railroad from Skagway to White-horse at the head of the Yukon, miners no longer had to cross the coast range at Chilkoot Pass on foot (map 4). They became "rich men" with regard to that particular journey. They simply took the train, consuming transportation over the mountains as a service rather than producing it themselves. Thus, miners who crossed the Chilkoot on foot one year only to return over White Pass by train the next experienced the sharpest possible contrast between the two ends of the transportation spectrum. That contrast in their experience of nature, recorded in their letters and journals, exaggerated and encapsulated the ways in which modern transportation technologies changed the human relationship with nature by drastically reducing bodily labor in nature. It seemed a nearly instantaneous conquest of nature, a magical transformation of a tough and deadly journey into a simple train ride.

That conquest, however, and the disappearance of the bodily production of transportation it brought are somewhat deceiving. They suggest that gold miners, and nineteenth-century Americans as a whole, underwent one simple shift from producers of transportation to consumers, one day struggling over icy or muddy trails, the next day comfortably ensconced in rail cars. It suggests that one day they were intimately engaged with nature, and the next day safely distanced from that nature, never to truly engage with it again. The Alaska-Yukon transportation economy as a whole, however, challenged those suggestions. Gold miners did not make that one stark shift one time, from the primitive labor of packing over Chilkoot Pass to the modern convenience of trains and steamers. In boarding steamers and trains at certain junctures, they did not completely abandon the bodily labor of transportation and its direct engagement with nature, seasons, ice, and mud. Instead, they made subtler and more incomplete shifts back and forth along the spectrum between wading through hip-deep mud and boarding steamers and trains, between production and consumption. Throughout their gold rush experiences, miners embraced both ends of the spectrum, shifting back and forth along it, producing their own labor one day, consuming invested capital and others' labor the next. Although they engaged less frequently in their own transport labor, they still, on occasion, were called upon to move their own bodies through nature. Such labor and the connections to nature that went with it remained part of their daily experience, and thus, by extension, part of industrialized life. The miners' diverse ways of moving themselves through the world jumbled together both consumption and the contrasting intimacy of production. It exemplified the mixture of diverse possible connections that made up the emerging industrial human relationship to nature.

INDUSTRIALIZED JOURNEYS

As part of a headlong plummet into industrial modernity, Americans by the 1890s were far more consumers of the work of transportation than producers of that work. With the exception of the bicycling craze that reinvented movement as recreation, Americans tended less and less to use their bodies, or even their bodies in conjunction with animals' bodies, as a means of getting anywhere. As investors poured the nation's accumulated wealth into an ever-expanding network of railroads, ship lines, and roads, transportation became an industry which sold movement as a commodity on its own market, something to be bought and sold. In the thirty years since the completion of the first American transcontinental line, rail lines had filled in the map to the point that Klondike miners in 1897 and 1898 could, with remarkable ease and very little cash, hop a series of trains that within hours or days deposited them on the Seattle waterfront and on northbound steamers (map 3).

In other words, gold rushers, whether rich or poor, traveled the initial legs of the journey north as symbolically "rich" men and women, as thoroughgoing consumers of capital, labor, and movement, free from their own bodily labor. Such travels sat at the consumption end of the spectrum of possible modes of transportation. When Bill Ballou, Mac McMichael, and Hunter Fitzhugh left home, they simply bought tickets, first on trains to the West Coast, and then on steamers to one of three Alaskan ports of entry on

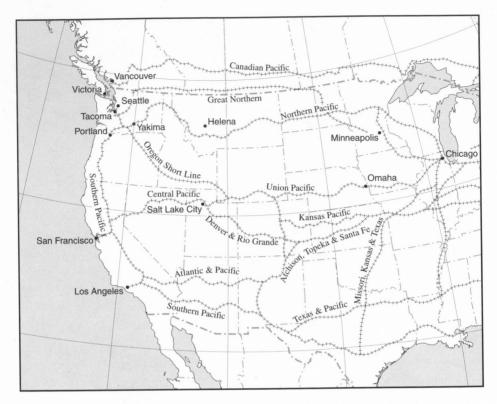

MAP 3. Transcontinental railroad routes in western North America, 1898

the Inside Passage: Wrangell, Skagway, or Dyea.[3] For those three, and thousands like them, the rich men's part of the journey ended there, and the poor men's bodily labor of transportation began. The found themselves suddenly and violently at the other end of the transport spectrum, facing immense bodily labor in the need to produce their own movement over the coastal mountain ranges. Others, headed for St. Michael and the mouth of the Yukon by steamship on the rich man's route, remained contentedly at the consumption end of the spectrum. They consumed movement as a commodity for the whole journey, on sternwheelers up the Yukon River to Dawson City and the goldfields (map 2). On trains or steamers, they purchased with their tickets an exact amount of transportation, at a fixed price, on a theoretically precise schedule. They also purchased a comfortable but not complete distance from the messy natural world through which they moved.

These trains, steamers, and schedules sped gold miners to Skagway, Dyea, St. Michael, and even Dawson City itself with remarkable ease. Thousands of miles from home, these miners had yet to do any physical work, for they lived in a relatively new world in which telegraphs, railroads, and steamers had transformed the meanings of distance, labor, time, and money. These "modern distance-diminishing technologies," as geographer Cole Harris describes them, had brought in the span of forty or fifty years a "time-space compression."[4] Seattle was no longer a three-thousand-mile summer journey from Boston by road, river, foot, and ox-drawn wagon. Instead, the coast-to-coast journey meant simply four days by train and a forty-dollar ticket, and the four days and forty dollars mattered far more than the actual physical space between Boston and Seattle. The distance to Seattle was so easily crossed that it seemed not to matter at all.

As a result, the meanings of distance itself were transformed. Historian Stephen Kern's study of notions of time and space between 1880 and 1918 notes that distance had long acted as a natural barrier to movement, requiring long spans of time to cross. By the 1890s, however, distance faded in importance when contrasted with speed and money. Because money could buy train and boat tickets, and hence the speed of rapid travel across distance, money became increasingly equivalent to speed and to time. Time and money merged, as time became money, and money, time. Americans paid closer and closer attention to shorter periods of time, and worried more and more about how fast they moved and worked.[5] This proved true for Alaska-Yukon gold rushers as well, at the start of their journeys. Their freshly minted guidebooks described the trip north in terms of time and cost, rather than distance. What mattered to miners was how quickly and cheaply they could reach the goldfields, not the actual mileage to be covered. In 1897, according to the *Chicago Record Guide Book,* the first-class fare to Seattle from Boston and New York ran about $80, the trip lasting about a hundred hours; from Chicago, it cost about $60 for a trip of eighty-five hours.[6] With the boom brought by the frenzy for Klondike gold, Canadian and American rail lines started a rate war, and the cost of the journey plummeted. When Bill Ballou hopped off the westbound train in St. Paul in March 1898, he found Great Northern Railroad tickets to Seattle selling for ten dollars. What once had required months of time and extraordinary effort now sold for a pittance. "It seems that every one who was able to beg, borrow, or steal ten dollars was on the way to the coast," Ballou wrote.[7]

This straightforward consumption of movement, concern for speed, and the accompanying unimportance of distance continued on the next leg of the journey. Steamer passage from Seattle to Dyea, a distance of about a thousand miles, ran about $40 for a cabin, or $25 for steerage, with an added $10 per ton of supplies. The much longer voyage to St. Michael, and then up the Yukon by sternwheeler to Dawson City, according to the *Chicago Record*, required at least $500 for transportation of self and outfit, but sometimes as much as $1,000.[8] A New York pamphlet, put out just days after the first Klondike news in August 1897, emphasized speed, stating that the all-water rich man's journey to the gold creeks took a mere fifty-one days.[9] Beyond speed and distance, transportation companies also advertised the freedom from labor, and from nature, provided by such a journey. A Tacoma steamer company's promotional pamphlet for the Stikine River route to the Yukon, which took miners part way to the interior by steamer, compared that superior route to the arduous foot and pack trails over the Chilkoot and White Passes: "Along this line the travel is THROUGH instead of OVER the mountains, and SITTING instead of WALKING—resting comfortably in chair and bed instead of toiling up steep acclivities."[10]

Modern technologies, especially railroads, freed gold seekers from such toil, at least up to a certain point. Railroads sped them westward, freeing travelers from the natural realities and constraints of weather, darkness, and seasons, and making travel possible at any time, day or night, winter or summer.[11] At the mouth of the Yukon, transportation companies operated 200–foot luxury sternwheelers, replete with mahogany-trimmed dining rooms and upholstered furniture in carpeted observation lounges. Cosseted passengers had little to do but socialize and observe the natural world as they were swept upstream toward Dawson City.[12] Their consumption of transportation did connect them to that natural world through the human labor and fuel required to build and run trains and steamers. For the passengers, however, those connections paled in intensity when compared with the linkages formed by their fellow miners, the "poor men" who, lacking the cash to purchase their way to Dawson City, set about the work of getting there under their own bodily steam.

"IT IS A TERRIBLE COUNTRY TO GET IN"

The thousands of gold seekers who disembarked steamers at Dyea and Skagway, at the head of the Lynn Canal, suddenly found themselves beyond the reach of their familiar industrial transportation network, with its tickets and schedules. As hopeful miners crossed the wharves and beaches littered with their supplies, they ceased, at least briefly, to be consumers of transportation. They became producers, dependent on their own bodies to move them over land and water. Their labor brought them into intimate contact with nature and forged connections with their environment that they would never forget. Both their labor and their intimacy were difficult and unfamiliar; such work mimicked an older, preindustrial world of slow, laborious movement in which distance, seasons, weather, and light suddenly mattered very, very much. However drastic the change, though, miners had not traveled backward in time to an earlier, primitive time in transportation history. They remained denizens of an industrialized world. Even at its most primitive moments, their bodily labor remained modern, for it occurred within an industrial economy as that economy reached north to incorporate the Yukon and Alaska.

Steamers disgorged miners at the transport boomtowns of Dyea and Skagway (map 4). From the cluttered beaches, miners, Native American packers, horses, dogs, and oxen hauled tons of goods up precipitous trails, fighting mud and streams in spring and summer, ice and snow in winter. For many, the Chilkoot became the place, as James Hamil wrote, "where men make horses and mules out of themselves."[13] As the ubiquitous images of the Chilkoot Pass suggest, that coastal mountain crossing was an almost pure expression of the bodily labor of transportation. The chain of bundled figures trudging upwards with grim effort revealed the miners' profound immersion in and struggle with the natural world. Edward S. Curtis, in *Century Magazine,* described the Chilkoot crossing in 1897 not only as a struggle with nature, but as an outright battle. Writing with the uncredited benefit of his brother Asahel's stories and photographs of the Chilkoot crossing, Curtis declared the 1897 trail as "the first shock of a great battle which is now waging between invading Man and defending Nature."[14] In ascending the Chilkoot and other passes and trails, miners pitched their bodies against nature and came away humbled and transformed, with what historian Richard White calls a "bodily knowledge" of this natural world.[15]

Through this physical engagement, the journey to the Klondike took miners to the other end of the transportation spectrum, far from the consumption represented by train and steamer tickets. The excruciating labor required to move, and the overwhelming slowness of that movement, did away with their accustomed, modern meanings of distance and time. For miners on the trail with 2,000 pounds of supplies, Lakes Lindeman and Bennett, on the far side of the mountains, might as well have been thousands of miles away, not thirty miles via Chilkoot or fifty miles via White Pass. Many of the miners could cross the distance on foot one-way in a day, but with outfits to be hauled, the familiar modern rules of distance and time ceased to have any meaning whatsoever. Nowhere in their lives had thirty miles, or even one mile, presented obstacles such as this. The average miner spent three months crossing the Chilkoot, doubling back again and again for another load, back and forth between two camps eight or ten times a day with small loads before advancing to the next stage. It could take days to move the whole lot just a few miles.[16] That slowness struck men and women accustomed to train travel as nothing less than an appalling *lack* of movement. Jonas Houck spent just over a month covering the fifty miles over White Pass. He wrote that it took "about 50 lbs. at a load over the same ground 60 times before we get our goods moved from one place to another." It was simply the "hardest work I ever did or ever see anyone else do," he wrote.[17]

As Hunter Fitzhugh had learned the hard way on the Teslin Trail, much of the miners' knowledge of nature came from seasonal changes. Packing and hauling required far less human and animal labor in winter, when frozen mud and ice provided a hard surface for sleds, wheels, snowshoes, and for the humans and animals that did the pushing and pulling. That seasonality extended to the trails at the gold camps, where freighting made little sense in summer due to mud, moss, bogs, and nasty, root-filled trails. Land transport proved to be winter work. Miners caught on the Chilkoot and White Pass Trails in the waning days of winter, in March and April, raced to get up over the pass before the snow and ice melted. In winter the frozen Dyea River constituted the first several miles of the Chilkoot Trail. Mac McMichael, one of at least five or six thousand people on that trail in late March 1898, noted the hurry to get up the river quickly and over the pass. "Every day is precious now for they are expecting the ice to break up at the canyon eight miles up. Then it will be much more difficult to pack and more expensive."[18]

Once the snow and ice melted, the Chilkoot and White Pass Trails turned "fearfully muddy," according to Harold Petersen. Petersen described the Chilkoot route in the summer of 1897 as "one of the many impressive places which my eyes have behold," where one "sees and hears the groaning of women, children, and horses alike . . . as they are passing by sinking now and again in muck to their knees."[19] Miners wrote home in disbelief after their experience of spring and summer on the trails. Rebecca Schuldenfrei, a wife and mother from the New York garment district, found herself at a loss for words after crossing the Chilkoot the same summer. "It certainly was never made for human beings," she wrote of the Chilkoot summit, "as any one who once went over it is either more or maybe less human, and no living being, who has not gone over it, can actually imagine or anticipate what it really is."[20] Jonas Houck had a similar reaction on the White Pass in 1898. "The hill coming up to the summit is beyond description. . . . The thick black mud runs down the trail on the mountain. . . . I tell you this is more than I bargained for. . . . If any person had told me I could stand this I would certainly have thought they were crazy." Houck packed between 50 and 125 pounds on his back, walking in rubber boots that reached to his hips. He tried to get his wife to imagine this, writing, "go through a canyon for two miles and with mud up to your ankles and then up a mountain 1600 feet high and so steep that you would fall backwards if you did not hang on and with slush and mud running against you." "I would not go through it again," he concluded, "for all the gold in Alaska."[21]

Nature's intensity continued on the far side of the passes. In the fall of 1897, hundreds of gold rushers descended from the Chilkoot and White Pass summits to the Yukon headwater lakes, Lindeman, Bennett, and Tagish (map 4). Here they decimated the local scrub forest to build a flotilla of small boats, nearly seven thousand by June 1898. When further hordes poured over the trails, the timber at Lindeman was already gone.[22] Searching for timber posed a challenge, but it was nothing compared to what came next. "The next work was to whip Saw Lumber so we built a pit which is simply a large scaffle made so one man can stand below and the other on top," James Hamil explained. The two men pushed and pulled a long crosscut saw between them, cutting the length of the log to produce a thick, rough board. The work proved horrendous. Sawing timber had for these men always been the work of sawmills, mechanized industrial plants. Now it fell back on their arms and backs, another source of physical connection to nature, this time to the tough fibers of stringy northern spruce. "It is trying," Hunter Fitzhugh wrote later, "this thing of making a saw mill of yourself." The man on top risked falling from the scaffold; the one on the bottom endured a constant shower of sawdust in his eyes. "We tried whipsawing, Boyd and I," wrote McMichael. "A trial is sufficient for me. I shall buy my lumber for the boat, if possible." Instead, he bargained with his two partners; they did the whipsawing while he cooked. "The Yukoners say," Fitzhugh wrote later,

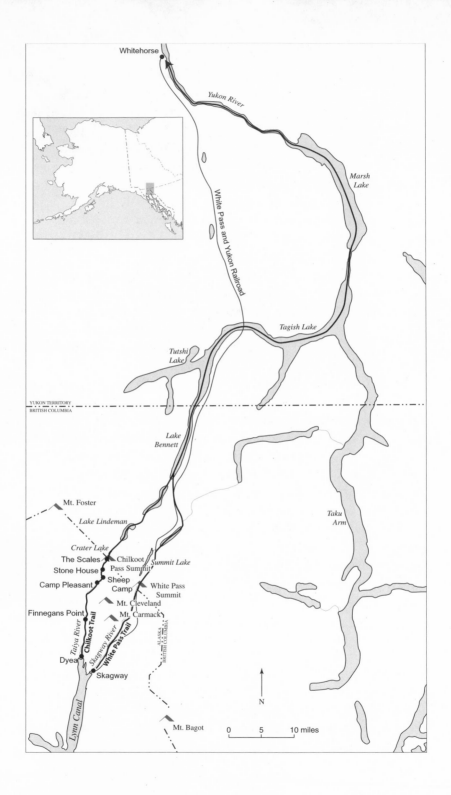

Whitehorse

Yukon River

*Marsh
Lake*

White Pass and Yukon Railroad

Tagish Lake

*Tutshi
Lake*

YUKON TERRITORY
BRITISH COLUMBIA

*Lake
Bennett*

*Taku
Arm*

Mt. Foster

Lake Lindeman

Crater Lake

The Scales   Chilkoot   *Summit Lake*
                    Pass Summit
Stone House
                    Sheep   White Pass
Camp Pleasant   Camp   Summit

                    Mt. Cleveland

Finnegans Point   Mt. Carmack

Taiya River   **Chilkoot Trail**
                 Skagway River   **White Pass Trail**

Dyea   ALASKA
                                     BRITISH COLUMBIA

        Skagway

Lynn Canal

                    Mt. Bagot   N

                    0   5   10 miles

spinning a yarn, "that when one of us who has not been as good as he should dies, the devil puts him to whipsawing; but if he is faithful and doesn't complain under the trial, he is then simply burned through eternity like an ordinary goat."[23]

The pressure to complete the boats quickly was greatest for those traveling in the fall of 1897. Temperamental whipsawers raced the winter and the ice to build boats and row 400 miles through tricky channels and rough rapids before the Yukon froze. Lakes Lindeman and Bennett remained open into October, but the Dawson-bound miners were headed north. They knew that the ice was forming ahead of them on the river, and they knew they had to beat it. For James Cooper, James Hamil, and Tappan Adney, three of the scores of men trying to get downriver in September and October 1897, the ice became an object of close observation and fierce debate. Gold seekers became sudden experts on how slow-forming ice affected small-boat navigation on lakes and rivers. Cooper despaired at the headwinds on Lake Labarge, which kept a hundred men pinned down at "Camp Detention" at the end of September (map 5). As they paced the shore, the ice gathered at their feet. "Are trying hard to get by Lake Labarge before it freezes over as that means either hauling our grub about 400 miles on sleds that we would have to build . . . or stopping here for 8 months and do nothing but devour our provisions."[24] "We were then in zero weather," wrote James Hamil below Labarge, "and the floating ice was running all around us but we had about six days more at least."[25] Tappan Adney and his partner found themselves creeping down Tagish Lake on October 12, knowing full well that the river would soon close. The shore ice had begun to form, reaching out toward the central channel of the river. The ice, Adney wrote, "creaks and cries . . . and it is indeed a dismal sound that bodes us no good." By the time they got to the Hootalinqua, the water had crystallized into fine crystals, and then slushy "mush ice." At the junction with the Pelly on October 23, they struggled to avoid the ice as it poured out of the smaller river, filling the Yukon. With temperatures below zero, they had to knock ice off the oars with an axe. The ice made an "ominous sound" rubbing against the boat, threatening to crush it or throw them into the bank.[26]

This desperate interest in ice continued the following spring. Through

MAP 4 (*facing page*). Transportation routes to the goldfields: the Chilkoot Trail, White Pass Trail, Yukon Headwater Lakes, Upper Yukon River, and White Pass & Yukon Railroad (built 1898–1900)

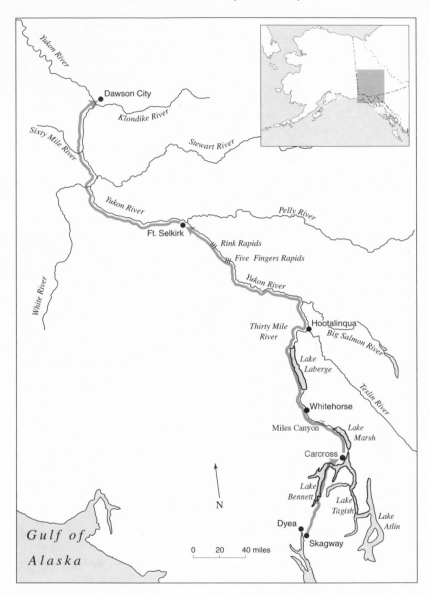

MAP 5. Transportation routes to the goldfields: the Upper Yukon to Dawson City

March, April, and into May, ice held impatient miners at the lakes, preventing forward movement. When not swearing at each other over saws, or pitching and caulking boat seams, or carving oars of spruce (not balsam, which broke under pressure), the volatile crowds paced the ice, awaiting the thaw and talking nonstop.[27] "Of course, the lake and ice are standard themes that are discussed continually," McMichael observed, "how soon, how late, is it open above or below; how thick or how thin the ice is; how much or how little it thawed to-day or will it freeze tonight. These are all a part of an interesting subject to us all for upon the movement of the ice depends our departure from these shores." In late May, the ice finally seized and cracked, and the milling crowds at Lakes Lindeman and Bennett burst their seasonal gates. They hoisted sails and sped down the windy lakes into the upper river. Fitzhugh and his partner christened their 21–foot boat the good ship "Evelyn Lee" and set her afloat with grand ceremony: "We broke a can of condensed milk over her (but saved the milk) and launched her."[28]

Open water meant high winds, dangerous swells, and, of course, mosquitoes. But it also meant progress, as the wind, water, and currents came together to sweep the boats forward. The miners, after months of slow, burdensome packing and then an endless wait for the thaw, rejoiced at the sheer motion. "It feels good to be on the move again," McMichael confessed from his boat on Lake Tagish. "We were a little over two months in making sixty miles of our journey. Pretty slow traveling is it not?" "Tremendous excitement in the crowd, to get away, and it is a great sight to see miles of boats, mast[s] with flags up, tied along the shore, some places 3, or 4 deep," wrote Bill Hiscock. The sheer numbers amazed them. "The boats are thick going down the lake today," wrote McMichael on May 25, 1898, "all rowing as there is very little wind."[29]

At Tagish Lake the Royal Canadian Mounted Police lined the boats and rafts up for inspection and issued registration papers. By mid-June 1898, the police counted 7,200 boats passing the post, most with four or five people aboard.[30] The crowd waiting for papers stretched for a mile along the lakeshore, boats two or three deep. That meant a half a day or more of waiting, torture for impatient miners finally set free from land and ice.[31] Charles Mosier's party sat out the wait on June 3, about three hundred boats back from the head of the line of seven hundred to a thousand boats. "Looks like New York harbor," Mosier wrote. Tom Boldrick bided his time in the same line, and made a telling comparison between the miners' boats and the flocks of passenger pigeons that had darkened midwestern skies earlier in the century: "It is astonishing the amount of them," he wrote, " as thick as pigeons in the old days."[32]

With the ice out of the rivers, the miners faced new natural obstacles, vicious mountain headwinds and crosswinds, and in the canyons and rapids, rocks and swift waters which smashed scores of hastily built scows. A short, turbulent canyon connected Lakes Lindeman and Bennett. Most miners portaged an easy two-thirds of a mile around it. In the "tremendous excitement" of May 1898, however, a reckless contingent shot the rapids in loaded boats, creating a spectacle for those on shore. "Today there are dozens of boats and scows coming through the canyon and getting smashed to pieces," Hiscock wrote, "not more than one in ten coming through safe, there were five outfits lost one after the other." Bill Hiscock and his fellow New Zealanders camped only a few yards from the canyon. He recorded in wonder and annoyance that "we . . . could not get through a meal without rushing to the bank when we heard the crowd yelling on the opposite bank, at the pleasure of seeing another wreck." Two days later he added that "the fun still continues only some smash ups and more outfits lost . . . excitement goes on from 3 a.m. in the morning till half past ten at night." One big scow "turned broad side on . . . the whole force of the current filled her entire length and she snapped in half like a rotten carrot."[33]

By the time they reached Miles Canyon, most of the daredevils had either been eliminated or come to their senses (map 5). Here the river narrowed from 300 feet to about 40, tumbling with concentrated energy through high rocky walls. Just below, it struck a stretch of threatening rocks at White Horse Rapids, named for the frothy crests of waves that resembled horses' manes. Scores of splintered craft and "acres of groceries and provisions spread out on canvas and blankets drying with scows turned up for repairs" convinced about three-quarters of the miners to hire experienced pilots (Indian and white) to take their empty boats through while they portaged freight around by pack and on tramways.[34] The fee, usually between twenty and forty dollars, was well worth it, because, as Tom Boldrick explained, "Loosing ones outfit is about equal to loosing ones life in this country."[35]

Although grateful for the river's six-mile-per-hour current, which speeded them on their way, miners nonetheless threw their bodies into rowing and steering. This was especially true at spots like the Thirty Mile River, the treacherous section of the upper Yukon below Lake Labarge. The Thirty Mile had a twelve-mile-per-hour current and "rocks and boulders whizzing past like ties under a moving train," as McMichael put it, using a more familiar image of transportation. "We bent our whole energy to the oars and by a close shave missed a large rock nearly in the middle where some poor fellow boat was lodged torn to atoms & dashed to pieces," Tom Boldrick wrote of this cauldron of "rocks & bars." "We were exhausted," agreed Hiscock in describing the Thirty Mile, "as during the whole distance, we barely had a minute without having to pull to avert wrecking and drowning." "It is a terrible country to get in," Boldrick wrote ominously, "& it may be a terrible country to get out of." Some looked forward to the respite of mining. "We were happy to know," admitted James Hamil as his boat approached the promised land of Dawson City, "that the past two months of the hardest work we had ever done was over so we laid back to rest."[36]

A sizable crowd chose not to abandon the labor of river travel, and left the Yukon to pole up the White, Indian, or Stewart Rivers in search of new gold strikes (map 5). At least three thousand went up the Stewart in the spring and summer of 1898. However intense the experience of nature while moving downstream on the Yukon, moving upstream against the Stewart's force brought a new level of struggle. The miners cached their supplies at the mouth, built small poling boats, and then pushed and hauled these boats against the spring currents of these smaller rivers, often stumbling alongside the boats for miles, waist deep in freezing water. Unable to row or paddle against the current in shallow, rocky water, they ran ropes to shore and crashed along through mossy bogs and tangled willow stands, over fallen trees, besieged by mosquitoes.

For most, this level of engagement with nature proved too much. Some lasted several weeks, others only days. Tom Boldrick's crew went first to the White, and then up the Stewart. The White, a swift and silty river named for its color, which looked like chalk or paint, proved so strong that after a few days, two parties combined their gear into one boat in order to have greater pulling power. "There is now eleven in our party & when they get all strung out on a rope they are a sight to see . . . we have not made over 10 miles in the two days pulling & dragging the boat." After a miserable day pulling up the Stewart, Boldrick's party watched other defeated boatloads careen back downstream at breakneck speed. "They came down in 5 1/2 hours on a boat and it will take us 3 days to go up to it which shows how swift the river is." That disparity proved the greatest example of the slowness of northern transport, and of nature's power to bring humans to a maddening standstill. At one point on the Stewart it got very bad, with "rocks straight up and down and with now and then one jutting out and as the current was very rapid we had to pull along close and hang on with our hands. We were over 2 hours making a few hundred feet." Boldrick's party lasted over a week before turning back down the Stewart for the Yukon, "which is pretty tough after wading 10 days in ice cold water but such is life in the gold diggins."[37] Mac McMichael's crew moved only eight miles a day up the Fortymile, hauling with bloody hands on 100–foot lines, sinking into quicksand in heavy boots. "Sometimes to get through the riffles we would have to stand in water nearly to our hips and pull until we could almost see stars and that way get the boat through inch by inch." He wrote of "a weariness that is almost beyond describing."[38]

"MAKING TRAVEL A JOY"

No matter how intractable going upstream or turbulent going downstream, the rivers provided the only feasible corridors for movement in the summer. Overland transport meant only mud and moss and thus even slower movement. Mac McMichael made his overland trip up Fourth of July Creek in the summer, to prospect the riverbed (map 7). An old Indian trail was not too bad, but when they left the trail for the banks of the creek, he wrote, "Then we would have great patches of deep moss, as hard to walk over as deep snow, or the tangled undergrowth of trees along the bank. But worst of all were the great bogs of a kind of bunch grass . . . from six inches to a foot and a half high. . . . If you can imagine yourself walking on inverted beer bottles and each one you step on falling in a different direction, then you can form some idea of walking a mile or two over such a bog. Below the grass is soft muck and often water." John Sidney Webb, writing for *Century Magazine,* described the trail up Eldorado Creek as "a miserable excuse for a path, leading over rough hummocks, up hills and over bogs, through sticky, oozy muck, by brambles and bushes, across creeks and corduroy paths." An Irish miner told Webb that he had paid a cheap price to have Indians pack his goods up the trail. " 'How much did you pay?' some one inquired. 'I don't know,' said he. 'Then how do you know it was cheap?' 'Oh, anything would be chape [*sic*] over that place!' he replied."[39]

With winter, everything changed. Once the rivers closed with ice and the muddy trails froze solid, both became feasible roadways for dogsleds, snowshoers, and even bicyclists, who took to the frozen Yukon as if to a paved street at home. Although dogs were crucial to hauling supplies and wood, men without the cash to procure a team could get along pretty well in the winter with a sled, good boots, and plenty of muscle. As Lynn Smith wrote during his first winter in the north, "Dogs are beyond my means, so I must play 'dog' myself." Rather than play dog, most miners imported a transportation work force in the form of malamutes, Newfoundlands, and retrievers, and hitched them to dogsleds to move food, equipment, mail, wood, and even gold over frozen creeks and rivers as well as frozen land. Once mail carriers broke trails over the ice and snow, dogsleds could move up and down the frozen Yukon River with relative safety. In November 1899, Fitzhugh wrote of the closed-up Yukon that "now its frozen corpse is marked all over with sled trails and the tracks of dogs and men." This became most apparent in the winter of 1900, when thousands abandoned Yukon mines to rush to the new goldfields at Nome, Alaska. Between January and April, miners poured down the frozen river, some with dogsleds, others on foot, moving from wood camp to mining town and from roadhouse to roadhouse. In early March, twenty parties a day passed Hunter Fitzhugh's camp. Some went by on bicycles, the tires fitted with canvas. In April, Bill Ballou, watching the Nome parade as it passed Rampart City, estimated five thousand headed to Nome, with up to a hundred teams passing in one day. The constant passing of sleds wore the trail down "as level as a table," according to John Cantwell, captain of the U.S. Revenue steamer, *Nunivak,* which patrolled the Yukon. They looked "like a procession of black ants crawling slowly over the white surface of the river."[40]

Dogsledding, like crossing the passes, proved to be an intense engagement with nature, especially nature in the form of the dogs themselves. Ever fond of adventure, Hunter Fitzhugh made several trips up and down the Stikine River by dogsled his first winter in the north, hauling heavy loads of supplies. He learned much about dogs and snow. "Another thing they are fond of doing is to sit on your snow shoes," he wrote, "as they are drier than the snow, and many a time I have started off after fixing their harness, or putting their feet over the traces, only to go head first into six feet of snow, owing to a sixty pound dog being perched on the heel of each of my shoes." Fitzhugh learned to feed dogs only once a day, tie them with chains (as they chewed through ropes), and keep his shoes from being eaten, as "any sort of dressed hides delight their souls." On the return trip up the Stikine in February, four dogs pulled eight hundred pounds on two sleds, leaving Fitzhugh and his partner to haul four hundred pounds on their own. On the lower river, in bad coastal weather, "we floundered along at an average rate of 2 1/2 miles a day. Some days the wind was so terrific that we had to stay in camp all day and have our eyes put out by smoke." The men had not yet learned to pack the sleds, which proved too heavy anyway. "The loads did nothing but turn over in the snow about twice a minute, and monkeying around a dog sled in seven feet of snow, with snowshoes on, trying to 'right' a 400 lb. load is one of the great trials of life."[41]

In the fall, when the season's first loose ice shut down boat travel, dog-sledders waited carefully until the trails froze and the ice in the creeks and rivers became strong enough to support a loaded sled, usually about the middle of October.[42] Sleds ran best over hard snow or smooth ice, and the exact consistency of the frozen surface of the earth profoundly shaped how much work it took from dogs and humans to move across that surface. Dogsledders thus tended to take careful note of the condition of the surface over which they moved. On open, smooth ice, a man or a few dogs could quickly pull a fairly heavy load for miles in a day. Fitzhugh worked a claim twelve miles up Big Manook creek, and moved his supplies up that far (map 7). "But," he explained, "that is nothing in the winter over 12 miles of smooth creek trail." "It is a joy to be alive now," he wrote with bounding enthusiasm after the first snow in October 1898. They were having "the most beautiful weather" which froze the trails, "making travel a joy." Just a few days earlier his trip out to the gulches led over fallen logs and through "a bottomless swamp, covered with this everlasting arctic moss," a nine-mile trek that took six hours. Once frozen, the trail proved a breeze, and the return trip took only two hours.[43]

Mid-winter conditions were perfect for transportation, but in March and April all movement ceased for a few weeks between the time that the hard-packed ice and snow turned to mush and the rivers cleared of ice. Spring made dogsledding a risky proposition. The sun warmed the snow and ice, making slush and covering the hard surface of the ice in water. Glad for his mail in April 1902, Bill Ballou nonetheless took note that there was "a great deal of water on the ice . . . in some places two feet deep through which the poor dogs have to swim."[44] Water also ran beneath the snowpack, threatening miners who broke through soft snow. "Even now the trails were impassable," Cantwell wrote, "rushing rivulets of water which cut miniature gorges in the hard, thin, packed snow and formed little lakes on the surface of the ice where hollows were."[45] For a few weeks, dogsledders and miners extended the winter by traveling at night, when colder temperatures refroze softening trails, or at least formed hard crusts over the slush below. Miners got out of bed at night to greet arriving mail sleds.[46] As temperatures warmed and days lengthened, freighters slept through the heat of day, and then packed from Dawson to the mining creeks at night, when it was cooler. "In this way they do not need to carry blankets, you see," McMichael explained. "Great country!!"[47]

"A CONTINUOUS PICNIC"

For miners caught up in these seasonal details of transportation, nature powerfully shaped their lives and work. In the space of two years, however, their connections to nature through transportation shifted. From the start, both the "rich men" who traveled by steamers and the "poor men" who struggled with packs, boats, and sleds combined their efforts and attracted the capital necessary to speed up transportation over *all* routes to Dawson and other gold camps. Entrepreneurs, investors, transport companies, and construction workers combined labor and nature to make it far easier to get to the goldfields. They cut roads, built tramways and railroads, and even calmed river rapids. As a result, these once daunting distances and obstacles shrank in meaning and importance. Gold miners became more consumers, rather than producers, of transportation.

In 1898, a conglomerate of British capitalists, American engineers, and laborers from everywhere began construction on the White Pass & Yukon Railroad from Skagway across the White Pass (map 4). By the middle of the winter of 1898–99, the rails reached the summit of the pass and carried passengers and their tons of freight quickly to the heights that had, the year before, taken miners weeks or months to gain.[48] Passengers took the train to the top for five dollars. At twenty-five cents a mile, Adney observed, this was "probably the most expensive railroad travel in the world."[49] Nevertheless, on July 6, 1899, the rails reached Lake Bennett, and the following season the railroad company announced a new rate of two and a quarter cents a pound for freight from Skagway over the pass to the lakes. By May 1900 workers were laying rail at a rate of two miles per day, and on July 29 they drove the final spike at Whitehorse, bypassing Lake Bennett, Tagish, and Marsh Lakes, where fleets of boats had battled high winds.[50] The journey over the passes was at last an item to be consumed, bought, and sold as a commodity.

Modern transportation technology transformed the journey from White-horse down the Yukon to Dawson City as well. Steamers moved onto the upper river in the spring and summer of 1898, and by the following year completely replaced the miners' small, handmade boats. The steamers ran in two legs, one boat back and forth above the Whitehorse Rapids, and a second between there and Dawson (map 5). The four hundred miles down the lakes and rivers turned into a distance to be consumed at a precise sched-ule, a commodity purchased at a standard price. Of course, not everyone could afford the purchase price, especially early in the season when demand was high. "The fare is $300 either way," McMichael wrote, on hearing of the steamers running on the rivers and lakes. "This is a big sum for the poor devils who are in here, broke and want to get out. There are many of them." With the increase in river traffic later in the season, however, prices dropped. When Angelo Heilprin came over the Chilkoot to a "deserted" Lake Bennett just a few weeks later, the fare to Dawson on the *Nora* was only seventy-five dollars.[51]

Trains and steamers changed the journey. When Mac McMichael fell ill at the goldfields in January 1899, he traveled upriver from Dawson to Lake Bennett by dogsled and sleigh. This man, who had crossed the Chilkoot on foot, built his boat, and rowed to Dawson, now boarded the train over White Pass, reached Skagway by dinner, and soon after took a steamer to Seattle. His purchase of a ticket—talisman of civilization and speed—marked the transition from movement as bodily labor to movement as consumption of a commodity. It also marked the further compression of distance and nature into mere time, as Dawson moved closer to the rest of the world. The Seattle *Trade Register* noted that the journey from Seattle to Dawson "will now occupy only six to seven days." Edward C. Adams took the train from Skagway to Lake Bennett in 1900. The thirty-mile trip took about five hours, complete with revealing views of the bones of dead horses that two years earlier had packed supplies on far slower journeys. When Bill Ballou traveled from Seattle back to Dawson in 1901, he returned through Skag-way, and took the train over the pass to Whitehorse. "So after sleeping on the Pacific one night," he wrote, "we were steaming down the Yukon the next traveling all the time." It took a total of six days and sixteen hours for him to reach Dawson from Seattle. Of Dawson, he remarked, "all business for this place now done by railroad," and by steamers on the upper river from Whitehorse.[52]

The journey to the Klondike goldfields thus became part of a familiar

American story. The "assault on time and space," as Cole Harris terms it, ended in victory, a conquest of time and space, the conquest of nature. In that conquest story, miners came west to the far boundary of civilization and struggled mightily against the land. They poured unimaginable amounts of physical labor into the task of making that land yield its treasures. Then, through human determination, ingenuity, capital, and technology, civilization arrived in the form of railroads and ships. "Nowhere else as on this gold trail has the genius of engineers wrought such beneficent and rapid change in so short a time," crowed engineer Harrington Emerson for the *American Monthly Review of Reviews*. The journey north no longer heeded seasons or weather, no longer required months of grueling labor. Rather than a dangerous experience of a savage environment, transportation became a pure expression of the progressive forces of civilization. Europeans took millennia to accomplish such a transformation, Emerson explained, but at White Pass, such progress unfolded in a mere twenty-four months. "The evolution from hunter's path to railroad, through the intermediate steps of pilgrim path, mule trail, wagon road, was 2,000 years in the making in the Saint Gotthard Pass. . . . Two short years as against 2,000 have evolved the same succession of improvements on the highway over the White Pass, back to a north hideous in climate, without history, without sentiment, without food, but abounding in gold."[53]

Such progress granted freedom not only from that hideous climate, but from labor as well, and the engagement with nature that went with such labor. The railroad ensured that no one—rich or poor—would ever make journeys that harrowing, that close to nature, ever again; they would simply take the train. The conquest won a victory not only over nature but over the work of moving through nature as well. In eliminating the physical effort of crossing passes and running rivers, humans conquered nature, or at least the need for work that immersed them in nature. When Arnold F. George, secretary of the Yukon Miners and Merchants Association, spoke in Seattle at the Alaska-Yukon-Pacific Exposition in 1909, he declared the days of struggle over. "Today," he explained, "the journey to these gold fields is a continuous picnic." Now, he continued, travelers stepped off the train at Whitehorse and boarded a stage on the government road to Dawson, or took a modern steamer down the Yukon, made "as safe as the Erie Canal" by the removal of rocks in Five Finger Rapids.[54]

Within this conquest narrative, the iconic photographs of miners crossing the Chilkoot Pass on foot take on a particular meaning, one associated with the human struggle against, and victory over, nature. In the conquest-of-nature story, the Chilkoot images provided the necessary starting point, a picture of the human descent into a tooth-and-claw battle with a primitive nature, a battle initially lost with the lives of those that died crossing the passes. The White Pass & Yukon Railroad thus represented an end to the story that began on the Chilkoot Trail, a victory over primitive nature, and the triumphant arrival of a civilized, consumer relationship with that nature. The power of the Chilkoot images thus lie, in part, with the human transcendence of nature and labor. Edward Curtis's article about the Chilkoot crossing in 1897 and 1898 made explicit use of this narrative of progress and conquest. In 1897, he wrote, the gold miner found nature at the Chilkoot "stern and repulsive, opposing his progress with all of her forces," a situation exacerbated by "the lack of transportation facilities." Looking forward to the spring of 1898, however, Curtis noted that "organization has displaced anarchy." In 1898, he predicted, miners "will cross the trails over prepared roads, steel bridges, and steam tramways, where the men of '97 waded through mud, forded streams, and painfully toiled over the summits."[55]

This conquest, this victory over the Chilkoot and nature, is far too simple a story about the human relationship to nature in Alaska and the Yukon, and to the industrial world as a whole. For one thing, the conquest could never be so complete. No matter how seamless the transport network in conveying miners by steamer, train, and sternwheeler from Seattle to Dawson City, downriver to St. Michael and Nome, and back to Seattle, there remained gaps in the system, places where miners remained producers as well as consumers of transportation. Whether mushing dogs from camp to camp, hauling wood to a claim, or simply waiting for ice to thaw around one such modern sternwheeler, miners were still immersed in the physical world and in bodily labor. In the interstices of their daily lives, just as at home in Boston and New York, they moved themselves and their belongings through nature, experiencing seasons and weather along the way. The production of transportation remained part of their labors, part of the spectrum of ways in which they moved through the world.

Although the conquest story oversimplifies the changes brought by railroads and other modern technologies, there is little question that such machines changed the human connection to nature in significant ways. Miners traveling home by rail experienced few of the dreaded challenges of seasons, mud, and ice afforded by their previous struggles; they grew more distant from the physical world. For most, gaining distance from messy nature seemed wholly positive, a beneficial mastery of distance, seasons, and time.

Such transformations were not universally hailed as progress, however. The changes were overwhelming. At the time, critics lamented the loss of character-building encounters with nature. A. A. Hill wrote in *Munsey's Magazine* in 1899, "It is a pity there is a prospect of a railroad being built from the coast of Alaska to the gold fields. I agree with Ruskin that going by railroad is not traveling at all. . . . It gives neither education, experience, nor character." Hill's analysis continued, with more than a touch of nostalgia. "The difference between the journey to Dawson as it was last year, and the same trip as it will be this season will be almost like the change from the age of romance to that of science. For there was romance, pathos, comedy, tragedy, and burlesque in the gold exodus of a year ago. The struggle . . . tempered character as the forge tempers the finest steel, or shattered it as if it were glass."[56]

More recently, scholars have moved beyond nostalgia to call the railroads' supposed mastery of nature into question. They have redefined it as part of a broader human alienation from nature. What appeared as a victory over distance and a conquest of nature and labor has also been interpreted as a profound alienation from nature. In speeding movement across great distances—the great distance, for instance, to Alaska—railroads and steamers made the space between the rest of the world and Alaska easily crossed. They thus made that space matter less and less until it hardly mattered at all, and indeed until it seemed not to exist at all. Geographer David Harvey quotes the nineteenth-century poet Heinrich Heine, reacting to French railroads: "Space is killed by the railways."[57] As historian William Cronon explains, this annihilation of space, whether the space between New York and Seattle, Seattle and the Yukon, or just between Skagway and Whitehorse, changed the ways in which travelers experienced space and the nature within that space.[58]

Both of these possible stories, one of conquest and victory, the other of annihilation, alienation, and loss, end with a fundamental separation of humans from nature. However, as much as both conquest and annihilation played a part in the gold rush transportation economy, a close examination of the gold miners' work as both consumers and producers of movement indicates that miners experienced neither a complete victory over nature nor a complete alienation from nature. They certainly annihilated space in their rapid travels north, and they certainly distanced themselves from the grueling physical labor of movement as quickly as possible, but neither their conquest nor their alienation were ever complete. As consumers of transportation, they shifted the production of movement to other workers, and through those workers they remained connected to nature. At the same time, the Alaska-Yukon transportation economy mixed the conquest and annihilation of space associated with industrial transportation with a strong dose of hard physical work. That work brought a direct physical engagement with nature along with a struggle to replace those labors with an expanded transport network, which would provide the industrial services to which gold rushers were accustomed. Altogether, their combinations of intimacy and distance, victory and defeat, consumption and production created a complex industrial relationship to nature that included all of these possible elements and shifted constantly between them.

3

THE CULTURE

OF THE JOURNEY

In the summer of 1897, a young woman named Nora Crane accompanied her husband to his new job as storekeeper in Circle City, Alaska. Steaming up the Yukon on the North American Trade & Transportation Company sternwheeler, Crane took great pride in the boat's pilot, his sartorial taste aside. "We have the best pilot on the river," she explained in a letter to her mother in Chicago, "a good looking Indian with a pumpkin colored tie that gives me a bilious start every glimpse I get of it. No wonder they give them good money for piloting, sometimes the river will be 5 miles wide and the deepest spot about ten feet and crooked, wind[ing] in around the base of great mountains until one thinks it is a lake we are riding on."[1] Nora Crane's sternwheeler voyage, so different from the miners' physically grueling crossings of the Chilkoot and Hunter Fitzhugh's trials on the Teslin Trail, was just one of the many types of Yukon transportation which combined all of the possible elements of such movement: intimacy with nature and distance from nature, production and consumption of movement, physical ease and physical hardship. Gold miners moved their own bodies and supplies through nature, but they moved in many other ways as well. They bought train and steamer tickets, and through those tickets hired woodcutters to provide steamer fuel, and steamboat pilots to thread them through dangerous sloughs and rapids. On the mountain passes and trails, they paid Native and Anglo-American packers to haul their goods for them; they bought and sold horses, mules, dogs, and goats as pack animals. This consumption of transportation services changed and expanded their relationship to the nature through which they moved. No matter how their consumption transformed such linkages to nature, however, the connections remained. Consumption could not completely separate Klondike gold miners from nature.

In hiring and consuming the labor of other human beings, gold miners not only formed new connections to nature, they also commodified nature in new ways. They commodified nature itself in the form of the physical distances through northern space across which they and their hired agents traveled. They commodified nature in the form of the seasonal changes that made various types of transportation labor easier or harder, cheaper or more expensive on the transportation market. They also commodified the human labor and human knowledge of nature necessary to move miners and their supplies through a challenging environment. Gold rush transportation revealed the industrial economy's power to commodify just about everything, from a steamboat pilot's knowledge of rock formations to the energy contained within animals' bodies, the energy stored in trees cut for fuel, and the energy saved by the low-friction surfaces of open water and hard-packed snow. This commodification of the journey unfolded piece by piece throughout the gold rush, as miners and transport workers took each segment of their journey and transformed it into an item to be bought and sold. In creating a market for all these transportation commodities, they extended their industrial economy to the Yukon interior.

When gold miners bought and sold transportation, the intimacy with the natural world that came with that labor changed hands, or rather, changed bodies. Railroads and steamboats did not eliminate the labor of moving through nature. They simply shifted that labor to other people. Nora Crane, after all, in paying her way up the Yukon River to Circle City, shifted that labor to the pilot who knew the river in detail, to the crewmen who knew how to move a boat through water, and to the boat builders in distant ports who knew the wood and iron that created the boat to begin with. Those workers' bodies came into close contact with nature so that Nora Crane's body did not have to. For Crane and other gold rush travelers who consumed rather than produced their own bodily transport, the simple, direct connections between their own arms and legs and the mud, snow, water, and ice of the journey gave way to more complicated connections, first to hired hands and wage laborers, and through them to nature. Transportation workers like Crane's boat pilot forged their own connections to nature through the labor of their bodies and the food that fueled their bodies. In hiring and consuming the labor of others, miners integrated those connections into their own expanding networks of linkages. Consumption certainly shifted the miners' connections to nature, but some connection nonetheless remained. As consumers, gold miners could no longer separate their connections to nature from their connections to other human beings. Hence, the miners' linkages to the environment were shaped by other human beings and the cultures and societies that came with them.

THE PASSES AND TRAILS: HIRED HELP

When gold seekers disembarked their steamers in Dyea at the foot of the Chilkoot Trail, those who could afford to hire help in moving their supplies immediately turned to local Native Alaskans and Native Yukoners. A photograph in Herbert Heller's collection of gold rush memoirs, *Sourdough Sagas,* shows an elderly Native Alaskan man in front of a small cabin in Dyea. Behind him a sign reads "Isaac, Chief of Chilkott. Packing a Specialty."[2] The photograph offers a stark contrast to the Chilkoot images, but the picture of Isaac rings just as true as those of miners on the Chilkoot Pass. Although thousands did haul their own bodies and supplies over the Chilkoot and White Passes, the "greatest feats of packing," as Harold Petersen wrote, were done by "a great many Natives," men, women, and children.[3] Natives and whites together created a market in the labor of moving tons of goods over the pass and together commodified each mile of the journey in the specific currencies of cash, time, and distance that ruled the gold rush transport economy.

The Chilkoot and White Passes had long been corridors for Native trade and transportation from the Lynn Canal to the Yukon interior (map 4). When Euro-American explorers and prospectors appeared in the 1880s, Tlingit bands on the upper Lynn Canal, along with Tagish groups from the upper Yukon lakes, reluctantly agreed to sell their services as packers.[4] Lt. Frederick Schwatka crossed the Chilkoot Pass on his exploration expedition in 1883, and reported hiring Tagish and Tlingit packers at an "ample" rate of ten to twelve dollars per pack of one hundred pounds.[5] By 1896, according to Josiah Spurr, "the natives had settled down into the habit of helping the white man, for a substantial remuneration."[6] In August 1897, Samuel Dunham counted 250 Indians and 150 white packers at work in Dyea using a combination of horses, boats, and packs to move freight fourteen miles up the canyon trail to Sheep Camp.[7] Over time, Native packers suffered increased competition from white packers and tramways, but in the first two seasons of the Klondike, Natives exerted significant control over the finances of transportation at Dyea and at the Chilkoot summit.

Within Tlingit culture of the 1890s, packing miners' goods across the Chilkoot for profit made great cultural and economic sense. The accumulation of material wealth increased an individual Tlingit man's status through the ritualized giveaway of gifts at a grand party and ceremony called the potlatch. By the 1890s, that acquisitiveness blended well with the opportunities presented by Euro-American fishing and trading, and Tlingit bands readily took part in both subsistence and market-oriented activities in southeast Alaska. They valued and sought U.S. currency, but also incorporated it into their potlatch ceremonies.[8] To white observers, who often described Tlingits as industrious, thrifty, and hardworking, this economic readiness looked like adaptation to Euro-American economic culture. Often, however, it represented as much cultural continuity as change.[9]

Most miners who hired Native packers immediately sensed the Tlingits' keen sense of the market and savvy knowledge of the economic value of their work. Journalist Tappan Adney did not trust Chilkoot packers at all; he described them as "shrewd, hard traders, who are making money fast and saving it." He found them "wholly unscrupulous" and unaware of what he saw as their inferior economic status. "They make no distinction between themselves and whites even for the same service," he wrote with some dismay. "If one engages them at a certain price and some one offers them more, they lay down their packs and take up the new ones; or if on the trail they hear of a rise in the scale, they stop and strike for the higher wages."[10] Josiah Spurr had a similar experience the previous year when he ascended the Dyea Trail with several other white groups. The Native packers got the freight as far as Sheep Camp, and then called a rate strike. They demanded a three-cent raise, from six to nine cents per pound. The whites refused, and all movement ceased for several days. Finally, one group of miners caved in and agreed to pay nine cents; Spurr and the rest had no choice but to follow their lead and pay up.[11]

Befuddled by the ups and downs of the packing market, gold seekers also took note of the Native packers' sheer physical strength, the product of long-term physical conditioning through frequent trading trips over the passes. This combination of trade sense and stamina proved impressive. Solomon and Rebecca Schuldenfrei hired eighteen Indian packers to take fifteen hun-

dred pounds of freight all the way to the lakes, paying a total of seven hundred dollars, or just over fifty cents a pound, a hefty price. In what must
have made a striking scene, the Native packers pulled Rebecca up the Dyea
River in a canoe. She explained to friends at home that "they charge like the
furies and a person is utterly powerless without them, as the white people
cannot pack and climb as they do; they take 150 lbs. on their backs easier
than Solomon can carry a basket of fruit."[12] James Hamil had planned to
pay only twelve and a half cents a pound to Indian packers in October 1897
to take twenty-four hundred pounds across; like many others, he could not
afford the going rate of twenty-five cents. Hamil and his partner set out to
do the work themselves. "So we started in to pack the first day," he wrote.
"We did not attempt to pack but 50 lbs at a load but the next we raised it to
75 but in four or five days we commenced to pack 100 lbs. The Indians pack
200 & 250 lbs. but 100 is all I can [manage] to pack."[13] Even Native children
and women, long part of an economy based on moving trade goods,
climbed to the summit with seventy-five-pound packs.[14]

In hiring Native packers, white packers, and pack animals, gold miners
entered a marketplace which commodified for sale the distance, labor, and
time required to cross the passes. Transportation turned out to be as much
about money as about nature, though the two were intimately intertwined.
Money mattered because it could purchase the human and animal energy
needed to move through the specific space of these trails at a specific time.
The Tlingits knew this well, and miners learned it quickly. Those with enough
cash could purchase faster transportation over the passes. Those without
had to do the work themselves at great costs of time and effort. James Hamil
wrote from the Chilkoot in the fall of 1897, "I have passed strong men on
the trail sitting down worn out and crying they did not have money enough
to [have] it done and could not possibly get their stuff over before the Lakes
and rivers froze over."[15]

Although miners paid close attention to the natural world, the mud and
snow and ice, they read and understood it in terms of how much money it
cost to move through it. The transportation market thus commodified the
very nature of the trails themselves. The amount of work required to cross
the passes, and thus the amount of money, varied with the seasons. Packing rates revealed how natural conditions themselves, in shaping the trails,
became commodities bought and sold. Sam Dunham, investigating for the
U.S. Department of Labor, hired four Indian packers in 1897 to transport
his supplies at a rate of thirty-eight cents a pound. His investigations

revealed that in the spring, when snow was still on the ground, packing cost as little as fourteen cents a pound, due to the ease of using sleds on snow and ice. In summer, when bare ground made the work far more challenging, rates soared as high as forty-seven cents a pound. These monetary differences reflected physical nature, certainly, but filtered through a market economy which controlled the production and consumption of transportation. "Warm and pleasant in the afternoon," wrote McMichael on April 8. "Softened trail up badly and rates for packing have gone up. We contracted for ours at three and a half cents to the summit."[16] When the snow melted at Sheep Camp, the rate jumped as much as fifteen cents per pound, by one report, because "this makes it more difficult for the horses."[17] Crossing the same distance with the same weight thus took vastly different amounts of work depending on ground conditions. Hiring that work similarly cost different amounts at different times. The same held true in Dawson and at the gold creeks. Samuel Dunham found the rate for winter hauling was just one quarter of the summer rate. Costs fell from thirty-five cents a pound at Dawson to only eight cents a pound once snow covered the trail of muck, roots, and water that led to Bonanza and Eldorado Creeks.[18] Those differences reflected the power of the natural world to shape transportation, but also the powers of commodification to bring new meaning—and new costs— to the physical world.

These powers of commodification proved innovative. At every step along the way, entrepreneurs found services to sell, whether food, horses, or dry places to sleep. This was especially true at the places which required the most drastic work, such as the Chilkoot summit itself, where the trail turned nearly vertical. In the winter, workers hacked a staircase a thousand feet high into the snow, but they charged a toll to ascend it.[19] Thus the iconic image of miners on the golden staircase represented not only nature's forces, but those of the market as well, which sold the final ascent to miners step by step. Such commodification was perhaps best exemplified by the several tramways, aerial cable cars for hauling goods, that entrepreneurs and transport companies constructed on the Dyea Trail in 1897 and 1898. Like the railroad on White Pass, the Chilkoot tramways offered the transport of tons of goods up and over the summit as a purchasable service. Adapted from cable tramways used in mining camps to carry ore, the trams consisted of towers built at four-hundred-foot intervals, up to thirty feet high; two cables, one to hold the loads and one to haul them, ran between the towers, the hauling cable powered by a steam plant which pulled the loads, in cable cars, at a rate of

250 feet every minute. They made the trip from Dyea to Lake Lindeman in eight hours, a powerful compression of time and space for foot-weary miners.

In December 1897, Archie Burns built the first of several tramways that used nonhuman power sources to carry freight by aerial trams up the trail to the summit. Burns's tramway operated first by horsepower; horses turned a capstan that ran a rope around a wheel.[20] According to Sam Stone Bush, writing in early 1898 for the *American Monthly Review of Reviews*, aerial tramways were well on their way to completion for the spring rush that year. The whole distance required six separate sections, powered by three power plants. As Bush explained, there was one company with four or five miles in operation; another company had just begun, but promised a line from the end of its docks in Dyea all the way to Lindeman, able to carry five hundred pounds per car, and even small boats. Such an operation, the writer claimed, would reduce the time taken to cross the passes from five or six weeks to eight hours, and reduce the freight packing rate from forty cents a pound to ten cents a pound.[21] In April 1898, as several thousand miners scrambled up the trail, the Dyea-Klondike Transportation Company, advertising itself as "the only successful tramway over Dyea Pass," promised transport "to any point between Dyea and Lake Linderman [*sic*]."[22] By March 1899, however, the Chilkoot tramways faced competition from the White Pass & Yukon Railroad, which had reached the summit and lowered freight rates to attract miners' business. One mode of commercial transportation, of buying and selling the journey, quickly replaced another.[23]

Such commodification of distance, time, and labor did not eliminate the miners' intimate experience of nature on the trails, however. On the Chilkoot, the culture of market profits collided with seasonal change on April 3, 1898. With hundreds of miners bivouacked in tents below the Chilkoot summit, and many working farther up the trail, a heavy spring snowstorm swept the pass. The wet snow soon gave way. A chain of avalanches swept down, killing between fifty and a hundred people, including about twenty white men who had been working for wages at the tramway at the foot of the summit.[24] Rumors spread that, despite the storm, the tramway bosses had not allowed the workers to leave, even when Indian packers sensed danger and descended to safety. Mac McMichael wrote on April 6, "It is said they forced the men out in the storm by saying they might work or call for their time at the office. Two refused to go. . . . The rest were lost and most of their bodies are yet to be found."[25] Fearing the worst, hundreds of men ran up the trail to try to dig out survivors; others dug out tons of buried provisions. The snow slides scared some miners enough to sell their outfits and head for home. Mac McMichael lost all desire to remain at Sheep Camp packing his own goods. With the avalanche scare and a sudden loss of business, packing rates dropped to under five cents a pound from Dyea to the Summit. "I find that freighting is so much cheaper than I thought, I am going to have mine all done and get out of this place as soon as possible . . . letting those who are used to it do the hard work."[26] Nature pushed McMichael to shift his own dangerous intimacy with snow onto the backs of more experienced laborers and to speed his journey through the threatening, unstable mountain spring.

COMMODIFYING ANIMALS

On the Chilkoot Trail, miners shifted the burden of their freight primarily to other humans, but on the nearby White Pass Trail and on interior trails between gold camps, they shifted it to animals, whose bodies and whose very lives became commodities in the transportation market economy. The lower elevation and rolling topography of the White Pass Trail, when compared to the Chilkoot, meant that horses, mules, and every other imaginable pack animal could trek all the way to the summit. Entrepreneurs in Skagway promoted and crudely improved the trail as an alternative to the Chilkoot, not only to create a more competitive transportation market, but also to make Skagway a boomtown. It worked. Skagway became a wide-open packtrain town, running hundreds of horses, mules, and dogs up the trail with miners' gear. Stewart Campbell called the Skagway Trail "the liveliest gold trail in the world," populated by "Horses, mules, jacks, bulls, oxen, cows, goats, dogs, men, women, and children, with sleds, packs, and every conceivable mode of conveyance zigzaging along a narrow trail."[27] The travelers paid from five to thirty-five cents a pound, and the packers made good money, up to twenty dollars a day.[28]

The market in packhorses extended from San Francisco, Seattle, and Victoria, British Columbia, north to Skagway. The horses, and the horses' energy, remained valuable only when and where they were cost-effective, or when and where the animals could do enough packing to pay the exorbitant cost of feeding them. This meant that horses considered worthless in Seattle or Victoria were worth high prices in Skagway. In Victoria, Tappan Adney saw decrepit "ambulating boneyards" rounded up for shipment to Skagway. "Till now they have been without value or price," he noted. Suddenly in demand for packing over White Pass, they sold for $125 or $200 at Skagway. In the winter of 1897, the tidal flats at the foot of the trail were "black with a thousand horses."[29]

These horses remained valuable only over the distance to the lakes, however. Those who tried to load them on boats and move them down the Yukon to Dawson City found the effort hardly worthwhile. As a result, once the horses completed the journey over the pass, they cost far too much to feed. Alpine terrain afforded no fodder, so merchants sold hay and grain shipped in from Seattle for between three to five hundred dollars a ton. Miners therefore bought horses for over a hundred dollars at the bottom of the White Pass Trail, and then abandoned them on the other side at the lakes as useless because they could no longer be fed or provide useful transportation. Horses did the work of reaching the lakes, but once there, they were "not worth 20 cents," Adney wrote.[30]

As a result, miners and packers not only commodified animals themselves, they commodified one brief episode of labor in the horses' entire lives, whatever life—or energy—the animals had left in them at purchase. They then wasted any other future life or value the animals held.[31] On the Chilkoot Trail, the miners needed the animals to last long enough to reach Sheep Camp, below the summit; on White Pass, they needed them to last all the way to the lakes, but no farther. After those points, animal feed represented certain cost. The miners' crude and careless treatment of the animals reflected this market reality. They had little economic incentive to care for horses in the long term, or even to feed them. At Skagway, Bill Hiscock observed "dead horses and mules and sick ones everywhere. . . . When the poor brutes can not work anymore, they are just turned out to die or get better, starved in the meantime."[32]

In the fall of 1897, on the Chilkoot Trail, miners abandoned used horses and mules at Sheep Camp. Cold weather and lack of feed brought disaster, as the animals slowly starved, stumbling around camp and breaking into miners' supplies. In mid-September, according to Tappan Adney, the men at Sheep Camp finally realized the situation and began killing the animals, leaving carcasses "lying on all sides." Miners also sold horses to packers, who took them back down to Dyea for another run up the trail. Adney sold his horse for twenty-five dollars, but noted that it paid its new owner back in one day of packing. A man with a horse could make forty dollars a day packing before the animal gave out. Even packers who used the animals for more than one trip worked them to death, and then replaced them. There was money to be made over the course of their dying.[33]

The toll in animal life at Sheep Camp on the Chilkoot was nothing compared to the Skagway Trail in 1897 and 1898, where the market in animal life combined with a narrow, muddy, disastrous trail to cause widespread slaughter. Creeks crossed the trail, creating bogs thirty feet wide, where, Adney wrote, "there is simply no bottom." The horses sank up to their tails. Fallen logs created roadblocks and bottlenecks so that loaded horses (and people) had to stand for hours with bone-crushing loads, waiting for any sign of movement. Slick rocks and roots provided poor footing, and heavily loaded horses slid and scraped, their shoes gouging the rocks like chisels. Many animals broke their legs and were shot. At one steep drop-off, hundreds of horses lost their footing and fell. "We are told that fifty horses a day fall here," wrote Adney. "No one thinks anything about it." The stench of rotting horse flesh grew unbearable. When Jonas Houck crossed back over the trail from the lakes to get his mail at Skagway in May 1898, he walked on carcasses to get down the trail, counting two thousand dead horses and mules. He could smell their rotting carcasses eight miles away.[34]

Similar market principles, though without the carnage, governed the labors and lives of sled dogs, who replaced horses and mules as the chief source of animal transportation once miners reached the gold creeks. As Hunter Fitzhugh and others demonstrated, the miners' relationships to their sled dogs were direct and intimate connections to the animals as part of nature. Like horses, dogs connected miners to nature, the nature in their very bodies and lives, and the nature in the food which fueled the dogs' bodies and their labor. Like horses, however, sled dogs also became commodities, given value on a specific dog-market that reflected both the nature of Yukon and Alaska seasons and the culture of capitalism.

The market in dogs, like that for horses, developed first in Seattle and San Francisco, where traders rounded up or stole every dog in sight, and then had more shipped in from all over the country. Seattle's streets were filled with dogs, dogsleds, and dog teams, all in training for the journey ahead. On the White Pass Trail out of Skagway, Bill Hiscock saw "every breed except poodles and greyhounds. . . . There were collies, retrievers, spaniels, Grt. Danes, Mastiffs, New Foundlands . . . many mongrels . . . and Malamutes and huskeys, the latter, a wolf strain in them."[35] Unlike horses and mules, who had brief economic value only on the Chilkoot and White Pass Trails, dogs had market value throughout the Yukon interior, but only by season.

Since miners found them useful only in winter, when they could pull heavy sleds over ice and snow, their market value rose and fell with the temperature. In late fall, when frozen earth, snow, and ice made overland movement possible, dogs became very useful. As McMichael explained, "To get food and supplies to some of the mines near Dawson . . . in the summer time costs $1.00 or $1.10 per pound," but, "in the winter a man with two or three dogs can get along very nicely."[36]

The dogs' market prices thus varied accordingly. In the off-season, spring and summer, dogs were worth a pittance, merely twenty or thirty dollars apiece, but by Christmas, the prices rose to fifty or seventy-five dollars, or more if they proved scarce. In October, at Rampart City, Alaska, a steamer unloaded a group of dogs which sold for a hundred and fifty dollars each.[37] For a prospector in Alaska for a year, five dogs could cost two hundred dollars, plus at least four hundred dollars more to feed them through the winter. McMichael further captured the heart of the matter when he wrote, "There is a lot of capital invested in these same dogs. Some could not be bought for $300. Many are worth $200 in this country, while a scrub is worth $50 or $75. . . . They will soon be invaluable to the men who have freighting out to the mines to do or want to start in haste on a stampede."[38]

For miners, the real economic question was not whether to make such a capital investment in the fall, but whether to keep and feed the pack through the summer. Dogs worked only in the winter, but, like the miners themselves, ate year-round. March and April brought melting snow, rotten ice, and the observation from one Dawson official that "the season of the dogs usefulness is about closing."[39] Many miners simply could not afford the expense of feeding them through the summer. After the thaw, they abandoned scores of animals, now deemed "worthless," Lt. Frederick Schwatka wrote in 1883, "except as scavengers for the refuse of decaying salmon."[40] Tom Boldrick, camped above Whitehorse Rapids, remarked on the night's quiet, the stillness broken only by "now & then the dismal howl of some poor dog left by some one on the shore to starve to death."[41]

Starving dogs not only made noise, they also threatened the human food supply. At Circle City in the summer of 1898, Mac McMichael noted the dogs' constant howling and fighting, and close attention to the miners' food. "When we cook," he wrote of cabin life, "there are always from one to three standing patiently with their heads in the door. . . . They are great at foraging too. They can get into a boat down on the river, tear open a bacon sack and rustle a side of bacon with neatness and dispatch."[42] Many dogs died, of course, whether of starvation, mistreatment, or poorly cleaned fish. Hunter Fitzhugh wrote that when the Yukon thawed in spring, the moving ice floes carried away heaps of trash and junk dumped on the ice, including "dead dogs of all nations and tongues" who died from eating dried salmon, the bones of which had punctured their stomachs.[43]

In consuming the labor of sled dogs by the dictates of the seasonal market, miners clearly consumed the dogs' lives as well. Their transportation consumption did not end there, however. It extended through the dogs themselves to the dogs' food supply, which added further to the miners' proliferating connections to nature. When they did take care to feed their sled teams, miners drew both from local ecosystems and from their own supplies, transported from hundreds or even thousands of miles away. They thus forged linkages with those local places, and with far distant places that produced imported dog feed. Tappan Adney described the feed one group of miners packed for a winter journey. For the dogs alone they carried 175 pounds of rice, 235 pounds of bacon, and 150 pounds of salmon, with an additional 100 pounds of dried salmon, 100 pounds of bacon, and 100 pounds of rice cached ahead along the trail.[44] According to John Cantwell, the best feed was a mixture of dried salmon, lard, and corn meal, mixed into a thick soup.[45]

Despite those loads of bacon and rice, which cost about one dollar a day per animal, dogs proved far cheaper to maintain than horses and mules because their main source of energy, salmon, came from the Yukon and other local rivers rather than from distant hay fields. In using salmon as feed, miners forged yet another connection to the Yukon environment. Not only did the river provide the miners with transportation during winter and summer, its ecosystem stored and provided the energy, through fish, to fuel winter dogsledding. Lt. Frederick Schwatka saw forty or fifty dogs at a Native village on the lower Yukon and reported that the packs survived on one salmon per day per dog through the winter.[46] The Native Yukoners' salmon harvest, which already reflected the need to feed their own sled dogs, increased further when local villagers began selling salmon to whites to feed the influx of new dogs that came with the gold rush. Miners commodified not only the dogs themselves and the dogs' seasonal labor, but also the salmon that fueled such labor. The new market in salmon connected humans to the nature that produced salmon, but it also revealed the culture which was fast transforming the ways in which humans harvested and used that nature. Several years later, when Clara Hickman Rust traveled up the Yukon

"Prospectors preparing for ascent of Chilkoot Pass—Spring of 1898." The base of the Chilkoot summit was as much a site of industrial transportation and industrial culture as an intense human engagement with nature. Workers who carved steps into the ice and snow sold use of those steps for a toll fee. Tramway companies charged to move supplies in overhead buckets slung on motorized cables. Packtrain operators commodified the energy in animals' bodies, trading on the market value of the animals' ability to travel the short distance from tidewater up the trail. MSCUA, Univ. of Washington Libraries, UW21254.

"Loading supplies into boat along the Thirty Mile River, Yukon Territory, 1898."
Alaska-Yukon transportation brought gold seekers into contact with nature on rivers
as well as passes. These miners, traveling down a section of the upper Yukon known
as the Thirty Mile River, had to learn the nature of the river to get themselves, their
small boat, and their supplies safely downstream to the goldfields. MSCUA, Univ. of
Washington Libraries, A. Curtis 46065.

"Klondiker with group of five Indian packers and a two-oxen packtrain on Chilkoot Trail, Alaska, 1897." Many miners hired Native workers to pack their supplies over the Chilkoot Pass. They also bought pack animals, including dogs, horses, goats, and oxen, to aid them in moving their supplies. The transportation economy showed the commodification of human labor, and of animals' lives and bodies, in the industrial gold rush economy. Of this image, photographer Frank LaRoche wrote, "In the foreground are four Indian packers returning from the summit of Chilkoot, having made $18 each for their day's labor. Oxen are regarded in some respects as the most desirable of all pack animals in summer, as when impossible to take them over the mountains they are not brought back, but bring a handsome profit for meat. One of these was killed at Lake Lindeman, and the heart sold for $7, the head for $12.50, and the balance of the animal 50 cents a pound." MSCUA, Univ. of Washington Libraries, La Roche 2018.

"Packers ascending the summit of Chilkoot Pass, 1898." The most iconic images from the Alaska-Yukon gold rush showed the mass movement of gold seekers and supplies over the coastal mountain range from the head of Lynn Canal to the Yukon headwaters in the late winter and spring of 1898. MSCUA, Univ. of Washington Libraries, Hegg 38.

(Facing page, top) "Blockade of Klondikers on Porcupine Hill, White Pass Trail (Skagway Trail), Alaska." Miners were overwhelmed by the intractable mud, mess, and chaos of the White Pass Trail. As hundreds of pack horses slipped, fell, and died, miners found themselves in the midst of a vicious market economy that traded on horses' brief usefulness on the trail. Once the horses reached the other side of the pass, they became useless, and were left to starve. MSCUA, Univ. of Washington Libraries, Hegg 181.

(Facing page, bottom) White Pass Trail. Asahel Curtis's famous photograph on what was also called the "dead horse trail." He wrote, "Three thousand horses were strewn along this trail, mostly on the two mile slope west of the pass." MSCUA, Univ. of Washington Libraries, A. Curtis 46112.

2354.

A.C. Co's. STR. LOUISE ARRIVING AT DAWSON
JULY 6~99.

"Alaska Commercial Company's Steamer *Louise* Arriving at Dawson, July 6, 1899."
Yukon River sternwheelers transported passengers upriver from St. Michael to Dawson City and other gold towns in relative comfort. They also pushed and pulled large barges with tons of food and supplies for the major trading posts along the river. These supplies from the industrial economy, along with railroads and steamers, made the gold rush possible. MSCUA, Univ. of Washington Libraries, Hegg 2354.

(*Facing page, top*) "Group of Yukon Natives employed to load cordwood fuel for the steamboats of the Alaska Commercial Company." On the "rich man's route," gold miners shifted the bodily labor of movement and the intimate knowledge of nature required for transport to the bodies of hired workers: steamboat pilots and crew hands, boatbuilders, and woodcutters, many of them Native Alaskans and Yukoners. Sternwheelers brought thousands of tons of food and supplies to the gold creeks, but burned immense amounts of cordwood in the process, all of it cut from the forests along the Yukon. MSCUA, Univ. of Washington Libraries, UW21253.

(*Facing page, bottom*) "Yukon Belles. Indian women and children at steamboat landing on Yukon River, Yukon Territory, ca. 1898." Native peoples were further integrated into the gold rush economy by supplying cordwood to fuel steamers along the Yukon River. Steamboat landings became places of interaction between Native and Euro-American peoples, and watersheds in the arrival of the market economy. MSCUA, Univ. of Washington Libraries, UW21252.

SSENGERS VIEWING THE SCENERY FROM PORCUPINE HILL . WHITE PASS AND YUKON ROUTE

"Passengers viewing the scenery from Porcupine Hill, White Pass and Yukon Route, February 20, 1899." The construction of the White Pass & Yukon Railroad over the White Pass from Skagway to Lake Bennett transformed the transportation of people and supplies into and out of the Yukon basin. By the winter of 1899, passengers, as tourists, took the train up the pass to view the scenery, where scarcely a year earlier miners had risked their lives to cross the passes on foot. This transformed humans' connections to nature through transportation. MSCUA, Univ. of Washington Libraries, Hegg 660.

"Bridge at Tunnel, White Pass and Yukon Route. Crew working on wooden trestle bridge connecting Tunnel Mountain with south portal of the tunnel during construction of the White Pass and Yukon Railroad, Alaska, ca. 1899." The White Pass & Yukon Railroad made it far easier to get to the upper Yukon, but it did not separate human beings from nature. It shifted direct, bodily connections to nature from those traveling over the pass to those laboring to make such transport possible, including railroad workers. The miners' intense experience of mud, snow, and rock on the Chilkoot was now shifted to construction workers on the railroad route. MSCUA, Univ. of Washington Libraries, Hegg 651.

"Steamboat *John C. Barr* at a boat landing on the Teslin River, Yukon Territory." In 1898 and 1899, steamer companies extended service to the upper Yukon, between Whitehorse and Dawson City. Travelers could combine railroad and steamer travel to transport themselves over the passes and downriver as "rich men," consumers of the labor of movement. MSCUA, Univ. of Washington Libraries, Hegg 2183.

(Facing page, top) "Mining claim No. 2 above Bonanza Creek, Yukon Territory, ca. 1898." Placer mining along gold creeks in the Yukon and Alaska required that miners disassemble the creeks piece by piece. They took wood from the hills, elevated the creeks into wood sluices, and dug gravels from the creek beds. MSCUA, Univ. of Washington Libraries, Hegg 3014.

(Facing page, bottom) "Mushing Wood." The key to winter mining work along the gold creeks was an ample wood supply. Miners not only lived in wood cabins and heated them with wood, they set fires to thaw through the frozen earth to bedrock, the solid subterranean layer that contained gold. All of their wood came from the riparian corridors and hillsides near the gold creeks. They transported wood either with their own bodies or by dogsled, commodifying the energy and lives of dogs who earned their keep in winter, but were often abandoned in the summer. MSCUA, Univ. of Washington Libraries, Cantwell 40.

No 2 ABOVE BONANCA

MUSHING WOOD

AT THE WINDLASS   40° BELOW

(*Facing page, top*) "Mucking thawed ground in a drift on 16 Eldorado, underground mining shaft, Yukon Territory, 1898." Winter work took miners underground, where they thawed shafts and horizontal drifts to expose gold-bearing gravels. MSCUA, Univ. of Washington Libraries, A. Curtis 46078.

(*Facing page, bottom*) "At the Windlass, 40 Degrees Below." For winter work, one miner would dig out thawed gravels underground while another worked the windlass, hauling gold-bearing dirt up in a wooden bucket to pile up in the winter's dump. MSCUA, Univ. of Washington Libraries, UW 21256.

(*Above*) "Gold miners operating sluice on claim No. 39 below Hunker Creek, Yukon Territory, ca. 1898." When the creeks thawed, the spring work of washing or sluicing the dumps of pay dirt began in earnest. The miners' cutting of riverside timber sometimes led, however, to erosion, flooding, and a wavering water supply. Sluicing depended on that water supply, and thus was often difficult to accomplish. MSCUA, Univ. of Washington Libraries, UW 21259.

Spring work was both exciting and daunting, as miners carefully extracted gold from their heaps of pay dirt. Everyone kept a close and careful watch on the sluices and riffles, ignoring the muddy, rocky results of their disassembly of the earth. MSCUA, Univ. of Washington Libraries, UW7326.

Gold Hill. A panoramic photograph of the Klondike gold creeks and hills shows the miners' effects on the landscape. MSCUA, Univ. of Washington Libraries, Cantwell 22.

BONANZA SHOWING PAY STREAK W.M. COWLEY'S C

"Bonanza Showing Pay Streak." Miners working with only shovels and sluices could still dramatically alter a stream in their attempts to expose the gold-bearing pay streak. MSCUA, Univ. of Washington Libraries, Larss and Duclos 65.

"Force of Miners Working on W. M. Cowley's Claim, 22 Above Bonanza." Alaska-Yukon miners sought escape from the pressures and losses of industrialized work through satisfying, independent, productive manual labor. In the end, however, gold mining reproduced industrial wage labor. Many miners worked for wages on claims owned by others, and often worked in large industrial forces. MSCUA, Univ. of Washington Libraries, Larss and Duclos 5.

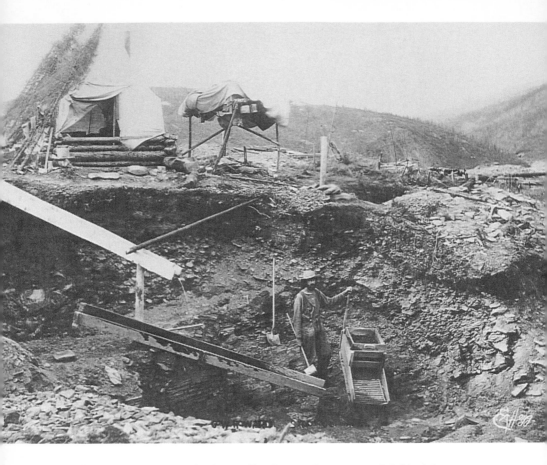

"Mining Operation on Skookum Hill, Yukon Territory, ca. 1898." Gold mining promised independence and wealth through hard work. It ended up providing something more akin to a fruitless gamble or, at best, hard work at hard wages. MSCUA, Univ. of Washington Libraries, Hegg 3016.

(*Facing page, top*) "Mountain sheep mutton on the way to Dawson from the Upper Klondyke." Euro-American hunters struggled to transport their kills to Dawson for sale to miners hungry for fresh meat. Some of the miners' food came from local wildlife populations, hunted by miners and by Native peoples. MSCUA, Univ. of Washington Libraries, UW21258.

(*Facing page, bottom*) "Peel River Indians' Dog Teams in Dawson with Wild Meat." Although some miners did hunt for themselves, most of their fresh meat from local ecosystems came from Indian hunters, who shifted their hunting cycles to supply a booming market in fresh caribou and moose meat at Dawson and in other gold towns and camps. MSCUA, Univ. of Washington Libraries, Goetzman 3012.

FROM THE UPPER KLONDYKE

Goetzman Photo

Pael River

"Barge on the Yukon River loaded with cattle for Dawson, Yukon Territory." The demand for fresh meat in the gold towns and camps inspired risky attempts to move live cattle over the Dalton Trail from the Lynn Canal, and then down the Yukon by barge. MSCUA, Univ. of Washington Libraries, A. Curtis 46066.

"California Market, Dawson, Nov. 1, 1901." This image of a thriving market in Dawson testifies to the abundance of fresh foods made available not only by local hunters, but by steamer and railroad transportation from the outside world. MSCUA, Univ. of Washington Libraries, Goetzman 3004.

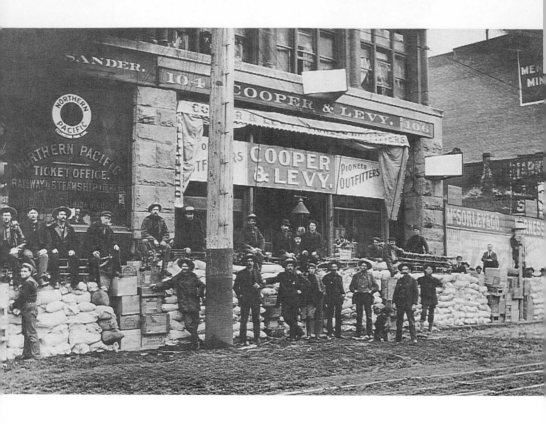

"Cooper & Levy Store, 104–106 First Avenue South near Yesler Way, Seattle, 1897. Also shows Northern Pacific Railroad Ticket Office." In response to the demand for gold rush supplies, Seattle retailers stocked literally tons of supplies, stacking them along the streets throughout the city. The railroad ticket office next door underscores the economic connections necessary to just such a supply operation. Most of the items that Cooper & Levy sold came from far-distant farms and factories and arrived in Seattle by rail. MSCUA, Univ. of Washington Libraries, A. Curtis 26368.

"Seattle Grocery Store, Dawson City, June 21, 1899." Seattle businesses not only expanded their supply networks to the East in order to equip gold miners, they also built networks in Alaska and the Yukon, taking supplies from Seattle and selling them retail in Dawson and other gold towns. This helped build and maintain the city's share of the gold rush supply business. MSCUA, Univ. of Washington Libraries, UW12851.

"Steamer *Roanoke* in Harbor Returning with Gold Miners from the Klondike, Seattle, July 19, 1898." Seattle's campaign to become the gateway to Alaska and the Yukon meant not only supplying miners on the way north, but also buying their gold and resupplying them on their way back south. The first returning boat of the season offered an annual burst in the Alaska trade as miners clamored to convert their gold to money at the Seattle U.S. Assay Office and then spend that money in Seattle. MSCUA, Univ. of Washington Libraries, La Roche 10022.

and Tanana Rivers to Fairbanks, the steamer stopped at Native villages along the way to load dry salmon for Fairbanks and Dawson: winter feed for the dog population.[47]

KNOWLEDGE AND WOOD:
CONSUMING RIVER TRANSPORTATION

As travelers, miners consumed the labor and energy of Native packers, and the energy and lives of countless horses, mules, and dogs. Such consumption did not, however, always look like consumption, mixed as it was with the miners' own bodily production of transportation, and their own labor in hiking alongside Native packers and mushing dog teams in the dead of winter. In steamboat transportation, however, there was no disguising the miners' consumption of nature. On their long boat journeys from Seattle to St. Michael near the mouth of the Yukon, then up the river to Dawson City, they consumed nature outright, as scenery and as fuel. Despite the "darndest rabble of kids and mosquitoes," Nora Crane found much pleasure in describing the nature that flowed past her as she steamed upstream aboard a comfortable ship. In a letter home to Chicago, she wrote, "After the second day out it is the most beautiful scenery I ever saw along a river . . . big tree covered mountains, bald tops very often snow yet on them and they come down to the waters edge in a precipice 500 feet high. . . . and the river is simply immense—sometimes 30 miles wide—and so crooked that the effect of land almost in every direction is that of an inland sea."[48] Crane saw plenty of the natural world, but, as on railroad cars, steamer passengers often experienced nature from a distance.

That distance did not always hold; real connections to nature remained. Steamboat transportation insulated wealthy travelers from some but not all exigencies of the northern environment. Yukon riverboats were relatively fast, inexpensive, and flexible. Pilots could run them anywhere, even in two feet of water. But river voyages still managed to bring passengers into very close contact with the physical world around them.[49] The river travelers' first direct contact with nature revolved, not surprisingly, around ice. The Yukon River froze solid at its mouth in early October, so sternwheelers had to obey strict seasonal limits. The boats traveled safely only from the time the ice "went out" each spring until the mush and cake ice formed in the fall, a period of about four months starting in late May. Eager miners pushed these seasonal limits, but without success. According to Tappan Adney, nearly two thousand people attempted to ascend the Yukon by steamer in the fall of 1897. Only forty-three made it to Dawson. The rest, their boats locked in Yukon ice, spent a long, restless winter in camps, cabins, and villages like Rampart City, fighting the cold.[50]

The Yukon's tricky but powerful nature made itself known to wealthy travelers in other ways as well. Even at the height of the summer season, nature constantly asserted itself. Steamer pilots cautiously maneuvered the Yukon's ever-shifting channels, but even shallow-draft, flat-bottomed steamers ran aground on sandbars and shoals, stranding miners and tons of supplies. Such delays made transportation slower and far more frustrating than the typically efficient train or steamer voyages closer to home. Late in the season, as tributaries froze, the river's level dropped significantly, even further limiting the steamers' movement.[51] A storekeeper on the upper river explained the difference between the Yukon and the outside world in 1897. "People outside talk as if steamers on this river run on a schedule; whereas they are liable to be stuck on a bar and not get off at all and be destroyed by the ice in the spring."[52]

Even on the rich man's journey, then, nature, in the form of ice, currents, water, and seasons, pervaded each moment of the miners' trip, even as they themselves did very little work. In order to steam up and down the river, though, someone had to do the work. Steamboats needed pilots and workers who knew the river, and the boats needed nature itself, in wood and coal. In shifting bodily labor to steamboat crews, passengers freed only themselves from direct bodily engagement with nature. In their places, pilots, crew members, woodcutters, and boatbuilders forged direct connections to nature. The miners' simple transaction of buying a ticket and boarding a boat for a labor-free passage masked this labor and the knowledge and intimacy that pilots and deckhands developed. Passengers remained connected to nature, however, through those workers, whose labors they purchased as commodities.

From the earliest days of Yukon steamboating, captains relied on Native pilots to guide them through a river that seemed more a tricky sea, "a terror to Steamboat navigation," according to one passenger.[53] The Yukon provided no clear path or channel, but rather a seemingly endless sea of sloughs, islands, and channels, and thus countless opportunities to end up in a dead-end inlet or aground on a shallow bar. The mouth of the river, its first few miles, and the Yukon Flats below Circle City provided particular challenges. James Anderson provided more detail on his trip upriver in

May 1898: "There is quite a current; you can see nothing but islands; if the water is high it is easy to get lost with a Steamboat and should the water fall quickly be left high and dry in some slough."[54] Because they traveled and fished the river, Native Yukoners knew the river's deep channels and treacherous rocks. Indians remained on the periphery of gold mining itself, but they were central to the work of moving gold miners to and from the creeks. Merchants, steamer captains, and miners recognized and valued Native peoples' knowledge, and the knowledge itself became a commodity in a trade economy, bought and sold as part of the price of movement. A man on the Yukon River steamer *Pingree* wrote a letter in July 1898 explaining that the boat was not yet at the mouth of the river and already aground in three feet of water: "Then an Indian pilot came aboard and brought us safely into the mouth of the river." As soon as the pilot left, they were again hard and fast aground.[55] On James Anderson's boat in August 1897, the captain "thought he knew more than the Indian; he proved he knew where the damn bars were by ramming the boat or barge on every one."[56] Walter Curtin reported that Indian pilots charged a hundred dollars to take a steamer through the Yukon Flats to Circle City. Their expertise seemed straightforward to Curtin. "The Indians travel over the ice when the water is low and study the channel. Who says the savages haven't any sense?"[57]

Miners traveling by steamboat clearly consumed the labor and expertise of Native Yukoners, but that consumption sometimes mixed with the miners' own labor in running the boats. On the upper Yukon in 1898, Stewart Campbell described the difficult labor and timing involved in running a steamer down a rapid. He and his mining party built one of the first steamers on the upper river, hoping to speed their journey down to Dawson and the goldfields. After running aground the first day out, they sought expert help. "Indians brought Tagish Jim, their chief, who we hired to go with us." Their perilous run through White Horse rapids, on June 8, 1898, required more than Indian guidance, however. It proved just how much work, and how many workers, it took to navigate a steam-powered vessel through a trouble spot. "Started with steamer at 1 p.m.," Campbell recorded, "with Schied fireing, Pierson running engine, Longwell keeping water in tank, Doyle hanging on to mast, pilot's helper at bow oar and pilot and myself at rear sweep on upper deck." They blew the whistle at the top to cheers from a crowd of spectators above on the cliffs.[58] At the Thirty Mile River, they wrecked it on a rock. Such complex and coordinated attempts, however, demonstrated the energy and labor that some miners produced in traveling by boat, but that most others consumed.

As Campbell's journey illustrates, Native pilots were not the only ones to work the Yukon's tricky passages. Those white pilots who first worked the river had lived in the North long enough to forge strong ties to Native communities and to gain knowledge from Indian canoeists and pilots. Mac McMichael was traveling upriver above Circle City when the *Victoria* got hung up on a bar for five hours. "A cold, snowy day and bad," he wrote. "Took on a white pilot with an Indian wife and child."[59] The market in such knowledge of the river intensified as whites and Natives increasingly saw such intimacy with nature as a valuable commodity, worth high wages. Young Harrison Kepner took a job as a crew member on a North American Trade & Transportation Company steamer in 1896, but, he wrote, "I am going to learn to steer the boat and learn the river then try and get a position as Pilot on the river. There isn't any white Pilots on the river yet they are all indians and I tell you what there is big money in Piloting."[60]

The increasing number of pilots inevitably led to conflict, as Native pilots faced competition from white deckhands and crews who had learned the river. A white pilot "cursed furiously" at the captain of the steamer *Yukoner* when he hired an Indian. In addition, new and different kinds of knowledge of the river's nature, recorded on navigation charts with scientific instruments, changed the ways in which humans knew and moved along the river. From 1899 to 1901, the crew of the revenue cutter *Nunivak* took soundings and charted the "narrow and intricate channels" of the Aphoon entrance to the Yukon.[61] Such records transcended any individual's or community's understanding of the river, taking the form, in charts and books, of knowledge even further commodified for sale as aids to travel and business. Native pilots, however, continued to work the river through those years.

For both Indian and white steamboat workers, the steamboat business meant knowing nature very, very well. John Callbreath ran a small sternwheeler on the Stikine River for over twenty years prior to the Alaska-Yukon gold rush, running supplies inland for his trading posts and packtrain operation (map 1). His diaries provide the most detailed example of the level of intense knowledge, experience, and connections to nature that became commodities during the gold rush. When miners purchased passage on Callbreath's boat, which ran from Wrangell, Alaska, to the head of Stikine navigation at Telegraph Creek, British Columbia, they purchased and consumed that knowledge and experience, the benefit of countless trips back and forth by both steamer and canoe.[62] Miners rarely took much notice of such expertise, though. Callbreath knew the Stikine's seasons and stages of high and low water and its currents, rocks, riffles, and turns. With his crews, both Indian and white, he developed his own geography of camps, wood piles, bends, and rapids, reflected in the names of places that marked movement up and down the river: Grand Rapids, Devil's Elbow, Boulder Bend; the shoals below Clearwater; Barley Cache. He even knew individual rocks, writing in July 1880, "The river was at a good stage; rock at head of canyon [a] foot above water." No matter how well he knew each rock and riffle, he also learned that they were subject to change. He took his steamer upriver in July 1892 and reported trouble finding the right channels as he "couldn't take the same ones as last time."[63]

Traveling miners benefited from Callbreath's knowledge of the river; they got what they paid for. They reaped even greater benefits from his knowledge of how to move a grounded steamboat, an enormous challenge that required both brute force and a delicate touch. That skill, too, had developed through years of trial and error. On May 30, 1894, Callbreath's steamer ran aground, high and dry with the river falling. "Can walk dry shod around the boat this morning," he remarked the next day. After ten days of using sills, cordwood, and soapy skids to move the boat, the crew was "overjoyed" to get it into water on June 11.[64] Steamers ran aground so often that, as Callbreath demonstrated, crews developed specific methods and tools for moving them. Nothing was more awkward and difficult than moving a loaded steamboat without benefit of water. John Cantwell described this gear on Yukon boats, a set of heavy spars and tackles which, with "skillful handling," made it possible to run a line to a short spar on the shoal in question and work that line to "crutch" the boat into deep water. This method, Cantwell explained, took "a lot of skill on the part of the man on shore." If undertaken by a novice, it was "liable to end in failure."[65]

With the exception of wrecks, groundings, and ice, passengers riding these boats up the Stikine and the Yukon to the goldfields remained relatively unaware of the knowledge and labor necessary to their journeys. Even in their oblivion as consumers, however, they remained connected, through the knowledge and labor they purchased, to that somewhat distant nature. What passengers *did* notice, and did frequently mention in their journals and letters, was the amount of fuel the boats—and hence they themselves as passengers—consumed in the course of their journeys. "We make quite a number of stops about every six hours or oftener we must stop and take on wood," wrote Nora Crane in 1897. "It is all drift wood that the Indians cut for them and pile up in cords."[66] All movement required a source of energy, and on steamboats that energy always came from the natural world, primarily in the form of wood or coal, but also in wind and current, and in the food that powered human muscles. Steamboats and steamboat passengers consumed their fair share of knowledge and labor, but mostly they consumed wood.

Far from conquering nature, steamboats moved by allowance of nature's energy, and depleted the forest along the way. In the Yukon transportation market, cordwood and the labor required to cut, haul, and load it became valuable commodities that travelers bought and sold as they consumed distance itself. A small boat burned a minimum of ten cords a day in high summer, but, according to Cantwell, the total ran to thirty cords a day for average-sized boats, and up to fifty a day for the luxurious vessels and larger boats that towed barges at the height of the gold rush.[67] The nearly two-thousand-mile trip from St. Michael to Dawson ran anywhere from twelve to twenty-five days, which meant anywhere from 150 to over one thousand cords for a one-way, upriver trip to Dawson. Such a quantity could cost fifteen thousand dollars.[68] On the upper river, a round trip from Lake Bennett to Dawson and back required at least 125 cords by one account, 260 cords by another. In 1901 the steamer *Dawson* made sixteen round-trip voyages for a total of about two thousand cords for the season.[69] At the height of the gold-rush sternwheeler era on the Yukon, as many as 250 boats and barges of all sizes ran on the upper and lower river.[70]

As a result of the steamboats' fuel demands, the riparian forest disappeared. Steamer companies and wood sellers cut trees as close to the river as possible, as wood cut at any great distance from the banks took a lot of labor to move to the fueling camps. Observing the Yukon in 1900 and 1901, John Cantwell wrote that "Great inroads have been made in the spruce forests along the immediate banks of the Yukon to supply fuel for the steamboats plying on the river, and in certain localities the shores have been almost entirely denuded of timber." Large timber had long since disappeared from areas in which miners had settled and built cabins. Much small wood remained throughout the region, but the forests "along the margin of the steamboat channels" were greatly depleted, he wrote. He predicted an imminent need to build tramways farther back from shore in order to bring cordwood to the riverbanks. "It will not be long before all the timber within easy reach of the steamers will be gone."[71] Other observers came to similar conclusions. U.S. Consul J. C. McCook reported between fifty and sixty thousand cords cut on the American side of the border in the summer of 1899.[72]

As much as steamboats needed the forest itself, and as quickly as they destroyed that forest, they required more than simply trees. To keep the boats and miners in motion, they needed those trees cut and stacked at convenient intervals along the river. True speed on the river required quick fuel stops with fast loading, and that required labor: workers who cut, hauled, stacked, and loaded cordwood. The demand for cordwood may have destroyed huge swaths of forest, but along the way it created a wood economy, a market in raw and processed materials and in labor. That wood economy connected steamboats not only to nature, but also to local Native peoples, who sold their labor within the wood economy.

That wood economy revealed the commodification of both labor and nature at the heart of industrial capitalist culture as it spread up the Yukon River. As with Chilkoot packers and steamboat pilots, the wood economy depended at first on Indian labor, and then shifted to include Euro-American workers as both demand for, and the value of, wood and labor intensified. As Nora Crane indicated in 1897, the first wood camps were simply Native villages, where the boats stopped to exchange cash and trade goods for driftwood. In these cases, the wood economy functioned as part of a broader, long-standing trade system between Native Yukoners and Euro-Americans. As early as 1883, Frederick Schwatka noticed that his steamer on the lower Yukon loaded "a considerable quantity of the wood it requires already cut at convenient points, the natives of course being paid for their labor."[73] Nora Crane noted in 1897 that the boats "pay $4 a cord to the Indians and they [the Indians] take goods from the storehouse in payment they charge them $6 for a pack of flour. The wood piles are generally at some little Indian village and it is a sight to see them come on board ship to trade wild ducks, Salmon, a sort of salmon berry, baskets and dried fish for food and clothes."[74]

As the Yukon transportation economy developed further, with more boats demanding more wood, cut and loaded faster with greater convenience, these barter and cash exchanges grew more complex. Native peoples continued to cut and trade wood seasonally when it fit into the cycles of their other subsistence activities. They also raised their prices. Wood that had sold for four or six dollars jumped to eight dollars per cord. When the demand outstripped the supply, Indians on the lower river raised prices to fifteen dollars a cord, or even as high as forty-five dollars a cord.[75] Such demands invited competition. Disillusioned miners, desperate for cash, turned to cutting cordwood as a last resort. A disheartened Will Childs wrote home from Dawson City in June 1900 that "I have made a failure of the gold mining business." He was headed for Nome, he added, to cut wood for steamers, as it sold for ten dollars a cord, although, he added, "wood is hard to get off the mountains."[76] After a small taste of winter mining, Thomas Moore gave up sinking shafts up the Koyukuk River and headed downriver to chop wood until spring. He and his partners built a flume to shoot the logs down hillsides to the riverbank, cutting mostly birch trees of four to eight inches around.[77] This work brought miners ready access to cash; a few cords of wood could buy a ticket home or an outfit for another season of mining.

White woodcutters and deckhands thus displaced some Native laborers and moved them even further toward the economic margins of the gold mining economy, toward, as one historian writes, "the bottom rung of a service industry."[78] John Cantwell sensed cultural differences amongst woodcutters and concluded in 1901 that independent white cutters pushed most Natives from the trade. "The more energetic white man has almost entirely driven the indolent and easy-going native from the field," he wrote. With that comment, Cantwell misread both the Natives' cycles of subsistence work and the whites' desperation. For most Indians, woodcutting was one of many seasonal activities, appropriate for certain times of year and for certain specific purposes. For most white men, on the other hand, woodcutting was a job of last resort, a desperate bid for cash. Those who ended up in wood camps in the winter suffered from isolation and lack of food. In March 1899 Lynn Smith heard reports of scurvy in and around Rampart City, "especially along [the] river among woodchoppers who have poor outfits and don't cook properly."[79]

While white miners and Native peoples competed for the lower rungs of the wood economy, the upper rungs of the industry were occupied by established wood camps, with direct ties to such major transport companies as the Alaska Commercial Company, North American Trade & Transportation Company, and the Empire Transportation Company of Philadelphia. The companies paid a fixed price per cord, and sent agents up and down the Yukon River to set contracts, which ensured a constant supply of wood in order to make movement as fast and efficient as possible.[80] Wood agents tried to tie up all the available wood to prevent others from getting it and to bring the competition to a literal standstill. When the large companies bought all of the cut wood along the river for the season, they forced other boats to cut their own wood. Mac McMichael took a steamer from Circle City up to Fourth of July Creek and found progress agonizingly slow, as the boat stopped at night while the crew went ashore to cut wood. On September 24 he recorded the boat starting off at 5 A.M. They stopped at 10 A.M. for wood. "Did not get through wooding up until 2. . . . Only making ten or fifteen miles per day." Lynn Smith was bored and impatient for news of the world in Rampart during August 1898, as the steamers worked their way upstream from below. "But the Boston and Alaska Co. and all other companys have to stop and chop wood for themselves which is the cause of the delay."[81]

Both the predominance of Euro-American woodyards and the ad hoc scrambling of cash-hungry miners disguised the ongoing presence of Native Alaskans and Native Yukoners in the wood economy. Captain John Cantwell took note of an operation at Greyling, Alaska, on the lower river, 427 miles up from St. Michael, where the river entered more forested land. Here a Mr. O'Shea maintained "one of the largest independent wood yards on the river," employing about half a dozen white wood choppers, but also about seventy-five local Indians who worked "from time to time" cutting wood "when hunting and fishing does not occupy them." The yard sold twelve hundred to eighteen hundred cords each year.[82] Indians' labor in fueling transportation became less and less visible over time, but Native woodcutters remained important in the wood economy that connected miners to nature.

By the time gold rushers reached Dawson City, whether as rich men or poor, producers or consumers of transport, their connections to the natural environment had expanded far beyond the initial cultural ties that made gold valuable and set them on their journeys in the first place. Through their own production of the bodily labor of transportation, they gained intimate knowledge of the seasonal vicissitudes of trails that turned from ice to mud and back again, and creeks that were solid one minute and liquid the next. In their far more widespread consumption of transportation, they consumed the energy, labor, experience, and knowledge of transport workers on trails and rivers, the lives of pack animals, and the abundance of energy stored in the forest. That consumption revealed the power of an expanding industrial economy to commodify nature in the form of distance, seasons, wood, and the energy in animals' bodies, and its power to commodify human beings' labors and knowledge. Transportation revealed the many ways in which consumption, rather than separating the miners from nature, created a proliferating network of connections, reaching out in every direction through the labors of hired workers.

Whatever slight distance from nature they might have gained through the hiring of workers and the consumption of transportation labor, that distance largely vanished when miners turned from their journeys to gold mining itself. Like the bodily labor of transportation, mining brought miners into direct contact with a challenging natural world. As they prospected and dug for gold, miners took their connections to nature directly into the earth. Their mining labors brought them a new knowledge of the creeks and hillsides of the Yukon basin. Along the way, those labors transformed that nature according to an industrial vision of a productive land.

4

THE NATURE
OF GOLD MINING

Bill Hiscock traveled for seven months from his home in New Zealand by way of Hawaii, Vancouver, B.C., Chilkoot Pass, and Dawson City before he finally reached Bonanza Creek in November 1898. Following a lead on a possible share in a mining claim, he and his two partners hauled their sleds from Dawson to "the center of the rich gold strike that had caused the rush." His diary recorded the scene:

> We got some miles up the Bonanza before we came to any claims being worked. Then we began to see a windlass with a heap of dirt; and gravel being frozen to all depths has to be thawed out, with wood fires, usually put in in the evening and left to burn during night time. In the morning the thawed earth, from 4 to 5 inches to 8 or 9 inches, is hoisted by windlass in a wooden bucket, tipped out and in 20 minutes it is frozen solid again and remains there until the spring comes.[1]

Like the labor of transportation, the labor of mining was an intensely cultural process through which miners carried their industrial economy north, including the commodification so characteristic of Yukon transportation. Like transportation, the actual work of digging gold from the earth also connected miners to nature, to heaps of dirt and gravel, frozen to all depths. Such labor brought miners new knowledge of the natural world and transformed the gold creeks into new places.

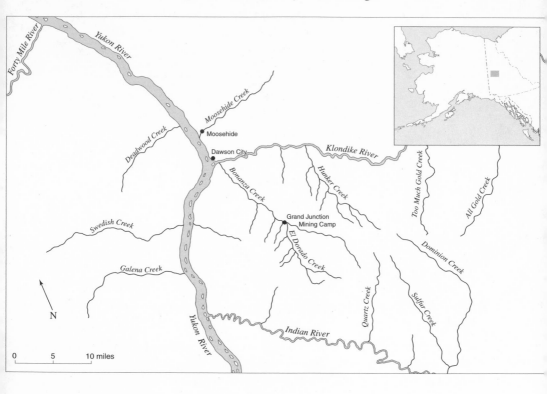

MAP 6. The Klondike goldfields, Yukon Territory

In Alaska and the Yukon at the turn of the twentieth century, the specific natural world in which placer miners worked was formed by riparian ecosystems, the rivers and creeks tributary to the Yukon on either side of the U.S./Canadian border, and the banks, forests, and bogs along those rivers and creeks (maps 6 and 7). Gold was literally embedded within these larger physical systems, which of course contained all sorts of nature besides gold: soil, rock, gravel, permafrost, ice, water, vegetation, forests, salmon, moose, caribou, and other living organisms. Northern ecosystems drew energy from the sun and produced all of these living things quite oblivious to the presence of gold.

Because their culture valued gold so highly, gold miners sought only one small part of the diverse organic and inorganic physical world that comprised the northern creeks, and that particular part usually lay deep underground. For centuries, yearly rounds of freezing, thawing, and erosion had

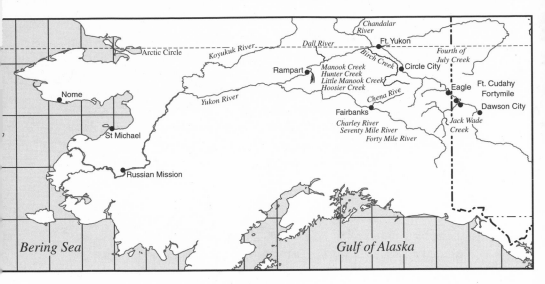

MAP 7. Yukon River gold creeks in Alaska

worked gold free from quartz or granite and washed it as dust and frag-
ments into creeks. Because gold was substantially heavier than anything
else, it sank into the gravels that formed the beds of the streams, and came
to rest when it hit something dense enough to stop it. Sometimes this was
heavy gravel, sometimes clay, sometimes solid rock. Miners called this
substance—whatever stopped the gold—bedrock. Although regular streams
like Bonanza Creek in the Yukon contained gold in their bedrock, gold lay
as well in the bedrock beneath older streambeds, which lay either underground, far below surface creeks, or far above them on hillsides. To get at
gold in all of these places, miners took the whole ecosystem apart. The work
of gold mining was the work of disassembly, and it left the creeks truly in
pieces.

Gold seekers stripped vegetation from the earth, rerouted streams, and
completely altered long stretches of stream valleys. In order to produce gold,
they consumed whole ecosystems, or rather the pieces of whole ecosystems,
broken into constituent parts in the form of endless piles of wood and dirt
and carefully channeled streams of water. Miners remade wood and water
into consumer commodities, to be used as tools for the extraction of gold.
They turned the solar energy in wood and water, stored and released in
annual cycles of growth and runoff, to this new and specific end. This dis-

assembly held consequences for the earth in which the miners worked. In taking the creeks apart, miners disrupted patterns of water flow and plant life, and transformed river ecosystems into almost lunar landscapes of mud, rocks, and silty, clouded water. In gold mining, the miners' connections to nature had a visible and transformative effect. Those connections remade the Yukon creeks in accordance with a culture that commodified both labor and gold and redefined the creeks as production sites for gold. As a result, gold mining made it impossible for humans along those creeks to do any other kind of work, and made it difficult for nature itself to produce anything besides gold.

Despite the disassembly of the gold creeks, the gold miners' labors did not constitute a complete separation or alienation from the nature around them. Here industrial work, even when environmentally destructive, constituted a new and particular set of connections with nature, albeit connections that had clear and often drastic consequences for nature itself. The miners' connections to permafrost, gravel, water, and wood constituted a very specific embrace of nature, one conditioned by a culture that valued certain natural elements—like gold—in very specific ways. That embrace of nature produced gold, sporadically, and also a "miners' knowledge" of the natural world, an increasingly sophisticated understanding of how to take the earth apart to find gold. Their knowledge of nature became so focused on gold, however, that miners paid little attention to the consequences of disassembling creeks, even when those consequences hindered their ability to produce gold itself.

For, as it turned out, dirt, muck, gravel, wood, water, and gold were not so easily divided from each other. They were components of interconnected natural systems and cycles, and intertwined with each other in ways miners recognized in their mining practices, if not explicitly in their writing and thinking. When miners altered one element of the system, such as flowing water, that water often reappeared in frustrating ways or disappeared just when it was needed. The very interconnectedness of the parts made disassembly a challenge, and the miners' ability to meet that challenge varied with their technology. At first, armed with shovels, picks, pans, sluices, and fire, they tore away at the riparian systems with remarkable energy and power. Within months of the initial rush, however, their need and ability to harness water moved them down an inexorable path toward full-scale hydraulic mining and stripping, which was followed after 1900 by dredging. Each step along this journey increased gold miners' ability to disassemble placer streams and rivers. Although the effects on the stream systems also increased dramatically with hydraulics and dredging, the principle was the same from the start in 1896 and 1897. Disassembly remained disassembly, whatever the tools. It was through that work of taking nature apart that gold miners came to know nature so well.[2]

DISASSEMBLY: WOOD, FIRE, EARTH, AND WATER

The first step in disassembling Alaska-Yukon gold creeks was deciphering the seasonal cycles of the place. Like most human labor, mining revealed one way in which human beings organized their lives within natural limits, and created new cycles of production and consumption that harnessed natural cycles. In the subarctic environment of the Yukon basin, all life was adapted to a climate of extremes, which brought long, dark, extremely cold winters and short summers, intense with light and heat. True daylight on the summer solstice lasted just over twenty-two hours.[3] Northern ecosystems cycled in ways that matched these conditions. In the summer, plants, animals, and of course mosquitoes grew in a frenzy of energy, concentrating their consumption of the sun's energy into a few short weeks of all-out growth and reproduction. Streams and rivers melted for a few brief months, cycling rain and snow quickly through watersheds. As every organic and inorganic element of the world sprang into action, Native Yukoners and gold-seeking newcomers followed suit, harnessing the abundance of the short summers.

Placer miners struggled to fit the basic tasks of gold mining into these seasonal extremes. First, they fought their way through layers of moss and other vegetation, surface muck, permanently frozen earth, and underground soil and rock to find the buried gold-bearing gravels. Second, they hauled those gravels to the surface by bucket and windlass, and piled them up in giant "dumps." Third, in the "wash-up," they ran water through sluices and rockers to wash away dirt and gravels and separate out the gold. The first two tasks were winter work; the third had to wait for spring and summer, when the creeks flowed free. Winter became the season of wood and soil, when the miners burned fires to thaw the earth. Spring and summer became the seasons of water and gold, when the long-awaited payday finally arrived. Northern gold mining hinged on these seasonal divisions, and miners divided their consumption of resources accordingly. In winter, they took wood and other plants and soil from the earth; in summer, they took water.

Together, the seasons of gold added up to an annual disassembly that left few resources untouched.

WINTER WORK

In Alaska and the Yukon, as in all gold rushes, miners began looking for gold on the surface, in the summer, along the banks of creeks and in sand and gravel bars in shallow water. They quickly turned, however, to the far more difficult project of prospecting and mining underground gravel deposits, and through that task began their attempts to take apart the earth. Scraping through the surface layers of muck and vegetation, they struck permafrost—permanently frozen soil—and gravel. Drawing on the experiences of northern prospectors in the 1880s and early 1890s, miners lit fires to thaw their way down through the frozen earth. Because thawing fires worked only in winter, they expanded mining beyond the summer months, making it far more productive. In December or January, once the world froze sufficiently, a miner picked a spot six or eight feet square to sink a shaft, and cleared the ground of trees, brush, moss, and soil.[4] "The top earth or muck can be done faster with a pick than by fire, but when the frozen gravel is struck," wrote Mac McMichael, "it must be burned to make headway at all." The distance to frozenness varied. Charles Mosier started work on a Meadow Creek claim in the Klondike, just after his arrival from upstate New York. "Started a hole near the line 9 & 10; dug about 3 ft.; frozen ground just under the moss."[5]

The repetitive, grueling labor of thawing and digging through foot after foot of frozen muck and dirt brought miners into intense physical and mental contact with the earth. They learned the frozenness of the earth through their muscles, as they dug and thawed and hauled with picks and windlasses. "Am working the hard graft," Bill Ballou reported to his brother Walt, "ten hours each day with pick and shovel."[6] "We worked out three fires today hard stuff to thaw muck and Rock mixed," James McRae scribbled in his diary. "This is what some people would call misery."[7] Tom Boldrick captured the drudgery succinctly in his record of July 4, 1898, a day spent prospecting on the Stewart River:

> We dig about 18 inches when we strike frozen ground. We gather wood build
> a fire in the hole which has thawed about 4 inches eagerly pan a pan of dirt

& get lots of glittering stuff in the pan but alas it is *mica*. We repeat the same thing for the whole day with the same results. There is gold here someplace.[8]

The first and most important tool in this misery, beyond the miners' tired bodies and worn shovels, was cordwood to fuel their thawing fires, taken from hillside and valley forests of spruce, birch, poplar, and aspen.[9] Winter work took miners down into the layers of the frozen earth, but before they could go into the earth they first had to go into the forest. Wood was the key resource for winter mining and for all aspects of survival during northern winters. In the Yukon Territory, each gold seeker purchased a license, or Free Miner's Certificate, which granted rights to cut wood for boats, cabins, and mining.[10] As a Rampart City newspaper put it in 1901, "The timber on a mining claim is as much a part and parcel of the claim, as is the gold contained therein."[11] In order to disassemble the creeks, they had to disassemble the forests as well.

Along many creeks, the first step was to start a forest fire. Thawing required dry wood, so miners heedlessly set fires in nearby forests to burn off branches, and dry and blacken trees for easy harvest and use. They then watched those fires spread and consume massive swaths of brush and timber along the rivers. These intentional fires added to the forest destruction that occurred all along the upper Yukon, where careless gold seekers lit camp fires and then left them to burn, igniting first ground cover and then the forest.[12] Tappan Adney hiked up Bonanza Creek early one winter morning to witness the work of gold mining. As he reached the sixtieth claim below the original spot where gold was discovered, called "60 Below," he found men cutting wood for the day, sawing away on "the slender blackened poles of spruce, cottonwood, and birch." "A heavy bank of smoke from the night's fires hung over the valley, and the air was laden with the smell of burned wood," Adney wrote later for *Harper's*. "Other men on the hill-sides were dragging down small poles for the fires, streaking the white snow with black."[13] Bill Ballou harvested wood in a forest swept by fire, and he found himself each night covered with soot, "Comming [*sic*] in as black as niggers." But the wood was dry due to the fire, and dry wood was always hard to come by.[14]

The wood that miners actually harvested from these burns came from the stream valleys and nearby hillsides, the narrow fringe along the waterways. Whether the wood was dry or green, the harvest for winter thawing, as with steamboat fuel, always began right along the water courses, and then worked up every nearby hill, gulch, and stream. Both humans and forests clustered in those corridors, and that confluence did not bode well for the forests. Miners took wood from the riparian zone because that was where the trees grew. Most nineteenth-century Euro-American explorers, observers, and miners were largely unimpressed with the boreal and sub-arctic forests of the arid Yukon interior. The trees did not seem a mer-chantable commodity. When Hudson's Bay agent Alexander Murray established a trading post on the upper Yukon in 1847, he had trouble finding large timber to construct his buildings. "The dry land," he wrote, "is mostly open, or having a small birch and willows, the only wood of importance is along the banks of the river or on the islands."[15] Like Mur-ray, observers consistently noted that the only worthwhile timber, domi-nated by white spruce, tended to hug the banks and islands of the great river itself and its tributaries.[16] In 1868 and 1869, William Dall noted that the white spruce was the "the largest and most valuable tree," spread over the "whole country a short distance inland," but "largest and most vigor-ous in the vicinity of running water."[17]

The thousands of gold miners who descended on the Klondike Valley and the scores that spread out to other valleys and the smaller creeks in the Yukon and Alaska cut, burned, and consumed this riparian forest at an unprecedented rate. Fire thawing consumed prodigious amounts of wood, and as with wood for steamboat fuel, this meant heavy harvesting. Alex McDonald, a wildly successful Klondike miner, told Tappan Adney that it took a half a cord of wood to thaw five cubic yards of gravel—equivalent to ten wheelbarrows—and that such wood cost twenty-five dollars a cord, cut and delivered to the mining site. Two men working holes through the winter could burn thirty cords of spruce, pine, and birch each season.[18] They often burned more. Bill Ballou reported in October 1901 that he was ready for winter work, having chopped "about sixty cords of nice dry logs."[19]

In addition to the wood for winter thawing, miners cut and purchased wood to build and heat their cabins and to construct tools and sluices for mining. Those who could afford to buy cordwood did so in a lively local market in which wood traders hauled "considerable quantities" from great distance to sell in Dawson and at the creeks. Those without cash, however, shifted for themselves, hauling wood on sleds. A local government report in 1898 stated that there was plenty of firewood in Dawson, "yet the extent to which the timber has been cut in the vicinity obliges the man who cannot afford to buy wood to travel further in quest of same."[20] When Maud Case visited her father's claim in June 1903, she walked up Eldorado Creek as far as Eureka Creek. "Not much timber on the mountainsides," she wrote, "for it had all been cut off for wood for these mines."[21]

For miners intent on gold, this wood served as a tool, a source of energy, a means to greater ends. They took that wood, however, from natural systems, and they burned it within natural systems. That massive wood consumption had consequences, both for nature and for the miners' own work. Along the creeks, wood and water were connected across seasons in ways that belied the miners' attempts to use them separately. Underground fires turned a frozen world into liquid just when the miners most depended on its frozenness. When spring came, and the snow and ice melted, deforested hillsides brought floods and dried streambeds when miners most depended on the streams' steady flow. Gold mining blurred the lines between the frozen and unfrozen seasons, and the local ecosystems proved far more complicated than the miners had expected them to be.

FIRE AND EARTH

Thawing through permafrost required not only stacks and stacks of cordwood, but also the skill to build fires that would thaw frozen earth in precise and predictable ways. As the *Klondike Nugget* explained, a good fire required specific knowledge of the different kinds of wood and the proper configurations of fire and earth. Once miners dug down to bedrock, they lit fires against the side of the hole to begin "drifting" laterally along that hard floor of earth. They started with kindling and shavings on the face of a drift, added small dry wood, and then covered that with green wood stood on end, to direct the heat against the frozen dirt. This "blanketing" supposedly ensured that only one part—the right part—of the miners' underground space would thaw.[22] Miners also tried to thaw or drift uphill, or "upstream," so that any threatening water would collect on the downhill side of the drift, away from the fires.[23] As the shafts got thirty feet down into the earth, and the drifts spread out to become underground tunnels, miners set two or three fires at a time, and the fires themselves got pretty big, with ten, twelve, or fifteen feet of banked flames. "Only twelve feet of fire burned," Charles Mosier noted on February 17, 1899, indicating plans for a bigger fire.

In building underground fires, miners gained knowledge of nature, but they encountered their share of problems as well, which brought further lessons in the seasons of mining and in the nature of wood, fire, and air. As they worked through the winter months, laying fires by night and cleaning gravel out of the holes during the day, the holes got deeper into the earth. In truly cold air, the deep shafts acted like chimneys, drawing hot air and smoke from the fires up and out into the winter stillness. When the temperature rose in the spring, however, carbon monoxide and smoke hung in the holes, stinging miners' eyes and lungs; it sometimes knocked them out, or worse.[24] Miners could immerse themselves in nature, but nature could just as easily drive them out. Charles Mosier and his father suffered badly from smoke and gas in the holes in March 1899, and had to quit work and rest in their cabin, blindfolded. On March 20 Mosier wrote, "Went down in the hole but it was too gassy to work." On the Rampart creeks, by the first of May 1899, all the men working for or near Bill Ballou were "driven out of the holes by water or gas." Gas and smoke signaled the effects of warming air, the change of seasons, and thus the change in work. On April 14 Mosier "quit the hole" and began preparations for spring sluicing. In mid-March, Frank Purdy stopped work due to sore eyes from gas. The next day he turned to spring work, whipsawing wood for rockers and mud boxes.[25]

Thawing fires posed other challenges as well. Permafrost meant that miners did not have to support their mining shafts and tunnels with timber scaffolds. Frozen creeks meant that they did not have to divert flowing water around their work. Miners thus depended on the frozenness of that earth for the structural integrity of the walls, floors, and ceilings of their holes and drift tunnels. Those holes and tunnels remained dry and safe only when the earth around them, and the creeks and underground springs they touched, remained frozen. The miners' chief tool in winter work, however, required them to light fires in this frozen earth, below frozen creeks and springs. In lighting those fires and digging holes, miners exposed frozen earth and frozen water to air and sunlight, and, of course, to fire. They thus threatened the very frozenness on which their winter work relied. To avoid the sudden collapse of thawing shafts and drifts, they had to limit fire thawing to its proper season. Flowing water, however, proved almost impossible to avoid.

In most cases, miners waited until at least November to begin thawing. Only in late November or December could they trust the frozen walls of their shafts and tunnels to hold firm, and trust running water to stay frozen.

As Mac McMichael explained in a letter home, "Many men start out in December to prospect their claims. In many places the ground does not freeze solid enough until about this time." Bill Ballou had to explain his summer laziness as well in September 1898, writing, "we can't work our claims until ground is well frozen."[26] Nevertheless, as the fires warmed and loosened the permafrost, walls and roofs loosened and fell, leaving debris and threatening miners' safety.[27] Miners lessened the danger by staying out of the holes during thawing. They lit the fires at night, and remained safely in their cabins through the most unstable part of the process, returning the next day to clean out the thawed material. "Put in evening fire but do not light until 9 p.m.," Asahel Curtis wrote in his diary for January 3, 1899. Some tried alternate thawing methods that applied more localized heat, including heated rocks and hot water. Stewart Campbell tried fire thawing in June 1899, with troubling results, which he recorded in a typically terse diary entry: "Hole badly caved in from last fire. Took 3 hrs. to remove debris. Have to burn with hot rocks after this. Down 18 ft." Frank Purdy heated rocks to put in the water that accumulated at the bottom of a shaft, finding them "better for firing for it dont thaw the muck."[28] Hot rocks rarely accomplished much, however, and hot water made for an even more difficult mess.[29] Miners timbered some shafts in winter as well as summer, to keep the walls from crumbling. They left earth pillars in drifts for structural support, and even used moss to insulate the walls, keep them cool, and prevent the steam from bringing them down.[30] They learned from nature. After laboring to strip thick, wet moss from the ground in order to warm the underlying muck, miners knew all too well its cooling, insulating ability.

The threat of caving worsened with the advent of steam thawing. To speed up the thawing processes, miners rigged long steel points to boilers, which forced steam into the points; they then drove the points into the permafrost and steamed the earth loose. This localized heat made it possible to thaw far greater volumes of dirt at far lower cost, and it made it possible, though not easy or safe, to mine permafrost in the summer.[31] Maud Case, a young woman from Minnesota, described the work on Eureka Creek in 1903. "They work all day under ground by candle light and in the steam and mud. . . . With the steam points they thaw the earth then they pick it to pieces and shovel the earth and rocks into wheelbarrows and out to the bucket to be hoisted into the sluice box. The disagreeable part is that the ground is thawing constantly and the mud falling down on them."[32] Mud, as it turns out, was never the only thing filling up the miners' hard-won holes in the ground.

In addition to the dangers of caving walls, the greatest threat to the mining itself came from water. As permafrost thawed, water seeped into the drifts, and, as one miner stated matter-of-factly, "water in the muck puts out the fire." Asahel Curtis explained, of his partner's attempts at thawing, that "When Charley goes to light he finds water dripping from Northwest corner and so did not dare to light the fire." "Water still dripping so we cannot fire at night," he added a few weeks later. Beyond the drips of melting ground, underground stream and spring water brought frustration beyond bearing. Every miner who dug more than a few feet into frozen gravel learned that no matter how frozen the world seemed, hidden waters had seasons of their own. Lynn Smith knew enough to wait for true winter, but in November 1901, he and his partner were "too anxious and tried to hurry nature. Put in five six foot fires and the weather is not cold enough so we started the water from above . . . and has been running ever since."[33]

To then make matters worse, once miners exposed underground water to the winter air, it of course froze, leaving them to face barriers of solid ice as well as permafrost. A group of Iowa miners working on Clear Creek in Alaska reported their progress to their hometown paper, the *Alton Democrat*. It was slow work, they explained: the "ground is only frozen two feet deep, and as soon as you get through that you strike water, then you have to lay off for three or four days, and let the ground freeze again, and so on. . . . So you see we really have to freeze a hole down as well as thaw it." Hunter Fitzhugh reported similar troubles in 1899: "I put my shaft down 6 ft. a few days ago, and was rejoicing at my good luck at not striking water as the rest have done, when lo! I hit one last blow with my pick and up gushed a stream of water. . . . I have four feet of solid ice to pick through when it freezes, if it ever does."[34]

Mac McMichael, James McRae, Lynn Smith, Frank Purdy, and all of their neighbors on multiple creeks saw days and days of labor destroyed when water broke through. "Everyone has had to quit on account of water," Smith reported in Rampart City, Alaska, in January 1899. "Some poor devil will get down nearly to bedrock and the water will run in and fill the hole up, and all his work has gone for naught," lamented McMichael. Fitzhugh told a similar tale: "the boys next door have five holes to bed rock, and all are

filled with water, making the work of six men for two months as nothing."
In the face of such frustrating battles with the natural world, Fitzhugh
yearned for regular work with a steady wage. "Only one hour is necessary
to fill our pay shaft with water," he continued, "and then we'll have all our
work to do over again, in which event I'll pack my sled . . . and look for
another job with wages." Running water was enough of a problem when
the weather stayed cold. Sudden winter thaws proved equally difficult for
work which depended on the frozenness of water and earth. "Had a thaw
of six days with rain," wrote Bill Ballou one February, as the temperature
caromed from sixty-one degrees below zero Fahrenheit to a striking thirty-
eight above: "Water running everywhere."[35]

LOST RIVERS

The miners' first goal in sinking holes was to reach bedrock, the solid bottom of old, buried streams, which had long ago caught and held the gold
washed by flowing water. If they followed the underground bed of the ancient
streams, they were most likely to find gold. The precarious task of locating
bedrock began with a more-or-less informed judging of the surface creeks,
which offered clues to the location of the subterranean beds that coursed
along invisibly under the miners' feet. Such guesswork could only get them
so far, however; they had to get down underground and have a look around.
Alaska-Yukon miners punched multiple trial-and-error holes downward,
like needles in an attempt to prick the right spot, tap the right gravels. It
was like fishing in a dark sea. Jonas Houck heard a story about a man digging down twenty-two times over a year and a half before he struck gold.
"I think about 5 holes to bedrock would satisfy me," Houck decided. Historian Rodman Paul described a similar task faced in California a few decades
earlier: "The miner had to gamble his intelligence against the unpredictable
whims of the lost river."[36]

Through this frustrating guesswork, and the labor it required, the miners' connections to nature took on cerebral as well as purely physical
aspects. As they worked their way into the ground, they learned not only
how hard the ground could be, but also how to read that ground for signs
of gold. This reading of the earth involved an ever-shifting combination of
instinct and experience. Finding ancient creek beds under twenty to sixty
feet of frozen dirt and gravel was nothing if not an education in the paths
that old creeks had, through centuries, cut through the Yukon plateau. As

they thawed and dug and hauled buckets, gold seekers carefully if not obsessively observed and read the earth, learning its layers and signs through constant contact and intense concentration. Frank Purdy, who left a job cutting lawns outside Boston to search for gold, proved particularly attentive. In his diary he recorded every kind of ground he dug through as he sank a hole forty-five feet down toward an old streambed: they included sand, black sand, gravel, ash, fine rock, coarse rock, coarse gravel, gravel with quartz, and muck with tree roots. All the while he tried to read the relationship of all of these strata to the presence of gold.[37]

Other miners were equally attuned to the earth in which they were digging, especially once they reached bedrock, and dug laterally to expose and trace the route of the underground creek. They read this ground by guesswork and analysis, but also by panning small amounts of gravel for traces of gold. These carefully noted amounts of gold gave the miners some idea of what kind of pay they were earning for their daily efforts, where to burn and dig underground, and where the richest ground was to be found. Lynn Smith wrote home on Thanksgiving eve that his work had exposed fourteen feet of bedrock. He used rising and falling yields from pans to detect the richest ground, the pay streak. "We . . . struck a different formation of gravel and we think we are getting into the old channel . . . three pans of dirt . . . five cents first, then 78 cents, then 40 cents. . . ." On February 2, 1899, Charles Mosier summed up the day with his usual reticence: "Cleaned hole; 14 buckets pay; 56 cents in 2 pans on west end; 76 cents on east end." These were not just economic reports. They were guides to the soil and gravel, a mapping of the earth in terms of gold dollars and cents.[38]

Learning where and how to sink into the frozen earth thus meant learning how to read and map the history of streams, to track their former paths from the clues provided by current paths, to read the history of erosion in the landscape. Old streambeds were not always buried. While some toiled downward to find gold, other miners thought to look up. On the Klondike River and its tributary creeks, flowing water had over centuries cut gulches and valleys down through the Yukon plateau. As the creeks worked downward, they washed and concentrated gold at each new level, leaving gold-bearing gravels at each bed, like a snake shedding and leaving behind a valuable skin.[39] A few miners figured out that many of their current creeks and gulches were the product of water cutting downward through the hills, and thus that other, older creeks must have flowed *above* them, and must

have left deposits of gold at those higher points. The story of hillside mining supposedly began in July 1897, when a former California miner named
Albert Lancaster risked the scorn of the Eldorado Creek community by
climbing the hillside above a rich claim to begin digging. He struck gold
four feet down, and the stampede to the hills began.[40]

For hillside, gulch, and creek miners alike, the location of creeks, bedrock,
and pay dirt proved to be a constant puzzle and a constant topic of discussion; theories abounded. In December 1900, a Rampart City newspaper proclaimed on its front page its thoughts on the source of the area's gold: "Instead
of the gold having been deposited in the creeks as they now exist," the article explained, "it is fed from the ancient channels running . . . at angles to
the streams." This knowledge came, the writer noted "at the expense of four
years of incessant prospecting, involving the labor and thought of hundreds
of miners and . . . almost as many theories, as to the source or the sources
of the gold." According to the Rampart miners' mapping of the underground
channels, one old channel had strung gold out underneath three different
sets of rich claims on three different surface creeks. "The famous No. 8 above,
Little Minook, appears to be above the center of the deposit along with 23
L[ittle] M[inook] jr. and 20 Hoosier, which seem to mark the crossing of
the channel on these creeks below which all of them have given good
returns."[41] Seattle photographer Asahel Curtis worked Sulphur Creek in the
Klondike during the winter of 1899 and was one of the miners mulling over
just such a theory. "The bench on west side of Sulp. must have discharged
gold on the surface," he wrote, "and perhaps there is still a deposit on the
hillside. This may be small but rich. Two small streams flow down the bank,
each seeming to carry gold and at the foot gold is found. This is not in bedrock but on muck which also carries a little gold."[42] However skillfully miners learned to read the earth for bedrock and gold and to trace underground
channels, winter work remained guesswork. Miners would not know the
true yield of their labors until the seasons turned, and the creeks ran.

SPRING AND SUMMER WORK

On March 16, 1900, Frank Purdy and his partner quit drifting underground
and began to build wooden boxes with slotted metal covers on bowed
rocking-chair legs— called rockers— in which they would, with water, sift
through their winters' accumulation of gold-bearing soil. By the 24th, after

a week of preparations, Purdy reported "water running on the hillsides and in the creek. Rockers are going everywhere.[43] Water defined the seasons of Alaska-Yukon placer mining, and the spring thaw signaled the year's great change, when running water allowed miners to switch from thawing the earth to washing it away to reveal the gold left behind. Once the ice began to soften, miners climbed out of their drifts, built dams to store spring runoff, and cut lumber for sluice boxes, rockers, and flumes in preparation for the great burst of concentrated, day-and-night work that would finally, they hoped, produce piles of gold.[44] Through the intense labor of the washup, miners forged new connections to water and earth, connections which transformed water and earth in significant ways.

For miners to harness the spring runoff to their own specific purpose, Tappan Adney wrote, "the same general principle is employed as by nature— namely, water in motion."[45] Miners redirected the flow of water through networks of sluices and boxes to wash their excavated gravel and separate out the gold. Streams and rivers did this work naturally, leaving gold scattered in bedrock, but after miners hauled that bedrock to the surface, they sped up the process by channeling the water, focusing the sifting, and concentrating the gold in their sluices, rockers, and pans. Miners built wooden sluices about twelve feet long, wider at the top than bottom, and slanted downward one inch per foot. To accommodate larger loads of dirt, bigger operations linked several sluices together to create long wooden chains. One worker designated to "shovel-in" threw thawed-out soil and gravel into the sluice, while another released flowing water down the wooden channel, using gravity to wash the loosened earth. Wooden slots and barriers in the bottom of the sluices— called "riffles"— caught the heavy gold as it fell out of the pay dirt, just as rocks had stopped its motion in the ancient streambeds.[46] The coursing water took the lighter dirt and gravel down the sluice and into pools or streams that quickly filled with silty waste; it left the gold behind. One or two miners tended the sluices to remove the larger rocks; others stirred the fine dirt and black sand with brushes to wash away small particles. At the end, nuggets and fine gold dust emerged from the sandy residue in yellowish bands.[47]

To manage the flow of water through earth, miners built flumes that diverted water from creeks to their dumps and sluices. They dug ditches to channel water, built small dams and reservoirs, and strung long chains of flumes that crisscrossed the creek valleys and gulches, carrying water from sluice to sluice. The aboveground scaffolds elevated the creeks themselves into high wooden pathways, a mine-to-mine, crazy-quilt circulatory system.[48] The work of sluicing changed the whole topography of the creeks, taking water from one path and sending it into another, and reaching out to distant creeks to divert them to more important gold-bearing sites. "Thus will the problem of getting water on Glen be solved," declared the *Alaska Forum* in Rampart City, referring to Glen Creek. "The Rhode Island [creek] water will be taken from 11 above and carried about 8000 feet to the west benches of Glen."[49]

Miners on hillsides such as Cheechako Hill and Gold Hill had no direct access to the creeks, so water became even more of a commodity for them, bought and sold with labor and cash. Because they lacked flowing water, they washed their dumps with buckets of water hauled or pumped from the creeks below. In place of sluices they built rockers. They shoveled pay dirt into the hoppers and rocked vigorously while ladling water into the mixture. The heavier gold and sand washed through the slots and holes to be caught on a blanket below. Those who did sluice dirt on the hillsides depended on and often paid for communal dams, flumes, and pumps, which carried water up to the hillsides and allotted a certain amount to each contributor. Frank Purdy explained in April 1900 that "Water is being pumped up on this hill from Bonanza a height of 305 ft. the stream is nine inches enough for 3 . . . sluice heads."[50] Purdy dug a ditch from his dump to this common water supply, and would open the ditch for certain periods when the water was running. Sometimes the water froze at night, and was slow to start in the morning. For Purdy, busy with his rocking in late March, this meant that "the water begins to run about 11 a.m. and runs till late in the afternoon." Shared water systems proved less than dependable when others controlled the stream. On April 13, Purdy noted, the "water didn't run very long today." But three days later he "rocked all day today. The water was running a good sized stream."[51]

A good-sized stream was good news, for spring sluicing required a steady water supply, and the Alaska-Yukon interior guaranteed no such thing. Miners worked in the rain shadow of the coast ranges, in a relatively dry climate with a fast spring thaw. Winter ice and snow melted in a few short weeks; the creeks thawed, flooded, then fell quickly and often dried up. This gave miners a narrow and unpredictable window in which to do the most productive work of the year. It also gave them a new knowledge of how water moved through the environment. The uncertain supply made for frantic periods of labor. U.S. Consul J. C. McCook, at Dawson City, described the cleanup on the Klondike creeks in May 1899, writing that a "full head of water is now running on all the creeks and every moment is put in shoveling the winters diggings into the sluice boxes. A majority of claim owners are putting on extra men so as to keep up the work continuously during the twenty four hours, as they are afraid the water may not last until they finish the washup."[52]

Even during the few hectic weeks of the thaw, creek levels could vary drastically. When the snow refused to melt, everyone sat idle. On May 2, 1900, Frank Purdy rocked for only half a day because of cold weather that slowed the water flow. By May 16th, the water was low in the ditch, then shut off for part of the day; on the 19th, the water was "nearly played out." In April 1901 the thaw came late again. John Lindsay wrote that the "season is so backward that we cannot get at it untill [*sic*] the snow goes off some more. . . . this time last year they were sluicing a week before this time and I think it will be a couple of weeks before we can start." Thomas Moore arrived at the Klondike creeks with hundreds of others in June 1898, and found Bonanza Creek miners restless and unoccupied, waiting for more water.[53]

Similar problems occurred later in the season when the creeks ran dry. In 1902, Bill Ballou wrote home from the Rampart creeks that the "creeks are dry with only about half of the dumps shoveled in and now Little Manook is the same." Such a drought had never happened before, and the financial threat loomed large. As Lynn Smith reported one June in Alaska, "everyone has stopped work on account of the dry season . . . no rain for three weeks now." The same held true for John Lindsay in June 1900 on Monte Cristo Hill above the Klondike creeks. He was limited to only eleven days of wage work "on account of not getting any water to wash with only for that I would have got my pay long ago." In other years, however, there were no such shortages. "The streams are all running gaily," the *Alaska Forum* recorded at Rampart in May 1901, "and the enormous quantities of snow still lying in the foothills assures us that they will continue to pour a steady stream into the Yukon long after the period when in times past they were almost dry."[54]

THE EFFECTS OF DISASSEMBLY

The miners' troubles with spring and summer water flow for the washup were rooted in more than just aridity, climate cycles, and weather. A steady flow of spring water, as part of the ecosystem's water cycle, depended on the various parts of the ecosystem—plants, soil, water—remaining relatively intact. As miners stripped vegetation from the river corridors, dug up stream beds, and diverted the creeks themselves, they took those ecosystems apart, separated plants from soil and soil from water, and put each to other uses. This disassembly affected the cycle of water flow itself, changing the creeks themselves. The resulting physical degradation of the gold creeks did not mean, however, that miners were disconnected or alienated from nature. Mining, after all, brought them new and intense connections to water, trees, fire, and dirt; it brought them useful knowledge about how to take gold from the earth. Clearly, such linkages directed toward such particular ends did not and could not leave nature unchanged.

Foresters and other conservationists in the United States and elsewhere had begun by the 1890s to link deforestation with the threat of floods, erosion, and drought. Miners discovered on their own small scale that their disassembly of forests and gold creeks did indeed have environmental consequences. Those consequences did not matter much to them in the long run, as they remained interested only in the short-term extraction of gold. But miners noticed consequences in offhand ways, as denuded hillsides brought spring water flooding down more quickly, eroded soil, and then dried the streams earlier in the summer.

The Yukon's riparian forests were by no means static or perfectly balanced ecosystems before the miners arrived to wreak their own brand of quick havoc. Native peoples hunted in the forests and harvested wood. They set fires to control mosquitoes, attract bear and moose, open up forests for travel, and counter the threat of larger fires.[55] In 1883, along the Yukon upstream from the Klondike, Lt. Frederick Schwatka found that "evidences of conflagration in the dense coniferous forests were everywhere frequent, the fires arising from the carelessness of Indian campers, and from the making of signal smokes, and even it is said, from design."[56] Indian burning had already shaped the forest, but the miners' burning and cutting along the Yukon, gold creeks, and nearby hillsides changed the composition of the forests and the forest floor even more dramatically. Miners took every piece of wood within reach; photographs of the Dawson region and the Klondike creeks from the turn of the century show deforested hillsides in every direction. Pierre Berton's edited photographic essay of the gold rush, *The Klondike Quest*, features a long series of views, both panoramic and closeup, of creeks, hills, and benches. Few trees stand visible in any of them, but wood is everywhere, in flumes, trestles, cribbing, and cabins, and as cascades of cut poles strewn down hillsides like pickup sticks.[57]

When it came to vegetation, miners did not limit themselves to the all-out harvest of useful timber. They also cleared and burned surface brush and moss. When James McRae and his partners built their cabin in Klondike City, across the Yukon River from Dawson, they repeatedly took a boat up Bonanza Creek and filled it with moss to insulate their roof. Miners and townspeople also recognized the connections between moss, wetlands, and mosquitoes, and they burned, drained, and cleared ground to eradicate the bugs. Tappan Adney noted that the mosquitoes menaced the islands that had yet to be cleared of trees and moss, but that in Dawson and on Bonanza Creek, on land which was "cleared partially," they were no worse than at home in upstate New York. In the spring of 1899, Bill Ballou noted that the clearing of timber and burning of moss near Rampart City mitigated the mosquitoes in town, allowing him to sit comfortably "on our piazza receiving callers and watching the steamers as they arrive and depart."[58]

As they cut timber, set fires, stripped moss, and dug up the soil, placer miners unleashed changes that rippled through the riverine ecosystems. Large-scale deforestation can increase stream flow five or six times in volume, and vegetation along river banks plays a particularly important role in regulating stream flow. Without those trees, plants, and mosses in place, snowmelt and rainwater ran more quickly into creeks in the spring and after storms, causing sudden floods which broke through the miners' earthworks, ponds, and sluices, foiling their attempts to harness runoff and to direct water through sluices.[59] Mining on hillsides and benches loosened vegetation, roots, and dirt, and caused additional problems when spring floods rushed downhill quickly, bringing debris and sediment with them, wiping out earthworks and flumes, and swamping trails and roads with mud.[60]

If miners were not plagued by floods, they suffered from dried-out creeks. The miners' thawing and clearing reduced the ability of soil and plants to absorb water and to regulate its flow by releasing it gradually over time.[61] Because permafrost prevented surface water from draining down into soils, the ground held much of the water at the surface, in heavy layers of moss which created soggy wetlands and bogs. The miners were all too aware of such wetlands. When Iowa clerk Thomas W. Moore first saw Bonanza Creek in 1898, he described it as "low marshy country, lying between the mountains that rose on either side . . . country covered by moss soaked with water. . . . Far from an inviting place, and the last place one would expect to find gold." Lynn Smith despaired over the land at the Rampart creeks, with its moss "18 inches thick and wet and soggy." Bill Ballou took note of some of these characteristics from the deck of a sternwheeler, coming up the Yukon to Rampart City. "It would seem as though the land itself . . . were a sponge, into which all rain and moisture from the heavens and melting snow are absorbed."[62]

This sponge of soggy moss drove miners crazy, but it also held moisture in place at the ground's surface. The surface water held by moss and other plants then fed slowly into creeks throughout the summer, through cycles of evaporation, rain, and runoff. In the heat of long summer days, water held in moss and bogs evaporated slowly, then cooled and condensed in low cumulus clouds. Such rain often fell as mist. Bill Ballou declared in May 1900 that "it can rain all day and not wet your hat."[63] On July and August afternoons, such clouds brought showers or even thunderstorms, a precious and often much-needed water supply for summer sluicing.[64] The moss and other surface plants thus kept rainfall in circulation in ways that could benefit humans in search of even and dependable seasonal water flows. But as miners removed the spongy layer of moss, they lost many of these benefits. Spring runoff ended up in the creeks too early and too quickly. As a result, streams dried faster and more permanently, earlier in the summer, sometimes preventing a full washup of winter diggings. The reduced evaporation of surface water then lessened summer mists and rainfall.

The increasing numbers of fires affected the riparian environment as well, beyond the mere consumption of wood. Fires cleared forests, thawed permafrost, and loosened soil, all of which increased runoff and flooded and muddied the creeks. An adventurous miner named C. O. Steiner went two hundred miles up the Stewart River, hunting and prospecting. At one point he noticed that a small tributary had suddenly turned muddy, and, assuming that there were men upstream mining, he went to look for them. Instead he found that a fire "had stripped [the] hillside for a mile." The trees, rooted only a foot deep due to permafrost, had collapsed, the earth had thawed out, and the whole hillside had thus slid into the stream. When Bob Marshall investigated gold mining around Wiseman, Alaska, in the late 1920s, he found that the flow of creeks in the Koyukuk region had been decreased by "forest devastation." Speaking of more recent cutting and burning in the local forest, an older miner explained that these careless activities affected sluicing. "Oh, yes," he told Marshall, "there's no doubt that since the timber's been cut and burned we don't keep our water the way we used to."[65]

The miners' overall disassembly of the gold creeks reached well beyond the problems of deforestation, flooding, and drought, however. The creeks and riparian zones were home to wildlife, birds, insects, and fish as well as to forests and wetlands, and the miners' labors affected all of them to some degree. Although the placer miners of 1896 to 1900, working mostly by hand, did not cause the level of environmental degradation brought on in later years by hydraulic mining and by gold dredges, they nevertheless changed the world around them. Their disassembly of the earth not only denuded the stream banks and riverbeds, but also changed the topography of the valleys and gulches. Miners diverted the creeks into flumes and exposed the beds for summer mining; they set streams on new courses in order to send water over new ground or get at rich ground. They dammed creeks into muddy pools, which then filled with castoff rocks and gravel. They dug ditches, created mounds of tailings, and left huge holes. Tappan Adney returned to Bonanza Creek in the summer of 1898 and described the very real mess:

> Summer had changed beyond recognition the winter's trail. Dams of crib-work filled with stones, flumes, and sluice boxes lay across our path; heaps of "tailings" glistened in the sunlight beside yawning holes with windlasses tumbled in; cabins were deserted—the whole creek, wherever work had been done, was ripped and gutted. Nothing but flood and fire is so ruthless as the miner.[66]

Another observer, Edward C. Adams, ventured up Eldorado Creek in 1900. "Rocks are piled up all over," he noted, continuing that "It is quite a sight to come up the Creeks and see how people are tearing up the earth"[67]

The most detailed picture of the miners' effects on the Yukon and Alaska landscape come from the hundreds of photographs made of miners' work and mining sites between 1897 and the early years of the twentieth century. Such images reveal a deadened landscape. The creek valleys, several hundred yards from side to side, formed an expanse of rocky rubble, dirt piles, and shallow wastewater pools, latticed by flumes. It is difficult in some images to locate the actual creeks flowing amidst the debris. Closeup views reveal a landscape of mud and rocks, with little else in evidence. Up on the hills, miners dug directly into benches and hillsides, piling up huge dumps which cascaded downhill as they grew, spreading rock and debris toward the valleys.[68] From a distance, the hills looked like they had been invaded by very large gophers.

This tearing up of the earth dramatically increased the flow of mud and sediment into rivers and creeks, silt which truly changed their nature as living communities of plants and other organisms. Muddied water made it difficult if not impossible for plants, fish, and insects to survive. When miners sluiced their dumps, waste water ran off into ditches or reservoirs to be recycled for more sluicing, or back into the creek. The bylaws of the Jack Wade Creek mining district in Alaska required miners to put used water back into the creek in order to maximize the flow for other miners.[69] Frantic spring days of sluicing dumps, however, left the water drastically muddied, more solid than liquid. Some miners dug sump holes to capture used water from sluices and reuse it, but again, the water ended up quite "thick."[70] Frank Purdy wrote while rocking dirt in December 1899 that "the water is pretty thick for rocking."[71] Miners so clouded the waters of the northern creeks that they themselves had to look elsewhere for clear water. Bill Ballou described using his steamer to thaw ice from the creek for the steam boiler, "the water we pump up from the drift being too muddy for that."[72]

The accumulated debris in the placer creeks did not, prior to 1900, reach the volume of earth that hydraulickers and dredgers would later process. Fire and steam-point thawing were comparatively primitive methods of hand labor, but they produced plenty of earth and sediment, enough to seriously affect water quality and the ability of streams to support insects, fish, and other living things. In a deep mining shaft, a big fire could burn up to forty-five buckets' worth of gravel and muck in a night. A few men working together with even more equipment could haul up over a hundred buckets a day.[73] "Wally has four six foot fires going every night and they thaw about 200 10 pan buckets a night . . . about 150 of them pay dirt," reported one miner of a partner in 1901.[74] A larger crew with boilers and steam-points could build an even larger pile. In January 1900, Frank Purdy and his partners took out fifty wheelbarrows of pay dirt a day, despite problems with water and waste in their tunnels.[75]

Miners unearthed and washed these volumes of dirt and gravel in fairly concentrated areas, which exacerbated the environmental effects. On Glenn

Gulch in 1901, a gold boom drew a sizable crowd. Lynn Smith wrote that there were twenty-four cabins on the gulch, "within a mile and a quarter." Over two hundred men worked this stretch of the creek, "every body busy and taking out gold" with "steam engines, thawers, and whistles [blowing] . . . three times a day all the same [as] big factories." The mining itself was accompanied by streamside clearing, woodcutting, and stripping for cabins and work areas. Bill Ballou hired twelve men to do the "dead work" of cabin building before mining began in 1899. They cleared brush and moss, and put up two big cabins. In October he had them at work again, clearing more moss and brush for the dumping ground, building cabins, and cutting wood.[76]

Given the intensity of this work and the amount of dirt removed and washed, placer mining and harvests of riparian vegetation seriously affected biological life in the streams as well as stream flow and topography. Miners, interested only in gold, reported only the extent of their labor, not its ecological consequences. They measured the earth under their feet only in terms of the gold it produced, with little value placed on anything else the landscape had to offer. Twentieth-century ecological studies have since revealed that riparian areas are characterized by high biological production, which means that many forms of life concentrate their energies along streams as they grow, feed, and reproduce. Wildlife, including moose, bear, and elk, came to streams and their banks for food, water, and cover. Birds and animals used them as travel and migration corridors, and to water, roost, and nest. In Alaska and the Yukon, riparian systems, especially the floodplains of rivers and streams, were particularly crucial to moose habitat. The tall shrub species clustered along banks provided both food and cover from predators, close to the water.[77]

Placer miners, through their disassembly of vegetation, water, and earth, transformed the creeks' ability to provide their usual range of biological functions for all of these living things. Mining works diverted and blocked creeks with sluices, flumes, and debris, and filled them with sediment, making it difficult if not impossible for salmon, grayling, and whitefish to feed, migrate, or spawn. The fish disappeared, and in many respects the most heavily mined gold creeks simply ceased to be truly living systems, at least temporarily.[78] When gold miners looked at the torn-up, muddied, lifeless landscape they left behind, however, they looked through the lens of their culture; instead of degradation, they saw riches, one of the most productive landscapes in the world. As Edward C. Adams wrote of Bonanza Creek in 1900, "You see great holes in the earth all over, some very rich."[79]

NATURE, CULTURE, AND MINING

In one sense, gold mining left creek valleys strewn with muddy debris; in another sense it made them the richest fields on the continent. In making them rich in this particular way, gold mining turned the creeks into places where fishing and hunting and gathering became more difficult and less successful, if not, at the time, impossible. Gold mining disassembled creeks like Bonanza and Eldorado to the degree that those systems could no longer produce the range of biological life present before 1896.[80] Mining changed the range of work possible along those creeks, and thus the very meaning of the places themselves. The two types of production, one that produced gold, another that produced living organisms, could not easily coexist. The miners' labor constituted a cultural decision that gold mining was unquestionably the most valuable and productive work to be done along those creeks and along others like them. That labor not only connected the miners to nature, it revealed their culture and the values at the core of that culture. Through the labor of mining, nature and culture came together to transform the earth.

The miners' new connections to nature thus made the creeks into new places, with new names. Traders and early explorers, including Lt. Frederick Schwatka, initially called the Klondike River the Deer River, for the abundance of caribou and moose in the region. The name "Klondike," as the story goes, was the Anglicization of a local Indian name for the river, spelled in English "Tron-diuck." The Native bands known as the Han came to the river's mouth each summer to fish, setting up weirs and traps. In their language, "Tron-diuck" meant "hammer waters," a reference to the stones they used to drive in stakes to hold the fish traps.[81] "On account of the large number of salmon who turn aside to enter the stream here," Josiah Spurr wrote, "the Indians called it Thron-duc or fish-water; this is now corrupted by the miners into Klondike."[82] The new names which gold miners brought to the Klondike's tributaries, names like Eldorado and Bonanza, spoke not of caribou or salmon, but of an abundance of gold. By the time the word Klondike reached Seattle, of course, the name meant gold, rather than hammers, weirs, or fish.

The various words Tron-diuck, Klondike, Deer River, Eldorado, and

Bonanza named both the place and the human work done there, whether hunting, fishing, or gold mining. Each type of work created connections between human beings and the places themselves; each connected human beings to nature in different ways. Of those different kinds of labor and different sets of connections, however, gold mining proved an especially powerful and transformative kind of labor. It was powerful because of the nature of gold, the way in which the earth held and distributed this one particular element. It was powerful because of the thorough disassembly required to find and extract gold from the earth. And it was powerful because of culture, a culture which shaped the labor of mining just as powerfully as it reshaped the nature of the creeks.

5

THE CULTURE
OF GOLD MINING

In September 1898, gold seeker Bill Ballou settled in for the long northern winter at Rampart City, Alaska. A letter home explained that he could not start winter work at the mines until later in the season, but that he was enjoying Alaskan life so far. He was working hard, he wrote, and he felt "a sense of freedom not to be had working for a corporation." A year later, after a summer of fishing, hunting, and boating, Ballou reported that "we have enjoyed the pleasant knowledge that we were our own masters and could do as we pleased—no corporation looking for a chance to jump on us at any minute." Ballou was so taken with Alaska that, unlike most of his compatriots, he remained for several years. In 1902 he spent a few days working for a local official on some account books, work that reminded him of his old railroad clerk job at home, but not favorably. "This is such a free and independent life," he wrote to his mother, "it spoils one for such a grind."[1]

Ballou's labor as a miner included new and intense connections to his physical environment, but the meaning and value of his work, as described in these letters back to Vermont, were about far more than nature, and far more than gold. For Ballou, gold mining meant not just monetary value and trying physical labor. It also meant freedom from corporations, escape, and independence. Alaska-Yukon gold seekers, like all human beings, understood and pursued their labors from within their culture, a broad and complex set of understandings, expectations, traditions, and rules that gave their work and their daily lives meaning, and helped explain their successes and failures. Ballou's labor, like all human labor, was as much about culture as about connections to nature. It revealed key elements of the broader industrial culture which shaped gold miners' lives, a culture in which corporations had gained unprecedented influence over daily life and daily labors. Gold mining thus brought miners not only to nature, but to the heart of certain aspects of industrial culture.

Ballou's and others' beliefs that gold mining offered escape, freedom, and independence were well-rooted in producer ideology, the powerful set of ideas about labor and wealth that Williams Jenning Bryan and Populist reformers loudly championed throughout the 1890s. In the midst of the "Battle of the Standards," as goldbugs naturalized gold as a divinely ordained source of wealth, Populists naturalized productive manual labor as the natural source of true value, human virtue, and real wealth. Since gold mining brought together both gold and manual labor, Klondike gold seekers like Bill Ballou could pursue both of the "natural" entities being celebrated around them in political life. As gold miners, they would be the ideal workers, mixing their labor with the earth to produce natural wealth.

The culture of gold thus filled the labor of mining with powerful political meanings, which made gold mining seem the natural thing to do. Beyond these cultural ideas about mining, however, gold really did have a nature, a nature which rendered it both extraordinarily scarce and very difficult to extract from the earth. Once in the Yukon and Alaska, miners collided head on with the true nature of gold: its scarcity. As they grappled with that scarcity, miners' ideas about their labor shifted. At the beginning, as with Bill Ballou, gold mining gave the miners an opportunity to do productive manual labor and to escape the poverty, boredom, and restriction of their lives in a depressed economy dominated by corporate-controlled, wage-labor jobs. Faced with a random supply of very scarce gold, however, miners changed their views of mining. It ceased to be a source of escape and freedom, and became a game of chance, an endless, frustrating, and often fruitless gamble. Then, faced with the uncertainties of gold mining as gambling, governed by luck rather than hard work, miners created a more predictable, familiar, and sustainable labor system. Mining became industrial wage labor, governed by clocks, watches, and whistles, and by a detailed accounting of time and pay. Although mining, for men like Ballou, continued to provide a sense of escape and was a frustrating but compelling gamble, most miners ended up doing the same kind of labor they had performed at home.

The northern goldfields became an integral part of the industrialized world rather than an escape from or a distant alternative to it. Alaska-Yukon gold mining was not only a replication of industrial work, it was a heightened example of it. Mining failed to forge any real connection between hard work and wealth; it thus captured the essence of wage labor in the late-nineteenth-century industrial economy.

"I HAVE CUT LOOSE": ESCAPE FROM INDUSTRIALIZED WORK

Nothing in the nature of gold, especially not its scarcity, made gold mining a natural source of escape from industrialized labor, but just such an escape attracted many men and women to the Klondike. Bill Ballou, Hunter Fitzhugh, and others like them expressed discontent with industrialized life and relished the freedom that the gold rush appeared to offer. Fitzhugh wrote home from the Rampart mining district in stalwart praise of his newfound freedom. "To be sure I long for home and civilization with a longing that 'is me doom' at times, but on the other hand if I was in the States I would be under the eye and hand of a boss, or out of a job. . . . I have cut loose and learned a new life, and I must stay with it at least another year."[2] Fitzhugh shared such feelings about bosses and unemployment with a wide spectrum of miners, many of them educated young men and women who had worked as lawyers, physicians, bankers, teachers, local politicians, farmers, storekeepers, clerks, and small business owners.[3] These men and women echoed Fitzhugh's belief that in the goldfields, they would work as free men and women and would get their rewards from nature, rather than from bosses or corporations. The ideas of cutting loose, making a mark, and escaping from dwindling opportunities at home ran through the miners' letters and diaries. They wanted and needed money and paying jobs, but miners also looked to gold mining for other things that they felt to be absent from industrial life: adventure, simplicity, freedom, independence, satisfaction, a connection between hard work and wealth, and an invigorating physical engagement with the natural world.

The miners' quests for these remedies from industrial ills shed a certain amount of light on their lives. Labor and cultural historians have established that nineteenth-century industrialization transformed American life, creating what Daniel Rodgers calls a "new world of work," with new restrictions and regulations that limited workers' autonomy in the workplace.[4] In the decades after the Civil War, workers' lives were revolutionized by corporate organization, standardization, mechanization, and also by the abundance of goods they produced, which made workers avid consumers as well as producers. According to Alan Trachtenberg, this period saw, literally, the "Incorporation of America," the shift in the basic organization of economic and social activity from the individual and family to the corporate body.[5] The decades following 1850 brought increasing numbers of factories and mills and expanding economic production and transportation networks. Industrial plants, factory gates, and workplace time clocks followed, along with centralized management, production gluts, and the paradox of increasing abundance accompanied by increasingly visible poverty.[6] Industrial culture created a whole new meaning for time, as managers used clocks to "keep" time and to regulate and discipline both work and workers. Time became an entity saved and spent like money.[7]

This new world of work brought clear gains. By 1894 the United States was by far the leading producer of manufactured goods in the world, nearly matching the combined output of Great Britain, France, and Germany.[8] Those gains were accompanied by social and cultural losses, however, as industrialization replaced older modes of work with wage work measured by time and controlled by bosses. That kind of work subjected Americans to what John Higham described as the "gathering restrictions of a highly industrialized society."[9] It also called into question the individual's power to ensure that his or her work would be productive. "Industrialization," writes Rodgers, "upset the certainty that hard work would bring economic success." It made it clear that "no amount of sheer hard work would open the way to self-employment or wealth."[10] By the 1880s, T. J. Jackson Lears explains, "genuine economic independence" for workers had become "a near impossibility."[11] Marxist labor historians such as Harry Braverman explain that the crucial loss with industrial capitalism was the alienation of the products of labor from the worker, and thus the worker's loss of control over the "inalienable property" of his own labor.[12]

Cultural historians such as Rodgers and Lears have tracked these economic shifts and their cultural effects among the late-nineteenth-century middle and upper classes. Lears writes that Americans lost their sense of autonomous individuality. City life, the dependence on others for food and shelter, the bureaucratization of white-collar work, and the secularization of intellectual life all reduced middle- and upper-class life to "a vapid, anonymous existence." Lears describes this loss of selfhood as "a sense that indi-

vidual causal potency had diminished, a growing doubt that one could deci-
sively influence one's personal destiny." Work, especially, seemed a source
of loss, as office jobs proved "strangely insubstantial . . . isolated . . . from
the hard substantial reality of things."[13]

Many working-class Americans responded to industrial transformations
with direct resistance, fueling the fervor and violence of the nineteenth-
century labor movement. Not all chose this path. According to Lears, the
nation's elite, intellectual, and bourgeois classes yearned for older, more
authentic work.[14] They sought renewal in the Arts and Crafts movement,
which idealized demanding, physical labor, a return to the work ethic, and
the simple, "virtuous and productive life" close to the soil.[15] Middle- and
upper-class gold miners, in heading for the Yukon, also sought escape
through work, but they looked to work they believed to be outside the industrial economy. For Ballou, Fitzhugh, and their contemporaries, gold mining promised to be an opportunity to put these vague yearnings into action,
to bridge the gap between a vicarious life of adventure and a real adventure. Fictional heroes of the period (including, a few years later, Jack London's Klondike heroes) took physical, even violent action. This attempt to
"recapture preindustrial vigor" had all sorts of racial and gendered meanings that took real and oppressive form as it shored up the power of the white,
Protestant male bourgeoisie.[16] But it all culminated, according to Lears, in
a cult of experience that led men in search of a way "to endow weightless
modern experience with gravity and purpose."[17] Gold mining offered one
such way. It attracted young men looking for adventure as a remedy for a
growing sense of weakness and emasculation. A Seattle newspaper described
the men gathered in the city en route to the Klondike as including " 'the ten-
derfoot,' who starts away for the first time from the home influences that
have until now hampered his growing manhood."[18] Dr. Sanden's Electric
Belt, a quack medical remedy of the day, ran advertisements in Seattle papers
that pictured a triumphant gold miner, pick on his back, revitalized in health
and wealth by the belt's "grand life-giving powers" (fig. 5.1). Together, gold
mining and the electric belt, it seemed, would save men with "weakened
nerves," those "who have wasted the energy of youth, who feel worn and
exhausted."[19]

The Spanish-American War offered a similar chance to regain strength
and manhood. The rush to the Klondike in the spring of 1898 unfolded nearly
simultaneously with the destruction of the *Maine* in Havana harbor, and
the United States' decision to go to war with Spain to liberate Cuba. Amer-

FIG. 5.1. "Dr. Sanden Is Here." A quack medical apparatus of the 1890s, Dr. Sanden's Electric Belt, offered to restore strength to "weak" men. Dr. Sanden shifted his advertising in Seattle newspapers to appeal specifically to gold miners headed north to Alaska and the Yukon. The electric belt and the gold rush struck familiar themes in offering men a remedy for feelings of physical weakness, boredom, and the general lack of vigor associated with urban life and industrial work. (*Seattle Post-Intelligencer,* February 28, 1898)

ican men were attracted to both mining and warfare in part because they felt lost, overcivilized, dislocated, and deprived of "intense experience." Trader John Callbreath noted that the wave of incoming miners on the Stikine River dwindled for a time with the outbreak of war. "I suppose the war had a deal to do with it too," he wrote to a business associate in July 1898, "in calling away the footloose crowd that would otherwise many of them drifted up here." Some miners wrote specifically of their choice between gold and war, indicating that they probably would have done one or the other. "Had I been at home very likely I should have gone to the war," Lynn Smith wrote to his sister. "I believe I had rather go to war than do what I am doing," Jonas Houck of Detroit declared on hearing of the declaration of war, "but of course the chances of getting money are greater here."[20]

Most men and women suffering industrial ills chose less extreme remedies than warfare or the Klondike. They sought relief and escape in a whole range of activities that together constituted what Theodore Roosevelt called the "Strenuous Life." This broad cultural trend found expression in everything from bird-watching and nature walks to college football, boxing, and bicycling. Roosevelt's western exploits as a cowboy and big game hunter served as a popular focus for his individual pursuit of "hard and dangerous endeavor."[21] All of these forms of bodily engagement with a real (or imagined) world offered a remedy for the unsatisfying existence of industrial life.

Despite the cultural trends of the era, gold mining did not hold any single meaning or group of meanings for the many different individuals who set off for the Yukon and Alaska. Most surviving letters and diaries come from literate middle-class and upper-class men and women, and historical interpretations drawn from such sources cannot hold true for all gold seekers. The thousands of men and women who went north constituted a diverse group. By all accounts from reporters, government officials, and miners themselves, between half and three-quarters of the participants came from the United States, but others hailed from the world over: Canada, Scotland, England, France, Austria, Australia, and Chile. Americans themselves came from New England, New York, Iowa, Nebraska, Michigan, Wisconsin, Illinois, Louisiana, Texas, Colorado, California, and Washington, just for starters.[22] Seattle photographer Asahel Curtis had his eye on social diversity when writing in his diary that "Seemingly every degree of the social scale has its representative."[23] Samuel Dunham reported to the U.S. Department of Labor on "gold fever," writing that "The contagion spread to all classes—

laborers, clerks, merchants, bankers, lawyers, physicians, ministers of the gospel—and even Federal and State officials were so charmed by the alluring picture drawn by the press. . . ."[24]

The only thing all miners shared was economic crisis. The financial slump of the 1890s left people of all classes in dire straits, toiling, in one government official's words, "for a bare subsistence" if they toiled at all.[25] Unemployment peaked at 18.4 percent in 1894, but remained as high as 14.5 percent in 1897, a year after wholesale farm prices bottomed out.[26] For thousands of men and women, the economy severely limited the possibility of steady work and steady income, let alone anything that could be called wealth. Gold offered a solution. In the United States, and in Canada, Scotland, England, and even Australia, men and women left jobs in banks, schools, corporate offices, and government to go in search of gold. They mortgaged farms and homes to purchase train tickets, food, clothing, and supplies.[27] Samuel Dunham's companions on a Yukon steamboat in 1897 included two doctors, three lawyers, a watchmaker, and six farmers from Iowa and Nebraska who sought enough gold to pay the interest on their mortgages.[28] Only some of these hopeful souls articulated broader goals of escape and renewal. Although there was considerable overlap among different social groups, middle-class miners tended to see Alaska and the Yukon more as an escape, and working-class men and women tended to see the northern goldfields more in terms of sheer hard labor.

Back at home, many middle- and working-class Americans reacted to the dislocations of industrialization not by trying to escape to the Yukon or Alaska, but by bolstering the ideals of an older Protestant work ethic. Daniel Rodgers defined this as the belief that work was both social duty and calling. While facing evidence to the contrary, industrial workers clung to the idea that work kept the evils of idleness at bay, and also provided the individual with the means to dignity, independence, advancement, self-sufficiency, and self-expression.[29] Gold seekers, who were very much industrial workers, echoed these beliefs. They praised work. In the Yukon, as Mac McMichael noted after just a few weeks on the trail north, "It is no disgrace to labor because all have to do it. . . . This is especially true of the trail and the lakes and rivers. In no country or place I have ever seen is there so much dignity in labor." The educated and literate miners who spoke glowingly of the good effects of hard work may not have represented all gold miners, but they spoke of feelings which had broad cultural appeal. "I am in here for work, and will get gold if it is to be found," wrote Lynn Smith in 1898. Jonas Houck agreed that hard work was an honorable and godly way in which to pursue wealth. He wrote home from the White Pass Trail, far from the goldfields, that "I shall commence prospecting right here for there seems to be gold everywhere . . . but it also seems that the creator intended us to work hard to get it."[30]

Some of these gold miners found what they were looking for. The outdoor work and adventure of gold mining gave them the chance to try many different kinds of work, to test their skills, and to discover what they could do: build boats, cabins, and sluices; cook, clean, chop wood, repair machines, fish, and hunt. Such labor granted them a better, broader sense of themselves and their capabilities. A former small-businessman-turned-miner from Detroit, McMichael, mused proudly about his efforts at boatbuilding on Lake Bennett. "I am quite proud of my handywork," he declared in a letter to friends at home. "You know, I never had any instructions in handling tools in any way. I never built a boat or saw one built and yet we have one here which is all my own planning. . . . I like boat building; it gives both the head and hands a chance."[31] Although always expecting to hear from home that his business had finally gone under, McMichael found in his new labor a heartening alternative to that failure.

Bill Ballou struck a similar theme of usefulness, fulfillment, and freedom when he wrote home in 1902 listing all the different types of work he was doing in Alaska. In the course of his mining labor, he fired and ran the boiler for steam thawing; he ran the engine for the hoist, saw, and water pump. He cut ice and sawed wood. He did the blacksmithing, sharpened the tools, refit the pipe lines, repaired all of the machinery, and did, as he put it, "a thousand and one other jobs." He especially enjoyed running the steam machines. It suited him "as well as any job." "I like to 'see the wheels turn'. You know, they wouldn't let me run this job out in the states—have to have a license etc." Walter Curtin spent the winter of 1898–99 on the lower Yukon, his steamer frozen in place by the ice. He cut wood, snowshoed, and hunted. "There is nothing I miss here," he wrote, "and I do not feel far away. It seems that the people on the Outside are far away. Think of a man sitting in a cage in a bank," Curtin continued, evoking white-collar work at home, "and thinking he is an important citizen instead of a slave." Not only did this winter life seem more free and real to Curtin, it fulfilled his cultural vision of a "wild" or "natural" life, as defined by nineteenth-century mythic icons such as Wild Bill Hickok. "Ever since I was a small boy I have wanted to live in the backwoods like Wild Bill . . . and this is the first chance I have had."[32]

Of course, the miners may have penned these earnest statements in letters home to assure their parents and wives that they *were* interested in work. When confronted with any prolonged idleness, miners wrote home of their anxiety about the lack of work and about their true dedication to hard labor. Bill Ballou took a steamer up the Yukon River in 1898. Of a two-week delay at the mouth of the river, he complained that "this idleness is worse than climbing Chilcoot Pass." The long steamer trip made him keenly aware of his own laziness. He called shipboard travel "a lazy, indolent life." Mac McMichael was eager for work as well when he arrived in Dawson City that same year. "I did not come to Alaska to loaf around," he declared to friends at home. "Do not worry about any danger," he added, "for there is no more here than in Detroit except what comes with hard work. . . . Plenty of that will be at hand. . . . I fully expected hard work and lots of it and I shall not be disappointed."[33]

This praise of work constituted more than a front for relatives waiting at home, however. The quest for gold may have looked to hometown folks, and to the nation at large, like a desire for escape *from* work through instant wealth. But at a deeper level, it was a desire for escape *through* work. Miners like Bill Ballou and Mac McMichael lamented the restrictions of the industrial world and praised gold mining as escape, but that need for escape existed alongside, and intertwined with, an equally potent search for hard, productive work. Superficially, escape and hard labor might seem antithetical, but when miners wrote about Alaska and the Yukon, the two merged. Escape, it seemed, involved work, and work promised escape from the industrial system because gold mining, at least at the start, seemed honest, independent, varied, self-reliant work, the kind of work unavailable at home.

These idealistic hopes for freedom and hard work contained a central paradox, however. All miners found hard work, and some found a sense of escape and freedom. Very few, however, found gold or wealth, and thus most miners faced a more ironic outcome. Hard work may have been a great virtue and the natural source of true value, but no amount of it guaranteed success in the goldfields. Along the Yukon, miners reproduced a system of spectacularly hard labor, usually wage labor, that rarely provided an industrial wage, let alone real wealth. Rather than escape through virtuous labor, the industrial grind of placer mining revealed an economic world governed not by hard work, but by chance, the slim chance of striking gold.

FROM RANDOM GOLD TO GAMBLING

Most Yukon miners, regardless of class, nationality, or race, did the same kinds of work in the same ways because they encountered the same natural environment and wanted the same thing from that environment: gold. They faced a common problem. The gold was there, but nature had distributed it in a random and unpredictable way. Whether miners expected to pick gold off the ground or earn it through hard work, they believed at the start that the gold itself was abundant. Those beliefs ran head-on into the natural world. The most common experience along the Yukon was *not* finding gold, or at least not finding very much of it. As they poured their labor into the northern creeks, miners realized that gold was abundant only in certain unspecified places. There were tiny amounts of gold in some places, great pockets of it in others, and every degree in between. As miners realized that gold was unsystematically scarce at best, they saw that no amount of hard work guaranteed a proportionate payoff. A small amount of work might produce riches; years of work might produce nothing. Miners could draw no direct cause-and-effect relationship between work and gold.[34] If, as Daniel Rodgers states, industrialization broke the cultural certainty that "hard work would bring economic success," then gold mining in 1898 represented an exaggerated metaphor for industrialization. It offered the chance, but only the chance, for hard work to bring success and wealth. It then delivered the reality that no amount of work, no matter how diligently pursued, guaranteed success in the goldfields. Mac McMichael put it succinctly when he wrote that "men, on arrival here, have suddenly found out that the unlimited opportunities for getting suddenly rich are not realized no matter how great their capacity for enduring work and hardships."[35]

The initial, exaggerated reports from the Klondike promised a river of gold. Reading newspapers at home, miners expected, as one reporter put it, "to get into the country and find the gold in buckets full."[36] Nora Crane, whose husband kept the store at Circle City, Alaska, wrote to a friend in 1898 that new arrivals expected to find gold without work. "Everyone who comes here has that same strained staring eyeball look as if they expected to find it in the trees or on top of a shack or some little old place where they only had to lift a leaf or a clod to be worth millions!!!! whereas ordinarily it means work of the hardest kind the like of which most of them never dreamed of doing."[37] Hard work was the first lesson of gold mining, but the realization of the utter futility of much of that work followed soon after.

Gold miners learned quickly that hard work governed their lives in the Yukon, but that chance governed their access to gold. Many noted the sheer inconsistency of gold in their diaries and letters. U.S. Consul J. C. McCook understood gold's nature. Of five thousand placer claims staked in the Klondike by August 1898, he reported, only two hundred had paid to work. "There is no doubt of the great riches of this country wherever gold is found. But its in pockets and there are a great many blanks." The blanks often showed up in maddening proximity to the riches. Lynn Smith reported the gold "as spotted as can be" and "very spotted" along Miwook (Manook) Creek in 1899 (map 7). Claims six through ten proved rich, but claims two, three and four had been worked three winters with no result. Hunter Fitzhugh suffered similar pangs, mining near rich claims in the Rampart goldfields: "And then the work on this claim seems to be a blank anyhow. The reports from Little Manook Jr. make me desperate. Why does the gold come so near me, and not near enough for me to get it. I dunno. Maybe tis Kismet." A year later, he bemoaned the same situation. "I picked up over $7.00 on another fellow's dump yesterday in less than half an hour."[38]

Other miners struggled to accept that expertise and experience played no role in their ability to locate rich claims. Old-timers thought they knew how to locate gold, but then, as Jonas Houck noted, "some green horn will dig where a person who knows anything about mining in other places would never think of looking and strike it rich." Geologists, writers, miners, and hangers-on worked their way toward theories of gold's distribution in the hopes of plumbing the secrets of placer deposits and the ever elusive "mother lodes." One miner mused to relatives at home about the theory behind his mining efforts at Circle City, Alaska. "There is supposed to be a gold belt running from Birch Creek (the mines back of here) up through Seventy Mile, Charlie River . . . Forty Mile River to the Klondike district. . . . Outside this line there has been little gold found. 4th of July and these other creeks are within or very close to this line. So much for indications. Next spring we shall know more about the reality."[39]

Even with constant reminders of the failures of these theories, miners continued to question why gold was not more evenly, or fairly, distributed along and amongst creeks. Almost every miner was plagued by the presence of others' rich claims next to their poor ones. Consul McCook, in Dawson, observed that "one may find a hundred thousand dollars in a claim, the next one to him . . . merely worthless."[40] Bill Ballou and his partner dug two shafts twenty feet down to an old stream bed without a "color" or sign of gold. Their neighbors, meanwhile, took out thousands of dollars, with the help of their hired hands.[41] One of Lynn Smith's claims "was supposed to clean up $3000 . . . but has been so at each piece of ground . . . good money below but I get shucko."[42] Hunter Fitzhugh put it quite succinctly in a letter from Hoosier Creek, Alaska, in 1899. "GOLD IS WHERE YOU FIND IT and nowhere else."[43] This natural unevenness drove miners to the far edge of frustration, but also kept them at work. If a neighbor on a nearby creek or claim could find a rich pocket, then anyone could. The gold worth $200,000 taken from one claim, number 8 on Little Manook, near Rampart City, bothered Lynn Smith, but kept him going. "Still I believe there is bound to be more found than in Little Miwook [Manook]," he puzzled. "It would seem strange if it was all in one place."[44]

Gold's random distribution changed the miners' ways of thinking and writing about their work. As they faced the disillusioning truth that success was not a matter of work but a matter of chance, gold mining slipped quickly from escape and freedom into the realm of gambling.[45] Gambling on gold did not mean, however, that there were no predictable patterns of economic life along the creeks. Those who owned rich ground succeeded far beyond anyone else. This frustrating inequality was part of the strangeness of gold's distribution. Sometimes it *was* all in one place. But any systematic predictions of who would succeed or fail proved problematic; any tendencies or patterns could be overturned in a moment by an individual's sudden stumble onto a rich pocket of yellow metal. No matter how poor the chances, some people did strike it rich. "This thing of placer mining is fascinating after all," admitted Hunter Fitzhugh, "for a man never knows when he is going to pick up the rarest nugget in the world. I MAY find it tomorrow, and I probably will not find more than a few cents. And I am likely to find our shaft full of water."[46]

The miners' adoption of the language and attitude of gamblers signaled this shift. Metaphors of gambling, bets, luck, and fortune indicated that miners saw their success as governed by chance and luck rather than by their social status in the gold mining hierarchy, or by their own labors. "I'm getting a little tired of waiting for Fortune to point her finger at me and say 'N-e-x-t'," Fitzhugh wrote. Bill Ballou admitted his own situation forthrightly in 1899: "We are all taking the rather desperate chance of running into something better . . . this mining business is a big gamble." The whole thing was indeed a gamble, according to McCook, and the odds were not good. You "go to work on a claim for three months and it's 20 to one you have drawn a blank," he explained. McMichael observed of the claims he worked near Dawson that "it is all chance, and there may not be much in any of them."[47]

The lure of the mines worked in ways similar to the lure of actual gambling. It was no surprise that so many miners became regular customers in the actual gaming halls that sprung up around them wherever they went. Miners found themselves in an economic world in which the expected ties between wealth and hard work weakened and disappeared. As Ann Fabian writes in her history of nineteenth-century American gambling, betting was about exactly that, the absence of any connection between work and value on one hand and monetary gain on the other, the tension over the role of luck and the role of hard work and "willful, responsible action" in worldly success.[48] And as with gambling, no amount of experience or loss of time and labor could completely erase the fascination with gold or the hope that a miner could, with luck, and against the odds, strike it rich. The hope and possibility, fed by others' success and the presence of gold on other claims, kept many men going for long periods of time. Each rumor, each new nugget, and each individual success held out all of the hope and excitement again. Ballou ended up with only $100 from a claim after the wash-up in 1899; "poor pay," he wrote to his brother, "and that is worse than none at all for by getting a little gold right along a man will stick to them for a life time." The possibilities were too tantalizing to leave behind. "You can't imagine a persons feelings when at this kind of work," wrote Lynn Smith. "Take a pan of dirt, wash it down to about a handful of dirt then it gets exciting and you are afraid to make a miss dip of water and lose part. Then as colors begin to show up your heart commences to go quicker and quicker until it is finished. Then a big sigh, dry the pan and weigh it out."[49]

The truly disillusioning lesson of placer gold mining was that it seemed very much like the industrial world that miners sought to leave behind. No amount of diligent effort guaranteed success when miners defined success as real wealth, enough gold to significantly improve their lives. One hundred miners could do exactly the same work, up and down a creek, at the same time. One of them might reap hundreds or even thousands of dollars; some might break even on the money spent on food and supplies. Others would get nothing. As a result, miners revised their hopes and expectations. They learned to look at gold mining not as a source of great riches, but, at best, as an uncertain source of wage labor. In April 1899 Lynn Smith described the fifteen hundred to two thousand men working on the creeks around the rich claim at Little Manook. "Not 25 of them will go out even and those will all be men who worked for wages on #8 or cut wood on the river."[50]

Experienced miners, working-class men who traveled from mine to mine, provided another source for this lesson. Farmers, clerks, and lawyers may have held out hope for a big strike, but when they listened to and observed the men around them, they were forced to reflect on the unsteadiness of mining as a permanent way of life. Ballou, a railroad clerk from Vermont and Boston, romanticized his mining partners in his letters home. They included an Austrian named Mike who had come from the Pennsylvania coal fields, a German named Meyers who had been all over the world, a minister, a prize fighter, and a cowboy from Oregon who had been all over the West. "I like this life with these free and careless people," he exclaimed, "any one of whom will take their winter's wages next spring and buck the first gambling table until not a dollar is left . . . and then work their way up or down the river to some other camp."[51]

Others clearly did not envy such a life, for transient miners revealed something of the true nature of mining, something that Ballou and others were in the process of discovering for themselves. Contact with "real" miners made it all too clear that mining was in no way a source of stable wealth or a stable way of life. About a third of the men along Fourth of July Creek in Alaska were migratory mine workers, and they clearly represented, both in the mode and meaning of their work, a different class. "When one sees the number of old miners on this stampede, it does not encourage one to make it a business," Mac McMichael wrote. "Out of ten men in this camp, three have made a business of mining all the way from five to fifteen years. They are all nearly broke. One has been [in] the quartz mines of Colorado, New Mexico and Arizona. Another has been in Australia, New Zealand and Costa Rica, Patagonia, Brazil and Lord knows where. He had mined within a few miles of Cape Horn and now here he is on the Yukon. . . . Half the men one meets have not enough grub to last through the winter, with but very little money to buy more."[52]

Such realities contributed to an inevitable shift in miners' attitudes toward gold mining. In its similarity to gambling, gold mining not only replicated industrial work, it delivered the final truth about all work. Success, defined as "striking it rich," was a matter of chance, not work. Miners worked hard, but few went home millionaires. Given this reality, Yukon miners again sought escape, but this time to return to the less adventurous path of paid work. Many miners who started out eager for adventure changed their minds. "I surely will not go after gold again," swore Mac McMichael. "There is too much uncertainty about it to suit me as a 'steady business'." Thomas Kearney thought along similar lines while working at a Dawson City bakery. "I do not intend to go prospecting," he wrote, "while I have steady work."[53]

DOES IT PAY TO WORK? FROM GAMBLING TO WAGES

The scarcity and randomness of gold and the frequency of failure made gold mining one of the most unproductive, unpredictable, and generally unpleasant occupations anyone could have chosen. At one particularly low point in his northern sojourn, Lynn Smith wrote in remarkably telling language that "This is no country, and mining in Alaska is no white mans work." James McRae ended his diary on just such sentiments. "I will now roll down the curtain on two years and four months of what has been the most miserable part of my life. I hope I will never again have to go through anything like what I have gone through during that period." The best route of escape from such misery was simply to go home, where conventional work now offered the better alternative. At his own discouraging moment, Bill Ballou wrote that as soon he got five hundred dollars, he would head back east, perhaps to the family orchard in Vermont. There "is more money in the cider business than this," he declared to his brother.[54]

The miners who did not go home right away, who stayed in Alaska and the Yukon for at least a season, found another response to the role of chance in gold mining. They shaped the work into industrial wage work, creating a hierarchy of work and wages similar to the industrialized work they had sought to escape. Within that hierarchy there were owners of rich mines, owners of poor mines, and owners of barren mines. There were also lay or share workers, who worked others' claims in return for a share of the gold produced. And there were hourly wage workers. Because of these different levels of work and workers, the overwhelming majority of miners quickly came to see their work as wage work, rather than free or independent work. Whatever gold mining was supposed to be, it quickly turned into a familiar round of hirings and firings and bosses, with too many men for too few jobs. In this structure of wage work, gold became wages, and often disappointing wages at that; Alaska-Yukon gold mining became hard work at hard wages.

There was plenty of gold in places, but as many disappointed seekers found out, few had direct access to it. Miners already in Alaska and the Yukon claimed much of the gold-bearing ground during the first few months of the initial strike in August 1896. By September 1897, miners had staked Bonanza Creek for twenty miles, and Eldorado for over eight miles.[55] For the three to four thousand who arrived the following spring and summer, and especially for the crowds that followed in May and June 1898, no ground on the world-renowned creeks remained to claim.[56] Hundreds and hundreds of potential miners, upon discovering that Bonanza, Eldorado, Hunker, and Dominion Creeks were staked, simply boarded steamboats down the Yukon and returned home. For them, the fact that they could not easily find claims and be assured gold, combined with the crowds and chaos, was enough to end the adventure at its start. "As I told you in recent letters," reported Thomas Kearney to his family in Ontario, Canada, in August 1898, "there are many disgusted people, many who wish they had never heard of Klondike. . . . There is no doubt the country is over done and people are leaving by the hundreds and still there are plenty left." Lynn Smith noted as well that "Every boat is loaded with disgusted people getting out." That level of disgust did not hold across the board, however, as hundreds took their chances at the labor of mining. "Just think of the thousands who are going out without even sticking a pick in the ground," wrote Mac McMichael. "Not that this is much of a pleasure in itself, I tried it a few days and found it hard work but that is what I came expecting."[57]

For those who stayed, a few options remained. Many headed for distant creeks in hopes of staking claims on new and equally rich ground. Some Americans trekked downriver into Alaska. Lynn Smith immediately left Dawson for Rampart City, Alaska. He went to the nearest creek, and followed it up the length of 112 claims, at five hundred feet each. He then climbed up a tributary creek or "pup" to a divide, then up another creek, where he found three or four unclaimed sites.[58] Others contracted with claim owners to work on lays or shares; the proportions shifted over time and from agreement to agreement, sometimes fifty-fifty, sometimes calculated according to the relative richness of the ground.[59] This made it possible for claim owners to avoid the labor of mining their ground, but also gave miners without any claims the chance to mine. Mac McMichael, full of hope, could not find a claim on the Klondike creeks, so he quickly took two lay claims for 50 percent of the output. Frank Purdy and his partners arrived in Dawson in August 1898, found no good claims, dug a lot of holes that produced only water, and eventually took a lay claim, "giving us the first two thousand that was taken out and 1/2 the rest." Another member of the group took a lay in Chief Gulch for 75 percent of the gold taken out.[60] Lay agreements gave miners only a distant chance of success, however. Even on the richest of creeks, some lay claims proved barren. "Many Bonanza lays are being abandoned," notes James Cooper's diary entry for December 13, 1897.[61] Bill Hiscock reported his misgivings about the people involved as well as the ground. "We went to see about taking a claim on, but didn't like the terms as there is seldom any pay till the washup in spring. One has to be careful with anything in work by percentage or contract here. Unless it is somebody you have known it is just as well to have nothing to do with many of them as there are men of every type."[62]

When miners could not secure lay claims, or when the claims they worked produced nothing, they looked for work elsewhere, with other miners or cutting wood. C. O. Steiner worked his way through 1899 in a series of jobs, sluicing on one claim on Dominion Creek, running an engine on another. The wages were a dollar an hour and he usually worked twelve, sixteen, or eighteen hours a day. Most miners did wage labor at one time or another. Frank Purdy and his partner spent most of the late winter and spring of 1899 scrounging for lays or jobs on the Klondike creeks. In May they found a lay claim on Bonanza Creek. Interrupted at times by sporadic stints of day labor for wages, they started stripping the ground and sinking shafts. The dirt they tested had "not a dollar in it." In June they began the washup, rocking dirt. On the worst day, they produced only $2.80. They soon gave up and moved to town to live in a tent on the Klondike River and fish. Hunter Fitzhugh looked to wage labor as a last resort when his claims failed to produce. After sinking several mine shafts that continually filled with water, he began to consider other options. "I really think we will lose our work," he wrote, "as only one hour is necessary to fill our pay shaft with water and then we'll have all our work to do over again, in which event I'll pack my sled with all my worldly goods and drag my slow length along to town, and look for another job with wages."[63]

There were never enough wage jobs, however, especially during the off-season months, summer and fall. As miners poured into Dawson City in 1898 and then rushed to each successive creek rumored to be rich, they found good jobs scarce. As one miner from the Maritime provinces wrote in April 1899, "There is a great many men here out of employment and they keep running around from one creek to another trying to get something to do but there are more men here than there is work for them to do." James McRae agreed. "There are 10 men for every job . . . there are men camped along the Creek waiting for work. There is very little work going on," he wrote while looking for work in Dawson and on Bonanza Creek in 1899.[64]

For the large proportion of Yukon and Alaska miners who became dependent on wage labor to survive, jobs and wages were a chief topic of concern. From the very start of the trail, they latched onto possibilities and rumors of jobs and pay, hungering for cash. Jonas Houck wanted to find gold, but more than that he wanted to send money home to his family. It did not matter where the money came from, and he was excited to hear news of Klondike jobs "at $10 to $15 a day" while he was still at Lake Bennett. Lynn Smith heard similar rumors. Of course, once Houck, Smith, and hundreds of others moved downriver from Lake Bennett to Dawson City, wages dropped precipitously to as low as five dollars per day. Thomas Kearney wrote from Dawson in August that "It is not likely that wages will be near as high from now on." Samuel Dunham investigated labor conditions in the Klondike in the fall of 1897, and reported the rumors of fifteen-dollars-a-day wages to be misleading. Wages were a dollar and fifty cents an hour, he wrote, and jobs uncertain at best. Consul McCook reported wages at a dollar an hour in August, but also "hundreds who cannot obtain labor at any price."[65]

Wage labor was thus central to gold mining, which made that mining a lot like every other kind of industrial work available in the late nineteenth century. Yukon miners worked for wages, by the hour, month, and season for other miners or claim owners. Even when they worked independently, however, gold seekers viewed their work as wage labor, as work performed in exchange for pay. The miners' primary criterion for all labor in the goldfields was simply whether it would pay, whether it was worth doing for the money gained. This focus on the exchange of labor and time for gold—for money—made mining even more like industrial work, with the exception that gold made particularly uncertain pay. The random scarcity of gold made miners constantly ask themselves whether their labor would pay, and whether they were likely to find enough gold to make their work and time worthwhile.

What miners looked for in the ground, then, was not so much gold as money, and not so much money as wages, a particular form of money earned in exchange for labor. Miners thought of gold as *naturally* money and wages. They naturalized gold as wages as easily and powerfully as any gold standard economist. In their minds, gold took the form of dollars and cents before they even got it out of the ground. Their diaries and letters were filled with the language of pay. They thought about gold and measured gold solely as dollars and cents, pay for their work. In the miners' common language, "pay dirt" was the term for dirt with enough gold in it to justify a miner's work, dirt that would pay wages at an acceptable rate for the work needed to get it.[66] Sometimes pay dirt was simply dirt with *any* gold in it. "Wally has had four six foot fires going every night," reported Lynn Smith of his partner's work at thawing through the permafrost on an Alaskan creek, "and they thaw about 200 10 pan buckets a night . . . about 150 of them pay dirt." Similarly, their term for gold-bearing gravel was the "pay streak" or simply the "pay." Smith continued, "Everybody estimates it at about $400 a foot. Our pay is now 19 feet wide and about 1 1/2 feet deep . . . and pans run from 10 cents to $4.60 each."[67] The pay streak was, according to *Harper's* correspondent Tappan Adney, "the part of the gold bearing gravel that is rich enough to pay to work."[68]

Along the Yukon gold creeks, nature was thus a fickle employer who paid only in gold, and nature never guaranteed good wages. Miners learned to evaluate a potential claim according to its ability to pay. The real question was always whether they could make as much working the natural world as they could working for another employer. The important thing was to find enough gold to make wages. As Fred Kimball wrote from Nome in 1903, "there is gold in all of it but whether there is pay remains to be seen." Miners thus developed a strong sense of whether they were making any money. The *Rampart Miner* hotly debated whether the goldfields around Rampart, Alaska, were worth miners' interest and labor, given that most of the ground contained from two to four cents of gold per pan. "There is a vast difference of opinion," the paper explained, "as to what constituted pay dirt." The article then set the community straight: "Few men will admit their inability to hoist from a 20 ft. hole, an average of from 50 to 75 ten-pan buckets a day. On that basis note the following: Fifty loads, 1 cent dirt, $5; 2 cent dirt, $10; 3 cent dirt, $15; 4 cent dirt, $20, per day. Seventy-five loads 1 cent dirt, $7.50; 2 cent dirt, $15; 3 cent dirt, $22.50; 4 cent dirt, $30 per day." According to the newspaper, only the lazy miner, unwilling "to expend his only capital, (muscle)" could overlook these mines as *not* worth working. "A certain class of miners must be shown the pay streak or they will not mine. They are well supplied with excuses."[69]

Miners clearly differed over what ground was likely to pay them enough money to constitute "wages."[70] On one creek Frank Purdy found gold, but only in fine dust. "The fine Gold was so hard to catch that it wouldn't pay to work." "Gus and Wally stopped on #8 and are in town," wrote Lynn Smith. "They will just about make wages." Bill Ballou hired fourteen men to work a claim on Little Manook Jr. He knew the claim would not "pay anywhere near day wages" but kept that a secret, telling the men that their pay would be in the spring cleanup. "Cleaned up last night," wrote Frank Purdy, "it wasn't very good only wages at $10.00 per day. . . ."[71]

By far the most commonplace example of this equation of gold with wages came in miners' careful notes on how much gold they found in each pan as they prospected new creeks or tested their "dumps," the piles of frozen dirt they accumulated in the winter. Daily panning provided a reading of the ground they worked, and miners judged the pans in terms of prospective wages. They knew how much gold per pan, and per cubic yard of dirt, was required to make a dollar an hour or ten dollars a day.[72] To strike "50 cent dirt" was a sign of rich ground.[73] Hunter Fitzhugh learned that fifteen cents to the pan was "splendid prospects," and later sent a twenty-eight-cent piece of gold home. "If every pan had one of these I would be a millionaire. . . . most claims in this country don't give more than a cent a pan." Frank Purdy gladdened at the good news from upper Eldorado Creek, "$1.40 to $6.00 a pan." James McCrae noted a neighbor's prospects as "they are getting good pay on #10 two dollar pans are common." The more common scenario of mere pennies a pan brought far more doubt. Lynn Smith worked a claim on Esther Creek in 1905 and reported the situation in typical language. "Got to bedrock and are on the edge of the Pay streak . . . have 3 ft. of 2 and 3 cents dirt and it won't pay to work . . . so we are drifting toward the creek. . . . we think we are getting into the old channel . . . three pans of dirt— five cents first, then 78 cents . . . and then 40 cents . . . we are over on the pay Streak. . . ." Many diaries consisted only of daily records of the results from sample pans. Charles Mosier's diary entry for March 15, 1899, read typically: "Cleaned hole. 32 buckets pay. 25 cents, 32 cents, & 37 cents to pan."[74]

Yukon miners had good reason to keep close track of how much gold they produced, for in most cases their wages proved stunningly low. The seasonal nature of the work contributed to their frustration. As they waited for the spring washup, they lived with the constant likelihood, James Anderson wrote in January 1897 from American Creek, that with "no good news along this creek. . . . we will have our winters work for nothing." On May 24, 1899, James McRae finished rocking on his partner Tucker's claim, and counted a total take of $579.80 worth of gold. His own claim produced about the same amount, $615.60 in gold. Their first act was to pay off a hired worker for the season's labors, with depressing results. "We paid Tucker's man off tonight. There was $29.00 left for Tucker's winter work." A year later, the same group, still at it, faced even more dismal results. After splitting up their small amount of spring gold, they went in search of another claim. As McRae explained, they "went up again this morning put down another hole but could not find anything that would pay us to work so we decided to try and sell it and get to work at something else where we can make something. We are pretty near tired of working for nothing."[75]

This preoccupation with gold as wages, and the desire for a rational connection between work and pay, revealed the affinities between the work of gold mining and work in the rest of the industrial world. Other work habits revealed other similarities. The miners' labor was not only wage labor, it was also structured and measured according to time. Some miners may have sought gold as an escape from regimented work lives, but they brought their watches and clocks with them. In diaries and letters, they reported their activities not only in terms of wages, dollars, and cents, but also in terms of minutes and hours. In a letter home, Mac McMichael explained that "During 'business hours' I am never out of a job. The pay streak is ever waiting to be found."[76] Miners paid close attention to hours worked, hours invested, and hours wasted; they reported their daily schedules in exact terms. On trails and rivers en route to the goldfields, they recorded what times they left one camp and arrived at the next, sometimes to the minute.[77] Bill Hiscock recorded his routine in 1898. "We work from about 9 a.m. till 3:20 p.m. It is just daylight at 12 noon, we stop work for lunch for 1 hour, and when we start at 1 oclock in the afternoon it gradually gets dark again, although it never gets very dark."[78] James McRae's diary entries were as specific as possible: "It was 1 p.m. when we got the first fire cleaned. I then put in a small fire we began at 7:40 p.m. to clean it out and got through at 9:40."[79] Even in mid-summer and mid-winter, when miners faced constant sunlight or constant darkness, they stuck with watches and clocks, asserting familiar industrial, time-driven work habits. The clocks had to work, of course. "We didn't get up until 9:30 this morning," Hunter Fitzhugh wrote of a December morning, "because it is so dark at that hour that we can't tell what time it is. Our alarm clock went back on us a day or two ago, and we are helpless."[80] Wage work, when combined with this attention to time, meant hourly work with hourly pay, familiar to men and women of the industrial age.

The men and women who tried their luck in the goldfields chose that work freely. Their actions were not determined by laws of nature, either laws that dictated that human beings desired gold above all else, or laws that dictated that an economy needing gold would naturally produce workers willing to travel far distances to dig gold out of the earth. Gold miners chose mining within a specific context of both industrialization and economic depression. Within that world, they faced a narrow range of choices for productive work and wealth. Once in the goldfields of Alaska and the Yukon, they realized that gold mining was exactly that, one choice among many similar choices, another form of industrial wage labor governed by hard work and chance. Most concluded that the odds were simply better at home. In the end, gold offered not the chance to escape life at home, but instead to return to it on slightly better terms. But that was all it offered: the chance. By the time they realized they were gamblers, they also knew that the gamble of industrial life made more sense at home than in Alaska or the Yukon, especially as the placer gold disappeared and the odds grew worse and worse. Home—even the Vermont cider business—became a better bet.

Through the labor of mining, gold seekers forged new connections to nature, but they forged those connections within the powerful context of their culture, for their labor was filled with culture, with industrial-era ideas and expectations about hard work, wealth, wages, and pay, about what work was worth doing, and for what gain. Their work as producers brought them to the heart of their culture. Their work as consumers did the same. Miners consumed wood and earth and water as they dug for gold. They also consumed vast quantities of food. To the labor of transportation and the labor of mining, they added the labor of supply, the project of outfitting, feeding, and sheltering their bodies. Their consumption of food and supplies connected them to nature along the Yukon creeks and to far distant natural places through a rapidly growing industrial economy that by the 1890s had transformed the scale and meaning of consumption itself.

6

THE NATURE & CULTURE

OF FOOD

W hen Charlie Chaplin happened upon photographs of miners
ascending the Chilkoot Pass, he was so taken by the power of
the images that he decided to make a film. Chaplin's 1925 silent,
The Gold Rush, opened with the classic Chilkoot shot, a long line of miners struggling up the trail. Despite the enduring draw of that scene, the film's
most famous and memorable moments came later, and they revolved entirely
around food. In one, Chaplin's character, the Lone Prospector, or "little fellow," snowbound in an isolated mining cabin with no supplies, meticulously
boils his shoe for Thanksgiving dinner with his partner, Big Jim. At the table,
Chaplin carefully consumes its sole, nails, and laces as if he were dining on
a fine steak, the most delicate chicken bones, and a lovely side of spaghetti
(the laces). In a later scene, the Lone Prospector dreams of entertaining his
imaginary New Year's Eve guests with a dance, an amiable soft-shoe number
performed by dinner rolls at the ends of two forks. Though Chaplin's hero
eventually strikes it rich, wins the girl, and returns home a millionaire, gold
and mining are entirely secondary to the story. Most of the tale is about hunger.

In this, Chaplin was right on the mark. Miners were forever hungry, and
they wrote constantly about food, craving it, buying it, cooking it, and eating it. As Charlie Chaplin must have surmised in portraying Thanksgiving
and New Year's meals in his film, food became a particularly intense topic
at holidays. For these special meals, miners made extra efforts to re-create
traditional, festive menus with whatever they had at hand. James Cooper's

diary for Thanksgiving 1897 best captured the humor and the reality of Alaska-Yukon holiday preparations.

> We propose to have a feast on Thanksgiving, have invited Ochs and Walter to come (and bring their dinner); following is "Bill-A-Fare" (as proposed). Fish-goose stew a-la-Bonanza . . . sour dough bread and weary Skagway butter. Potatoes, solid, a-la-evaporated. . . . Boiled Cabbage a-la-tough, Apple-pie (if you can eat it), Mush Straight, Vegetable soup a-la-can, Citric acid on the side, Dawson Floats, lemon flavor, Klondyke Strawberries [beans] and Coleman's mustard, Stewed Peaches, Boiled Apricots, Liver and Bacon (minus liver), Eldorado Flapjacks and maple syrup (if Ochs brings it). . . . The foregoing may be modified or extended depending somewhat on our ability to rustle more tomato cans to complete our silver service.[1]

Cooper's Thanksgiving did not proceed as planned, however, "owing to scarcity of grub." The men tried to maintain levity but, he wrote, "we find it impossible to keep from being sober."[2] Other miners made similar efforts. The Mosier party served a moose roast on Thanksgiving Day, with plum pudding, cranberry sauce, and potatoes.[3] Mac McMichael's crew, down the Yukon in Alaska, sat down that day to "moose stew with dumplings, bread, ginger cookies and apple pie. All luxuries with us."[4]

Meals like these holiday feasts revealed the miners' creative culinary efforts. They also revealed the nature and culture of food during the gold rush. The miners' food, like all food, was natural; it came from nature. Fish-goose stew a-la-Bonanza, moose roast, and moose stew came from local nature, from nearby creeks, rivers, and forests, provided most likely by Native hunters who fueled a steady market in fresh salmon, caribou, moose, and other game. Such foods forged direct connections to local ecosystems and to local peoples. Moose and goose notwithstanding, however, most of the miners' food—bacon, beans, flour, sugar, potatoes, canned vegetables and fruit—came across great distances from the agricultural empires of North America. Miners had at their service a vast integrated economy that harvested, preserved, stored, and then transported the energy of sunnier southern ecosystems to their far north dinner tables. Klondike miners were industrial consumers par excellence in that, in the words of Daniel Boorstin, they were simply "no longer local."[5] Through nonlocal foods, miners forged connections to far distant natures, to all the myriad places and myriad workers who produced, preserved, and carried that food north to the gold creeks.

Those connections to nonlocal nature took concrete form in a surprising variety of foods. In the summer, when sternwheelers brought in loads of ham, canned meats, and fresh fruits and vegetables, miners with a ready supply of cash lived well. When the Yukon froze in the fall, though, the food supply from Seattle and San Francisco dwindled, and diets grew more monotonous. According to Mac McMichael, the "regulation Alaskan dinner" was pork and beans with bread and rice, or, as Bill Hiscock put it, "the inevitable bacon and bread and treacle."[6] Tappan Adney quoted a miner admitting he had eaten so much bacon he was "ashamed to look at a hog in the face."[7] The Alaska Commercial Company and North American Trade & Transportation Company maintained warehouses full of preserved foods, however, which, while they lasted, supplemented the winter bacon-beans-and-bread diet. McMichael's party of three had "a good supply of condensed beef" on hand, "plenty of evaporated fruits, apples, peaches, apricots, pears, prunes and raisins," as well as maple syrup, maple sugar, corn meal, rolled oats, canned butter, and condensed milk.[8] Dogsledding down the Stikine River, Hunter Fitzhugh traded with two white men for "12 pounds of prunes and apricots, and we nearly made ourselves sick eating them raw and stewed."[9] These more diverse diets, so heavy in preserved foods, still grew tiresome. "We have all eaten pickle, onion, and cauliflower until our very clothes are sour," Lynn Smith complained in a letter home. He added with irony, "I actually ate an apple Oct. 5th."[10]

Early spring brought relief. At the first sign of a thaw, or even before, daring speculators brought much-treasured lots of fresh food over the Chilkoot and White Passes and down the Yukon River, just behind, or sometimes on the breaking ice, to capitalize on the winter's scarcity at the goldfields. "Most of the small boats coming down bring a surplus of provisions," Army Captain W. P. Richardson reported in June 1898, "including fresh vegetables, eggs, and fruit, and it is to these small but numerous additions to the supply of the commercial companies that the people owe their comfort at the present time."[11] Such supply work promised great profits, but it was dangerous in more ways than one. Food's status as a market commodity in a capitalist economy left early- and late-season speculators vulnerable to extremely volatile markets and prices operating in an uncertain and severe natural environment. In one of Jack London's lesser-known tales, "The One Thousand Dozen," a hustler named David Rasmunsen tries to strike it rich by carrying twelve thousand eggs from San Francisco—where eggs cost fifteen cents a dozen—to "the Golden Metropolis," Dawson City, where they sell for an unimaginable five dollars a dozen.[12] Rasmunsen explains to his skeptical wife that even given the costs of transportation (fifty dollars shipping to Dyea; one hundred and eighty dollars for Indian packers from Dyea to Lindeman; three hundred dollars for a boat downriver to Dawson) he could easily turn a four-thousand-dollar profit. At the Chilkoot, however, the Indian packers charge fifty cents, not twelve cents per pound. Rasmunsen suffers frostbite at the summit; the Yukon closes with ice. Obsessed by the possibility of wealth, he starves himself and his sled dogs en route to Dawson, where hungry miners pay a dollar fifty each for the eggs, a miraculous eighteen dollars a dozen. But the eggs had spoiled, every single one. Rasmunsen turns the dogs loose and hangs himself.[13]

Once the Yukon ice broke fully in the spring, however, the big stern-wheelers steamed into Dawson laden with fresh potatoes, fruit, sugar, eggs, milk, hams, butter, and even livestock, all only a few weeks out of Seattle and San Francisco. "In the brief space of a few days," Tappan Adney wrote at Dawson in 1898, "there seemed to be nothing that could not be purchased in Dawson, from fresh grapes to an opera-glass, from a safety-pin to an ice-cream freezer."[14] "Mostly anything can be bought here and pretty cheap to[o] even green cucumbers," marveled Frank Purdy. Mac McMichael wrote, "I see that I can have ice cream and cake at 50 cents a dish so we need not pine for luxuries in this blessed country." Some had their doubts. "They have some bananas here," wrote Fred Kimball from St. Michael, when the spring boats arrived in 1904, "but they don't look good to me. They are too far from home." But Stewart Campbell noted with relish in August 1899 that "[a] boat load of Anhuiser [*sic*] Busch beer just arrived today and it tasted finer than cream."[15]

All of these foods, whether Cooper's and Mosier's holiday feasts or a regular old can of pork and beans, revealed connections to nature, but also to culture. There was culture in the miners' customs and preferences, their desire for fresh meat and cranberries, ice cream and bananas and beer, their yearnings for familiar brands and products. Those yearnings created markets in the gold rush economy for hundreds of particular foods, whether fresh beef, cucumbers, watermelon, or other standard items in the late-nineteenth-century North American diet. There was industrial culture in the power of the North American economy to transport those familiar foods thousands of miles for consumption along the gold creeks so very far away. There was culture as well in the miners' ability to effortlessly mix local and nonlocal foods at their tables, such as in a Christmas Day menu which included "Roast Cariboo Au Jus" and "Roast Ptarmigan dressing" as well as Boston baked beans and English plum pudding. Such mixtures meant that miners could forge simultaneous connections in a single meal to a Yukon caribou herd, a Central American banana plantation, Chicago's stockyards, California's Central Valley, and New England's dairy farms. At Christmas dinner in 1898, Mac McMichael reported a meal of "Pea soup . . . boiled salmon with drawn butter sauce, moose stew with dumplings, Cudahy [canned] roast, beef brown gravey, mashed potatoes, scalloped tomatoes, green peas, bread and butter, ginger bread, peach short cake, Detroit fruit cake, apple pie, [and] seedless raisins."[16]

Although these various foods came from vastly different places, what made this meal so clearly modern was that, to the miners, it hardly mattered at all where it came from. For miners as industrial consumers, it did not really matter that eating moose and eating canned roast beef constituted vastly different acts of consumption with vastly different ecological and social consequences. It did not matter that one dish connected them to an irrigated tomato field in California and another to a local Native hunter working just a few miles away. It did not matter that those connections helped to transform the natures, cultures, and societies of local and far-distant places and peoples. To the miners, it was simply another meal, a celebration, a source of energy to fuel their search for wealth through gold. Food was the essential capital of the gold rush, the wealth consumed in order to produce more wealth. Such meals captured the essence of industrial consumption.

WHERE DID THEIR FOOD COME FROM?

Although gold miners rarely thought about the source of their food, it did matter where that food came from. All of it came from nature, but the question of *which* nature made all the difference in the world. A Cudahy roast and a can of Van Camp's pork and beans were very different from salmon steak, moose stew, or a caribou roast; they connected miners to nature in very different ways. A canned Cudahy roast was the product of distant cattle ranches. It came thousands of miles, absorbing along the way the labor not only of food processors, but of ranchers, cowboys, slaughterhouse workers, and railroad shippers. It contained a small fraction of the millions of dollars in capital invested over decades in the land, factories, and railroads which made the consumption of canned meat possible. A caribou roast, by comparison, traveled only a few miles, absorbing the solar energy captured by a large but local ecosystem, and also the labor and knowledge of local Yukon peoples. When miners consumed these foods at the table, they consumed all of the capital and labor poured into processed meat, and the knowledge and energy contained in fresh caribou steaks. Yet in the miners' casual consumption of such foods, both the nature and the culture which they consumed became invisible.

By the 1890s, industrial food processing had reached new heights of volume and efficiency as patterns of consumption shifted toward mass-produced foods, bringing a revolution to the American diet. Nowhere was this more evident than along the Yukon during the gold rush, where canned and dehydrated food became the basis of the miners' diets. "We lived high," Bill Ballou bragged to his brother Walt, at home in Vermont, "on canned chicken, turkey, mutton, roast beef, tomatoes, corn, sweet potatoes, peaches, and dried apples, prunes, apricots, peaches, and plums. . . . fine butter and condensed milk . . . evaporated potatoes and onions . . . granulated eggs and prepared soup stocks." Canning, dehydration, and condensing made meats, fruit, and vegetables impervious to decay. Once dried, condensed, or sealed and boiled, they could not spoil, so they traveled thousands of miles with impunity. They thus escaped older natural limits of time, seasons, and geography; they became "portable through time," as Daniel Boorstin puts it. Transported by rail, ship, and human packers, such foods made it possible for miners to eat deviled ham and apricots thousands of miles from the feed-lots and orchards in which pigs and apricots actually grew. The evidence of such consumption appeared everywhere in the goldfields. "There is a layer of about one foot of tin cans over the whole place . . . ," Nora Crane reported from Circle City." "Most everything is canned," she continued, "and makes one think of three picnics in a day . . . everything in fact one can think of can be sent here without spoiling." As Hunter Fitzhugh remarked, the "five gallon evaporated potato can" was nothing less than "the national wash tub of Alaska."[17]

Each tin can represented a strand of connection that reached from the Yukon and Alaska across great distances to the places where all of those potatoes, apricots, and pork products actually came from. Where they did come from rarely seemed clear to the gold seekers, though. Hunter Fitzhugh voiced a theory on sources as he described the trash heaped on the Yukon ice awaiting the clean sweep of the spring thaw. "There will be tin cans in all sizes. . . . sealed and said to contain extract of beef (said beef used to wear iron shoes and pulled a street car in Chicago)."[18] His jests captured some truth. The miners' canned meats, meat extracts, and bacon may not have been former streetcar horses from Chicago, but a lot of it was nevertheless from Chicago, Indianapolis, Cincinnati, and Omaha, the nation's meat-packing centers. Processed-food companies recognized gold miners as a perfect market for their products, and pursued that market energetically. Michael Cudahy, of Chicago's Cudahy meat-packing company, knew he could sell thousands of his famous Cudahy roasts to Alaska miners. To further increase his profits from the gold rush, he invested heavily in the North American Trade & Transportation Company (NAT&T), whose sternwheelers undoubtedly shipped crate loads of processed meat up the Yukon. Cudahy's company also provided jobs in Alaska for Cudahy's friends and business associates, including Nora Crane's husband, who worked at the NAT&T store in Circle City.[19] In a letter home Nora Crane imagined the dividends to be earned on her family's Cudahy investments, given the situation at her own dinner table. "When I think of four years of canned corn beef & beans I think we will earn ten times more than I will ever get out of it."[20]

Through such volumes of canned meats, the miners were connected to other meat-packing and canning corporations, including Van Camp's in Indianapolis, Swift, Armour, and Libby, McNeill & Libby in Chicago, and smaller operations like the Omaha Packing Company. In January 1898, Swift sent its Pacific Northwest agent, Harry L. Strong, to set up his sales headquarters in Seattle in order to oversee the sale of pork products to mining outfitters.[21] That May, Van Camp's dispatched Willard B. Cook to advertise its products, all "choice and ready sellers," to wholesalers on Puget Sound.[22] From the 1870s to 1910, canning and packing grew into a global business dominated by these industrial giants in meats, Heinz in condiments, Campbell in soups, and the California Fruit Grower's Exchange in fruits and vegetables.[23] By the 1890s, the canned and prepared foods that gold miners ate, like Van Camp's pork and beans (the "best known prepared food in America") and macaroni and cheese, were easy to prepare and, more important, "cheaper than the average housekeeper could buy the ingredients of the can uncooked."[24] By 1910 in the United States, sixty-eight thousand workers produced over three billion cans of food a year, providing milk, meat, fish, and vegetables year-round to working and poor classes— and miners—who until the 1870s had subsisted mainly on salt pork, cabbage, and potatoes, with fresh food only in season.[25] By the 1920s, U.S. canners packed more food, writes Daniel Boorstin, than "all other countries combined."[26]

FIG. 6.1 Van Camp's Advertisement. Although miners did harvest some of their food from local ecosystems in Alaska and the Yukon, the great bulk of their supplies were processed foods from the American West and Midwest, such as the popular Van Camp's pork and beans. Seattle outfitters Cooper & Levy featured this product with an advertisement evoking a gold seeker headed up the Chilkoot Trail. (*Seattle Post-Intelligencer*, May 27, 1898)

These large integrated corporations fed miners well, but in consuming the capital and labor commanded by such industrial giants, the miners' connections to nature proliferated so far and wide as to become untraceable. Meals on Yukon dinner tables led back to midwestern packing plants; the connections then branched out in yet more directions, as meat-packers and food processors drew cattle, sheep, hogs, and poultry from all across the American and Canadian West and Midwest, thus extending the miners' connections to those farms and ranches.[27] Meats were not, however, the only heartland products to reach the Yukon. LaMont's crystallized eggs— simply powdered or dehydrated eggs—became a well-advertised Klondike novelty. They came from a St. Louis factory, which collected up to sixteen thousand eggs a day from farms along the Tennessee, Ohio, Missouri, and Mississippi Rivers.[28] Some of the miners' dinner meats extended their connections to nature even farther afield. "Australian canned meat has always

FIG. 6.2 LaMont's Crystallized Eggs Advertisement. To promote their brand of crystallized eggs, LaMont's contrasted the deadly fate met by miners victimized by inexperienced outfitters with the hardy success of those who pursued proper outfitting. The packs of the fortunate miners spell out "Crystallized Eggs" in an orderly fashion. (*Seattle Post-Intelligencer,* March 9, 1898)

stood high in Cassiar where we deal," John Callbreath wrote from his Stikine River trading post, "and I doubt not it has a good standing in the Youcon country."[29]

When miners sat down to fruit, vegetables, and flour, they expanded their connections to nature to include new areas of the American West brought into cultivation since the Civil War. From 1870 to 1900, railroads through Minnesota, the Dakotas, and the Pacific Northwest opened up a wheat-producing empire. Under the auspices of corporate giants like Pillsbury and

Gold Medal, automated factories produced refined white flour which sold at much lower prices and became the key ingredient in the nation's baked goods. In 1872, one dollar bought fifteen pounds of flour. By 1897, when the gold miners went north, that dollar bought thirty-four pounds of flour at home, though far less at Yukon trading posts.[30] With the application of mass-production technologies, rice, beans, tea, coffee, and sugar all saw similar drops in price, as did milk. As grain production moved west, dairy production expanded in the Northeast and Midwest, assisted by railroads that could move fresh milk quickly to market. In 1856, Gail Borden, an inventor and land agent from Texas, patented a process to condense and can milk. Borden's Eagle Brand Condensed Milk quickly caught on in the 1850s and then fed the Union Army during the Civil War. This breakthrough made dairy products available to a far broader segment of the population, regardless of its proximity to actual cows. From 1870 to 1900, American milk sales jumped from two billion to eighteen billion pounds a year.[31]

Although the miners' condensed milk came from dairies and milk plants as far away as New York, and their processed meats from Chicago's western hinterland and packers, some of their other staples, particularly beans, fruits, and vegetables, connected them to ecosystems and workers slightly closer at hand, in California's Central Valley. Although local growers in Washington State grew a few beans, wholesalers in Seattle bought the great bulk of beans of all varieties from California brokers and producers, along with walnuts, almonds, and honey. Fontana and Company of San Francisco and Haight Fruit of Redlands and Riverside advertised their packed and canned fruits and vegetables, including peas, tomatoes, asparagus, peaches, and pears, to Seattle wholesalers. California so dominated the nation's production of fresh and dried fruit that every time a miner ate fruit, he forged a link directly to that state's growing agricultural empire, which in one month, July 1897, shipped over 2.8 million pounds of dried fruit.[32] A few weeks later, California producers shipped ten tons of dried fruit from Santa Rosa directly to Dawson City.[33] By 1899, California was producing 121 million pounds of dried prunes, peaches, apricots, apples, pears, and plums, in addition to 30 million cases of canned fruit.[34]

Alaska-Yukon gold miners did not bring California's—or the entire West's—agricultural empire into being. They did not provide the capital, labor, and resources to farm the Central Valley or provide much of the demand for the products of that capital and labor. Gold miners may not have been the most powerful or numerous consumers remaking the West,

THE KLONDIKE DRINK

GHIRARDELLI'S COCOA——Easier carried and takes up less room than any other food. Keeps you warm and strong during the long, cold marches. Made in a minute——costs less than one cent a cup. More nourishing than meat or any other solid or liquid foods. Be sure you get Ghirardelli's. It's the strongest and freshest.

FIG. 6.3 "The Klondike Drink." Producers of brand-name products like Ghirardelli's chocolate advertised to gold seekers with specific gold rush images and motifs, claiming that their brands were especially well suited to the Alaska-Yukon environment. (*Seattle Post-Intelligencer* March 6, 1898)

but when they opened cans of pork, beans, beef, and apricots, they nonetheless linked themselves to and profited from changes that had been happening all across California and other western states since the Civil War. In consuming canned beef and white flour, dried peaches and roast beef, miners linked themselves to a West remade by intensive capitalist agriculture, and to the resultant changes in the region's environment.[35] Like typical industrial consumers across North America, gold seekers benefited directly from the nineteenth-century ecological transformation of the region.

For just as gold miners disassembled Yukon creeks to produce gold, western producers reorganized tallgrass and shortgrass prairie, high desert, and rich valley bottoms to produce the imported plant and animal species that constituted Euro-American food. In doing so, they drastically changed the West's plant and animal communities. As William Cronon explains, wheat and corn farms were "radical simplifications of the grassland ecosystem." Ranchers converted buffalo range to cattle and sheep range, overgrazed big- and little-stem grasses, and spread exotic weeds shunned by the stock. In

California, fruit and vegetable growers diverted rivers to reclaim desert lands for raisins and peaches. Cattle and grain and fruit absorbed the accumulated "stockpile" of solar energy stored in rich western soils, and gold miners drew on that organic energy in their search for an entirely different sort of natural wealth.[36]

As a group, Yukon gold miners represented only a tiny fraction of the population supported by this transformed West, as the great bulk of western foods traveled east by rail to rapidly growing cities. The miners' food demands did connect them to all of those transformations, however, particularly in the Pacific Northwest. Here their consumption linked them to ecological and economic changes that, while well under way before 1897, nonetheless proceeded with great energy thanks to the gold seekers. Many of the miners' supplies, including much fresh food, came from the Pacific Northwest, where a growing agricultural hinterland centered on Seattle boomed during the rush.

By the 1890s, Washington and Oregon had developed fruit and vegetable industries that grew pears, prunes, and apples in the rich valleys west of the mountains, and tomatoes, peaches, grapes, watermelons, and more apples on the irrigated borders of the Columbia River and its tributaries.[37] The gold rushers' meals connected them directly to this growth, stimulating capital investment in agriculture, which brought a sudden explosion in the production of dried and dehydrated produce. By 1898 at least four Seattle companies, including the Washington Evaporating and Preserving Company, produced evaporated potatoes, onions, and canned soup vegetables for sale to miners.[38] In 1898 Seattle and Yakima plants packed 311,000 pounds of dried fruits and vegetables, 200,000 of which were Hunter Fitzhugh's favorite, potatoes.[39] The potato craze spread across the state. Coupeville, Washington, on Whidbey Island, long known for its ample potatoes, set up a vegetable drier in 1897 and made heavy shipments to gold rush markets. By 1898 the drier at Coupeville was running day and night.[40] Another drier at Whatcom produced twenty thousand pounds of dried spuds that winter, but still could not fill all incoming orders.[41] Fresh and evaporated onions became huge items as well. "A large number of Yakima farmers this year propose to grow onions extensively for the Klondike trade," a Seattle trade paper announced in the midst of the spring 1898 rush.[42] Fruit growers as well invested heavily in driers, building plants all over the state, including six in Seattle by the end of 1898. Other producers dried apples, prunes, peaches, plums, and cherries in plants at Tacoma, Puyallup, Colfax, Wenatchee,

Chelan, Yakima, Orting, Sumner, Monroe, and Vashon Island, with at least twenty-five in Clark County around Vancouver, Washington.[43]

In 1897 and 1898, Washington was well on its way to developing a wheat production empire to rival older wheat regions in California and the northern Midwest. From 1890 to 1900, Pacific Northwest wheat production grew from twenty million bushels a year to over fifty million bushels. When gold miners flocked to the West Coast demanding tons of flour for their bread and pancakes, they forged connections to this emerging empire, aided by the Great Northern and Northern Pacific Railroads, which were already delivering shipments of Big Bend and Palouse wheat from eastern Washington to Seattle and Portland for milling and export to England, South America, Hawaii, Alaska, and even to San Francisco. Almost four thousand carloads of wheat—or 1.6 million bushels—arrived by rail in Seattle in 1898.[44] In that year Seattle boasted five flour mills producing flour, oats, and cereals, one of which, the Centennial Mill, doubled its capacity to two thousand barrels of flour a day.[45] Much of this flour went into pasta and baked goods. Whether Klondike miners bought supplies in Seattle or San Francisco, they may well have bought cereals or flour made from Washington grains. A cartoon in the *Seattle Post-Intelligencer* on September 12, 1897, during the first wave of gold outfitting, depicted the "King of the Klondike," a crowned sack of flour, standing imperiously over the figure of a gold coin. The gold coin bowed prostrate in abject surrender and worship before flour, the true source of Seattle's wealth that first gold rush summer.[46]

THE CULTURE OF FOOD

Whatever combination of far-distant places provided each miner with his daily bread, the miners' collective connections to those places were shaped by more than just hunger and geography. Culture, as well as distance, shaped what miners ate, and culture shaped the connections they forged to distant ecosystems and economies. Like all human beings, Alaska-Yukon miners filled their food with a host of cultural meanings and values quite apart from its basic stores of nutrition and energy. Miners, for instance, sought certain familiar foods simply because they offered a comforting link to home and to their accustomed lives. "For supper last night I had something which reminded me of Sunday tea at home—sardines," wrote weary Mac McMichael, "the first I have tasted since leaving home. They were a French brand and delicious."[47] Such items were often readily available to gold miners. The amazing thing about Dawson City in July 1898 was that it was pretty easy for miners to find almost all familiar foods, to buy and eat an egg, a steak, macaroni and cheese, even cake and ice cream. By 1899 and 1900, miners, as consumers, wielded the power to eat just about anything they desired, from anywhere, in any season, as long as they could afford the market price. This consumer world, like the emerging transportation economy, was one in which distance, time, and season—nature itself—mattered less and less in determining what miners ate. Culture, desire, and markets, on the other hand, mattered more and more.

What miners ate thus came to reflect what they *wanted* to eat, and corporate food producers played an increasingly powerful role in directing those wants. Miners trusted and bought products like Van Camp's pork and beans in part because the names and labels were very familiar, part of the emerging world of national advertising, brand loyalty, and the new science of sales. Like other industrial consumers, miners preferred certain brand names and colorful labels, such as Swift, Armour, Eagle and Magnolia Condensed Milk (both from the New York Condensed Milk Co.), Baker's Chocolate, Royal Baking Powder, and Vermont Maple Syrup.[48] That cultural familiarity was as much a corporate product as was the food itself. New processing technologies produced flour, sugar, and canned goods that were "absolutely uniform in appearance, quality, and taste," according to one historian. Companies used brand names, advertising, and creative packaging to distinguish their products from the crowd, and to create "consumption communities," which forged intangible links between people in part through the shared consumption of identical products and in part by producers and advertisers striving to build brand loyalty.[49] Producers, wholesalers, and grocers worked together to provide miners with brands that connected them not only to the comforts of home, but also, through the shared consumption of certain foodstuffs, to each other.

At one extreme, then, nature and culture came together in the gold rush economy to provide Alaska-Yukon miners with every sort of food their hearts desired. At the other extreme, however, nature and culture sometimes left them without the basic nutrients they needed to survive. Miners took risks early in the gold rush, and especially in the winter, in depending on a narrow range of foods that had to come thousands of miles to the dinner table. Miners could eat their fill of bacon and bread and beans all winter long, and still, with no source of vitamin C, become frighteningly ill with scurvy. Their legs swelled, making it difficult to walk; their gums bled, and their teeth loosened. These were sure signs that gold miners were ecologically out of place, out of easy proximity to the usual sources of ascorbic acid—fresh fruit, potatoes, tomatoes—and to the ecosystems that produced those foods.[50] Bill Ballou got scurvy his first winter in Alaska; his legs turned black, but with medicine and fruit he recovered. He found scurvy "quite prevalent" in Rampart City in 1898–99.[51] The U.S. Consul at Dawson reported scurvy in Dawson as early as August 1898, and reported the cases increasing at an "alarming" rate by December 1898, especially amongst destitute miners without proper food.[52] The most famous of poet Robert Service's moilers for gold, Sam McGee, is a fictional creation of a man who dies of scurvy and is cremated in the firebox of a steamer.[53]

The miners' displacement from accustomed sources of ascorbic acid was a matter of culture as well as the nature of their bodies and food supplies. There were less familiar local sources at hand, but most Euro-Americans failed to recognize them. According to all reports and observations, Native Yukoners rarely if ever suffered from scurvy. They derived an adequate supply of ascorbic acid in part from moose and caribou liver, but mostly from berries, wild rhubarb, spruce bark, and a plant called mousenut.[54] Gold miners, though, tended not to see this diversity in the Indians' diet. They saw local peoples eating fish and meat, and assumed that Natives were physiologically different from whites and did not require other foods like potatoes and oranges. Josiah Spurr saw Eskimos on the lower Yukon eating only fish. "White men can hardly become so simple in their diet," he wrote, "without some danger of dying in the course of the experiment."[55]

In searching for the dietary cure for scurvy, miners did resort to local as well as nonlocal foods. The most commonplace hospital cures in Dawson and Rampart, spruce leaf tea and raw potatoes, drew from both categories.[56] Although chemists had yet to truly identify vitamin C, sailors and other adventurers had long known that citrus fruit prevented scurvy, and most Klondike outfitters sold lime juice or citric acid as part of every gold miner's prepackaged set of supplies. Walter Curtin's party, in winter quarters on a stranded steamer, used citric acid and lime juice to ward off scurvy; a nearby party, from Chicago, lost an elderly man to the disease. Miners also ate canned tomatoes and dried apples and prunes as preventatives. Thomas Moore, cutting wood on the Koyukuk River, ate dried fruit two or three times a day to keep scurvy at bay. After hearing of scurvy among woodchoppers and at Rampart City, Lynn Smith immediately sat down and "ate a quart of canned cherries." And stories about the curative powers of potatoes circulated quickly. Mac McMichael purchased an expensive load of evaporated potatoes at Circle City in August 1898. "They come high though, but, in spite of that, I am going to take fifty pounds with me to camp, at 50 cents a pound. Boyd will think this awful extravagance but I think it economy for they are a good scurvy preventative. Raw potatoes eaten every day will cure scurvy. That is what they feed patients at the hospital here, two or three raw potatoes a day." Still others turned to fresh meat, believing somewhat falsely that it, too, cured scurvy. In January 1899, Frank Purdy sent his partner to town for fresh meat and potatoes, as "we have both got scurvy." McMichael's partner, Boyd, came down with symptoms of scurvy in October 1898. "Well, soon after they began to catch salmon," McMichael wrote, "and the fresh fish drove every symptom away in a few days." His faith in fresh meat, which contained comparatively little vitamin C, led him to trade sixty pounds of bacon to a neighbor for forty-five pounds of moose meat."[57] "We will have plenty of fresh meat this winter," he wrote in another letter, "and that will drive it away."[58]

Whether it cured scurvy or not, miners craved fresh meat, a desire that was often as much about cultural preferences as a need for protein. Miners resembled other late-nineteenth-century consumers in their cultural predilection for fresh beef, and by the 1890s, advances in meat-packing, transportation, and refrigeration had made it possible for urban consumers to purchase and serve fresh beef at low prices.[59] Middle- and upper-class consumers rejected salt pork as an inferior, lower-class, unhealthy food, and celebrated beef as the healthful, high-status alternative, for three meals a day.[60] Gold miners carried those preferences to the Yukon, where they ate bacon and beans, but aspired to beef and potatoes. Caribou and moose meat provided a certain middle ground, but did not meet the cultural standards required for high-status dining. Shipping live cattle, sheep, and hogs to Dawson City, Rampart, and Nome was a dangerous and expensive endeavor, however, and the price of fresh meat did not approach feasible levels until 1899 and 1900, when natural and economic barriers yielded to capital investment in new means of transport, including the White Pass & Yukon Railroad.[61] In 1899 the Arctic Meat Company of Seattle fitted ocean steamers and river sternwheelers with liquid ammonia refrigeration, and shipped fresh-cut meats directly to Dawson City. Another transport company, Alaska Meat, contracted with Frye-Bruhn in Seattle to supply two hundred tons of fresh meats for the 1899 Yukon season, including ten thousand turkeys, ten thousand chickens, sixty tons of beef, and forty tons of mutton; the order also included ten tons of butter and eggs.[62] In the summer of 1900, John Cantwell's *Nunivak* inspected the steamer *Michael Kerr*, en route to Dawson with fresh meat and eggs. The crew happily accepted a gift of turkeys.[63] By 1900 meat shippers using refrigerated cars on the White Pass & Yukon Railroad competed with cattle drives over the Dalton Trail and cold storage boats from St. Michael. In June 1901, when the railway announced advance contracts for the new season, it reported a capacity for a thousand tons of perishable merchandise.[64] The railroad so lowered the cost of shipping dressed meat to Dawson that eating it was almost as cheap as eating moose and caribou.[65] Beef prices at Dawson City fell from a high of over two dollars a pound in the early days of 1896 and 1897 to as low as thirty cents a pound.[66]

With cold storage trains and steamers, Yukon suppliers broke the final seasonal limits on fresh food from the outside world. In historian Margaret Archibald's words, it "freed meat from cans."[67] Miners at the creeks could sit down any time to a roast beef, or fresh fruit or eggs, that came from anywhere in the country, if not the world. A beefsteak now seemed no different—better, in fact—than a moose or caribou steak. Because the Yukon River still froze, such shipments remained seasonal, but storage facilities at Dawson extended the supply of fresh food for months.[68] When it came to food, the Yukon interior was now fully part of the industrial world. Space, time, and distance had truly ceased to matter when it came to the cultural demand for fresh beef. Yet beefsteaks came from somewhere. No matter how easy it was to simply buy fresh beef, no matter how invisible the connections became, those connections to nature remained, branching in myriad directions to myriad natures, with consequences for every meal.

LOCAL FOODS, LOCAL PEOPLES

In the months before fresh beef arrived to complete the miners' industrial diets, fresh meat meant not beef, but caribou and moose. No matter how easily miners mixed caribou stew and moose steaks with beef and Whidbey Island potatoes at the dinner table, local foods meant different sorts of connections to nature. When miners consumed from the nature around them on the creeks, they transformed that nature, and the lives and cultures of the Native peoples who depended on that nature. As hunters and fishers, gold miners reduced wildlife and fish populations, diminishing the resources available to Native Yukoners and Alaskans. As paying customers, they created a sudden and demanding market for Native hunters and fishers, who shifted their own fishing and hunting practices to take advantage of the miners' demands. As a result, Native peoples increased their harvests of fish and wildlife and reoriented their own annual cycles of subsistence activities to meet the miners' quite different cycles of supply and demand. Over time, Yukon Indians became increasingly dependent on imported Euro-American food commodities. In reaching into local ecosystems and communities to feed themselves, gold miners irrevocably changed the world of Native peoples.

Although Alaska-Yukon miners purchased most of the fish and game they consumed from Indian hunters and fishers, some hunted for themselves, to fill their meager or monotonous larders and to save their expensive store-bought supplies.[69] "My rifle is a bacon-saver," Hunter Fitzhugh wrote at Teslin Lake, where the swans, geese, and ducks were plentiful, "and each successful shot saves nearly a dollar."[70] Miners gathered other local foods as well, such as rose hips and mushrooms, not to mention the profuse berries that Bill Hiscock found growing wild along the upper Yukon: strawberries, raspberries, gooseberries, blueberries, and cranberries.[71] Tom Boldrick found and ate goose eggs, an act far different from paying a dollar and a half for an egg from Seattle or San Francisco.[72] Miners and merchants even took advantage of the summer's long light on south-facing slopes to plant and harvest lettuce, turnips, radishes, onions, cauliflower, spinach, beets, and, with some success, potatoes. By 1899, there were twelve market gardens in the Dawson area.[73] "You can almost see the lettuce grow," Maud Case wrote in 1903. Hunter Fitzhugh explained further that "ten pound turnips are not uncommon in Alaska."[74]

Although miners consumed from local ecosystems in all these ways, their hunting had the greatest impact. From the start, they found themselves surrounded by an abundance of game species. Taking fish, geese, and ducks on Tagish Lake and trading at Fort Yukon for fish and moose, Lynn Smith wrote that "with game as it is here we will not need near as big an outfit." "If we stay here this winter," Mac McMichael wrote on arrival at Fourth of July Creek, "there will be no lack of game to eat and that will help our grub out wonderfully. Moose, caribou and bear seem to be very plentiful. A number have been seen here abouts, but none have been killed because all are busy prospecting and that does not go with hunting which is a specialty." Dogsledding up the Yukon to Dawson, McMichael wrote, "150 reindeer passed us last night."[75] In addition to the caribou herds, moose were a common sight along the Klondike and other Yukon tributaries. In the summer they clustered along the waterways, seeking relief from bugs. In winter they sought sheltered valley bottoms.[76] Frank Purdy saw moose and caribou tracks "very thick" on the Stewart River, and shot four caribou near Dawson in August 1899. Tom Boldrick saw many caribou and moose tracks on the White River in 1898, which impressed him with their size and impact. "There are regular beaten paths up the creek made from wild animals," Boldrick observed. "It looks like some farmers cattle had been turned loosed in the mountains but we never got sight of one we see also lots of bear & lion tracks & they must be large ones from the size of the tracks." "The boys saw three bears today but could not get a shot at them," Boldrick continued. Three days later another group killed a moose, and Boldrick found them "living high." "They divided it with us & it was a great treat to have fresh meat after living 4 months on salt meat."[77]

Wild game was abundant, but fish proved even more plentiful. The annual migration of king salmon arrived at the mouth of the Klondike the second week of June, followed by silver and dog salmon later in the year. "You would enjoy the beautiful long red steaks from the king salmon," Hunter Fitzhugh wrote to his mother, "sometimes 16 inches long and six inches wide and one inch thick, without skin or bone."[78] Miners harvested for their own larders, and for the emerging local market in fresh food. In 1896 one of James Anderson's companions fished for two and a half hours one night in May and brought back 1,040 grayling, which he sold at a dollar a dozen.[79] When the salmon arrived at Dawson in the summer of 1899, off-season miners choked the rivers with 150- or 250-foot drift nets.[80] James McCrae and his friends bought a net, and drifted briefly "without results." "The River is full of fishing boats," McCrae explained. "We put new sinkers on our net this afternoon and we went out again this evening, but no fish. There were 16 nets stretched across the River. All the Dagoes and Frenchmen from Hill are here fishing," he observed, referring to miners from the hill claims up the Klondike. "There are a lot of Salmon being caught now," he finished.[81] Bill Ballou netted fish at Rampart that fall, getting three or four fifteen-pound fish each morning that he sold to local restaurants for a dollar apiece.[82] They fished through the winter as well, catching brook trout through the ice on the creeks and storing the fish frozen through the winter.

The miners' sporadic and seasonal hunting and fishing provided some relief to the monotony of nonlocal processed foods, but the great preponderance of their fresh local foods came not from the miners' own labors, but from Native suppliers. Native Yukoners and Alaskans had long supplied Euro-American fur traders, explorers, and gold prospectors with food in exchange for trade goods. Local peoples greatly expanded their role in the supply economy, however, with the gold rush boom of 1897–1900. The crowds provided a large and instant market for Indian hunters and fishers.[83] When Tappan Adney hunted with the Han in 1897, the band killed eighty moose and sixty-five caribou over the winter, "the main part of which," Adney wrote, "was hauled by dogs to the starving miners at Dawson."[84] In addition, he wrote, "much game was killed by white hunters; but on the whole the best of them lacked the consummate skill of the Indian."[85] In November 1898, following the fall hunt, a group of Tanana Indians brought seventeen sled loads of moose into Rampart City, "and it was all sold in short order," for a dollar a pound. A new supply of moose and caribou arrived in spring, selling for fifty cents a pound.[86] Those prices held through the fall of 1900, when there was "plenty of game meat around" at Rampart City.[87]

In the early stages of Yukon and Alaska mining, before the Klondike rush itself, the work of supplying miners with meat and fish fit within Native subsistence practices, and some groups of Native Yukoners created an economy that encompassed both direct subsistence and trade with Euro-Americans. Supply work was short-term and seasonal, after all, and Natives were already hunters and fishers. They could choose whether to sell or consume the products of their hunt, and by and large they continued to hunt and fish as usual, regardless of the demand. Hungry miners asked for fresh local meat in the summer of 1898, but, as Tappan Adney pointed out, "the Indians do not usually hunt in the summer," and did not this time. Instead, "numbers of white men proceeded to the upper Klondike and hunted moose with considerable success."[88] The miners who did buy fish and meat from local bands gave Indians direct access to cash and trade goods, however, and some Native hunters and fishers accumulated considerable wealth by combining hunting and fishing with seasonal wage work on steamers and in wood camps.[89] As historian Kenneth Coates writes, this "successful and remunerative" adaptation to gold mining meant that Native peoples played a "significant economic role" in the gold mining economy without losing long-held means of subsistence, especially if they experienced little or no competition from white laborers.[90]

In creating this sudden gold rush market for fresh meat and fish, however, the miners' food demands eventually reached out to refocus, and then disorient, the ways in which Native peoples harvested food from the natural world. The changes were neither wholesale nor identical for the diverse groups spread along the river from the lakes to the delta. Yukon Natives had already adapted their subsistence economy to the fur trade, and in some ways the addition of an active trade in meat and fish constituted a broadening of adaptations already under way.[91] Before the gold rush, for example, many Native bands had already adopted rifles and dogsleds for hunting, and had already increased their salmon harvests to feed the dogs; many already considered flour, sugar, and alcohol to be regular parts of their diets.[92] The arrival of repeating rifles in the 1890s, however, available at the Alaska Commercial Company, made it far easier to kill moose, which were difficult to stalk at close range with less effective arms. The rifles also made it possible to kill larger numbers of caribou. As a result, Indians shifted away from cooperative, communal hunting techniques, such as the use of long caribou fences, into which whole bands, howling and running, drove the reindeer herds. As such practices disappeared, fewer hunters took larger numbers of animals.[93] The guns, combined with the miners' preference for moose and caribou over fish, may have drawn some Indian groups away from fishing toward more big-game market hunting.[94] But caribou herds' migration patterns were unpredictable, and slight shifts left Indians without this major source of food. U.S. Army Captain P. H. Ray found Native peoples starving near Fort Yukon in December 1897. "They report that the caribou migration did not come their way and that the fish catch last fall was almost an entire failure."[95] When the southern Yukon caribou herds shifted migration patterns around 1900, this change, combined with over-hunting along the upper Yukon, brought about a shift toward moose as the more important game species. It was a shift made both possible and necessary by the new market for meat and by better rifles.[96]

With the gold rush, Native peoples shifted their hunting and trading patterns in other, more specific ways as well. Within this general supply market, certain bands of Natives established supply connections with companies like the North American Trade & Transportation Company, delivering meat to trading posts seasonally. They built customary economic relationships with mining towns. "Our Indians came in a few days ago," Lynn Smith wrote in 1901 from Rampart, where he worked for the NAT&T. The Natives sold "lots" of meat for twenty or thirty cents a pound. In March 1899, Stewart Campbell traveled by dogsled from Fortymile to Gold Creek. He shared a cabin with a couple of Indians. "They were headed for forty mile," Campbell wrote, "with some caribou meat on sleds." A few days later he had another guest, a Tanana Indian headed home from Fortymile. Campbell explained that the Indians made the trip each spring to trade meat for flour. Native hunters brought a load of meat to Rampart City in late September 1901, but, as Lynn Smith noted, "unless it turns cold will lose it all." Maud Case's father, George, on the other hand, stored meat in an old mining shaft in the summer because, as all miners knew, the "walls are all frost."[97]

Indian supply work was not limited to gold creeks and towns, but extended all along the main routes of gold rush transportation. From the moment they came ashore at Dyea, miners on the White Pass and Chilkoot Pass Trails and on the lakes bought fish and meat from Native suppliers.[98] In 1896 Josiah Spurr frequently bought fish, ducks, moose, and berries from Indians along the upper Yukon, who approached Spurr's boat in canoes in order to conduct trade.[99] James Cooper and others traded for jerked caribou, marten skins, and goat meat. "Have mt. sheep for supper," he wrote, "positively the finest meat I ever tasted, got it from the Indians on the Big Salmon River." "Indians very foxy on trade," he added.[100] Frank Purdy traded with Indians for moose meat near McQuesten Creek, up the Stewart River. "They are very sharp in trading," he wrote, "knowing the value of things surprisingly well."[101] At St. Michael at the mouth of the Yukon, Eskimos brought ptarmigan, fresh salmon, and trout down the coast from the Unalakleet River to sell to miners and settlers.[102] All of the frustrated steamboat passengers frozen in on the lower Yukon in the winter of 1897–98 traded with local bands for fresh meat. Walter Curtin's boatload of grumpy shut-ins traded flour and food for fish with a band from nearby Russian Mission, as did the crews of at least two nearby steamers.[103] "Each man buys his own birds from the Siwashes," Walter Curtin explained when visiting a neighboring steamer camp, "and when he gets hungry . . . roasts it at the fire."[104] "We were almost entirely dependent on native men for fresh moose meat" during the winter, "and on women for moccasins," reported Captain John Cantwell, wintering his ship on the Dall River.[105] His crew also bought fresh meat and fish throughout the year, at prices from fifty cents to a dollar per pound for meat, and twenty-five cents a pound for dried salmon, grouse, and ptarmigan. Cantwell's men also advanced flour and other supplies to local bands, to be paid for later with meat and fish.[106]

These increased harvests by both Indian suppliers and white miners took their toll on caribou, moose, and other wildlife populations after the turn of the century. Game became scarce in densely occupied areas, particularly around Dawson City. The moose population first increased as the caribou shifted elsewhere, but then the moose came under greater hunting pressure and declined.[107] Historian Robert McCandless estimates that with a 1904 population of 9,000 people, Dawson City consumed about 600 moose and 2,300 caribou in a year. In 1899 and 1900, with a population of over 15,000, the gold miners would have consumed far greater numbers.[108] After John Cantwell sent men out to hunt moose in February 1900 or 1901, he wrote that the "persistent hunting of the animal in the vicinity of Dall River has no doubt driven it into less accessible localities, and the few killed hereabouts are probably stragglers."[109] Hunting was not the only factor in decreasing wildlife populations. Forest cutting and massive forest fires "devastated" the Yukon valley, destroying habitat and driving game farther from the mines. Native hunters complained of having to travel farther and farther to find meat.[110] McCandless's history of Yukon wildlife notes "a general widespread decline in game and fur bearers" with the Klondike rush.[111] One Mounted Police inspector wrote in 1899 that "A great many moose were brought to town during the past summer and sold. . . . The Game Ordinance was not enforced here last summer. This I think was a mistake as if the quantity of moose that was brought in last summer is brought in every year very few will shortly exist in the country."[112]

Such shortages had limited impact on miners' diets, as improvements in transportation and cold storage ensured their access to fresh foods imported from Seattle, San Francisco, and beyond. In addition, most white miners left the Yukon within a year or two of arrival and thus remained unaffected by wildlife declines. The impact on Native peoples proved more serious. Yukon miners eventually brought chaos and dislocation to much of Native life, especially to bands directly in the miners' path, which included the Tagish and Inland Tlingit at the upper lakes and along the Upper Yukon, and the Han around Dawson City and Fortymile. The Han, who fished at the site of Dawson City, experienced what anthropologist Cornelius Osgood describes as "one of the more concentrated invasions of white men into the north that history has recorded."[113] Within a very brief time, the Han bands and their neighbors gained and then lost a large and profitable market for their meat and fish, and with it a key source of cash and trade goods. Depleted wildlife populations disrupted Native subsistence patterns, and the white hunters and fishers who remained in the goldfields competed with Natives for those resources that remained, for specific fishing sites, and for the right to sell food to miners.[114] In 1902 a Mounted Police officer notified the Dawson Fish Inspector that two "Frenchmen" with licenses were shipping fish to Dawson from Little Salmon Lake, a lake "much resorted to by Indians" as one of their summer camps. The Indians complained that it was "not right for these white men to come there as the lake belongs to them, and that if they continue fishing they—the Indians—will not be able to catch enough to keep them from starving."[115]

As long as the miners' demand for fresh local food remained high and local wildlife remained abundant, the Indians' niche in the supply economy remained flexible and profitable. But the gold mining economy was too short-lived and unstable to sustain that niche, and when the bulk of the gold miners left for home, Native hunters and fishers found themselves shunted aside in the economy that remained. At certain key harvest sites, most notably the Klondike, white fishers did more than compete with Indians; they displaced them. When Josiah Spurr floated past the Klondike in 1896, before the Klondike strike, he noted a Han fishing camp of about two hundred. "At the time we were there most of the male Indians were stationed along the river, eagerly watching for the first salmon to leap out of the water."[116] Fish sold for as much as two dollars a pound early in the season, but the price dropped to twenty-five cents in mid-summer.[117] Two years later, James McRae railed at the nets of "Dagoes and Frenchmen" stretched across every available spot. McRae revealed more than his sense of ethnicity; he revealed the absence of Native fishers, a particular problem for the Han, who depended more on fish than on caribou and moose.[118] The Canadian police removed the Han from the Dawson site and placed them on a government reserve down the river at Moosehide. From there, the Han actively traded and worked in Dawson, but they lived separately.[119] The displacement had clear effects. As Charlene Porsild points out, Spurr observed two hundred Indians at the mouth of the Klondike in 1897, but in 1901 there were only eighty-one people living at Moosehide.[120] Even where Natives continued to fish and hunt in accustomed places, they did so alongside whites. "An Indian has just left me . . . as he had a salmon camp a few hundred feet from my cabin," Hunter Fitzhugh wrote from near Rampart City in July 1900. "I like to be near the Indians. They are good neighbors and are always finding something queer in the way of fish or animals—I mean flesh. The salmon are running now, and I saw an Indian woman catch two yesterday, one weighing 45 pounds and the other 25. I will set a net too, and catch a lot this summer." A month later he reported catching "a great many salmon," up the river. "Every day I go up to my nets and take out from three to ten salmon weighing between 12 and 30 pounds."[121]

Indians not only found themselves squeezed out of fishing sites, they also faced competition when they went to sell their fish. White suppliers sold meat and fish as well, and thus sought to exclude Indian sellers in order to maximize their own gains. As a result, Natives were pushed to the social and economic margins of white northern society.[122] Although the white population of the upper Yukon and Alaska dropped considerably after 1900, the competition for fish continued. After all, there were fewer whites buying fish, so they were more easily supplied by a few white fishers. The Indians' supply niche, established in the population boom of the initial rush, slowly closed.

The gold rush affected how, where, and why Native peoples hunted, fished, and marketed their catch, but it also changed the Indians' own connections to nature through the foods that they themselves consumed. Although some Yukon bands had incorporated European foodstuffs into their diet before 1897, the scope and scale of Indians' use of imported foods increased dramatically with the Klondike rush. According to Cornelius Osgood, who studied the Han in the twentieth century, the rush began an "almost complete displacement of the aboriginal foods by the ones sold in stores."[123] Natives continued to hunt and fish, but they sold fish and game to miners for flour, bacon, tea, sugar, butter, syrup, and dried fruit.[124] These exchanges proved far from even. Miners expanded their resource base and their food supplies by eating salmon and caribou and berries, the richest and most nutritious foods the northern ecosystem had to offer. Indians benefited from flour and sugar and crackers in that they took much less labor to procure and were less seasonal and perishable than local foods. Because they often lacked cash, however, Native peoples adopted only the most inexpensive foods of the miners' diet rather than the more expensive and nutritious imported foods. As miners' tables grew richer and their health improved, the Indians' tables and their health grew poorer.[125]

Native peoples not only lacked the whites' formidable resources and outside support, they also faced repeated waves of infectious diseases that, in combination with shifting subsistence patterns and food supplies, left them susceptible to ill health and social disintegration. Yukon Indians had had no historical exposure to Euro-American diseases, and thus no biological immunities or defenses. As Frederick Schwatka noted, the Yukon was "a great thoroughfare for contagious disease."[126] Epidemics swept the Yukon interior at contact and throughout the fur trade period, reducing an interior population estimated between seven to nine thousand people to about three or four thousand people by 1895.[127] The great influx of white miners in 1897 and 1898 brought new epidemics, including measles, influenza, diphtheria, dysentery, and typhoid.[128] Native peoples' work in the supply economy brought them directly into the paths of these diseases. As they moved in and out of mining camps and towns, selling and trading for food, they were constantly exposed to illness, which prevented further hunting and fishing. This led to ongoing cycles of sickness and hunger and to increased reliance on Euro-American store-bought food. Angela Sidney, a Native Yukoner born in 1902, recounted how her parents lost four young children to a German measles epidemic at Skagway in 1898. "Oh . . . lots of kids died off, they say, in Juneau and all over," Sidney recalled her mother saying. Her father was working as a packer on the trails. "They're freighting over the summit toward Bennett," Sidney explained in an oral history. "They get paid for packing stuff, flour, soap, everything like that."[129]

The intersection between Euro-American food, disease, and culture among Native Yukoners was borne out in a tragic story from 1898 told by Yukon elder Kitty Smith. According to her story, a Tagish family at Marsh Lake (adjacent to Tagish Lake and on the main route to Dawson) came across a miner's cabin and found some baking powder in a can. They had some flour, and used the baking powder to make bread. The can contained arsenic, however, which miners used to refine gold, and a young boy and his grandfather died from eating the bread. One version of events recognized this as an accident. Another saw it as deliberate poisoning. Four Athapaskan men avenged the deaths, killing one white prospector and wounding another. The Mounted Police quelled this "uprising" by arresting and trying them for murder at Dawson; two died in the hospital, and two were hanged. Members of the immediate band came home to Marsh Lake to deal with the tragedy, but were caught up in an influenza epidemic. Many of them, including Smith's own mother, died as well: "She came back to Marsh Lake that time the rush started. Dawson was just full of white man! Nobody knows what kind of sickness Indians got. They just got sick. *Lots* of people died at Marsh Lake. That's the time she died, too."[130]

Sickness swept the lower Yukon as well. John Cantwell and the crew of the *Nunivak* traded with Indians at the Dall River in 1899 and 1900. Cantwell reported that the Indians suffered unduly in the middle of the winter from lack of food. Native groups often went through periods of starvation or near-starvation in late winter when stored food resources dwindled, but Cantwell observed that some sort of illness, characterized by rashes and skin disease, had prevented them from catching and storing the fish that usually saw them through until the late-winter hunt. Cantwell provided the Indians with food, but felt they had to work for it, inducing some to cut wood for the Revenue Cutter. This was unsatisfactory to Cantwell, however, who found them "shiftless" and unwilling to work hard for the food they needed.[131] Just downriver at Rampart City in December 1903, Lynn Smith described the Indians trading furs at the NAT&T store as suffering from an unidentified disease. They were "half starved and almost naked all sore eyed and jerking with disease. Leprosy or something of that order."[132]

In the summer of 1900, American officials at St. Michael made a valiant effort to prevent smallpox from reaching the mouth of the Yukon and spreading upriver. They quarantined all incoming ships and fumigated the mail. But they could not control all diseases. While smallpox was contained, measles spread a thousand miles up the river from the coast, followed by a wave of pneumonia. Cantwell reported Indians "dying like flies" as he traveled upriver with supplies for the sick in August 1900. He saw much evidence of suffering, including corpses left unburied at Native camps. When he arrived at Dog Fish Village, he found only seven survivors of twenty-seven people he had met before.[133] He also saw empty Indian food caches, which indicated a lack of food stored for the winter, due to illness.[134] There were dysentery, typhoid, and smallpox outbreaks, nonetheless, at Nome in 1899 and 1900, as the city was plagued by sewage and garbage, and had no drainage ditches.[135] In the summer of 1900 whites fled Nome by ocean steamer, but Native peoples, according to Fred G. Kimball, died "like poisoned rats."[136]

FOOD AND CONSEQUENCES

As the Native Yukoners' subsistence practices, food supplies, and health all deteriorated, gold miners, some of them at least, thrived. They found themselves surrounded by a more and more complete version of their familiar industrial diets, right down to the roast beef and ice cream. One of Asahel Curtis's more lighthearted Alaskan photographs, taken in 1913, shows the six children of a Yukon River woodchopper, in summer hats, holding fresh slices of watermelon.[137] Watermelon, like roast beef and fresh eggs, came from nature, and in consuming it, those children forged linkages to far-distant people and far-distant natures. They also embraced culture, both that of traditional picnic treats, and that of the industrial economy which made it possible to eat watermelon in Alaska. Whatever its source, most likely Washington or California, the children's watermelon traveled a great distance from the field in which it grew through a complex set of networks and exchanges, at great costs in money and energy, to end up at a picnic along the Yukon's banks, where the trees were cut away to fuel the boats that carried watermelons. The value and importance of gold production in their culture and economy meant that miners had at their command the infrastructure, capital, and relentless energy of the industrialized world. At the dinner table, they easily and readily consumed that world, and all of the natures from which it drew its wealth, so that they might turn their bodies to the production of gold. Everything that they consumed connected them to nature and to other human beings, whether local or far away. Everything that they consumed brought consequences, as well, for Native peoples along the Yukon, for wildlife populations, and for the distant natures and laborers that produced their food. A complete accounting of those consequences is impossible, however, without consideration of yet another place which shaped, and was shaped by, the consumption at the heart of the gold rush economy: Seattle.

7

THE NATURE & CULTURE

OF SEATTLE

I n the spring of 1898, a gold miner bound for the Yukon walked into
Stetson Brothers in Seattle, Washington, and spent $517.16 on mining
supplies. O. S. Johnson's purchases, remarkable only in that his manuscript record of them has survived to this day, ranged from the usual bacon,
flour, rice, and evaporated potatoes to a rip saw, claw hammer, shovel, camp
stove, needles, and yarn. He bought rubber boots, suspenders, blankets, a
rifle, and, of course, a gold pan.[1] When Johnson purchased supplies, packed
them on his back over the Chilkoot Pass, and consumed them along the
gold creeks, those supplies placed him at the center of a network of connections to nature which led in all directions. They led to the wheat and
potato fields, rice paddies, and hog farms which produced the food, and to
the farmers who labored in those places. Others led to flour mills and meat-
packing plants, cotton fields, rubber plantations, and iron mines. Still others led to processing plants, rifle factories, rail yards and shipyards, and to
workers who transformed raw natural resources into marketable commodities for sale to gold seekers in Seattle. Yet Johnson and gold miners like
him did not have to go to all those places and all those natures to assemble
what they needed to produce gold. Seattle did that for them.

As hundreds like Johnson poured into and out of the city on their way
north and on their return trips south, Seattle's business community turned
its wealth and capital, its warehouses, buildings, railroads, banks, wharves,
ships, and streets, to the work of supplying miners and buying their gold.

The city's economy, with its linkages to the national economy, made it possible for miners to outfit themselves quickly and to forge all of the real, material connections to nature and labor contained in their long lists of needed supplies. But that economy also made it possible for the miners to ignore those connections. For the crowds of gold seekers on Seattle's streets in 1897 and 1898, food, clothing, and tools came not from distant farms and factories, and not from nature and human labor, but simply from Seattle. For Johnson and his fellow gold miners there was, in the words of William Cronon, "no need to wonder where such things came from—how they had been created, by whom, from what materials, with what consequences for the place in which they had been made."[2] The city's boosters and businessmen made Seattle's markets seem the only possible source of pork and beans, potatoes, rubber boots, blankets, rifles, and gold pans. At the same time, through a thoroughgoing advertising campaign to establish the city's prominence in supplying miners, the city's promoters naturalized the gold rush supply trade. They made it seem as though Seattle was the *natural* source of mining supplies. Through those naturalizations, Seattle's commercial leaders made claims about nature and the natural that left real, material connections to real nature and labor increasingly unimportant. Their claims about the nature of Seattle left the city's industrial economic culture out of the picture. As industrial consumers of food and supplies, however, and as industrial producers of gold, the miners remained immersed in that culture, and, as ever, irrevocably connected to nature.[3]

Meanwhile, Seattle saw some wild times. When the first shipload of happy Klondike miners unloaded their gold at Seattle docks on July 17, 1897, excited crowds surged through the streets to greet the returning miners and then to supply themselves to follow the golden trail north. Seattle's growing trade with Alaska and the Yukon exploded. The *Seattle Post-Intelligencer* headline said it all: "Gold! Gold! Gold! Gold!" A few inches down the front page, the paper listed the supplies necessary to go to the Klondike. The city emptied out. "They Are All Going," the *P-I* exclaimed, "The Population Preparing to Move to Klondike." Steamers left on July 18, 19, 22, 23, 25, 27, 28, 31, and August 2, 3, 5, 7, 9, 10, 12, and 13.[4] The Seattle Chamber of Commerce estimated, perhaps quite liberally, that eight thousand miners left Puget Sound in the fall of 1897, with the initial wave of the rush. The city's suppliers and shippers brought in sixteen million dollars in the last few months of 1897 alone, an amount equal to all of their business in 1896.[5] A reporter noted a few days later that "A delivery wagon rolling up the street does not usually attract any attention. Yesterday one loaded to its fullest capacity with tents was almost overturned by the curiosity it inspired. The tents were all marked Dyea. That was enough to set the crowds wild."[6] "Prosperity is Here," the *Post-Intelligencer* announced, with news of economic recovery from Seattle to New York.[7] The Seattle *Trade Register* commented on the political implications: "Free silver isn't in these days with free gold." The trade paper added, to sum it up, "The country wears a great, big smile."[8]

Through the winter and early spring of 1898, hundreds of gold-hungry miners arrived in Seattle, eager to outfit themselves with the requisite sleds, stoves, bacon, flour, and apricots, and ship out for the Chilkoot and Skagway Trails. The streets became an open miners' market, choked with men, dogs, sleds, tools, and endless sacks of flour. As Bill Ballou wrote, "all the stores have their K.[londike] departments. . . . hotels are all K. houses and fellows give their girls K. nugget breast pins."[9] In January, February, and March 1898, steamers left Seattle in droves as waves of miners, fifteen thousand of them, headed north. Two thousand miners departed in a week in January, with "hundreds arriving daily by all trains."[10] On March 11, the Great Northern and Northern Pacific Railroads together deposited thirty-five coaches of passengers, eighteen hundred people, on Seattle's doorstep. That weekend fifteen hundred left for Alaska. After the ice broke at the Yukon's mouth, another wave of miners and supplies headed for St. Michael, along with "no end of river craft for prospecting and freighting."[11] Seattle thus supplied up to two thousand pounds of goods apiece to well over twenty-five thousand miners in 1897 and 1898, more, according to Seattle boosters, than any other city. Wholesale grocers alone took in $6.5 million.[12] In a year, clearings at eight banks increased from $33.3 million to $67.3 million.[13]

The miners themselves marveled at the crowds, the activity, and the frenzied consumption. Hunter Fitzhugh, having already spent a winter up north, arrived at Seattle's Hotel Northern the first week of January 1898 and bragged to his family at home. "I am besieged by dozens of people who call at the hotel to talk to me about the trail. . . . On all subjects as snow-shoes, moccasins, camp fires . . . I am standard authority. . . . They are all going crazy about Alaska."[14] Stewart Campbell reported on February 7, 1898, "Everything hustling for the Gold Rush. Carloads of people and freight arriving all the time."[15] Bill Ballou wrote home on March 29—with the Spanish American War brewing—that "Seattle is all Klondike, everybody and everything pertains to it nothing is talked or thought of but Klondike, the war question takes a second place. . . ."[16] Mac McMichael visited Vancouver and Victoria in Canada before outfitting in Seattle. "This is a busy town," he wrote. "Vancouver and Victoria were like country villages in comparison. At all times the streets are like Woodward Avenue on Saturday nights."[17] After two weeks, though, McMichael had had enough. "I shall be glad to get away from 'Klondike Supplies,' 'Alaska Outfitting' and the hundreds of other signs which have been staring us in the face so long."[18] Miners had plenty of complaints, many of them justified, about the swindles perpetrated on Klondike-bound consumers. Bill Ballou didn't mind, though. "I like Seattle," he reported, "all its different fakirs trying to sell you a gold washer, a K. stove, or a dog team with one lame dog which would get well by tomorrow."[19]

Seattle merchants prided themselves not only on their bustling streets, but on the speed with which the city's "20 or more first-class outfitting houses" could assemble supplies for the smallest and the largest parties of gold seekers. Miners looked to outfitters for a range of clothing, food, and equipment, and Seattle retailers captured their business by organizing that consumption. They marketed complete outfits as single units so that miners did not have to go to a long list of different retailers to purchase all their individual items. As early as July 1897, Z. C. Miles, Fischer Brothers, and the Seattle Trading Company ran advertisements for "Complete Alaska Outfits," and Seattle Trading printed special forms for Alaska outfitting, listing all necessary supplies; miners simply read down the columns and checked off their purchases. The Columbia Grocery Company put together outfits for fifty-six miners from Lancaster, Wisconsin, in only twenty-seven hours.[20] The Seattle *Trade Register* celebrated these retail achievements with a typical photograph of miners perched five feet off the ground on piles of sacks and boxes stretching fifty yards along a storefront, bearing signs that read: "Alaska supplies."[21] Such scenes, however, had not always been so common.

THE NATURE OF SEATTLE

When Josiah Spurr traveled down the Yukon in 1896 for the U.S. Geological Survey, Native Alaskans at the future site of Rampart City, Alaska, spoke a few telling words of English. These included "yes," "no," "steamboat," and "San Francisco," this last term, Spurr explained, "being . . . a general name for the world of the white men."[22] Before the Alaska-Yukon gold rush, San Francisco stood for the "outside" world. It was the gateway city, the entrance and the exit, the place you had to go first and last on your way to or from Alaska and the Yukon.[23] San Francisco organized Euro-Americans' consumption and production in Alaska and the Yukon. The city's storekeepers sold the supplies that miners, fur sealers, and fishers needed to consume in the north country, and bought the miners' gold, furs, and fish when they returned. With the gold rush, however, Seattle emerged as the most prominent urban gateway to Alaska and the Yukon, the new place to stop on the way north, the new name for the first stop on the way back to the outside world. Seattle came to command the markets which sold the supplies that miners consumed, and Seattle bought the gold that the miners produced.[24]

During the gold rush, the Seattle Chamber of Commerce led a more than energetic campaign to secure Seattle's status as the commercial gateway to Alaska and the Yukon. Fearful that San Francisco, Portland, Victoria, or Vancouver would capture the nation's attention and the miners' business, the Chamber's campaign worked to advertise the city's superiority as a supplier of mining supplies, to demonstrate Seattle's superior transportation network, and to secure a federal assay office to buy and refine raw gold. The city's commercial boosters also declared Seattle the *natural* gateway to the northern goldfields.

This particularly focused group of boosters, led by journalist Erastus Brainerd, defined the city's gold rush boom as more than the expression of an industrial market economy in action. They declared it an expression of natural law. Just as Americans and others defined gold and gold money as naturally valuable by decree of God or nature, so, too, Seattle boosters and journalists, and miners as well, anointed the city the divine and naturally ordained gateway to the Yukon's great store of golden wealth. Naturalizations of gold made gold mining seem the natural thing to do. Naturalizations of Seattle made Seattle the natural place to buy supplies, the natural place to travel en route to the Yukon and Alaska, and the natural place to sell raw gold. Thus Seattle's economic growth took on a hallowed status, ordained by nonhuman forces such as nature or destiny. "The hand of destiny seems to guide to sure and certain success," the *Trade Register* argued in July 1898, "for she has opened up to the world the great Alaskan gold fields, the pathway to which lies directly through the heart of the Queen City."[25] With its gateway status made clear, Seattle so successfully routed gold and supplies through its streets and across its wharves that the city's Alaska-Yukon trade, which was a thoroughly cultural exchange of commodities within a

capitalist economy, quickly came to seem a naturally occurring phenomenon, integral to Seattle's very being. "Seattle is the gateway to Alaska," read
an article in the *National Magazine of Boston* in June 1900. "You may get
there by way of other west coast cities, but you will be as a man using a side
door."[26]

As with naturalizations of gold, however, naturalizations of Seattle's gold
rush economy masked the real connections to nature and labor, and to the
nation's industrial economy, that underlay the city's success. The language
and imagery of those arguments papered over the markets, institutions, and
sheer human labor, the East Coast buying trips, full warehouses, new docks,
and brick buildings, which actually did make Seattle the gateway city to
Alaska and the Yukon. The industrial economy that defined Seattle's growth
at the turn of the twentieth century certainly transformed the natural world
in Alaska and elsewhere, but that economy itself was anything but natural.
It was the creation of an industrial, capitalist culture, of an industrial people
prone to creating powerful naturalizations. Those naturalizations distanced
them from the cultural assumptions and economic connections that defined
their relationship to the natural world.

From the moment news of the Klondike gold strike reached Seattle's
docks, city businessmen and boosters actively naturalized the city as the pre-
ordained gateway to the newfound land of gold. These naturalizations took
several forms, including printed language, advertisements, other promotional materials, drawings, cartoons, and maps. Some newspaper articles
stated the situation outright. A 1900 trade summary declared that "Seattle
has, in fact, by a most natural order of things, become the great northern
territory's emporium and metropolis."[27] Other reporters chose nature
metaphors to explain the city's growth. In December 1897, four months into
the gold rush, the Seattle *Argus* used such metaphors to place the gold rush
boom in relation to other sources of economic growth. "The sudden
change," the *Argus* stated, "was wrought by a fast-swelling stream of
gold. . . . but the sight of it, and the news of it, brought forth other streams
from the many hidden sources . . . and they all flowed towards Seattle."[28]
In addition to employing nature metaphors, the *Argus* author also included
a more historical explanation of good fortune. History and nature were at
work together:

The current had set strongly towards Seattle, for the people of that city had
been working for years and dug their channels wide and deep, foreseeing what

a great stream might flow through them. . . . year by year it grew in volume . . . until now . . . it has become a mighty torrent. For trade, like water, follows the line of least resistance, and when the laws of nature, seconded by the energy of man, have cleared the way for it, flows along the channel thus created, and any obstacles placed in its way in defiance of natural law will give way before it as the ramparts of sand before the incoming tide.

The author continued to use nature metaphors as the editorial concluded, stating that "Seattle had been wide awake and had made ready to grab the ripening plum when it should drop from the tree."[29]

Thus the first step in gaining a monopoly of the Alaska-Yukon supply trade was to claim that Seattle already had it, by nature. "Alaskan Trade Absolutely Controlled by this City," the *Post-Intelligencer* declared on July 25, 1897, a week after the first gold arrived. "Naturally and inevitably," the paper explained, "the great bulk of adventurers who propose to seek fortune . . . will flock to Seattle."[30] "Why Outfit in Seattle?" the paper asked in the summer of 1898. It answered, "This City the Natural Supply Base." "By sheer force of circumstances Seattle has come to be well recognized . . . as the natural point of supply and departure for the Klondike and all Alaska mining points. . . . This is but the natural result of natural causes."[31] The campaign to secure a federal assay office in Seattle naturalized the city as the best location for such an institution. "Seattle, being the outfitting point for the Yukon and the port of departure and arrival for the steamers plying to Alaskan ports," the Seattle *Argus* asserted, "is the natural market for the great quantities of gold which will come thence during the next few years. The location of an assay office here is therefore the logical outcome of the city's position."[32]

Seattle's trade press and business community next extended their naturalizations of the city's economic prominence well beyond the gold rush trade. As the national economy recovered from the depression of the 1890s, Seattle's economy boomed across the board. This rapid economic growth, too, fell under the increasingly common rubric of the natural. By the turn of the century, the city found itself exporting increasing amounts of wheat, flour, and lumber to the United Kingdom, Peru, Chile, Hawaii, Tahiti, and Japan, coal and lumber to San Francisco, and shingles and salmon east by rail to Chicago and beyond, as well as to South Africa and Australia. The amount of wheat and flour shipped from Seattle and Tacoma doubled between 1899 and 1900, reaching over 14 million bushels—a close approach to Portland's 17.7 million bushels.[33] Imports boomed as well. A 1900 trade report even went so far as to declare that with new Japanese export and import connections, "Seattle is a natural rice center." By the middle of 1900, the city stood second only to San Francisco among Pacific ports in exports and imports, and was listed the tenth most active city in the nation. All of this "tremendous" economic growth, the *Trade Register* declared, "is not one of accident; it is one of absolute commercial naturalness."[34] "We are not building upon any chance or happy accident," claimed the *Post-Intelligencer*, "but on a foundation furnished by nature herself and guaranteed by all the laws of trade."[35]

Beyond headlines, articles, and promotional tracts, Seattle newspapers deployed hundreds of cartoons, drawings, and pictorial advertisements which naturalized the city's commercial strengths in general, and its gateway status for Alaska and the Yukon. Newspaper drawings depicted gates of every variety, often labeled "Seattle" or "Gateway to Alaska," with long columns of miners, laden with supplies, marching through those gateways toward a golden Alaskan sunset. Such images meshed well with the papers' headlines, such as that of October 3, 1897: "Seattle Opens the Gate to the Klondike Gold Fields." Beyond straightforward gateway images, newspaper artists, like writers, deployed natural metaphors to describe the sudden wealth pouring into the city. A January 1898 cartoon showed dollar coins, having sprouted wings like birds, flying in dense flocks into Seattle. An image a few months later showed a man with a huge watering can marked "Gold" watering a scraggly tree labeled "Prosperity." The caption read "Arbor Day in Seattle."[36] Shifting to the increasingly common metaphor of physical union between a female Seattle and a male Klondike, the *Post-Intelligencer* in July 1898 reported the summer's return of gold-laden Yukon and Alaska miners with a special edition. The front page featured a large illustration in which a rugged "King Klondike" empties a huge sack of gold into the lap of the female "Seattle," the "Queen City" (fig. 7.1).[37]

Seattle's press continued its claims to natural power over Alaska and the Klondike in published maps of the region. Illustrators of maps naturalized the city's power and its command of the trade by inscribing that power on depictions of the physical space itself. A newspaper illustration from November 1897 shows a map of the gulf of Alaska, tightly bounded by the curve of the Northwest coast, with Skagway, Dawson, and the Yukon River clearly marked (fig. 7.2). In the center of the map sits a large steamship, the *City of Seattle*, filling the entire gulf. Here the city, in the form of a steamer,

King Klondike Pours His Treasure Into the Lap of the Queen City.

FIG. 7.1. "King Klondike." This metaphoric image naturalized the relationship between the Klondike and Seattle, the Queen City. It depicts a physical union of the royal couple as King Klondike pours his golden wealth into the lap of Queen Seattle. A steamship, undoubtedly bearing more gold, approaches from the golden north. (*Seattle Post-Intelligencer*, July 21, 1898)

thoroughly dominates the geography of the gold rush. The *Post-Intelligencer* reprinted a map from the popular magazine *Judge*. It shows the United States with the face of Uncle Sam formed out of the shape of the state of Washington. Upon his head sits the crown of Alaska, with a garland of the Klondike. The caption declares "U.S. Crowned with Gold."[38]

In drawing prospective miners to Seattle, guidebook and promotional

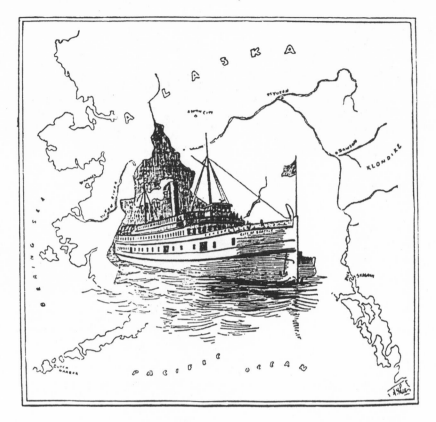

FIG. 7.2. "City of Seattle." Maps as well as cartoons and drawings naturalized Seattle's place as the gateway city to Alaska and the Yukon. Here a steamer named *City of Seattle* dominates the geographic space within which the gold rush unfolded, linking all the key locations through which miners traveled. (*Seattle Post-Intelligencer*, November 29, 1897)

maps were never simply maps. Boosters in San Francisco, Portland, and Tacoma also mapped the Northwest in different ways as part of their promotional attempts to establish the true and natural gateway city. In early 1898, news of the rival cities' efforts arrived at Erastus Brainerd's Seattle office. "Seattle's rivals are in the field," wrote Brainerd's business associate Eugene Higgins in a letter from New York. "The ticket bookers have books on the Klondyke with maps showing *Portland only* as a starting point."[39] In late 1897 the *Tacoma Daily News* ran headlines and drawings which claimed

FIG. 7.3. Like Seattle, Tacoma sought to capture the business of miners bound to Alaska and the Yukon by claiming that the city was already the gateway to the golden north. Seattle papers ran with the same exact headlines. (*Tacoma Daily News*, December 14, 1897)

gateway status, and also published a map—an age-old ploy—which showed all the major national railroads converging on Tacoma. The caption on the map, much like the paper's headline (fig. 7.3), read "Tacoma the Gateway City—All the Great Railroads Lead to Tacoma." Seattle had pulled the same gag just weeks earlier with a map entitled "Seattle the Gateway—All Great Rail Lines Lead to Seattle" (fig. 7.4) It showed all of the same railroads converging on Seattle instead of Tacoma.[40] Neither map was accurate. "Look at your map!" another advertisement demanded. "Seattle is a commercial city, and is to the Pacific Northwest as New York is to the Atlantic coast. All railroads in United States connect with three great transcontinental lines running to Seattle." "Every steamship line but one leaves Seattle," the paper continued. "You must go there before you can get to Alaska. Do not be deceived by misleading or false statements to the contrary."[41] All of this, according to the *Trade Register*, "made plain all over the United States" the "general conviction" that Seattle "was the starting point for Alaska and the return point from Alaska."[42]

Advertising, rather than nature, explained the success of Brainerd's campaign. The Chamber of Commerce spared no expense in harnessing the power of advertising to link Seattle with the gold rush. Brainerd placed adver-

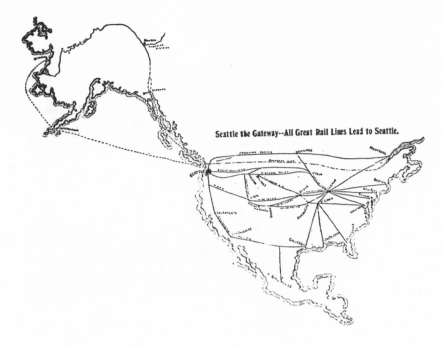

Seattle the Gateway--All Great Rail Lines Lead to Seattle.

FIG. 7.4. End of the Line. Seattle citizens naturalized their location as the Gateway City to Alaska in newspaper headlines and illustrations by claiming the city's geographic position as the end of the line for all major transcontinental rail lines. Compare this image with map 3 (p. 46). (*Seattle Post-Intelligencer*, October 13, 1897)

tisements in 6,244 weekly newspapers, consisting mainly of three words linked together in bold print: Seattle, Klondike, Alaska. He ran a larger, five-inch advertisement in daily papers in Butte and Anaconda, Montana—mining centers—and in Denver, Chicago, and St. Paul. In December 1898, he followed up with quarter-page advertisements in several national magazines, including *McClure's, Cosmopolitan, Harper's,* and *Century.* The Seattle Bureau of Information, the Chambers' key committee on the Alaska trade, also distributed over 200,000 copies of a special Klondike edition of the *Seattle Post-Intelligencer,* mailing it to postmasters and libraries in cities all over the country. Ten thousand went to the Great Northern Railroad, and five thousand to the Northern Pacific.[43] The advertising campaigns of 1897 and 1898 succeeded. They declared that the supply-hungry miners already in Seattle were there by nature. In doing so, they drew even larger crowds to town. Despite the frequent naturalizations of Seattle's mining supply economy, however, these miners did not appear in Seattle by nature or because of natural law.

THE CULTURE OF SEATTLE

Seattle won gateway status during the gold rush in part because of advertising, but also because the city had in previous years linked itself to markets, manufacturers, and a transportation network that made it possible, by 1897 and 1898, for miners traveling through Seattle to succeed as industrial consumers. Those commercial networks did not emerge either naturally or instantaneously with the Klondike gold strike. They had grown slowly through the 1880s and 1890s as investors from across the nation and the world poured capital into the railroads, ships, buildings, and urban infrastructure necessary to an industrial gateway city. Before the 1890s, San Francisco commanded key railroad supply networks, a rich agricultural hinterland, and the only regular Alaska steamer line, the Pacific Coast Steamship Company. Trader John Callbreath's buying patterns revealed San Francisco's and Seattle's relative positions in the West Coast trade hierarchy of the 1870s, 1880s, and 1890s. Callbreath ran trading posts along the Stikine River and in the Cassiar and Dease Creek areas of interior British Columbia. For years before the Klondike gold rush, Callbreath depended on merchants and bankers in Victoria, San Francisco, Portland, and Seattle to supply his posts. Because Callbreath did most of his business with gold miners and fur traders in Canada, he banked and deposited gold dust in Victoria. His annual buying trips for groceries, clothing, and hardware, however, took him farther south. Records of his 1878 spring trip, for instance, indicated heavy purchases in San Francisco, at establishments that included Cutting and Company wholesale foods, Levi Strauss and Company, and Goodyear Rubber Company. He bought apples and bread in Portland, liquors, drugs, and dry goods in Victoria, and everything from two thousand pounds of onions to silk handkerchiefs in San Francisco. His order books listed only three Seattle purchases that year: cheap jewelry, dried beef, and salt pork.[44]

Over the next fifteen years, however, Callbreath recorded more and more transactions in Seattle. He came to depend exclusively on Moran Brothers' Shipbuilding for hardware for his beleaguered river steamer, and after 1890 was a regular customer of Schwabacher Brothers grocery and hardware supplies, ordering a wide range of items by mail and in person: copper pipe, coal, potatoes, washers and bearings, a pump. The rise of Schwabacher Brothers and other wholesalers reflected Seattle's expanding transportation linkages: rails from the east and steamers to the north.[45] Fischer and MacDonald and Schwabacher Brothers grocers both expanded from retail to wholesale operations in 1887 and 1889. In 1893 Fischer and MacDonald became Fischer Brothers, and Schwabacher Brothers added wholesale hardware to their operations. These were the years when eastern rail links—the Northern Pacific Railroad in 1884 and the Great Northern in 1893—opened direct Seattle access to eastern producers. Fischer Brothers did most of its buying in Chicago.[46] Schwabacher Brothers initially supplied their stores from San Francisco. Once the Northern Pacific reached Seattle, however, they opened a buying office in New York, built a second warehouse, and expanded their wholesale grocery and hardware operation around the Puget Sound region.[47]

In the early and mid-1890s, the grocery supply and transportation sectors of Seattle's northern trade grew in tandem. Railroad-supplied jobbing houses and their eastern goods drew Callbreath increasingly to Seattle, and the expanding steamer network provided the other half of the transport system necessary to the Alaska trade. New boats brought goods north to Alaska and Alaskan consumers south to Seattle. The first regular steamer service between Seattle and Alaska started in 1886, and in 1891 Seattle businesses began sending salesmen and agents to Juneau. Those agents could offer consumers lower freight rates for goods, since shipping took only four days from Seattle, as opposed to seven days from San Francisco.[48] In 1892, the Pacific Coast Steamship Company moved its headquarters north from San Francisco to Tacoma, and the same year the North American Trade & Transportation Company chose Seattle as its West Coast headquarters. The North American Trade & Transportation Company brought its ships to Seattle's Elliott Bay, along with the business of supplying its trading posts at St. Michael and Fortymile. This set up direct competition between Seattle and San Francisco, which remained home to the more established Alaska Commercial Company. Much of the NAT&T's merchandise came directly from Chicago by train, but the company patronized Schwabacher Brothers and Fischer Brothers as well, helping to shift the flow of Alaskan business toward Seattle.[49] In 1894, the U.S. Postal Service switched Alaska mail service from its former coastal terminus at Port Townsend to Seattle, which improved mail orders for Seattle businesses.

John Callbreath's supply purchases reflected these developments. In 1895 Callbreath ordered peaches, fresh eggs, and navel oranges from Schwabacher

Brothers, and both Schwabacher Brothers and Fischer Brothers sent sales-men to Alaska. To save time and money, these and several other Seattle whole-salers combined forces to send a single salesman north to take orders for groceries, dry goods, drugs, and hardware.[50] That same year, with the found-ing of the Alaska Steamship Company in Seattle, the city gained its own direct Seattle-Alaska steamer line. This made it possible for Seattle merchants to compete directly with San Francisco for Alaskan markets.[51] Although Call-breath continued to patronize certain favorite San Francisco establishments, his routine orders for fresh food and bacon, as well as for hardware and ani-mal feed, went directly to Seattle's leading wholesalers. He also traveled to Seattle to buy mules, feed, and Winchester rifles. Victoria and Seattle, only a brief steamer ride apart, formed one combined market, and on buying trips Callbreath moved back and forth between them, comparing prices and patronizing specialists in both cities for various products. In March 1896 he wrote to relatives from Wrangell, at the mouth of the Stikine, "I will start for Victoria and Seattle tomorrow on the Steamer City of Topeka to buy our seasons outfit."[52]

Thus Seattle was already serving as a gateway in 1896, when minor gold strikes at Circle City and Cook Inlet spurred a two-month supply boom in Seattle, with heavy sales of lumber, animals, hardware, and food.[53] These smaller gold rushes, along with continued mining at Fortymile, turned out to be brief but significant pre-Klondike "dry runs" for Seattle merchants. Cooper & Levy grocers ran front-page advertisements in the *Post-Intelligencer* in March 1896, announcing "ALASKA. We are supplying a great many Alaska outfits."[54] "'To the Alaska Gold Fields is the cry,'" the paper reported as it listed ships bound for Cook Inlet. "No Abatement in the Rush to the Alaskan Mines: Schooner Lincoln Sets Sail. Three More to Sail Soon—Steamers Crowded Every Trip." Seattle papers also listed arriving and departing min-ers: 19 men from Pennsylvania and 16 from Michigan going to Fortymile, Six-tymile, and to Cook Inlet; 186 on the steamer *Mexico*; a crowd of 411 on the steamer *City of Topeka*; and 2,000 total going to the Cook Inlet mines.

Seattle supplied most of them. By 1897 the city's businessmen were vig-ilantly alert to the benefits of the gold-boom trade. Wholesalers sat ready at the crucial transportation junctures. Stetson Brothers—who would sup-ply O. S. Johnson in 1898—ran an advertisement stating that "The location is one of the best in the city, being within 200 ft. of the railroad depots of the roads entering the city, and is also near the landings of the various Sound and sea-going Steamers."[55] The *Post-Intelligencer* reported that "Seattle merchants . . . well know the value of the Alaska trade, and are making every effort to hold it. They have a bureau of information open at all hours, and whenever a person makes inquiries about Alaska he is told it is the best country in the world and that Seattle can furnish all supplies needed for a trip to the north."[56] Nora Crane passed through Seattle in June 1897, a month before the *Portland* arrived with the first news of the Klondike gold strike. "There is [sic] about 46 Alaska headquarters here going to Alaska is about all one hears."[57] By the spring of 1898, when new waves of customers, including Hunter Fitzhugh, came up the Stikine to John Callbreath's posts en route to the Klondike, Callbreath's business showed Seattle's wholesale and transportation sectors at work together within the Alaska trade. On May 6, he posted a letter to Schwabacher Brothers requesting by the first Pacific Coast Steamship Company steamer a large shipment of groceries, including a thousand pounds of butter and three thousand pounds of bacon and hams.[58]

THE GATEWAY BOOM

Seattle wholesalers, wholesale buyers (jobbers), retailers, and transportation agents met the demands of the gold rush by drawing on well-established trade patterns and rail, shipping, and communication networks. Those patterns and connections revealed the extent to which Seattle's boom was linked to a national industrial economy, to a continent-wide if not worldwide system of mass production. They also revealed more about where the miners' supplies came from. As the gold-hungry crowds gathered, Seattle jobbers and wholesalers like Schwabacher Brothers, Fischer Brothers, and Stetson Brothers dispatched telegraph orders and buyers east to Chicago and New York to fill their warehouses with clothing and dry goods. In September 1897, Seattle Woolen Manufacturing sent Thomas Eyanson east to buy "heavily of such lines as they do not manufacture," which would ensure the company's ability to "outfit from foot to head any man intending to go to the mines."[59] Mr. Fraser of Fraser and Wilson dry goods went "to New York and other cities" and made the "largest purchases in underwear as well as in other lines ever made by any house in the West." Mr. and Mrs. Nordhoff, buyers for the Bon Marché department store, spent two months in eastern cities the following spring; they returned to find the store moving to bigger quarters. J. Berkman and Company, Seattle's first wholesaler of "gentleman's furnishings," bought a large stock from eastern suppliers in September, especially goods required by miners.[60] Wholesale buyers had strategies beyond mere increases in stock. They ordered American brands, preferred over Canadian products by American miners in the north. Wholesalers also repackaged existing products to meet gold-related demands, creating Alaska brand names of their own. Seattle's leading grain and feed dealer, Lilly Bogardus, sold sacks of dog feed from the Chicago stockyards as "Alaska Dog Feed."[61]

Seattle jobbers met competition, however, from national companies who bypassed wholesale middlemen and instead sent agents to market their goods directly to Seattle's storefront retailers. Sprague, Warner & Company of Chicago installed an agent in the Pioneer Building, ready to sell canned goods and syrup directly. "You know that most everything comes from the east, anyway," the advertisement read, "and you can buy so much cheaper in Chicago."[62] Philip F. Kelley brokered Baker's Chocolate, Ivory Soap, and Lea and Perrin's Worcestershire Sauce. M. J. Connell was one of the city's more successful grocery agents, judging from his volume of advertising. Connell represented food processors from all over the country, including Columbus Canned Fruits, Del Monte Milling Company, Omaha Packing Company, and Crystal Salt Works. Dealers looking for these companies' products went to Connell to place orders. In May 1898, Connell announced that he had moved to a larger office due to a rapid increase in business. Such agents flocked into the city in 1897 and 1898. Charles T. Battelle brokered "eastern and California canned goods by the carloads."[63]

As the center of these networks of buying and selling, Seattle shaped what gold miners consumed, and hence how they were connected to the places in which all of these products originated. Some Seattleites extended that power through trade ties to Chicago and New York. Others built new trade and supply networks in the Yukon and Alaska, which further cemented the flow of money and goods between Seattle and its emerging northern hinterland, and further determined what miners could and would consume. Seattle supplied miners along its own First Avenue, but also through retailers in Skagway, Dyea, Dawson, and Nome, who stocked their shelves from Seattle. This ensured that when miners bought supplies in northern mining towns, the profits, and the connections to nature, spun back south through Seattle. Some of these retailers had direct ties to Seattle, including M. K. Kalem, who in 1897 moved his grocery stock from a store on Pike Street in Seattle to Dyea at the foot of the Chilkoot Trail. From there he reported that business was booming; he was always running out of goods.[64]

F. W. Hart of Dyea purchased fifty tons of merchandise in Seattle in December 1897, and thirty thousand feet of lumber.[65] Gordon & Company, a Western Avenue supplier, opened a wholesale commission house at Skagway; George R. Adams left the Alaska Transport Company, bought a grocery and outfitting stock in Seattle, and went into business at Dyea. A. A. Anderson left his job as a hardware clerk in Seattle, opened his own store at Skagway, and by 1900 had one of the largest stores there, having become "a capitalist."[66] In 1900, Seattle's expanding supply network shifted to Nome to meet the miners rushing down the Yukon River to the new goldfields on the Bering Sea. A. Dinklespeil, an outfitter on Washington Street in Seattle, shipped his whole stock to Nome in July 1899.[67] As the northern retail network expanded, Seattle became more and more a wholesale center for Alaska in general. "The outfitting will likely be done more and more by Alaska firms," the *Trade Register* speculated in 1899, "while they in turn will buy supplies mainly from Seattle jobbing houses. We will get the trade just the same."[68] The following year, Fischer Brothers opened a branch at Nome. With large shipments of goods from Seattle, it supposedly became the "northernmost wholesale store of any in the world."[69]

Seattle storekeepers and wholesalers created these economic ties to the north, but transportation companies and boat builders actually carried people and goods from place to place. The city profited from moving miners' outfits as well as selling them. "Steamer passage has to be engaged weeks before hand," Hunter Fitzhugh reported from Seattle in January 1898, "and every boat is loaded to the gunals."[70] The Pacific Coast Steamship, Alaska Steamship, and NAT&T boats on the Alaska run were quickly joined by new competitors, each of them capturing, in their chosen names, the linkages being forged between Seattle, Alaska, and the Yukon. In January 1898 "eastern capitalists" formed the Seattle & Yukon Steamship Company. Grain dealers Lilly Bogardus found partners to form the St. Louis and Alaska Transportation Company. The Alaska Transportation and Development Company arrived from Chicago, planning six modern steel ocean boats and six light Yukon steamers. Others followed: the Upper Yukon Transportation Company, the Boston and Alaska Transportation Company, the Washington and Alaska Steamship Company, and the Empire Transportation Company of Philadelphia.[71] Schwabacher Hardware's 1898 accounts ledger listed over twenty companies, most of them transport operations with names referring to the Yukon or Alaska or gold.[72]

The capital investment for all of these companies came from eastern and midwestern cities, but the new Alaska fleet itself came out of Seattle's burgeoning shipyards. Some companies bought steel steamers from the Union Iron Works in San Francisco, and from yards in Pennsylvania and New York, but Seattle produced eighty-four new vessels in 1898: fifty-seven steamers, twelve schooners, and fifteen barges.[73] In this, the city did prove to be a site of direct production, of direct human engagement with wood and steel. Moran Brothers, the leading shipyard, built twelve Yukon river sternwheelers simultaneously, including three for the NAT&T and three for the Seattle & Yukon Steamship Company. Such intense demands transformed Seattle's waterfront from a gateway entrepôt into an industrial production site, complete with labor strife. Labor conditions at Moran Brothers led to a strike in April 1898, when steam fitters and helpers walked out, demanding higher wages and a nine-hour day.[74] "There is hardly a question," the Seattle Chamber of Commerce declared in 1900, "that Seattle will continue to be the shipbuilding center of Puget Sound, and further that it will be in due time one of the shipbuilding centers of the world."[75]

With so many boats and passengers mobbing the waterfront, the city expanded and improved its wharves, roads, and sidewalks to withstand the wear and tear of thousands of feet and millions of boxes and sacks of supplies. Such improvements revealed the gold miners' connections to nature in the city itself. The wood, stone, rock, and iron that went into new infrastructure reshaped Seattle's physical landscape. In 1898 A. A. Denny announced plans for a new wharf, and Amos Brown and Schwabacher Brothers both rebuilt and extended their wharves. Large-scale improvements followed, though not necessarily for the Alaska trade alone: a realignment of all wharves on the waterfront, and a new Great Northern Railroad facility with grain elevator, docks, and warehouses. Such economic growth spread away from the steamer docks as well, with a "phenomenal increase in new buildings," from the new Denny Hotel, to the new Vulcan Iron Works manufacturing plant on the tide flats by Fifth Avenue. G. W. Folsom of the Novelty Mill Co. went off "to get a fortune to put into flour mills in Seattle."[76] Brick buildings sprung out of the ground, including a $60,000, six-story building at First and Spring, three on Second Avenue, one adjoining the Rainier-Grand Hotel, and another on the Collins Block, along with the Great Northern Railroad's new stone and brick warehouses on Jackson Street.[77] In a telling shift, the Seattle National Bank, at the corner of Yesler Way and Occidental, carved a new name over its entrance in 1899: Pacific National Bank.[78] In March 1900, Thomas Lippy, one of the first miners to strike gold in the Klondike, obtained a building permit for a $30,000, five-story brick and stone building on First Avenue South in Seattle, to be leased to a paint and glass dealer and a harness store.[79] And in 1904, a beneficiary of the 1900 gold rush at Nome, Alaska, Jafet Lindeberg, helped finance the Alaska Building, Seattle's first steel skyscraper. It became, according to historian Terrence Cole, "a symbol of the economic ties between Seattle and Alaska." The Alaska Club on the building's twelfth floor became a meeting place for Alaskan businessmen working in or visiting Seattle. Above the front door they placed a gold nugget.[80]

A MARKET IN GOLD

That gold nugget above the Alaska Building door represented more than the wealth brought to Seattle by the Alaska-Yukon trade. It also symbolized the actual gold itself. As a gateway city, Seattle had to do more than just organize industrial consumption for miners headed to its northern hinterland. It also had to become a market for the raw materials that the hinterland's industrial workers produced: timber, fish, and gold. In the midst of their efforts to supply miners as consumers, the city's bankers and other businessmen realized that the continued growth of their Alaska trade depended on drawing those same miners back to Seattle as producers and providing them with a market in which to exchange their hard-won raw gold for actual currency.

Under McKinley's gold standard, the federal government controlled much of the market in gold. As a result, in order to capture more of the wealth brought south by returning miners, the Chamber of Commerce lobbied vigorously in Washington, D.C., for a federal assay office in Seattle to measure, certify, and purchase the miners' raw gold. When the *Portland* tied up in Seattle in July 1897, loaded with the first Klondike gold, the nearest U.S. Assay Office lay either in San Francisco or Helena, Montana. Although a few Seattle banks, jewelers, and private smelters bought miners' gold, San Francisco had served as the best and nearest market for gold throughout the 1880s and early 1890s. Although the *Portland*'s arrival galvanized the city, sending hundreds of prospective miners into frenzied preparation to head north, most of the arriving gold itself traveled on to California without stopping. N. H. Lattimer of the Dexter Horton Bank—the one bank which could purchase large amounts of gold in 1896—explained that all his bank could do for returning miners was advance a rough estimate of the gold's value,

ship the actual gold to San Francisco, and await assay returns before paying miners the full value. "So the miner goes on to San Francisco," Lattimer
lamented, "where he can at once get the full assay value." "Every miner thinks
his gold is the best and he will not believe otherwise until he gets returns
from a government assay office." Lattimer continued that, "If we had a government assay office, the miners could sell their gold to the banks and they
could get returns on it the same day. Then the miners would buy their goods
here, spend the winter here and outfit here the next spring, so that every
branch of business would gain by it."[81] As the *Post-Intelligencer* put it in January 1897, Seattle was well on its way to controlling the supply trade, but
one thing was missing: "Some bank or business which will purchase the placer
gold and prevent its passing on to San Francisco."[82] With an assay office,
Seattle would be the point at which gold was turned into liquid cash. Miners would sell their gold for money, and spend at least some of that money
in Seattle.

Within days of the *Portland*'s arrival, the Seattle Chamber of Commerce
redoubled its pleas to Congress, pledging both a site and a building for the
assay office, free to the government.[83] Less than a year later, by the end of
March 1898, word arrived that Seattle was to have its office. It opened on
July 15, just days before the summer's gold shipments began to arrive.[84] In
late July, the *Trade Register* reported that "large amounts of gold from the
Klondike and Alaska gold fields continue to arrive and the assay office and
safe deposit are kept busy taking care of the fortunes of the fortunate ones."[85]
Miners went directly from the wharves to the assay office, or turned gold
in at the banks, which then deposited it with government assayers. From
July to December 1898, the assay office took in $5.6 million in gold. At times,
the summer rush made the service slow. Even two years later, in July 1901,
Bill Ballou had a long wait at the Seattle office. "Delay here is caused by the
mint," he wrote, referring to the assay office, "which is a little one horse
affair which at this time of the year can't handle the biz—that is, with any
speed."[86] By the end of the rush, however, according to historian Margaret
Archibald, Seattle dominated the process of buying Alaska-Yukon gold.[87]
In 1898, the Seattle U.S. Assay Office's $5.5 million represented about 40 per-
cent of the total $13.5 million of Alaska-Yukon gold that entered the United
States for processing. In 1899, the Seattle office and private smelters in Seattle took in 60 percent, and in 1900, 71 percent of Alaska and Yukon gold.[88]

As they returned to the city with gold, miners often wanted nothing more
than to get rid of it as quickly as possible. The nature of gold made it very,

very heavy. When miners found gold, they had to carry it wherever they went, and thus their first task was to exchange it for something easier to handle. Tappan Adney met some men hauling eighty-five pounds of gold dust, on foot down the Skagway Trail. "They told me that they threw the sack of dust down fifty times, not caring if they ever picked it up again."[89] Beyond its burdensome weight, raw gold was not at all uniform in its quality, and thus its monetary values fluctuated, depending on its purity and source. In 1897, Bonanza Creek gold ruled the Klondike, with values between $15.75 and $18.50 per ounce (map 6). Hunker Creek gold was valued at $17.50 per ounce, with Dominion Creek not far behind at $17.00, Eldorado at $16.50, and Bear at $15.00.[90] Gold from Claim 26 Above Discovery on Bonanza assayed at $18.35 per ounce; from Claim 18 Below on Sulphur, $15.17; and from the bench on Monte Cristo hill above Bonanza, $10.68. The clerks at the Canadian Bank of Commerce in Dawson City could look at gold dust and tell which creek it came from. Even arriving in San Francisco or Seattle, the gold was Bonanza or Sulphur gold, still the product of nature, of a specific creek.[91]

In the Klondike and Alaska, miners traded on these useful natural differences in gold's value. Banks and merchants along the Yukon set a standard value between fourteen and sixteen dollars per ounce for generic "trade dust," no matter what its actual purity. "I went over Town this afternoon and changed my gold dust for currency," James McRae reported from the Klondike after the cleanup in 1899. "I could only get $15 an ounce for it."[92] Miners saved money by using the "cheapest," least pure dust as trade dust to pay for goods. It might be worth only twelve or thirteen dollars an ounce, but it bought fifteen dollars' worth of goods. Miners saved their better dust and nuggets, worth seventeen or eighteen dollars an ounce, to take to Dawson banks, or out to the Seattle assay office.[93] They also used gold's natural variability to play fast and loose with the 10 percent Canadian royalty on all Klondike gold, payable along the creeks and at the Dawson branch of the Canadian Bank of Commerce.[94] The bank accepted low-purity dust, high-purity dust, and coin in payment for the royalties. Miners paid with the cheapest available form of currency, either trade dust or coin. "A considerable amount of Royalty this year is being paid in Currency," the Gold Commissioner wrote to Ottawa in 1900, "and I find that the Creeks that produce the most valuable gold are paying largely . . . in currency, while the Creeks which produce inferior gold pay almost altogether in dust."[95]

Gold's nature thus worked for and against the miners, as they hauled heavy sacks of dust but also turned a profit on its changeable value. The Seattle assay office, however, functioned, as Erastus Brainerd put it, "to convert a bulky and inconvenient article of uncertain value into coin or its equivalent."[96] The government relieved miners of their weighty load. When Charles Mosier and others like him took their raw gold to the U.S. Assay Office, they exchanged it for a receipt which tied them to ownership of their specific lot of gold, still from a specific creek, still with specific characteristics and impurities. When they returned a few days later, however, they exchanged that receipt for U.S. currency, cash or check, equal to the assayed value of their gold. "Got returns from U.S. Assay Office in morning," Mosier wrote in July 1899 in Seattle.[97]

Here again, Seattle served to make the miners' connections to the nature of gold increasingly invisible and intangible. Miners carried not only the raw metal itself to the Seattle assay office, but with it all of the connections to nature contained in that gold, inherent in the work of gold mining. They carried with the nature of gold, all of their intimacy with and knowledge of soil, gravel, wood, and water. They carried as well the connections to nature forged on the trails, and the food they consumed to fuel their bodies for that labor. In that moment of exchange at the assay office, miners transformed their direct, one-on-one connection to the nature of gold and the labor which had produced their gold. They replaced that connection with a far less tangible one. They now held paper and coin, which represented the value of labor and nature, but no longer held that value in the specific physical form of gold. With the miners off to spend their cash, assay workers melted down the gold and cast it into uniform bars to be shipped to the United States Mint. The gold became a standardized market commodity, and Seattle became the place where gold disappeared, the place at which it ceased to matter where that gold came from or where it was going. And for the nation as a whole, gold now came not from Alaska-Yukon nature, but simply from Seattle.

FULL CIRCLE

Despite the grand welcome afforded the assay office by Seattle's businessmen, the office itself had its share of troubles. When miners flooded into the city with their gold, the government clerks scrambled to keep enough paper money on hand to pay off the eager miners, who clamored to be loose in the city with cash. It was so costly to ship paper bills from New York to

Seattle that, according to a 1910 letter, the assay clerks sometimes ordered gold coin from the Denver or San Francisco mints, which was apparently cheaper to ship the shorter distance to Seattle. They then paid off the miners with gold coin.[98] Such an exchange brought gold full circle. Raw gold arrived in Seattle from Alaska and the Yukon as nuggets and dust, was assayed, melted, and sent on to Denver as bars of bullion, only to return to Seattle as coin, to be exchanged once again for dust. Miners must have been thrilled when this happened; they deposited burdensome, irregular nuggets and dust, and walked away with U.S. gold coins, an official (and lightweight) version of the metal they had just labored to wrest from the earth. Those miners who chose to return to the goldfields then turned their hard-won golden cash back over to Seattle merchants in exchange for more mining supplies, another round of flour, potatoes, pork and beans, shovels, and rubber boots. The cycle continued. Miners bought food and supplies, which they consumed to mine gold, which they exchanged for gold money, which they spent for more supplies, which then fueled their bodies to mine more gold.

Such a satisfying round of exchanges would have been impossible without Seattle. The gold rush demonstrated the importance of this gateway city in the industrial production of gold. The city made it increasingly convenient for miners to travel to the gold creeks, quickly assemble the necessary supplies, and consume the wealth of a modern industrial economy in order to produce gold. The city provided the geographic center and financial and trade institutions which organized and structured the exchanges by which producers and consumers traded the myriad products of their individual labor—whether meat or fruit or gold—for every other product they required.[99] The city connected producers and consumers to each other through a national and world economy, a transportation system, a growing federal government, and a powerful industrial culture. If gold mining was at its core an exchange of gold on the one hand for everything consumed in the production of gold on the other, Seattle sat at the center of that exchange, organizing it and keeping track of the profits and losses.

The city also made it easy to forget where everything came from. Seattle's businessmen embraced and profited from the seasonal cycles of the Alaska-Yukon trade, and they called it all natural. The boosters looked at miners like O. S. Johnson and the $517.16 he spent at Stetson Brothers, and they called both his presence in Seattle and his exchange of cash for supplies natural. In naturalizing the gateway city and all of the work that the city contributed to the gold rush economy, that booster rhetoric erased from the story the actual physical nature and human labor which built that economy. It erased the nature in the flour and bacon itself. It erased the labor of growing wheat and raising hogs. It erased the nature in gravel and permafrost, in riparian forests, in the bodies of pack horses, sled dogs, and caribou herds. Human labor and nature brought gold, clothing, meat, flour, and tools together in the city's streets, warehouses, and storefronts, but the simple acts of buying supplies and selling gold made it easy for miners, and for everyone, to forget or ignore where those things actually came from. They made it easy to forget what William Cronon writes of as "the web of economic and ecological connections that stretched out in all directions."[100] They made it easy to forget the history, the slow and gradual change, which had made Seattle the gateway to begin with. And they made it easy to forget the culture of gold, the very human process by which gold was deemed valuable in the first place.

CONCLUSION

Nature, Culture, and Value

What, then, was the nature of gold? If you asked that question of a miner crossing the Chilkoot Pass in 1898, toiling upward in fervent pursuit of wealth and burdened by a heavy load of flour and bacon, you might get a curt answer. For miners, the nature of gold made it valuable, eternal, beautiful, and pure. That nature, though, was largely a cultural creation. The nature of gold more broadly defined included not only gold's physical attributes and culturally created value, but also every single part of the earth to which miners were connected, however distantly, in the labor of mining gold. When we see the long chain of miners ascending the pass, we see them immersed not only in cultural beliefs about gold's value, but also, literally, in the nature of gold, in the rock, snow, and ice of Chilkoot Pass itself, through which miners moved their bodies to reach the gold-bearing creeks of the Yukon and Alaska. The flour and bacon in their packs were part of the nature of gold, as were the wheat fields and hog farms which produced their food. The wool and cotton clothes on their backs were part of the nature of gold. The nature of gold included the forests which fueled Yukon River steamboats, the dogs and horses that hauled sleds and packs over trails, and the hay and bacon and rice and salmon which kept those animals alive. Along the creeks of the Yukon basin, forests, soil, muck, gravel, moss, moose, caribou, fish, and insects became part of the nature of gold. And all of the human beings who labored to bring those miners to the Chilkoot and to the creeks, who grew their food, made their clothes, transported, bought, and sold their supplies, carried their burdens, built and piloted their boats, those people, too, ate food and wore clothes and turned their hands to nature. The natures in which they worked were also part of the nature of gold.

This nature of gold suggests that, stripped of its profound cultural meaning, gold was not much different from any other part of the earth. One could trace everything produced and consumed in making a can of pork and beans, or a watermelon, or a pair of rubber boots. One could write a book called *The Nature of Pork and Beans,* detailing all of the nature and labor that human beings put into each can of Van Camp's much-favored dinner. Aside from a slight loss of drama, such a book might not look all that different from this one. Everything that human beings produce from the earth has a nature, not only in its physical qualities and in its usefulness, but also in all that people consume to produce it. All acts of production are unequivocally linked to myriad acts of consumption; all acts of consumption are further connected to other acts of production, and thus to other natures. We all take the earth apart in one way or another as we move through nature, as we labor, and as we consume food and supplies to keep ourselves alive. The connections and the disassembly may not always be easy to see, but in everything we do, they are inescapable.

This nature of gold suggests, likewise, that gold miners were not all that different from other industrial workers. When they thawed a drift or piloted a flimsy boat down the Yukon, they created networks of connections to nature and culture not fundamentally different from those formed by factory workers, farmhands, or office clerks walking down a city street half a continent away. The miners' networks resembled other such networks, not in their precise connections, but in their complexity, their shifting mix of production and consumption, their annihilation of space, and their inclusion of the labor of other workers, both close at hand and far away. Like all human beings in an industrialized economy, gold miners formed connections to nature that ran the entire spectrum, from a fierce, physical, seemingly preindustrial engagement with the physical world to the far more mediated and complicated set of connections represented by eating fresh roast beef or canned pork and beans on a Yukon sternwheeler. Their connections to nature were fully industrialized from start to end.

Gold miners also shared with other North Americans the powerful naturalizations of gold, the gold standard, and gold money which made up the culture of gold. Like other workers, miners naturalized productive labor in the earth through a producer ideology. Like others' labor, the gold miners' labor was shaped by cultural ideas about hard work, production, nature, labor, virtue, chance, luck, and wages. Just as in the wider industrial world, gold miners' labors in transportation, mining, and supply were shaped by markets, commodification, and technology.

Alaska-Yukon miners resembled more conventional late-nineteenth-century North Americans in other ways as well. Just as factory workers assembling bicycles knew where bicycles came from, gold miners, as producers, knew all too well just where gold came from, or, more likely, where it failed to come from: the creeks. On the other hand, mass production, national and global markets, and modern transportation made it more difficult for them, as for other industrial workers, to keep track of where their food and other supplies came from. Industrial technology, markets, and gateway cities like Seattle made the miners' connections to nature and human labor difficult to see and acknowledge, and easy to forget, just as they did for other denizens of the industrial world. Steamboat journeys obscured the immense energy, labor, and skill required to carry tons of freight upriver against the Yukon current. Dinner tables loaded with processed food, whether in Rampart City or Kansas City, offered few clues as to where that food came from. Seattle, like other gateway cities, organized workers' buying and selling of just about everything they produced and consumed, but the city's outfitting emporia and advertising blitzkrieg made it seem that food and clothing simply came from Seattle. Like other industrial cities, Seattle obscured and naturalized all of the nature and labor that went into consumer goods.

Finally, Alaska-Yukon gold miners, like many other industrialized North Americans in the 1890s, faced limited economic choices when it came to labor and the chance for economic success. At no point, however, no matter what work they chose, could gold miners or anyone else choose not to be connected to nature. At no point could they choose not to be connected to the other human beings who labored in their service. At no point can any of us be fully separated from nature, from other human beings, or, for that matter, from culture. Neither through any supposed conquest of nature, nor through apparent alienation from nature, could such connections disintegrate completely or free modern, industrial human beings from nature. Those connections became difficult to see and trace, but they did not disappear. Instead they became ever more complex, with ever more complex consequences.

Thus the available choices in 1898, just as the available choices now, were not about whether to produce and consume within the material world, but about how to do so, whether as a hog farmer or a gold miner or a railroad clerk. In that group, hog farmers and gold miners might have appeared more connected to the physical world than did railroad clerks, but all, at some point along the spectrum, through some combination of consumption and production, stood like the miners on the Chilkoot, tethered securely to the earth by the strands woven by their own labors and by the labors of those who served them. Just how any individual chose (or chooses) which work to do, however, and which connections with nature to form, is a broader question that leads us back once again to questions of culture and of value.

What value, in the long run, did human beings gain from the gold rush? Given the complicated mix of consumption and production necessary to mine gold, was it worth it? The gold rush's greatest storyteller, Jack London, asked that very question, unromantic and calculating as it might seem. In January 1900, London's short article in the *North American Review of Reviews* asked, "Did the Yukon district return to the gold-seekers the equivalent of what they spent in getting there?" The answer was no. According to his calculations, miners extracted $22 million in gold from the frozen creeks, while spending ten times that amount to do so, $220 million dollars. Most of it went to supplies and transportation. Yet London went on to claim that the gold rush had been worth it. It was an economic success, if not for the individual miners themselves, then for the interests of civilization as a whole. "It has been of inestimable benefit to the Yukon country," he wrote, "to those who will remain in [the Yukon], and those yet to come."[1] His arguments for this success drew from powerful late-nineteenth-century beliefs about value, nature, and civilization.

The gold rush was a success, London explained, because the massive outpouring of capital and labor it brought to the Yukon and Alaska had by 1900 overcome all barriers to further economic development. The railroad and river steamers made it easier to move in and out of the Yukon interior, and they gave industrial consumers year-round access to inexpensive mass-produced goods. Thanks to the sacrifices and investments of thousands of gold miners, few of whom reaped any profits, gold mining could now proceed on a rational economic basis. "With the necessaries and luxuries of life cheap and plentiful," London wrote, "with the importation of the machinery which will cheapen many enterprises . . . , with easy traveling and quick communication between it and the world and between its parts, the resources of the Yukon district will be opened up and developed in a steady business like way."[2]

Part of London's argument echoed the sentiments of those who célebrated the White Pass & Yukon Railroad as a conquest of nature, a triumph of technology and capital over a savage environment. Gold rush miners, London implied, with their primitive methods, bodily toil, and closeness with nature, had themselves been primitive, uncivilized, and unsystematic in their pursuit of success. They wasted their energies in this disordered rush, he implied, participating in a "harum-scarum carrying on of industry." In their wake, however, modern technology and business methods had eliminated the need for physical labor in nature, such as that of crossing the Chilkoot. In the post-rush Yukon basin, London proclaimed, "natural obstacles will be cleared away or surmounted, primitive methods abandoned, and hardship of toil and travel reduced to the smallest possible minimum."[3] We know from the gold miners themselves that railroads and steamers could not actually eliminate human beings' connections to nature. Modern technology shifted bodily toil from the miners' bodies to the bodies of workers who built and ran railroads and ships, and packed supplies. London missed the ongoing presence of those workers. He missed the ongoing presence of nature in industrial consumption and industrial life. In his view, nature and hard labor had both been eliminated, leaving the field clear for modern economic development.

Buried not so deeply within London's article were echoes of even more powerful ideas about miners, nature, and Euro-American history. In his rhetoric of a country "opened up," London echoed Frederick Jackson Turner's 1893 essay "The Significance of the Frontier in American History," presented at the World's Columbian Exposition in Chicago. Westward expansion into unsettled territory, Turner argued, had long formed the basis of the United States' economic and political development. In Turner's vision of westward movement, early settlers on the frontier, at the meeting point of civilization and savagery, regressed into more primitive stages in order to garner the skills and strength necessary to then overcome that savagery and progress to later stages of settlement. Adopting Turner's powerful plot line, London described how frontier gold miners had confronted nature with sled dogs and other primitive methods, but would now, by a quite natural order of things, disappear. Now, London wrote, "The frontiersman will yield to the laborer, the prospector to the mining engineer, the dog-driver to the engine driver, the trader and speculator to the steady-going modern man of business; for these are the men in whose hands the destiny of the Klondike will be intrusted."[4]

It is easy to understand, given the power and currency of Turner's ideas in 1900, how London and his readers interpreted the individual failures of the gold rush as unimportant in the face of the broader victories of technology over nature, and of civilization over primitive savagery. It is also easy to understand how Euro-Americans as a whole continued to see gold rushes as natural. Embedded in Turner's story of the stage-by-stage progress of American civilization, this gold rush, like all gold rushes, fulfilled the necessary role of the first stage. When put in the context of that touchstone mythology of American identity, the individual miners' experiences and losses in the gold rush hardly mattered at all. Likewise, the millions of dollars invested in the gold rush with little return hardly mattered. The miners were necessary participants in the much broader and more important process of bringing civilization to the frontier. Failure and loss were necessary sacrifices to that civilized future.

It is also easy to understand why London's readers, and anyone else who considered the question, failed to consider any negative consequences of the gold rush.[5] With gold naturalized as the most valuable and moral earthly element, the "most precious thing that men crave or covet," as one writer claimed in 1908,[6] and with gold rushes naturalized as the first step toward civilization in an inevitable expansion of Euro-American capitalism and democracy, Americans would never have questioned those values or stopped to think of the environmental consequences of gold mining for riparian ecosystems or any other part of nature. Nor would they have considered the connections to nature forged by miners as producers and consumers, or the consequences of those connections. Those of London's contemporaries who did take note of the social consequences for Native peoples along the Yukon often dismissed those dislocations and personal tragedies as the necessary costs of the advance of white civilization. London did not even mention Native peoples in his article.

Yet even as he gave the gold rush his wholehearted approval as an economic success, Jack London suggested ways in which such approval might be challenged. His central questions in this one article concerned production and consumption, profit and loss, value and profit. What did the gold rush produce, and what was its value in the long run? Did the gold rush produce as much as it consumed? Did it turn a profit? Was it worth it? While London argued that this gold rush was indeed worth it, he did ask such questions, and in doing so he opened the door to other possible answers. His questions, after all, were about comparing values, costs, and benefits. The answers to such questions are always subjective, shaped by culture, ideology, experience, and opinion. They depend entirely on how any society, culture, or individual assigns value, how people decide the comparative worth of all that human beings produce and consume. The answers also depend on how human beings acknowledge and calculate the costs and consequences of their production and consumption. For London, gold and the progress of civilization were together of far greater value than the economic failures and losses experienced by individual miners and Native peoples. They were worth the loss. His measurements and calculations were powerfully shaped, however, by late-nineteenth-century American mythology and by the culture of gold. Other values, other mythologies, other cultures, and other considerations of the consequences of gold mining might have led to different conclusions.

In 1996 and 1997, exactly one hundred years after the Alaska-Yukon gold rush, automobiles in and around Missoula, Montana, began sporting bumper stickers that read "The Blackfoot River Is More Precious Than Gold." The slogan referred to an ongoing political and environmental battle which divided the state in the 1990s, and has continued to draw both local and national attention. The fight involves a dogged and so far successful fight by a coalition of western Montanans to stop a proposed heap-leach cyanide gold mine, known as the McDonald mine, on the headwaters of the Blackfoot River. In November 1998, Montana voters passed Initiative 137, a law banning all new cyanide-based gold mines in the state. Although that law is under constitutional challenge, the latest western gold rush, for the time being, has ground to a halt. In at least one western place, gold mining is no longer the natural thing to do.[7]

It would be silly, of course, to directly compare the battle over the McDonald mine on the Blackfoot with the Alaska-Yukon gold rush. By the 1990s, gold and gold mining had come to mean very different things from what they meant in the 1890s, and nature had accumulated some new cultural meanings as well. The intervening century brought revolutionary transformations in the human relationship with nature, and with them drastic changes in the earth's landscape and atmosphere. It would be folly as well to compare the effects of late-twentieth-century, open-pit, cyanide heap-leach gold mining, a fairly recent technological feat, with those of 1890s Alaska-Yukon placer mining. The two, while both technically gold mining, could not be more different in their methods, scale, technology, and environmental effects; they constitute two entirely different human relationships to the gold-bearing earth. Nineteenth-century gold miners in the Yukon and Alaska tore up and muddied creeks, stripped hillsides of timber, and depleted wildlife populations. The proposed McDonald mine in Montana, if built, will replace mountain meadows and buttes with eight square miles of industrial development, consume 2.5 million gallons of water a day, and sink a pit a mile wide and a mile long over a thousand feet into the earth. The mine will require fifty tons of low-grade ore to extract every ounce of gold, and will, as David James Duncan writes, "explode, move or process 245 *tons of rock*" for each of those ounces. To keep the pit dry, the mine will pump thousands of gallons of groundwater a day, lowering the water table beneath the valley by 1,300 feet. Despite the proposed containment technology, the mine will constantly threaten to leak deadly cyanide, sulfuric acid, and nitrates into the river.[8] Gold mining these days is an entirely different story.

What gold mining looks like has changed dramatically, but the questions we might ask of it remain very much the same. In debating the Blackfoot River mine, Montanans in the 1990s asked many of Jack London's questions from 1900. What would the McDonald mine produce, and what would be the value of that production? What would it consume? Would it turn a profit, producing more than it consumed? Who would benefit? The answers were relatively clear. The mine would produce a good amount of gold, worth a great deal of money, most of which would become jewelry. It would produce 390 jobs for ten to fifteen years, and with them the income to support workers and their families for a decade or two. The mine would also produce waste, something nineteenth-century miners never considered, in the form of toxic runoff, debris, and sediment. In order to produce gold, jobs, wages, and waste, the mine would consume nature in many forms, including chemicals, earth, vegetation, fossil fuels, and large pieces of the landscape itself.

In laying out their arguments against the McDonald mine, Blackfoot-loving writers and activists weighed the value of what the mine would produce against what it would consume. In a political move that would have mystified gold miners and nineteenth-century Americans as a whole, Montanans concluded first that a huge open-pit gold mine which produced toxic, cyanide-laced runoff threatened the health of the Blackfoot River, particularly its prized fish, beloved by flyfishers. They then argued that the health and beauty of the Blackfoot River as a living ecosystem was more valuable to the people and other living creatures of Montana than any amount of gold. For those fighting the mine, that one bumper sticker said it all: The Blackfoot River Is More Precious Than Gold.

Although worlds apart, the Alaska-Yukon gold rush and the proposed Blackfoot headwaters mine thus raise similar questions about value, production and consumption, and human connections to nature. In the 1890s, Americans and others rushed to the Yukon River to mine gold without ever questioning the value of gold. In the 1990s, in an admittedly different economy, Montanans directly questioned the value of gold and compared it directly to the value of other parts of the natural world: a healthy river and healthy fish. Another bumper sticker read—imagine this in 1898—"Boycott Gold." That bumper sticker demonstrates unequivocally that the ways in which Americans have valued gold is historical; it has changed over time. That change is unfolding before us. Such a shift in values, in *what has value*, indicates once and for all that the value of gold was and is *not* natural, as some Americans so fervently believed in the 1890s. It was and remains cultural, a human decision, embedded in social, economic, and political contexts, the product of history and of markets that were themselves human creations.

Of course, in asking and answering Jack London's questions about value and worth, Montanans fighting the Blackfoot River mine cast those questions in a very different light, bringing to bear the cumulative cultural, social, and economic weight of the twentieth century. Beyond questions of value, chief among the differences are issues of work, jobs, and wage labor. In the 1890s, the work of gold mining revealed not only connections to nature—soil, water, wood, and gravel—but also important elements of industrial culture. For Alaska-Yukon miners, like their fellow industrial workers at home, work was about more than work; mining was about more than simply gold. It was about freedom, independence, identity, and satisfaction, and about seeking a connection between hard work and wealth. It began as an escape from industrialized wage labor, but quickly became something more akin to gambling before being reinvented as just the type of wage labor miners had sought to leave behind. The miners' work reflected their values and their desires, and thus the results of their work, their disassembly of the creeks, expressed and reflected those values and desires. The muddy, silty, transformed landscapes they left behind were a direct result of the ways in which the miners thought about labor. But of course, 1890s gold miners never gave the environmental consequences of their work, or their cultural beliefs about work, a second thought.

Although miners in the Klondike never considered the question of what type of work was the *best* work to be done on gold-bearing creeks, Americans in the 1990s, particularly western Americans, grappled head-on with such questions. Western communities struggled, and continue to struggle, with the environmental consequences of mining, logging, farming, ranching, tourism, and fishing. In divisive debates over the ways in which these labors disassemble western ecosystems, westerners have become fully aware that work is full of issues of class, culture, history, and human values. Montanans on both sides of the gold mining issue have asked directly what would be the best work for human beings to do along the Blackfoot River. Some argue that gold mining is good and productive work, just the sort of work to be done on the Blackfoot. Writing in fervent opposition to the McDonald project, however, David James Duncan acknowledged the 390 "new jobs" promised by the gold mine, but argued that these were not simply "new jobs," but also *"bad jobs."* Duncan then went on to define bad jobs quite clearly: "Building Love Canal, Hanford, Chernobyl, and Bhopal were jobs. Clearcutting the Amazon . . . stealing Africans from their homes and selling them at auction, were jobs. . . . Unconscionable jobs. In no century soon will we undo the damage wrought by three centuries of unconscionable jobs. Why create 390 more?"[9]

Things have changed, indeed, although not for everyone. In the 1890s, Americans defined gold mining as moral and respectable work, full of the miners' hopes for success and independence. At worst, some saw gold mining as risky and foolhardy. A century later, however, writing from deep within his own moral, environmental convictions, David Duncan ranked gold mining with the nation's greatest historical crimes. The differences between the two gold rushes, a century apart, show us that while all work does and will disassemble the earth through production and consumption, human beings do and can make choices about the best work to do in any given place. They make those choices within their cultures, based on their values and on their understanding of what has value. Those values have consequences. The values that made up the culture of gold put those miners on the Chilkoot Pass. Those values spurred the thousands of connections to nature that made up the labors of transportation, gold mining, and supply. The choice to value and mine gold brought change to individual miners' lives. It brought change to the passes and trails. It brought change to the creeks and villages of the Yukon River, and to the people who lived along them. In Montana, on the Blackfoot, the choice between a moderately healthy river and a heap-leach gold mine will have consequences. It will forever shape the ways in which people will know, experience, consume, and transform nature along the Blackfoot.

Of course, we do not always get to decide, individually, how to value the earth, how to produce or consume from nature to sustain our bodies and souls, how to connect ourselves to nature. Such values are often so rooted in broader cultural and historical patterns, beliefs, markets, and economies that they are impossible to see, let alone to challenge. Human beings rarely agree, either, on values, labor, or connections to nature. We do not always agree on the best job to do in any one place. Likewise, we cannot fully predict the consequences of what we choose to value, of our production and consumption, of our labors in the earth. Those who chose the Alaska-Yukon gold rush acted within the midst of an economic culture which offered a narrow range of choices and which valued gold and the labor of finding it in particular ways. Individual miners saw gold as offering what they wanted, and thus chose to pursue it, knowing neither the particular set of relationships with nature they would build, nor the consequences of their actions.

What we do have, as human beings, is an enormous capacity and predilection to think carefully about what we value, and to shift the ways in which we value the earth to meet our best moral vision of our place on the earth, and to match our best understanding of how the earth works. Even in the midst of the gold rush, immersed in the culture of gold, more than a few gold seekers stopped to reflect on and even question the dictates of that culture. The last word belongs to Nora Crane's husband, Edward, who wrote to his mother from Circle City in June 1898. "It gives me great pleasure to hear of your good health and happiness, and they are the good things that count in this world," he told her. "Gold dust is not it, comparatively speaking."[10]

ABBREVIATIONS FOR ARCHIVAL SOURCES USED IN NOTES

DCM   Dawson City Museum and Historical Society, Dawson City, Yukon
Territory

UAF   Elmer E. Rasmuson Library, University of Alaska, Fairbanks, Alaska
and Polar Regions Department, Manuscripts, Historical Photographs,
and University Archives, Fairbanks, Alaska

UW   University of Washington Libraries, Manuscripts, Special Collections,
University Archives Division, Seattle, Washington

YA   Yukon Archive, Department of Education, The Government of Yukon,
Whitehorse, Yukon Territory

NOTES

INTRODUCTION: ON THE CHILKOOT

1. Automobile advertisement in author's possession.

2. James H. Hamil letter, October 8, 1897, Vertical File Manuscript, UAF.

3. Herman Ferree letter, February 19, 1898, Vertical File Manuscript, "Dyea and the Dyea Trail," UAF.

4. Hamil letter, October 8, 1897.

5. Ferree letter, February 19, 1898.

6. Alfred "Mac" McMichael letter, April 1, 1898, Alfred McMichael Diary and Letters, Juliette Reinicker Papers, MSS 100, Acc. 79/68, YA. McMichael's letters have also been published in Juliette C. Reinicker, ed., *Klondike Letters: The Correspondence of a Gold Seeker in 1898* (Anchorage: Alaska Northwest Publishing Co., 1984). My references are all to the typescripts of the letters in the Reinicker Collection in the Yukon Archive.

7. Ibid., April 5, April 14, April 15, 1898.

8. On the distance between the sites of production and of consumption, and on the annihilation of space, see William Cronon, *Nature's Metropolis: Chicago and the Great West* (New York: W. W. Norton, 1991), ch. 5 and ch. 7, especially pp. 339–40.

9. Virginia Scharff, "Man and Nature! Sex Secrets of Environmental History," in John P. Herron and Andrew G. Kirk, eds., *Human Nature: Biology, Culture, and Environmental History* (Albuquerque: University of New Mexico Press, 1999), 40–41.

10. On the industrial relationship to nature, see Cronon, *Nature's Metropolis,* and Jennifer Price, *Flight Maps: Adventures with Nature in Modern America* (New York: Basic Books, 1999).

11. See especially Donald Worster, *Dust Bowl: The Southern Plains in the 1930s* (New York: Oxford University Press, 1979).

12. Cronon, *Nature's Metropolis,* xv.

13. Jack London, "The Call of the Wild" in *Novels & Stories* (New York: Library of America, 1982), 15, 21.

1 / THE CULTURE OF GOLD

1. David Goodman, *Gold Seeking: Victoria and California in the 1850s* (Stanford: Stanford University Press, 1994), xiv.

2. Paula Mitchell Marks, *Precious Dust: The American Gold Rush Era, 1848–1900* (New York: William Morrow, 1994), 15.

3. Pierre Berton, *Klondike: The Last Great Gold Rush, 1896–1899* (Toronto: McLelland & Stewart, 1958; rev. ed., 1972), 94–95.

4. Paolo E. Coletta, *William Jennings Bryan,* vol. 1, *Political Evangelist* (Lincoln: University of Nebraska Press, 1964), 140–41.

5. Stefan Lorant, *The Presidency: A Pictorial History of Presidential Elections* (New York: The Macmillan Company, 1951), 438; Paul W. Glad *McKinley, Bryan, & The People* (Philadelphia: Lippincott, 1964), 139. It was not the speech alone which won Bryan the nomination; his nomination was well sought and well planned prior to the convention. See James A. Barnes, "Myths of the Bryan Campaign," *Mississippi Valley Historical Review* 34 (December 1947): 367–404.

6. Alfred "Mac" McMichael letter, June 19, 1898, Alfred McMichael Diary and Letters, Juliette Reinicker Papers, MSS 100, Acc. 79/68, YA.

7. David Harvey, *Justice, Nature, and the Geography of Difference* (Cambridge, Mass.: Blackwell, 1996), 173–74.

8. Irwin Unger, *The Greenback Era: A Social and Political History of American Finance, 1865–1879* (Princeton: Princeton University Press, 1964), 14.

9. Milton Friedman and Anna Jacobson Schwartz, *A Monetary History of the United States* (Princeton: Princeton University Press, 1963), 7, 25, 85. On the general history of American monetary policy and the gold/silver debate, see also Gretchen Ritter, *Goldbugs and Greenbacks: The Antimonopoly Tradition and the Politics of Finance in America* (New York: Cambridge University Press, 1997); Robert A. Degen, *The American Monetary System: A Concise Survey of Its Evolution Since 1896* (Lexington, Mass.: Lexington Books, 1987); Richard Timberlake, *Monetary Policy*

in the United States: An Intellectual and Institutional History, 2nd ed. (Chicago: University of Chicago Press, 1993); and Anna J. Schwartz, ed., *Money in Historical Perspective* (Chicago: University of Chicago Press, 1987). Prior to the Civil War, the nation used a bimetallic monetary standard. In 1792, on the sage advice of Alexander Hamilton, the United States established a coin system based on silver and gold, coined at a ratio of 15:1. The treasurer coined dollars in both silver and gold. The gold dollar contained 24 3/4 grains of gold, grains being an age-old system of measuring the weight of precious metals, based originally on grains of wheat. The silver dollar contained fifteen times that weight, or 371 1/4 grains of silver. The two different dollars were equal in value, or each worth one dollar, and thus interchangeable. Edwin Walter Kemmerer, *Gold and the Gold Standard* (1944; reprint, New York: Arno Press, 1979), 61–63. For a general source on currency history in the United States, see Herman E. Krooss, ed., *Documentary History of Banking and Currency in the United States,* 4 vols. (New York: Chelsea House, 1969). The mint produced coins of various denominations, from ten dollars to a half cent, in gold, silver, and copper; gold was used for the higher denominations, silver in the middle range, and copper for pennies. Each coin contained the amount of metal equal in value to the denomination of the coin. See Kemmerer, *Gold and the Gold Standard,* 67.

10. Friedman and Schwartz, *Monetary History of the United States,* 26–27.

11. Unger, *Greenback Era,* 16.

12. Timberlake, *Monetary Policy in the United States,* 88–89; Lawrence Goodwyn, *Democratic Promise: The Populist Moment in America* (New York: Oxford University Press, 1976), 17–18.

13. On issues of prices, see Timberlake, *Monetary Policy in the United States,* 166–67, 183; on Panic of 1873, see ibid., ch. 8.

14. This was an old practice. When a gold coin was worth more as raw metal than as coin, then the person holding it melted it and sold it as a commodity for profit. This was particularly dangerous to bimetallist nations coining both gold and silver. The relatively more valuable coins tended to disappear as entrepreneurs took either gold or silver coins out of circulation to cash in on their commodity value. Gold was always more valuable than silver, but their relative values varied with the rise and fall of supply and demand. Gold could be twelve times as valuable as silver, creating a silver-gold ratio of 12:1. If the gold supply increased, and gold's value decreased, the ratio fell. An ounce of gold was still worth more than an ounce of silver, but not as much more. This, of course, complicated the value of coins. As early as the fourteenth century, economic writers including Nicole Oresme and Henry of Ghent noted that the shifting ratio of value between gold and silver caused coins of one or the other metal to vanish from circulation, leaving the other to serve as

currency by default. An anonymous fourteenth-century source described the problem in pithy terms: "Sometimes silver eats gold, sometimes gold eats silver." See Arthur Eli Monroe, *Monetary Theory Before Adam Smith* (Cambridge: Harvard University Press, 1923), 37. In the late sixteenth century, a British economist, Sir Thomas Gresham, codified the problem as "Gresham's Law," which stated simply that "bad money drives out good." In a bimetallist economy, the more plentiful, or cheaper, currency always replaced the scarcer, more valuable metal, especially when bimetallist nations set different silver-gold ratios. This practice made one or the other metal more valuable across national borders than at home, and led to the rapid disappearance of the more valuable metal from a national economy.

15. Silver had been quite rare, relative to gold, throughout the mid-nineteenth century, so much so that Congress, in the 1873 currency act, indeed ended the government's coinage of silver. Only later, when silverites demanded the use of silver as currency, did this 1873 act become known as part of an eastern capitalist conspiracy against western producers, particularly silver producers. As a result of this "Crime of '73," as it was soon pronounced, Greenbackers, silver producers, and other soft money supporters attacked Republican gold resumptionists as having criminally deprived the nation of a valuable source of hard currency, which, if freely coined by the U.S. Treasury, would increase the money supply and counter the combined effects of the panic and the loss of currency caused by gold resumption.

16. Walter T. K. Nugent, *Money and American Society, 1865–1880* (New York: Free Press, 1968), 195–200; Friedman and Schwartz, *Monetary History of the United States,* 48–49, 113–14. For an in-depth discussion of the silver issue in western states and the role of the West in the silver debates, see Robert W. Larson, *Populism in the Mountain West* (Albuquerque: University of New Mexico Press, 1986). For the general role of silver and Greenbackers in the politics of resumption, see Timberlake, *Monetary Policy in the United States,* 113–15.

17. Major works on the currency issue, including Nugent's *Money and American Society* and Unger's *Greenback Era,* which are important sources here, focus on the debates of the 1870s. Both make clear that the fundamental ideologies expressed in that decade remained consistent in the debate of the 1890s. Many of the same writers were active in both periods, and many pamphlets written in the 1870s were distributed widely in the 1890s. For further information on the 1870s as a "seedtime" for silver issues, see Allen Weinstein, *Prelude to Populism: Origins of the Silver Issue, 1867–1878* (New Haven: Yale University Press, 1970).

18. Goodwyn, *Democratic Promise,* 517.

19. From Thomas Aquinas to John Locke to gold standard advocates of the 1890s, some economic thinkers argued that the value of a coin was determined by the mar-

ket value of the metal it contained. They believed in money's intrinsic value for a reason. In Aquinas's time, European princes coined gold and silver, marking the coins with a standard value that rested on the power of their decree. The problem with this regal value was that the monarchs systematically devalued the coins for their own profit. They reduced the amount of silver or gold in the coins, kept their face values the same, and pocketed the difference. Knowing this, merchants ignored the marked face value of the coins, the extrinsic or socially created value, and instead judged their worth by the weight of the metal they contained and the market value of that metal—a lower value. This lower value prevailed, and with it the practice of giving coins not face value, but value according to their metal content. See Monroe, *Monetary Theory*, 25–27.

Most of these arguments over money's intrinsic or social/cultural value, like the 1890s debates, emerged from problems with national currencies, particularly gold supply crises brought on by the effects of Gresham's Law. In the late 1690s, British Parliamentary factions tried to change the value of English shillings because currency traders were slipping across the channel to trade silver (which was worth more as bullion in France than as coin in England) for gold. They also clipped silver from silver coins, melted the shavings, and traded that for gold in Europe. See Joyce Oldham Appleby, "Locke, Liberalism, and the Natural Law of Money," *Past and Present* 71 (May 1976): 45–46. See also Glyn Davies, *A History of Money: From Ancient Times to the Present Day* (Cardiff: University of Wales, 1994), 244–47. Davies discusses Locke's 1695 *Short Observations and Further Considerations Concerning Raising the Value of Money* on pp. 245–46. These currency problems left London with a battered and dwindling supply of money. In order to maintain a functional level of currency, and with a clear belief in the socially created value of money, the government moved to cast new silver coins with less silver in them. According to those officials, it did not matter how much silver was in the coins; the government could legislate the value of coins in the national interest, regardless of the weight of the coin or the value of the metal.

John Locke disagreed. He argued that the gold and silver coins had intrinsic value, which came from the "unique esteem" that human beings had for gold and silver. That esteem for precious metals was universal, natural, and inherent in both human nature and the nature of gold and silver. See Appleby, "Locke, Liberalism," 49–50, and 66–67, where Locke is quoted: "'A Law cannot give to Bills that intrinsick Value which the universal consent of Mankind has annexed to Silver and Gold.'" The intrinsic value argument continues to this day among gold standard advocates. See Anna J. Schwartz, "Alternative Money Regimes: The Gold Standard," in Schwartz, ed., *Money in Historical Perspective*, 370. People used gold and silver as money not by choice, but because intrinsic value made it possible for the metals to measure and store the value of other commodities. The value of money came from its being made of precious metal, not from legislation or from government; it came from nature, not culture. See Appleby, "Locke, Liberalism," 48–49.

20. Michael O'Malley, "Specie and Species: Race and the Money Question in Nineteenth-Century America," *American Historical Review* 99 (April 1994): 377.

21. O'Malley's "Specie and Species" provides a more sophisticated and thorough discussion of the intrinsic value of gold as a nineteenth-century issue. See also Walter Benn Michaels, "The Gold Standard and the Logic of Naturalism," in *The Gold Standard and the Logic of Naturalism: American Literature at the Turn of the Century* (Berkeley: University of California Press, 1987), 147–155. There is, of course, a voluminous literature on the question of value in general and whether it is inherent or intrinsic in nature. See Harvey, *Justice, Nature,* ch. 7.

22. See note 19 above and Monroe, *Monetary Theory,* 25–27.

23. Barnes, "Myths of the Bryan Campaign," 383. As errant coin-clipping princes demonstrated, and as the American people would learn after the Civil War, the dual identity of metal coins—that they could be given value as coins (social value) or as metals (intrinsic value)—caused real economic havoc.

24. Karl Marx, *Capital: A Critique of Political Economy,* vol. 1, trans. Ben Fowkes (New York: Random House, 1977), 177.

25. Adam Smith, *An Inquiry into the Nature and Causes of the Wealth of Nations,* vol. 1, ed. R. H. Campbell and A. S. Skinner (Oxford: Clarendon Press, 1976), 25–26, 29.

26. Quoted in Maria Cristina Marcuzzo and Annalisa Rosselli, *Ricardo and the Gold Standard: The Foundations of the International Monetary Order,* trans. Joan Hall (New York: St. Martin's Press, 1990), 42.

27. David A. Wells, *The Silver Question: The Dollar of the Fathers versus The Dollar of the Sons* (New York: G.P. Putnam's Sons, 1877), 41–42.

28. Ibid., 15.

29. Nugent, *Money and American Society,* 185.

30. Wells, *Silver Question,* 37–38. Historian David Goodman writes that in the 1850s, during the California Gold Rush, this idea of natural laws operating to draw the labor of miners and thus adjust the gold supply was an emergent mode of thought, but not yet dominant. He quotes Thomas Hart Benton as saying "It is no matter who digs up the gold or where it goes. The digger will not eat it, and it will go where commerce will carry it." Goodman, *Gold Seeking,* 28.

31. Wells, *The Silver Question,* 37. On Wells, see Stanley L. Jones, *The Presidential Election of 1896* (Madison: University of Wisconsin Press, 1964). Another key

economist on the gold side of the debate was J. Laurence Laughlin, whose text, *The History of Bimetallism in the United States* (New York: D. Appleton and Company, 1896), laid out the principles supporting a gold standard.

32. The idea that people would mine for gold when the economy needed gold, and that its value stemmed from adjustments in the total supply, was the general economic belief of the late nineteenth and early twentieth centuries. See David Kinley, *Money: A Study of the Theory of the Medium of Exchange* (New York: Macmillan, 1904), and Amasa Walker, *The Science of Wealth: Manual of Political Economy* (1866; Philadelphia: Lippincott, 1872). The labor theory of value affirmed both the socially created value of a gold coin, and the natural, intrinsic value of that coin, but, in factoring labor value into the latter, it drastically shifted the basis of the theory of natural value. In postulating that gold's natural value as a commodity came from the labor of gold miners, labor theorists for the first time made those miners part of the question of value. By making labor the ultimate source of economic value, labor value economists expanded the idea of natural value beyond the somewhat archaic idea of a physically identifiable or chemical value intrinsic to gold or another commodity.

Karl Marx and other theorists of labor value thus affirmed the idea of a natural value, but it was not Locke's natural value. They recognized that money, no matter what it was made out of, had a different kind of value, a social value. True value came from labor, and money simply represented that value. A unit of money, a coin, was a unit of labor, a store of labor value, distinct from the work itself. Money was crystallized labor value, not value itself; money represented value, and it made it possible to move and exchange labor, and thus value, through space and time. Marx and John Stuart Mill affirmed that money was a social tool and a social creation. Marx wrote of the real distinction between "the specific natural form of the commodity gold" and money, or "the universal equivalent form" of value (Marx, *Capital*, 162–63). That form could be made of gold, or any other substance. The commodity gold became money through social action, by social consensus (183–84). Using an apt governmental analogy, Marx wrote that "coins are like uniforms worn at home but taken off when gold and silver appear on the world market" (222).

The labor theory of value affirmed certain aspects of both natural value and social value, but it only partially solved the paradox of the dual identity of gold and silver money. Gold and other precious metals contained natural value created by miners through the labor of production. Gold and silver coins, however, remained distinct from gold and silver as commodities; those coins were social agents, in uniform, with social purpose. The true source of gold coins' natural value remained problematic. Was it labor value, created by gold miners, or government-declared social value? One of John Locke's contemporaries, William Petty, offered an early indication of why this question proved vexing. Petty tried to figure out how to measure the actual labor value of silver and corn. To start, he asked how much corn was actually worth in labor (natural) value, as expressed in money. In response, he proposed that it was worth "as much as the money which another man producing money (i.e. the money commodity) can save during the same time above his expenses of production." See Eric A. Roll, *A History of Economic Thought,* 4th ed. (London: Faber, 1973), 104–105.

To illustrate, Petty proposed that one man mined silver for a certain amount of time. After feeding himself during that time, he took the silver that remained to a field of corn. The corn produced by a farmer, in the same period of time, would be worth the amount of silver the miner had left. Both had labored the same amount. If the farmer produced twenty bushels of corn, and the miner brought twenty ounces of silver, then a bushel of corn was worth an ounce of silver, measured essentially by labor time. This was its natural, labor-based value, or price.

Petty ably demonstrated why this system could never work. The value of gold and silver (or corn) might come from the labor needed to produce them, but the economy could not function if that labor had to be measured and compared every time someone wanted to exchange gold or silver for another product. There was no direct way to translate the value of one kind of labor into the value of another kind of labor. They were incomparable, and hence money was useful to make labor values easily comparable.

The key revelation here on the question of gold mining, though, was that in practice the market value of gold and silver did not stem directly from the time and physical effort necessary to dig them out of the ground. According to the labor theory of value, the labor of mining gave gold its true and natural value, but that natural value was hard to quantify and ultimately unimportant in setting gold's market price. In practice, gold's day-to-day value came not from miners' labor, but from the operation of market laws of scarcity, supply, and demand. The gold miners' labor, then, seemed to disappear from the problem of intrinsic value, social value, and labor value; it played no role in the value of gold or of gold money.

John Stuart Mill confirmed the unimportance of gold miners' labor in 1852, after observing gold rushes in California and Australia. It did not really matter, he wrote, how much labor and capital it took to produce gold. Sometimes, he noticed, miners found gold with very little effort; in other cases, the extraction required immense labor. In either case, gold's market value remained the same. The market price really depended on the quantity of gold produced and the total supply of gold available in the market, no matter what it cost in labor to produce. See John Stuart Mill, *Prin-*

ciples of Political Economy, ed. W. J. Ashley (1848; reprint, London: Longmans, 1940), 503–504. Why, then, did miners work so hard to find gold? An ounce of gold was not worth more if it took ten times the usual effort to produce that nugget. There appeared to be no direct linkage between the labor of gold mining and the value of gold and gold money. In the late nineteenth century, gold standard supporters and Alaska-Yukon miners faced that disjunction head-on in their struggle to understand the place and role of gold mining within the laws and realities of the natural world.

33. Nugent, *Money and American Society*, 180–81; Unger, *Greenback Era*, 124, 129, 143–44.

34. Unger, *Greenback Era*, 123–24.

35. Wells, *The Silver Question*, 37.

36. Unger, *Greenback Era*, 121.

37. Goodwyn, *Democratic Promise*, 522.

38. David A. Wells, *Robinson Crusoe's Money*, rev. ed. (New York: Harper, 1896), 42–43.

39. See cover of Wells, *Robinson Crusoe's Money*.

40. Unger and Nugent make clear in their studies of the 1870s money debates that gold contained a wide range of Protestant moral and economic meanings, above and beyond its status as naturally valuable and naturally money. On the moral discourse concerning money, work, and honesty, especially within the Horatio Alger canon, see Carol Nackenoff, *The Fictional Republic: Horatio Alger and American Political Discourse* (New York: Oxford University Press, 1994), 146–61.

41. *Republican Congressional Committee, Republican Campaign Textbook, 1896* (Washington, D.C.: Republican Congressional Committee, 1896), 317–18.

42. John Higham, "The Reorientation of American Culture in the 1890s," in *The Origins of Modern Consciousness*, ed. by John Weiss (Detroit: Wayne State University, 1965), 27.

43. For McKinley poster, see John Mack Faragher et al., eds., *Out of Many: A History of the American People*, 3rd combined ed. (Upper Saddle River, N.J.: Prentice Hall, 2000), 594. According to a popular magazine digest, newspaper cartoons played a larger part in this election "than ever before in our political history." See *American Monthly Review of Reviews* 14 (November 1896): 557, 541.

44. Cartoon from *American Monthly Review of Reviews* 14 (November 1896): 541.

45. Wells, *Robinson Crusoe's Money*, 98–100; illustration on p. 7.

46. Goodwyn, *Democratic Promise*, 10–11.

47. *American Monthly Review of Reviews* 14 (November 1896): 542; *American Monthly Review of Reviews* 22 (November 1900); Goodwyn, *Democratic Promise*, 11–12;

Nugent, *Money and American Society*, 189; William McKinley, "Letter of Acceptance of Republican Party Presidential Nomination, 26 August 1896," Republican National Convention, *Official Proceedings of Eleventh Republican National Convention* (Pittsburgh: James Francis Burke, 1896), 151.

48. Goodwyn, *Democratic Promise*, 370–71.

49. Ignatius Donnelly, *The American People's Money* (Chicago, 1896; reprint, Hartford: Hyperion, 1976), 133. On Donnelly, see Jones, *Presidential Election of 1896*, 32–33.

50. Donnelly, *American People's Money*, 133. As many undergraduates are aware, several historians have argued that L. Frank Baum's *The Wonderful Wizard of Oz* is an allegory of the Populist Movement of the 1890s. Hugh Rockoff's 1990 article argued that the story is actually more specifically an allegory of the monetary debates, or at least contains numerous details that are direct references to the specifics of the monetary debates. See Hugh Rockoff, "The 'Wizard of Oz' as a Monetary Allegory," *Journal of Political Economy* 98 (August 1990), and Ritter, *Goldbugs and Greenbacks*, 21–25. The word Oz, for instance, refers to ounce; the tornado is the free silver movement; the witch wears silver shoes, and so on.

51. Donnelly, *American People's Money*, 183; on appeal of these ideas in the campaign, see Ritter, *Goldbugs and Greenbacks*, 58–61.

52. Nugent, *Money and American Society*, 28. For a broader view of producer ideology and the labor theory of value in the United States, see T. J. Jackson Lears, "The Concept of Cultural Hegemony: Problems and Possibilities," *American Historical Review* 90 (June 1985): 574–77.

53. *Puck* 41 (August 11, 1897).

54. Daniel T. Rodgers, *The Work Ethic in Industrial America, 1850–1920* (Chicago: University of Chicago Press, 1974), 213–14; Nugent, *Money and American Society*, 195. On the agrarian West, South, and Midwest in the election, see Jones, *Presidential Election of 1896*, 90.

55. Friedman and Schwartz, *Monetary History of the United States*, 8, 97. For a concise analysis of the price trends and deflation in relation to the money supply, see Rockoff, "The 'Wizard of Oz,'" 741–45.

56. Economists with a more skilled understanding of the way the economy grew after the Civil War have since argued that a bushel of wheat selling for thirty cents was not the social evil that the farmers perceived—though the perceptions were real and deeply felt. Scholars argue that it was not the contraction of the currency supply alone, but rather a combination of factors that caused price declines, including the increase in production of the post-war industrial expansion. The economy simply grew faster than the money supply. Lower prices hurt producers, but they

benefited consumers—a group that included farmers and urban workers. But falling prices in relation to a gold-based dollar were real, and had real repercussions for many of the Americans who expressed mounting discontent with monetary policy. See Unger, *Greenback Era,* 49; Ritter, *Goldbugs and Greenbacks,* 74–78.

57. Donnelly, *American People's Money,* 93.

58. Donnelly, "Gabriel's Utopia," in George Brown Tindall, ed., *A Populist Reader: Selections from the Works of American Populist Leaders* (New York: Harper & Row, 1966), 110. Other document collections that provide equally rich material include Vernon Carstensen, ed., *Farmer Discontent, 1865–1900* (New York: Wiley, 1974), and Arno Press, comp., *Gold and Silver in the Presidential Campaign of 1896* (New York: Arno Press, 1974).

59. William H. Harvey, *Coin's Financial School* (1894; reprint, ed. Richard Hofstadter, Cambridge, Mass.: Harvard University Press, 1963), 87. On William Harvey, see Jones, *Presidential Election of 1896,* 32–33. William Jennings Bryan referred to this illustration in his speeches, stressing the unlimited abundance of agricultural products in contrast with this paltry cube of metal. See Arthur M. Schlesinger, Jr., ed., *History of American Presidential Elections, 1789–1968,* vol. 2, *1858* (New York: Chelsea House, 1971).

60. Donnelly, *American People's Money,* 92. Donnelly's and Harvey's hyperbolic rhetoric was not without basis in reality. Gilded Age economic thinkers realized that there was rarely enough currency circulating in the country to purchase the abundant crops that farmers produced each season. They noticed that the annual demands for currency ran in cycles, attuned to the natural cycles of planting and harvest. Demand for cash reached its highest during and after harvest, when farmers moved their crops to market, buyers sent back to banks for currency, and banks sent to New York for currency. Each year saw an annual flow of crops toward the city and money away from the city. This caused panic over whether there was enough money to cover the incoming crops. See Unger, *Greenback Era,* 66. The two "natural" cycles, one based on crop harvests, the other based on the amount of gold that represented the value of those crops, failed to match up, creating financial imbalances. Some economists asked themselves whether the money supply might be made more flexible, and less natural, in order to handle the seasonal give-and-take of farm production without crisis. See Edwin Walter Kemmerer, "Seasonal Variations in the Relative Demand for Money and Capital in the United States: A Statistical Study," Senate Doc. 588 (Washington, D.C.: National Monetary Commission, 1910).

61. Nugent, *Money and American Society,* 51, 39–41.

62. Charles D. Lane, "The Gold Miner and the Silver Question," *Overland Monthly* 28 (November 1896): 585–88.

63. On general issues in the election and the moral importance on both sides, see Jones, *Presidential Election of 1896,* 338–40.

64. Kemmerer, *Gold and the Gold Standard,* 104.

65. *American Monthly Review of Reviews* 17 (March 1898): 266.

66. *San Francisco Examiner,* July 25, 1897.

67. Berton, *Klondike,* 94–95.

68. "The Northern Gold Fields," *The Nation,* 29 July 1897, 83.

69. A. C. Harris, *Alaska and the Klondike Gold Fields* (Chicago: Monroe Book Company, 1897), 110–11.

70. Hunter Fitzhugh letter, Rampart, Alaska, July 5, 1900, Robert Hunter Fitzhugh Collection, Box 2, UAF. Fitzhugh's letters were later published in Ann Carlisle Carmichael, ed., *Hunter: The Yukon Gold Rush Letters of Robert Hunter Fitzhugh, Jr., 1897–1900* (Montgomery, Ala.: Black Belt Press, 1999).

2 / THE NATURE OF THE JOURNEY

1. Hunter Fitzhugh letter, Lake Teslin, May 5, 1898, Robert Hunter Fitzhugh Collection, Box 2, UAF.

2. Pierre Berton, *Klondike: The Last Great Gold Rush, 1896–1899* (Toronto: McLelland & Stewart, 1958; rev. ed., 1972), 95, 90.

3. Some miners attempted to travel overland from the Canadian interior. This discussion focuses on three major routes of river transportation used by the majority of American miners (and the majority of all miners): the ascent of the Yukon from its mouth at St. Michael; the ascent of the Stikine River to Telegraph Creek, B.C.; and the descent of the Yukon from its headwaters beyond the Chilkoot and White Passes.

4. R. Cole Harris, *The Resettlement of British Columbia: Essays on Colonialism and Geographical Change* (Vancouver, B.C.: University of British Columbia Press, 1997), 161–62.

5. Stephen Kern, *The Culture of Time and Space, 1880–1918* (Cambridge: Harvard University Press, 1986), 15, 110–11, 125. As Kern points out, Jules Verne wrote of going around the world in eighty days. As William Cronon writes of the railroad, "No earlier invention had so fundamentally altered people's expectations of how long it took to travel between two distant points on the continent, for no earlier form of transportation had ever moved people so quickly." Cronon continues that railroad and telegraph systems "together . . . shrank the whole perceptual universe of North America." See William Cronon, *Nature's Metropolis: Chicago and the Great West* (New York: W. W. Norton, 1991), 76.

6. *Chicago Record, Klondike: The Chicago Record's Book for Gold Seekers* (Chicago: Chicago Record Co., 1897), 100–104.

7. William B. Ballou letter, March 24, 1898, William B. Ballou Papers, 1889–1918, UAF. Pierre Berton also reports a fare drop to ten dollars for tickets from Chicago to the coast in *Klondike*, 95.

8. *Chicago Record, Klondike*, 96–97.

9. *Ho! for Alaska: How to Go, What to take, What It Costs, What You Find* (New York: Republic Press, 1897), University of Washington Microfiche Collection, M-2501, no. 14011.

10. Tacoma–Port Orchard Navigation Co., "Stikine River Route to the Klondike: Shortest, Safest, Quickest, and Best" (Tacoma, Wash., 1898). University of Washington Microfiche Collection, M-2501, no. 15918.

11. Cronon, *Nature's Metropolis*, 74–81.

12. Barry C. Anderson, *Lifeline to the Yukon: A History of Yukon River Navigation* (Seattle: Superior Publishing, 1983), 48.

13. James H. Hamil letter, Oct. 8, 1897, Vertical File Manuscript, UAF.

14. Edward S. Curtis, "The Rush to the Klondike Over the Mountain Passes," *Century Magazine* 55 (February 1898): 692–93. In this article, Curtis claimed credit for photographs from the trail actually taken by Asahel Curtis, and this caused a serious fraternal rift.

15. Richard White, *The Organic Machine: The Remaking of the Columbia River* (New York: Hill & Wang, 1995), 9.

16. Berton, *Klondike*, 243–44.

17. Jonas B. Houck letters, March 29, 1898; April 28, 1898, Jonas B. Houck Papers, UAF.

18. Alfred "Mac" McMichael letters, March 31, 1898; April 3, 1898, Alfred McMichael Diary and Letters, Juliette Reinicker Papers, MSS 100, Acc. 79/68, YA. On numbers on the trails in spring 1898, see Tappan Adney, *The Klondike Stampede* (1900; reprint, Vancouver, B.C.: University of British Columbia Press, 1994), 360.

19. "Diary of Mr. Harold Petersen," August 28, 1897, Vertical File MS, UAF.

20. Rebecca Schuldenfrei letter, Sept. 25, 1897, Schuldenfrei Family Papers, MSS 166, Acc. 84/47, YA.

21. Houck letters, 29 March 1898; 28 April 1898.

22. Margaret Carter, "A History of the Use of Wood in the Yukon to 1903" (Ottawa: National Historic Sites Service, 1973), DCM, 102. For wood, miners traveled further and further upstream from the lakes, searching out the last patches of spruce, poplar, birch, and balsam for what seemed to all of them an "astonishing" number of small craft. Samuel Dunham confirmed in 1897 that there were sawmills

operating at the lakes, but no wood left to buy. Frank Purdy found the number of boats lined up "astonishing" in June 1898, in a line two or three deep for over a mile below the landing. See Frank Purdy Diary, June 1, 1898, Vertical File MS, UAF. James Hamil reported going up a river four and a half miles in 1897 to cut timber near Lindeman. Hamil letter, Oct. 8, 1897. Jonas Houck walked seven miles back into the mountains from the lakes to find boat timber in 1898, as did Mac McMichael. All along the trails, McMichael wrote, "Men are continually asking . . . 'Do you know where there is any good timber?' A few men will camp in a cove where there is a grove of passable timber," he lamented, "and within a week, from twenty to forty tents will go up until the timber is gone." McMichael letter, April 24, 1898. In the spring of 1898, Thomas Moore reported forests of heavy timber, including poplar, birch, and spruce a hundred feet high, on the shores of Lake Labarge, the northernmost of the big lakes. A year later the Yukon Territory timber agent sent Corporal Evans of the Mounties to inspect timber berths along the lakes in 1899. On berth #7 on Lake Laberge, Evans found "four miles of timber more or less cut through." See Thomas Moore account, 1898, MSS 007, Acc. 82/121, YA; and Timber Agent Reports, 1899–1900, Govt. no. 1683, File 43 1(2), Government Records, YA.

23. Hamil letter, October 8, 1897; McMichael letter, April 29, 1898, YA; Fitzhugh letter, Oct. 29, 1900. Fitzhugh was actually cutting wood for a cabin, not a boat, at the time.

24. Diary of James S. Cooper and Associates, TS, Sept. 28, 1897; Oct. 1–4, 1897, Diaries File, File Collection, DCM.

25. Hamil letter, October 8, 1897.

26. Adney, *Klondike Stampede,* 136–38, 151, 165–66.

27. Diary of F. Wm. Hiscock, June 5, 1898, "The Youkon Trail of Year 1898," TS, Diaries File, File Collection, DCM. Hiscock learned that balsam would not do for oars from a helpful "Yank."

28. McMichael letter, May 19, 1898; Fitzhugh letter, May 24, 1898.

29. Hiscock diary, May 31, 1898; McMichael letter, May 25, 1898.

30. Adney, *Klondike Stampede,* 386.

31. Purdy diary, June 1, 1898.

32. Charles P. Mosier diary, June 3, 1898, MSS 012, Acc. 82/168, YA; Tom Boldrick diary, June 2, 1898, Vertical File MS, Klondike Miners, UAF.

33. Hiscock diary, May 31, 1898.

34. McMichael letter, June 10, 1898. When James McCrae arrived at Five Finger Rapids, further down the river, he found some friends working as pilots: "Found the boys there running boats through the Rapids. They had turned Pilots. Their experience down the River on a raft had given them courage." See James A. McRae diary,

"Bound for the Klondyke," June 14, 1898, MSS 104, Acc. 80/1, YA. Lynn Smith had a pilot take his boat through White Horse Rapids and used a tramway for freight. See Lynn Smith letter, June 2, 1898, Robert Lynn Smith Correspondence and Diaries, Box 1, Herbert Heller Collection, UAF. Various sources mention the hiring of Indian pilots on the upper river. See also Charlene Porsild, "Culture, Class, and Community: New Perspectives on the Klondike Gold Rush, 1896–1905" (Ph.D. diss., Carleton University, Ottawa, 1994), 93.

35. Boldrick diary, June 4, 1898.

36. McMichael letter, July 13, 1898; Boldrick diary, June 7, 1898; Hiscock diary, June 11, 1898; Boldrick diary, June 3, 1898; Hamil letter, Oct. 8, 1897.

37. Boldrick diary, July 13, June 14–21, June 29, July 2, June 16, 23, 1898; White, *Organic Machine,* 7.

38. McMichael letters, July 1, 9, 1898.

39. McMichael letter, July 13, 1898; John Sidney Webb, "The River Trip to the Klondike," *Century Magazine* 55 (February 1898): 685–86.

40. Smith letter, Dec. 1, 1898; Fitzhugh letter, Nov. 12, 1899; Fitzhugh letter, March 2, 1900; Ballou letter, April 12, 1900; John C. Cantwell, *Report of the Operations of the U.S. Revenue Steamer "Nunivak" on the Yukon River Station, Alaska, 1899–1901* (Washington, D.C.: GPO, 1904), 146.

41. Fitzhugh letters, Jan. 7, Feb. 24, 1898.

42. Cantwell, *Nunivak,* 155.

43. Fitzhugh letters, Oct. 29, Oct. 5, 1898.

44. Ballou letter, April 25, 1902.

45. Cantwell, *Nunivak,* 95. Adney wrote, "At night, however, enough winter returned to freeze the trails for the dog-teams hurrying supplies and lumber to the mines before the final break-up." See Adney, *Klondike Stampede,* 359. At the end of March, Bill Ballou wrote that "about a week more will end our darkness, then all the 'mushing' will be done at night when it is cool." Ballou letter, March 31, 1902. O. G. Herning hauled wood to Willow Creek at night in April 1903, "working in the middle of the night to sled on the crust." O. G. Herning diaries, March–April, 1903, O. G. Herning Collection, UAF.

46. Ballou letter, April 25, 1898.

47. McMichael letter, Dawson City, June 22, 1898.

48. *Trade Register* (Seattle), 25 February 1899, 10.

49. Adney, *Klondike Stampede,* 385.

50. Roy Minter, *The White Pass: Gateway to the Klondike* (Fairbanks: University of Alaska Press, 1987), 347; *Trade Register* (Seattle), 7 April 1900, 17; 5 May 1900, 7.

51. McMichael letter, June 23, 1898; Angelo Heilprin, *Alaska and the Klondike:*

A Journey to the New Eldorado with Hints to the Traveler (London: C. Arthur Pearson, 1899), 25.

52. McMichael letter, March–April 1899; *Trade Register* (Seattle), 11 August 1900, 22; Edward C. Adams, "Dairy [*sic*] of the Tripp from Seattle to Dawson City and also for the whole year of 1900," 1900, Vertical File MS, UAF; Ballou letter, Sept. 12, 1901.

53. Harris, *Resettlement of British Columbia,* 161–62; Harrington Emerson, "The Rail Route to the Klondike," *American Monthly Review of Reviews* 20 (September 1899): 350.

54. Arnold F. George, Alaska-Yukon-Pacific Exposition Address, Govt. no. 1641, File 16721, YA.

55. Curtis, "Rush to the Klondike," 697.

56. A. A. Hill, "The Klondike," *Munsey's Magazine* 20 (February 1899): 704.

57. Cited in David Harvey, *Justice, Nature, and the Geography of Difference* (Cambridge, Mass.: Blackwell, 1996), 242.

58. Harris, *Resettlement of British Columbia,* 183; Cronon, *Nature's Metropolis,* ch. 5.

3 / THE CULTURE OF THE JOURNEY

1. Nora Crane letter, July 9, 1897, Kepner-Crane Collection, Microfiche, UAF.

2. As visible in a photograph printed in Henry Davis, "Recollections," in *Sourdough Sagas,* Herbert L. Heller, ed. (Cleveland: World Publishing, 1967), 31.

3. "Diary of Mr. Harold Petersen," fall 1897, Vertical File MS, UAF; Kenneth S. Coates, *Best Left as Indians: Native-White Relations in the Yukon Territory, 1840–1973* (Montreal: McGill-Queen's University Press, 1991), 35.

4. Tlingit bands along the coast of the Lynn Canal crossed the Chilkoot to trade both local and European goods with the Tagish or "Stick" Indians of the interior, with whom they shared trade, linguistic, and cultural ties, as well as a high rate of intermarriage; both groups were accustomed to carrying trade goods over the Chilkoot Pass, though the more powerful Tlingit exerted significant political control over the area, dictating who could cross and effectively excluding both Tagish people and whites whenever they chose to do so. In 1880, however, a direct confrontation with the U.S. Navy, in which a Gatling gun was displayed but never fired, convinced the local Tlingits to allow gold prospectors up the Chilkoot Trail. The Natives also cautiously extended their services as packers to miners and explorers. Sources on trade and cultural contact over the passes include Catharine McClellan and Glenda Denniston, "Environment and Culture in the Cordillera," and Cather-

ine McClellan, "Tagish," in *Handbook of North American Indians,* vol. 6, *Subarctic,* ed. June Helm, gen. ed. William C. Sturtevant (Washington, D.C.: Smithsonian Institution, 1981), 481–82, 489–90; Frederica De Laguna, "Tlingit," in *Handbook of North American Indians,* vol. 7, *Northwest Coast,* ed. Wayne Suttles, gen. ed. William C. Sturtevant (Washington, D.C.: Smithsonian Institution, 1990), 372, 150; Julie Cruikshank, *Life Lived Like a Story: Life Stories of Three Yukon Native Elders* (Lincoln: University of Nebraska Press, 1990), 8; Cruikshank, "Discovery of Gold on the Klondike: Perspectives from Oral Tradition," in *Reading Beyond Words: Contexts for Native History,* ed. Jennifer S. H. Brown and Elizabeth Vibert (Peterborough, Ontario, Canada: Broadview Press, 1996), 442; and Cruikshank, "Images of Society in Klondike Gold Rush Narratives: Skookum Jim and the Discovery of Gold," *Ethnohistory* 39 (winter 1992): 22–25.

On conflict over the passes and the Gatling gun incident, see De Laguna, "Tlingit," 150; Morgan Sherwood, *Exploration of Alaska, 1865–1900* (New Haven: Yale University Press, 1965; Fairbanks: University of Alaska Press, 1988), 123, 146; and Josiah Edward Spurr, *Through the Yukon Gold Diggings: A Narrative of Personal Travel* (Boston: Eastern Publishing Company, 1900), 37. Spurr dated the Navy-Chilkoot negotiation at 1878, however. Henry Davis remembered another story from 1886. He arrived at Dyea to find a crowd of Indians, mostly Hoonahs and Chilkoots, milling around. The Chilkoots were blocking all forward movement over the Chilkoot because they did not want the Hoonahs to pack for white men. Stalemated, the miners sent for John Healy, who got some soldiers to come up to Dyea from Haines Mission, just south on the Lynn Canal. Negotiations ensued between two officers, Healy and the "head man" of the Hoonahs and Chilkoots. Two hours later, they came out, having made peace, "saying they were all ready to pack." See Davis, "Recollections," 38–39.

5. McClellan, "Tagish," 482; Cruikshank, "Discovery of Gold on the Klondike," 436; Lt. Frederick Schwatka, *Along Alaska's Great River, Together with the Latest Information on the Klondike Country* (Chicago: G. M. Hill Co., 1898), 61–62.

6. Spurr, *Through the Yukon Gold Diggings,* 39.

7. Samuel C. Dunham, *The Alaskan Gold Fields* (1898; reprint, Anchorage: Alaska Northwest Pub. Co., 1983), 11–12. This was originally published as "The Alaskan Gold Fields and the Opportunities They Offer for Capital and Labor," *Bulletin of the Department of Labor,* no. 16 (May 1898): 297–425.

8. David Arnold, "Work, Culture, and Environment: Tlingit Fishing and Economic Change, 1890s–1940s" (paper presented at the annual conference of the Western History Association, Lincoln, Nebraska, October 5, 1996), 3–4.

9. David Arnold, "'Putting Up Fish': Environment, Work, and Culture in Tlin-

git Society, 1780s–1940s" (Ph.D. diss., University of California, Los Angeles, 1997), ch. 3, 34–35.

10. Tappan Adney, *The Klondike Stampede* (New York, 1900; reprint, Vancouver, B.C.: University of British Columbia Press, 1994), 96, 95.

11. Spurr, *Through the Yukon Gold Diggings,* 47.

12. Rebecca Schuldenfrei letters, Sept. 16, 20, 1897, Schuldenfrei Family Papers, MSS 166, Acc. 84/47, YA.

13. James H. Hamil letter, October 8, 1897, Vertical File MS, UAF.

14. Adney, *Klondike Stampede,* 92.

15. Hamil letter, Oct. 8, 1897.

16. Alfred "Mac" McMichael diary, April 8, 1898, Alfred McMichael Diary and Letters, Juliette Reinicker Papers, MSS 100, Acc. 79/68, YA.

17. McMichael letter, April 8, 1898.

18. Dunham, *Alaskan Gold Fields,* 27–28.

19. Pierre Berton, *Klondike: The Last Great Gold Rush, 1896–1899* (Toronto: McLelland & Stewart, 1958; rev. ed., 1972), 244.

20. Ibid., 247.

21. Sam Stone Bush, "The Rush to the Klondike," *American Monthly Review of Reviews* 17 (March 1898): 299–300.

22. *Trade Register* (Seattle), 23 April 1898, 25.

23. Ibid., 4 March 1899, 9.

24. Charles P. Mosier Diary, April 4, 1898, MSS 012, Acc. 82/168, YA. Mosier reported that heavy snow caused the slide.

25. McMichael letter, Sheep Camp, April 6, 1898.

26. McMichael letter, April 3, 1898.

27. Diary of Stewart L. Campbell, Feb. 21, 1898, MSS 122, Acc. 81/129, YA.

28. Bill Hiscock's party arrived in Skagway in April 1898 and paid five and a half cents a pound to a firm that packed their 2,600 pounds on horses and mules to the top of the pass. Diary of F. Wm. Hiscock, April 16, 1898, "The Youkon Trail of Year 1898," TS, Diaries File, File Collection, DCM; Adney, *Klondike Stampede,* 46, 56.

29. Berton, *Klondike,* 143–45; Adney, *Klondike Stampede,* 18–19.

30. Adney, *Klondike Stampede,* 46–47.

31. On energy and work, see Richard White, *Organic Machine: The Remaking of the Columbia River* (New York: Hill & Wang, 1995), 6–7.

32. Hiscock diary, April 26, 1898.

33. Adney, *Klondike Stampede,* 109; Berton, *Klondike,* 238–39, 242.

34. Adney, *Klondike Stampede,* 80, 62–63; Berton, *Klondike,* 142; Jonas B. Houck diary, May 15, 1898, Jonas B. Houck Papers, UAF.

35. Hiscock diary, April 29, 1898.

36. McMichael letters, July 22, July 9, 1898.

37. Lynn Smith letter, Sept. 19, 1898, Robert Lynn Smith Correspondence and Diaries, Box 1, Herbert Heller Collection, UAF.

38. McMichael letter, August 26, 1898.

39. U.S. Consul letter, March 1898, "Despatches from U.S. Consuls in Dawson City, Canada, 1898–1906," Microfilm no. 199, UAF.

40. Schwatka, *Along Alaska's Great River,* 220.

41. Tom Boldrick diary, June 2, 1898, Vertical File MS, Klondike Miners, UAF.

42. McMichael letter, August 26, 1898.

43. Hunter Fitzhugh letter, May 18, 1899, Robert Hunter Fitzhugh Collection, Box 2, UAF.

44. Adney, *Klondike Stampede,* 221.

45. John C. Cantwell, *Report of the Operations of the U.S. Revenue Steamer "Nunivak" on the Yukon River Station, Alaska, 1899–1901* (Washington, D.C.: GPO, 1904), 159.

46. Schwatka, *Along Alaska's Great River,* 313; Dunham, *Alaskan Gold Fields,* 63.

47. Clara Hickman Rust, "To Fairbanks by Steamboat," *Alaska Journal* 1 (winter 1971): 20–26.

48. Crane letter, NAT&T Steamer, July 1897.

49. R. Cole Harris, *The Resettlement of British Columbia: Essays on Colonialism and Geographical Change* (Vancouver, B.C.: University of British Columbia Press, 1997), 169–72.

50. Adney, *Klondike Stampede,* 190–92; Paula Mitchell Marks, *Precious Dust: The American Gold Rush Era, 1848–1900* (New York: William Morrow, 1994), 130.

51. Capt. W. P. Richardson, Eighth Infantry, U.S.A., "The Mighty Yukon as Seen and Explored," in U.S. Congress, Senate, Committee on Military Affairs, *Compilation of Narratives of Explorations in Alaska, 1869–1900* (Washington, D.C.: GPO, 1900), 745.

52. Adney, *Klondike Stampede,* 163.

53. Thomas W. Moore Account, summer 1898, MSS 007, Acc. 82/121, YA.

54. James Lynn Anderson diary, May 1898, vol. 2, James Lynn Anderson Diaries, 1895–1899, Vertical File MS, UAF.

55. Letter, July 18, 1898, Boston-Alaska Transportation Co., Vertical File MS, UAF.

56. Anderson diary, vol. 1, Sept. 29, 1897.

57. Walter R. Curtin, *Unofficial Log of the Steamer Yukoner* (Caldwell, Idaho: Caxton Printers, 1938), 226.

58. Stewart L. Campbell diary, May 31, June 4–5, 8, 1898, MSS 122, Acc. 81/129, YA.

59. McMichael letter, Sept. 22, 1898.

60. Harrison Kepner letter, Dec. 23, 1896, Kepner-Crane Collection, UAF.

61. Curtin, *Unofficial Log*, 226; Cantwell, *Nunivak*, 37.

62. Steamers began plying the Stikine in 1862, carrying supplies for fur traders and miners, but became firmly entrenched in 1874 with the Cassiar Gold Rush to Dease Lake in British Columbia, for which the river provided direct access and transport. At the height of the Klondike rush on the Stikine, fourteen steamers plied the 150–mile stretch of the river above Wrangell. John C. Callbreath letter, July 18, 1898, Callbreath, Grant, & Cook Papers, Charles Hubbell Collection, UW; R. N. DeArmond, "Riverboating on the Stikine," *Alaska Journal* 9 (autumn 1979): 68–81; William P. Blake, *Geographical Notes Upon Russian America and the Stickeen River, Being A Report Addressed to the Hon. W.H. Seward, Secretary of State, with a Map of the Stickeen River* (Washington, D.C.: GPO, 1868), 5–6.

63. Callbreath diary, 1880; July 2, 1892.

64. Ibid., May 30–June 11, 1894.

65. Cantwell, *Nunivak*, 131–32.

66. Crane letter, July 9, 1897.

67. Melody Webb, *The Last Frontier: A History of the Yukon Basin of Canada and Alaska* (Albuquerque: University of New Mexico Press, 1985), 26; Cantwell, *Nunivak*, 133.

68. Cantwell, *Nunivak*, 134.

69. "Wood Reports, Steamer Dawson, 1901," Steamer Wood Reports, British Yukon Navigation Company, 1901, Govt. no. 1684, File 65, YA; Bruce L. Willis, "The Environmental Effects of the Yukon Gold Rush 1896–1906: Alterations to Land, Destruction of Wildlife, and Disease" (Master's thesis, University of Western Ontario, 1997), 40.

70. A typical steamboat burned a cord an hour moving downstream, but moving against the current demanded far more energy, and thus far more wood. For the steamer *Dawson,* running between Whitehorse and Dawson City, the ratio of cords burned going upstream to those burned running downstream was about 2.7 to 1. The captain purchased over two and a half times as much wood to move against the current, a measurement in cut trees of the nature of the river itself. On rivers and energy, see White, *Organic Machine,* chaps. 1–2, esp. 10–15 and 30–38. I calculated this ratio from the numbers provided in "Wood Reports, Steamer Dawson, 1901," and "Wood Reports, Steamer Dawson, 1902," Steamer Fuel Reports, British Yukon Navigation Company, 1902, Trips 1–18, Govt. no. 1683, File 47 1(2), YA; William R. Hunt, *Whiskey Peddler: Johnny Healy, North Frontier Trader* (Missoula, Mont.: Mountain Press Pub. Co., 1993), 147.

71. Cantwell, *Nunivak,* 118, 91.

72. U.S. Consul letter, July 28, 1899. When the Canadian government at Dawson stepped in to regulate timber cutting, the office of the Crown Timber Agent granted parcels in the form of five-square-mile "timber berths" for cordwood and larger timber in exchange for a nominal fee and a tax of fifty cents per cord. Because none of the land had been surveyed, the Timber Agent recorded the location of timber berths the only possible way, by simply describing them, and the only way to find or designate land was in relation to rivers. The berths in question all consisted of huge swaths of riparian land, which indicated again how intensively woodcutting focused on the rivers, and how important it was to cut wood close to the water in order to sell it to boats and to transport it to Dawson and other town markets. One berth included all of the timber in an area, starting on the "East bank of Yukon 2 1/2 miles above Indian [River] running up 1 mile with a depth of one mile on the East bank." Overall, wrote one historian, wood during the gold rush "was carelessly cut and functionally abused by inexperienced hands. It was consumed in unprecedented quantities in congested areas by a proportionately unprecedented increase of population." See Timber Berths, 1898, 19 August 1898, Govt. no. 1684, File 68, 1(2), YA; and Margaret Carter, "A History of the Use of Wood in the Yukon to 1903" (Ottawa: National Historic Sites Service, 1973), DCM, 157.

73. Schwatka, *Along Alaska's Great River,* 334–35.

74. Crane letter, July 9, 1897.

75. Webb, *Last Frontier,* 745; Northern Design Consultants, "A History of Logging in the Yukon, 1896–1970," vol. 1 (Whitehorse, Yukon Territory: Northern Design Consultants, 1993), 11–12, DCM; Cantwell, *Nunivak,* 132.

76. Will Childs Letters, MSS 166, Acc. 84/65, YA.

77. Moore account.

78. Carter, "A History of the Use of Wood in the Yukon to 1903," 70.

79. Smith letter, March 2, 1899.

80. Carter, "A History of the Use of Wood," 118; Webb, *Last Frontier,* 26; Cantwell, *Nunivak,* 133.

81. McMichael diary, September 24, 1898; Smith letter, August 21, 1898.

82. Cantwell, *Nunivak,* 144.

4 / THE NATURE OF GOLD MINING

1. Diary of F. Wm. Hiscock, April 1898, November 1898, "The Youkon Trail of Year 1898," TS, Diaries File, File Collection, DCM.

2. For a recent detailed account, see Bruce L. Willis, "The Environmental Effects of the Yukon Gold Rush 1896–1906: Alterations to Land, Destruction of Wildlife, and Disease" (Master's thesis, University of Western Ontario, 1997).

3. U.S. Department of the Interior, National Park Service, *Final Environmental Impact Statement,* vol. 1, *Mining in Yukon-Charley Rivers National Preserve, Alaska,* (Washington, D.C.: GPO, 1990), 32.

4. John A. Gould and Richard C. Stuart, "Permafrost Gold: A Treatise on Early Klondike Mining History, Methods and Technology," Microfiche Report Series No. 11 (Ottawa: Parks Canada, 1980), Microfiche, 18, DCM. At the start, in the 1880s and early 1890s, Yukon placer miners accomplished both these tasks during the brief northern summer. Then, mining had only one season: summer. Miners waited out the long frozen winters for the summer sun's thawing heat and the creeks' free-flowing water. Working long days and nights, they gathered what surface gravels the sun— and muscles—could loosen, and washed them before the streams dried and froze in the fall. When miners introduced fire-thawing of the permafrost, however, they created a more complicated, two-season pattern of work. They harnessed the duality of the northern climate in which the world was either frozen or unfrozen. Miners divided their work accordingly.

Gold miners in search of productive labor had initially chafed at the limits imposed by waiting ten frozen months every year for two unfrozen months of mining. Winter—frozen water and frozen earth—dominated life in the Yukon basin, and gold miners soon figured out a way to harness that frozenness to the task of mining and to extend the seasons of their own work. Harnessing the solar energy stored in wood, miners began to use small fires to thaw through the permafrost alongside and even underneath creeks in order to gain access to deeply buried gravels, which proved far richer than surface deposits. Accounts of the introduction of wood thawing vary. Michael Gates, *Gold at Fortymile Creek: Early Days in the Yukon* (Vancouver: University of British Columbia Press, 1994), reports that the first recorded use of fire thawing was in 1882 along the Sixtymile River. See Gates, 18, 62–63. In 1887, according to another version of the tale, a miner at Franklin gulch in the Fortymile district decided to try his hand at winter mining on a creek bed. After the creek surface froze, he chipped slowly downward through the ice, allowing the exposed water to freeze at each step. Eventually he reached the creek bed, through his vertical shaft of ice that kept the running water at bay. He then built a fire to thaw his way into the stream bed, initiating fire thawing, and thus winter mining, along the Yukon. Another version of the story was that Canadian government explorer and official William Ogilvie, sent to the Yukon to survey conditions, suggested building fires on frozen ground, thawing a layer, then building another fire deeper down, to slowly burn a mining shaft into the permafrost. Ogilvie had seen this used to expose burst water pipes in the winter streets of Ottawa. See Thomas Stone, *Miners' Justice: Migration, Law and Order on the Alaska-Yukon Frontier, 1873–1902* (New York: Peter Lang, 1988), 140, citing Ogilvie.

5. Alfred "Mac" McMichael letter, Fourth of July Creek, Oct. 27, 1898, Alfred McMichael Diary and Letters, Juliette Reinicker Papers, MSS 100, Acc. 79/68, YA; Charles P. Mosier diary, June 30, 1898, MSS 012, Acc. 82/168, YA.

6. William B. Ballou letter, Dec. 10, 1901, William B. Ballou Papers, 1889–1918, UAF.

7. James A. McRae diary, Sept. 1, 1899, "Bound for the Klondyke," MSS 104, Acc. 80/1, YA.

8. Tom Boldrick diary, July 4, 1898, Vertical File MS, Klondike Miners, UAF.

9. Willis, "Environmental Effects," 12.

10. James E. Beatty Papers, MSS 122, Acc. 82/390, YA.

11. *Alaska Forum* (Rampart), 28 Sept. 1901.

12. Willis, "Environmental Effects," 35–37.

13. Tappan Adney, *The Klondike Stampede* (1900; reprint, Vancouver, B.C.: University of British Columbia Press, 1994), 257.

14. Ballou letter, Oct. 19, 1901. When miners switched from fire thawing to steam thawing, they simply shifted wood consumption from underground shafts to boilers on the surface. Steam-powered operations excavated more ground with less wood, but the combinations of steam-driven thawers, pumps, and hoists managed to burn plenty of wood nonetheless. "I saw the wood myself," wrote Bill Ballou of his steam machines, "I keep the hoist running all the time . . . and the pump whenever it is needed . . . and at the same time I have to be constantly firing that old boiler which eats up a lot of wood in the twenty four hours." Ballou letter, Jan. 29, 1902.

15. Harold John Lutz, *Early Forest Conditions in the Alaska Interior: An Historical Account with Original Sources* (Juneau, Alaska: U.S. Department of Agriculture, U.S. Forest Service, Northern Forest Experiment Station, June 1963), 26.

16. U.S. Department of the Interior, National Park Service, *Mining in Yukon-Charley Rivers,* 32–33; J. Lewis Robinson, "Agriculture and Forests of Yukon Territory," ca. 1946, Govt. #2078, vol. 8A, File 20, 5–7, YA.

17. Lutz, *Early Forest Conditions,* 27.

18. Adney, *Klondike Stampede,* 251; Gould and Stuart, "Permafrost Gold," 69, citing Adney. See also Northern Design Consultants, "A History of Logging in the Yukon, 1896–1970," vol. 1 (Whitehorse, Yukon Territory: Northern Design Consultants, 1993), 11–12, DCM.

19. Ballou letter, Oct. 19, 1901.

20. Report on Wood, 1898, Govt. no. 2078, vol. 8A, File 3, YA.

21. Maud Case letter, June 29, 1903, George E. Case and Family Letters, MSS 172, Acc. 81/91, YA.

22. Gould and Stuart, "Permafrost Gold," 19.

23. Ibid., 19, 85.

24. On the dangers of drift mining, see Gates, *Gold at Fortymile,* 62.

25. Mosier diary, March 20, 1899; Ballou letter, June 10, 1899; Mosier diary, April 14, 1899; Frank Purdy diary, March 15–16, 1900, Vertical File MS, UAF.

26. McMichael letter, Dec. 10, 1898; Ballou letter, Sept. 18, 1898.

27. Gould and Stuart, "Permafrost Gold," 19.

28. Stewart L. Campbell diary, June 1899, MSS 122, Acc. 81/129, YA; Purdy diary, Dec. 8, 1898.

29. Gould and Stuart, "Permafrost Gold," 67–68.

30. Ibid., 89–90.

31. Ibid., 74.

32. Maud Case letter, July 26, 1903.

33. Purdy diary, Dec. 8, 1898; Asahel Curtis diary, Jan. 3, 17, 1899, Asahel Curtis Collection, UW; Lynn Smith letter, Glenn Gulch, Nov. 10, 1901, Robert Lynn Smith Correspondence and Diaries, Box 1, Herbert Heller Collection, UAF.

34. Iowa miners' letter, Nov. 21, 1898, reprinted in *Alton Democrat* (Iowa), May 13, 1899, William Michaels Collection, Iowa-Alaska Mining Company, UAF; Hunter Fitzhugh letter, Nov. 20, 1899, Robert Hunter Fitzhugh Collection, Box 2, UAF.

35. Smith letter, Jan. 11, 1899; McMichael letter, Jan. 3, 1899; Fitzhugh letter, Jan. 1900; Ballou letter, Hoosier Creek, Alaska, Feb. 17, 1901.

36. Jonas B. Houck letter, Dawson City, June 30, 1898, Jonas B. Houck Papers, UAF; Rodman Paul, *California Gold: The Beginning of Mining in the Far West* (Lincoln: University of Nebraska Press, 1947), 148.

37. Purdy diary, 1898 entries.

38. Smith letter, Esther Creek, Alaska, Nov. 1905; Mosier diary, Feb. 2, 1899.

39. Gould and Stuart, "Permafrost Gold," 7–10.

40. Adney, *Klondike Stampede,* 398–400.

41. *Alaska Forum* (Rampart), 27 Dec. 1900. Another example comes from the *Alaska Forum* of 11 July 1901: "A large number of men are over the divide staking and, from reports just to hand, the gold-bearing channel has been followed into Kentucky creek, where prospectors are working hard to find the place where the old channel crosses the creek."

42. Curtis diary, Jan. 2, 1899.

43. Purdy diary, March 1900.

44. Ballou letter describing spring work, June 10, 1899.

45. Adney, *Klondike Stampede,* 228.

46. Gould and Stuart, "Permafrost Gold," 82.

47. Adney, *Klondike Stampede,* 233–35.

48. Gould and Stuart, "Permafrost Gold," 48.

49. *Alaska Forum* (Rampart), 28 Sept. 1901.

50. Purdy diary, Cheechaco Hill, April 26, 1900. Many miners used pumping systems, but the steam engines that ran the pumps required enormous amounts of wood to maintain adequate water pressure. Some investors ended up building pumping stations, but charged customers for water, which often proved too expensive for individual miners. They measured water by the amount needed for sluicing, and paid by the sluice head. A sluice head of water could cost between four to eight dollars an hour during the placer mining rush. Gould and Stuart, "Permafrost Gold," 24–25, 53, 82.

51. Purdy diary, March 31, 1900, April 16, 1898.

52. U.S. Consul letter, May 1899, "Despatches from U.S. Consuls in Dawson City, Canada, 1898–1906," Microfilm no. 199, UAF.

53. Purdy diary, May 1900; John H. Lindsay letter, Eldorado Creek, April 17, 25, 1901, Lindsay Family Papers, MSS 12, Acc. 82/173, YA; Thomas W. Moore Account, June 12, 1898, MSS 007, Acc. 82/121, YA.

54. Ballou letter, June 16, 1902; Smith letter, June 18, 1902; Lindsay letter, June 10, 1900; *Alaska Forum* (Rampart), 23 May 1901.

55. Willis, "Environmental Effects," 16–17.

56. Lt. Frederick Schwatka, *Along Alaska's Great River, Together with the Latest Information on the Klondike Country* (Chicago: G.M. Hill Co., 1898), 168.

57. Pierre Berton, ed., *The Klondike Quest: A Photographic Essay* (Boston: Little Brown, 1983), ch. 7.

58. Adney, *Klondike Stampede,* 450; Ballou letter, June 10, 1899.

59. Gould and Stuart, "Permafrost Gold," 45–46.

60. Willis, "Environmental Effects," 44.

61. Andrew Goudie, *The Human Impact: Man's Role in Environmental Change* (Cambridge: MIT Press, 1981), 127.

62. Moore account, 1897–1898; Smith letter, July 9, 1898; Ballou letter, August 19, 1898.

63. Ballou letter, May 31, 1900.

64. U.S. Department of the Interior, National Park Service, *Mining in Yukon-Charley Rivers,* 33, 57.

65. C. O. Steiner Diary, "A Journey to Dawson in 1898," Vertical File MS, UAF;

Robert Marshall, *Arctic Village: A 1930s Portrait of Wiseman, Alaska* (1933; reprint, Fairbanks: University of Alaska Press, 1991), 162, 174; Willis, "Environmental Effects," 64–65.

66. Adney, *Klondike Stampede*, 404.

67. Edward C. Adams, "Dairy [*sic*] of the Tripp from Seattle to Dawson City and also for the whole year of 1900," August 15, 1900, Vertical File MS, UAF. For more details on the two eras of Yukon mining, the gold rush and post-1900 dredging, see Willis, "Environmental Effects," ch. 3. Paula Mitchell Marks discusses the effects of gold mining in western rushes in general. Gold miners, she writes, left the earth "attacked, rearranged, washed, and dumped." See Paula Mitchell Marks, *Precious Dust: The American Gold Rush Era, 1848–1900* (New York: William Morrow, 1994), 151.

68. See for instance, Norm Bolotin, ed., *Klondike Lost: A Decade of Photographs by Kinsey & Kinsey* (Anchorage: Alaska Northwest, 1980), 35, 46, 51, 53, 88, 92–93; Berton, ed., *Klondike Quest*, ch. 7.

69. Bylaws amended and adopted by Miners Meeting, June 15, 1899, Jack Wade Creek Mining District, Box 5, Herbert Heller Papers, UAF.

70. Gould and Stuart, "Permafrost Gold," 46.

71. Purdy diary, Dec. 9, 1899.

72. Ballou letter, Jan 29, 1902.

73. Smith letter, Dec. 2, 1901.

74. Ibid., Oct. 29, 1901.

75. Purdy diary, Jan. 19, 1900.

76. Smith letters, Oct. 22, 29, 1901; Ballou letters, Aug. 31, Oct. 5, 1899.

77. U.S. Department of the Interior, National Park Service, *Mining in Yukon-Charley Rivers*, 77–80.

78. See Willis, "Environmental Effects," 69–72. The literature on the effects of placer mining on fish populations dates from the 1930s in California and the 1980s in Alaska. None of these studies, of course, apply directly to Yukon and Alaska placer mining during the 1890s gold rush. All of them conclude, however, that mining sediment increased stream water turbidity (cloudiness) in such a way as to significantly impair the lives of many native fish species. See Francis H. Sumner and Osgood R. Smith, "Hydraulic Mining and Debris Dams in Relation to Fish Life in the American and Yuba Rivers of California," *California Fish and Game* 26 (January 1940): 2–22; Henry Baldwin Ward, "Placer Mining on the Rogue River, Oregon, in Its Relation to the Fish and Fishing in that Stream" (Portland: Oregon Dept. of Geology and Mineral Industries, 1938), 4–31; Almo J. Cordone and Don W. Kelley, "The Influences of Inorganic Sediment on the Aquatic Life of Streams," *California Fish*

and Game 47:2 (1961): 189–228; James E. Morrow, "The Effects of Extreme Floods and Placer Mining on the Basic Productivity of Sub Arctic Streams," Report No. IWR-14 (Fairbanks: University of Alaska Institute of Water Resources, 1971); David M. Bjerklie and Jacqueline D. LaPerriere, "Gold-Mining Effects on Stream Hydrology and Water Quality, Circle Quadrangle, Alaska," *Water Resources Bulletin* 21 (April 1995): 235–43; Stephen M. Wagener and Jacqueline D. LaPerriere, "Effects of Placer Mining on the Invertebrate Communities of Interior Alaska Streams," *Freshwater Invertebrate Biology* 4 (November 1985): 208–14; Denby S. Lloyd, "Turbidity in Freshwater Habitats of Alaska: A Review of Published and Unpublished Literature Relevant to the Use of Turbidity as a Water Quality Standard" (Juneau, Alaska: Alaska Dept. of Fish and Game, Habitat Division, January 1985), 10; Erwin E. Van Nieuwenhuyse and Jacqueline D. LaPerriere, "Effects of Placer Gold Mining on Primary Production in Subarctic Streams of Alaska," *Water Resources Bulletin* 22 (February 1986): 91–99; D. J. McLeay, G. L. Ennis, I. K. Birtwell, and G. F. Hartman, "Effects on Arctic Grayling of Prolonged Exposure to Yukon Placer Mining Sediment: A Laboratory Study," *Canadian Technical Report of Fisheries and Aquatic Sciences,* no. 1241 (January 1984): xi; I. K. Soroka and G. Mackenzie-Grieve, "A Biological and Water Quality Assessment at a Placer Mine on Barlow Creek, Yukon Territory," Environment Canada, Environmental Protection Service, Pacific Region, Yukon Branch, Regional Program Report 84–16 (Whitehorse, Yukon Territory: Environment Canada, 1984), 46; and U.S. Dept. of Interior, Federal Water Pollution Administration, Northwest Region, Alaska Water Laboratory, "Effects of Placer Mining on Water Quality in Alaska" (College, Alaska: Alaska Water Laboratory, 1969), 4, 18.

79. Adams diary. ·

80. In the late 1980s and early 1990s, with the rise in gold prices and the revival of gold mining, placer miners, fishers, and government agencies in the Yukon were embroiled in the "goldfish" debate, the fight over whether placer mining harmed Yukon salmon stocks and should be more heavily regulated to protect fish and wildlife (also called the "moose vs. nuggets" debate). Miners argued for the historical and economic importance of placer mining—how mining creates wealth, and how five generations of miners had "farmed the ground" and created money, rather than just moved it around, as in service industries. At the time, the Yukon government classified streams on a scale from "A" to "D," where "A" was a salmon-spawning stream or river and "D" was a stream with no significant fish value. Most of the creeks around Dawson City were classified as "C" streams, which meant they were historically degraded and historically mined. See *Whitehorse Star,* 5 Sept. 1979. Regulations on the books required placer miners to reduce their output of sediment below certain levels—set differently for class A, B, C, and D streams—and to restore fish habi-

tat. A 1986 newspaper article argued that only two operators in the entire Yukon Territory operated on salmon streams, and that all others operated on "historically mined streams" or "non-salmon" streams and met the sediment standards for those streams.

Miners argued that they were being scapegoated for declining salmon stocks, that the fish returned to creeks when the sediment cleared, that the fish were accustomed to high levels of natural sediment, and that the slopes revegetated with willow. See "Mining-Placer-1989," and "Mining-Placer-1984–86," DCM; *Whitehorse Star*, 16 May 1986, 2 June 1989, 26 August 1992, 31 August 1992, 2 Sept. 1992, 11 Sept. 1992.

81. Terrence Cole, "Klondike Visions: Dreams of a Promised Land," *Alaska Journal* 16 (1986): 82–93.

82. Josiah Edward Spurr, *Through the Yukon Gold Diggings: A Narrative of Personal Travel* (Boston: Eastern Publishing Co., 1900), 106.

5 / THE CULTURE OF GOLD MINING

1. William B. Ballou letters, Sept. 18, 1898, Sept. 20, 1899, June 15, 1902, William B. Ballou Papers, 1889–1918, UAF.

2. Hunter Fitzhugh letters, summer 1899, Nov. 20, 1899, Robert Hunter Fitzhugh Collection, Box 2, UAF. Paula Mitchell Marks notes in her history of western gold rushes that many miners reveled in and celebrated "the freedom of mining," and thus implicitly criticized the "noise and artificiality of civilization" that they left behind. See Paula Mitchell Marks, *Precious Dust: The American Gold Rush Era, 1848–1900* (New York: William Morrow, 1994), 372–73.

3. Samuel C. Dunham, *The Alaskan Gold Fields* (1898; reprint, Anchorage: Alaska Northwest Pub. Co., 1983), 9.

4. Daniel T. Rodgers, *The Work Ethic in Industrial America, 1850–1920* (Chicago: University of Chicago Press, 1974), xii.

5. Alan Trachtenberg, *The Incorporation of America: Culture and Society in the Gilded Age* (New York: Hill & Wang, 1982).

6. Rodgers, *Work Ethic*, 24–27, 125–126.

7. T. J. Jackson Lears, *No Place of Grace: Antimodernism and the Transformation of American Culture, 1880–1920* (New York: Pantheon Books, 1981), 11. On time, see Stephen Kern, *The Culture of Time and Space, 1880–1918* (Cambridge: Harvard University Press, 1986).

8. Herbert Gutman, *Work, Culture, and Society in Industrializing America: Essays in American Working-Class and Social History* (New York: Vintage Books, 1976), 33.

9. John Higham, "The Reorientation of American Culture in the 1890s," in *The*

Origins of Modern Consciousness, ed. John Weiss (Detroit: Wayne State University Press, 1965), 27.

10. Rodgers, *Work Ethic,* 28–29.

11. Lears, *No Place of Grace,* 18.

12. Harry Braverman, *Labor and Monopoly Capital: The Degradation of Work in the Twentieth Century* (New York: Monthly Review Press, 1974), 54–58.

13. Lears, *No Place of Grace,* 33–34, 60.

14. Ibid., xix, xx, 4–8.

15. Ibid., 75.

16. Ibid., 108–9.

17. Ibid., 121.

18. *Seattle Post-Intelligencer,* 28 Jan. 1898.

19. Ibid., 4 Feb. 1898. Other advertisements for Dr. Sanden's Electric Belts promoted them with more conservative rhetoric simply as "Klondike Heaters." See ibid., 16 March 1898.

20. Lears, *No Place of Grace,* 48, 138; John C. Callbreath letter, Wrangell, Alaska, July 18, 1898, Letterpress Copy Books, vol. 6, Callbreath, Grant, & Cook Papers, Charles Hubbell Collection, UW; Lynn Smith letter, 31 August 1898, Robert Lynn Smith Correspondence and Diaries, Box 1, Herbert Heller Collection, UAF; Jonas B. Houck letter, June 30, 1898, Jonas B. Houck Papers, UAF.

21. Higham, "The Reorientation of American Culture in the 1890s," 26, quoting Roosevelt.

22. Henry Dow Banks, "Account of Voyage, ca. 1898," MSS 40, Acc. 82/240, YA.

23. Asahel Curtis diary, Asahel Curtis Collection, UW.

24. Dunham, *The Alaskan Gold Fields,* 9.

25. Ibid.

26. For economic figures, see Hugh Rockoff, "The 'Wizard of Oz' as a Monetary Allegory," *Journal of Political Economy* 98 (August 1990): 742.

27. Tappan Adney, *The Klondike Stampede* (1900; reprint, Vancouver, B.C.: University of British Columbia Press, 1994), 6.

28. Dunham, *Alaskan Gold Fields,* 43.

29. Rodgers, *Work Ethic,* 6–8, 11–12, 125.

30. Alfred "Mac" McMichael letter, Fourth of July Creek, June 22, 1898, Alfred McMichael Diary and Letters, Juliette Reinicker Papers, MSS 100, Acc. 79/68, YA; Smith letter, 29 April 1898; Houck letter, March 20, 1898.

31. McMichael letter, Fourth of July Creek, May 19, 1898.

32. Ballou letter, January 29, 1902; Walter R. Curtin, *Unofficial Log of the Steamer Yukoner* (Caldwell, Idaho: Caxton Printers, Ltd., 1938), 141, 147.

33. Ballou letter, 19 August 1898; McMichael letters, 22 June 1898, 1 July 1898.

34. This, of course, was not unique to the Alaska-Yukon gold rush, but applied to gold mining in general. David Goodman's study of California and Australia in the 1850s notes that "On the goldfields the quantity of labour bore no necessary relation to the magnitude of the reward—months of diligent labour might bring no reward, a lucky swing of the pick might bring comfort for life." In the Victorian era, this threatened the idea that labor was "the necessary and controlling mediator between the individual and wealth." David Goodman, *Gold Seeking: Victoria and California in the 1850s* (Stanford, Calif.: Stanford University Press, 1994), 53. The same themes cropped up in the 1890s, but in the later stages of industrialization, the belief that labor was the individual's route to wealth was already in the process of being severely undermined.

Susan Johnson also discusses the relation of the California gold rush to ideas of labor and wealth, and gold mining as a reaction to economic changes brought by industrialization. As she argues, the free labor ideology stressed upward mobility away from wage labor, as wage labor became acceptable as a stage in a man's life, rather than a lifelong condition. Gold miners embraced California as a way out of lifelong wage work. See Susan Johnson, "'The gold she gathered': Difference, Domination, and California's Southern Miners, 1848–1853" (Ph.D. diss., Yale University, 1993), 294, 333.

35. McMichael letter, July 13, 1898.

36. "St. Michael, July 1898," Vertical File MS, UAF.

37. Nora Crane letter, July 11, 1898, Kepner-Crane Collection, Microfiche, UAF.

38. U.S. Consul letter, August 2, 1898, June 8, 1899, "Despatches from U.S. Consuls in Dawson City, Canada, 1898–1906," Microfilm no. 199, UAF; Smith letters, Jan. 29, 1899, April 30, 1899; Fitzhugh letters, Dec. 21, 1899, Rampart District, January 1900.

39. Houck diary, June 30, 1898; McMichael letter, Circle City, Alaska, Sept. 11, 1898.

40. U.S. Consul letter, August 2, 1898.

41. Ballou letter, Nov. 10, 1898.

42. Smith letter, Jan. 6, 1905.

43. Fitzhugh letter, Hoosier Creek, Alaska, Nov. 12, 1899.

44. Smith letter, Nov. 29, 1898.

45. There are hints in journals and letters that middle- and upper-class miners sensed the moral dangers of mining because it seemed to them so much like gambling. They did not seem overly anxious, however. In *Gold Seeking*, David Goodman analyzed Victorian anxieties about gold mining in the 1850s in Australia and

California. Reactions to those gold rushes revealed the belief that gold digging was an illegitimate form of work because luck (fortune), rather than the miner's own virtue or diligence, rewarded the miner.

46. Fitzhugh letter fragment, Jan. 1900.

47. Fitzhugh letter, July 5, 1900; Ballou letter, Sept. 20, 1899; U.S. Consul letter, winter 1898–99; McMichael letter, June 22, 1898.

48. Ann Vincent Fabian, "Rascals and Gentlemen: The Meaning of American Gambling" (Ph.D. diss., Yale University, 1982), 10, 22. Fabian, too, points out that in the gold camps of California and the West, "gambling bore a close relation to the economic and cultural life of men in mining camps." Writers in California during the gold rush made it clear that gambling was a metaphor for gold mining as a whole. Fabian quotes Dame Shirley's observation that mining was "'nature's great lottery scheme.'" See Fabian, 54–56. On western gambling and American culture, see also John M. Findlay, *People of Chance: Gambling in American Society from Jamestown to Las Vegas* (New York: Oxford University Press, 1986).

49. Ballou letter, June 12, 1899; Smith letter, Glenn Gulch, Alaska, Oct. 29, 1901.

50. Smith letter, April 30, 1899.

51. Ballou letters, Feb. 21, 1902, Dec. 3, 1898.

52. McMichael letter, Fourth of July Creek, July 13, 1898.

53. McMichael letter, July 29, 1898; Thomas J. Kearney letter, August 4, 1898, Diaries File, File Collection, DCM.

54. Smith letter, January 1, 1899; diary of James A. McRae, June 1900, "Bound for the Klondyke," MSS 104, Acc. 80/1, YA; Ballou letter, March 11, 1901.

55. Dunham, *Alaskan Gold Fields*, 25.

56. Ibid., 39, on arrivals in summer 1897.

57. Kearney letter, August 4, 1898; Smith letter, June 1898; McMichael letter, August 6, 1898.

58. Smith letter, July 9, 1898.

59. "Chapter 10," untitled Klondike manuscript, Vertical File MS, UAF; R. W. Cautley, "Highlights of Memory. Incidents in the life of a Canadian Surveyor," MSS 005, Acc. 82/97, YA. In 1897 Sam Dunham described lays as "ground worked on shares," with the usual terms an equal division of the output, the lessors paying all expenses of operation. Dunham, *Alaskan Gold Fields*, 25.

60. Frank Purdy diary, Aug. 30, Sept. 2, 1898, Vertical File MS, UAF.

61. Diary of James S. Cooper and Associates, Dec. 13, 1897, TS, Diaries File, File Collection, DCM.

62. Diary of F. Wm. Hiscock, Jan. 23, 1899, "The Youkon Trail of Year 1898," Diaries File, File Collection, DCM.

63. C.O. Steiner diary, "A Journey to Dawson in 1898," Vertical File MS, UAF; Purdy diary, Feb.–April 1899, May 12, 17, 28–29, 1899, July 1899; Fitzhugh letter fragment, Rampart City District, Alaska, Jan. 19, 1900.

64. John H. Lindsay letter, Fox Gulch, Yukon Territory, April 3, 1899, Lindsay Family Papers, MSS 12, Acc. 82/173, YA; McRae diary, June 14, July 14, 1899.

65. Houck letter, May 15, 1898; Kearney letter, August 4, 1898; Dunham, *The Alaskan Gold Fields;* Smith letter, June 1898; U.S. Consul letter, August 2, 1898.

66. Adney, *Klondike Stampede,* 230–31.

67. Smith letter, Oct. 29, 1901.

68. Adney, *Klondike Stampede,* 235.

69. Fred G. Kimball letter, Oct. 12, 1903, Fred G. Kimball Letters, 1899–1909, UAF; *Rampart Miner* (Alaska), 17 Sept. 1901.

70. Lynn Smith wrote on January 4, 1902, that "We are on good ground and hope to make good wages at least."

71. Purdy diary, July 2, 1898; Smith letter, June 18, 1902; Ballou letter, April 15, 1902; Purdy diary, July 15, 1900.

72. John A. Gould and Richard C. Stuart, "Permafrost Gold: A Treatise on Early Klondike Mining History, Methods and Technology," Microfiche Report Series No. 11 (Ottawa: Parks Canada, December 1980), DCM Microfiche, 81.

73. Cooper diary, Dec. 13, 1897.

74. Fitzhugh letters, Rampart District Creeks, Oct. 5, 1898, Jan. 1900; Purdy diary, Jan. 22, 1899; McCrae diary, Sept. 17, 1899; Smith letters, Nov. 25, 1905, Thanksgiving Eve, 1905; Charles P. Mosier diary, March 15, 1899, MSS 012, Acc. 82/168, YA.

75. James Lynn Anderson diary, vol. 1, Jan. 8, 1896, Jan. 17, 1896, James Lynn Anderson Diaries, 1895–1899, Vertical File MS, UAF; McRae diary, May 27, 1899, May 2, 1899, May 29, 1900.

76. McMichael letter, Jan. 3, 1899. One sidelong indication of the miners' time-regulated work was the presence of watchmakers in the gold camps. Miners owned watches, and when those watches broke, they spent money to get them repaired. Canadian miner James McRae lived and worked with a partner named Tucker, who in addition to mining spent long evenings fixing watches for pay. McRae made note of his steady business, mostly in complaining that Tucker kept the cabin heated at night in order to work, thus depriving his roommates of comfortable sleep. Lynn Smith was a watchmaker by profession, and used that work to support himself in Rampart City. He, too, did a steady business, and wrote consistently that with more tools and watches, he could be doing even better business. For Smith, as for wage laborers in industrial society as a whole, time was literally money. He charged customers for his time. At one point he reported buying a five-dollar creek claim after

news of a gold strike, but doubted that it was money well spent. "But I think I burned up $5 and 13 1/2 minutes work on a watch for nothing," he commented in a letter home. Smith letter, Rampart City, Alaska, Oct. 18, 1898.

77. Joseph H. Cavanagh diary, "Journey to Alaska-Yukon 1898–1900," Vertical File MS, UAF; Diary of Stewart L. Campbell, MSS 122, Acc. 81/129, YA; McMichael letters.

78. Hiscock diary, Dec. 23, 1898.

79. McRae diary, Jan. 9, 1899.

80. Fitzhugh letter, Dec. 19, 1899.

6 / THE NATURE OF CULTURE AND FOOD

1. Diary of James S. Cooper and Associates, Nov. 22, 1897, Diaries File, File Collection, DCM.

2. Ibid., Nov. 25, 1897.

3. Charles P. Mosier Diary, Nov. 24, 1898, MSS 012, Acc. 82/168, YA.

4. Alfred "Mac" McMichael letter, Nov. 24, 1898, Alfred McMichael Diary and Letters, Juliette Reinicker Papers, MSS 100, Acc. 79/68, YA.

5. Daniel Boorstin, *The Americans: The Democratic Experience* (New York: Random House, 1973), 112.

6. McMichael letters, Jan. 1, 3, 1899; Diary of F. Wm. Hiscock, June 6, 1898, "The Youkon Trail of Year 1898," TS, Diaries File, File Collection, DCM. On staple diet, also Paula Mitchell Marks, *Precious Dust: The American Gold Rush Era, 1848–1900* (New York: William Morrow, 1994), 175.

7. Tappan Adney, *The Klondike Stampede* (1900; reprint, Vancouver, B.C.: University of British Columbia Press, 1994), 378.

8. McMichael letters, Jan. 1, 3, 1899. A U.S. Department of Commerce and Labor, Bureau of Statistics report, *Commercial Alaska, 1867–1903* (Washington, D.C.: GPO, 1903), reported that the principal food articles shipped from American Pacific Coast ports to Alaska between 1880 and 1890 were flour, sugar, butter, coffee, tea, potatoes, onions, fruits, pork, beef, salt, canned goods, and canned vegetables. About halfway through the decade, canned meats appeared on the list. In 1890, 2,137 cases of canned meats were shipped to Alaska. See *Commercial Alaska,* 114.

9. Hunter Fitzhugh letter, Jan. 7, 1898, Robert Hunter Fitzhugh Collection, Box 2, UAF.

10. Lynn Smith letters, Oct. 13, Sept. 19, Oct. 9, 1898, Robert Lynn Smith Correspondence and Diaries, Box 1, Herbert Heller Papers, UAF. It was hard to keep fruit through the winter. When Smith worked in the North American Trade & Trans-

portation store at Rampart in the winter of 1902–3, he had to keep fires stoked in the storage rooms to try to keep the oranges, apples, and cider from freezing when temperatures reached from thirty to sixty degrees below zero.

11. Capt. W. P. Richardson, Eighth Infantry, U.S. Army, "Report of an Expedition into Alaska," in U.S. Congress, Senate, Committee on Military Affairs, *Compilation of Narratives of Explorations in Alaska, 1869–1900* (Washington, D.C.: GPO, 1900), 506.

12. Jack London, "The One Thousand Dozen" (1904), in *The Bodley Head Jack London,* vol. 4, *The Klondike Dream,* ed. Arthur Calder-Marshall (London: Bodley Head, 1963–66), 232–49.

13. Lynn Smith recorded a real-life version of this story in two letters, Nov. 10, 1898, and Dec. 2, 1898, from Rampart City. "Last night a man who brought 1500 doz. eggs packed in lard and opened a restaurant was found unconscious and first report was apoplexy, but it was an attempt at suicide. His eggs were too ancient for use and he could not sell them so he grew despondent." The second letter read that the "egg man succeeded in suicide." He "severed an artery and then hung himself to the cross log of his cabin." Smith letters, UAF. Another source, the short-lived newspaper *Dyea Trail,* mentioned two men with five hundred dozen eggs, all of which ended up at the bottom of the Thirty Mile River. *Dyea Trail,* 12 Jan. 1898, "Dyea and the Dyea Trail," Vertical File MS, UAF. Whether London based his story on Smith's particular man or not, or on similar events elsewhere, is unclear. But he did base it on actual events. See Franklin Walker, *Jack London & The Klondike: The Genesis of an American Writer* (San Marino, Calif.: The Huntington Library, 1966), 234–35.

14. Adney, *Klondike Stampede,* 378–79. According to Adney, two women had indeed set up an ice cream business in the summer of 1898, using ice and condensed cream.

15. Frank Purdy Diary, July 27, 1898, Vertical File MS, UAF; McMichael letter, June 23, 1898; Fred G. Kimball letter, June 27, 1904, Fred G. Kimball Letters, 1899–1909, UAF; Diary of Stewart L. Campbell, August 5, 1899, MSS 122, Acc. 81/129, YA.

16. Menu printed in Henry Davis, "Recollections," in Herbert Heller, ed., *Sourdough Sagas* (Cleveland: World Publishing, 1967), 81; McMichael letter, Jan. 1, 1899.

17. William B. Ballou letter, June 12, 1899, William B. Ballou Papers, 1889–1918, UAF; Boorstin, *The Americans,* 309, ch. 35; Nora Crane letters, July 9, 24, 1897, Kepner-Crane Collection, Microfiche, UAF; Fitzhugh letter, Little Manook Creek, summer 1899. For general information on canning, see also Boorstin, *The Americans,* ch. 35.

18. Fitzhugh letter, May 19, 1899.

19. When Lynn Smith worked at the NAT&T store in Rampart City, he asked

family members in Seattle to send him money through the company, at the Rookery building in Chicago, or through the offices in Seattle. Smith letter, August 31, 1901. The Chicago connection to the miners' food supply, through Cudahy meatpacking and its subsidiary, the NAT&T, also took the form of the name of the 1893 NAT&T trading post across the Yukon from the mouth of the Forty Mile: Fort Cudahy. See Virginia S. Burlingame, "John J. Healy's Alaskan Adventure," *Alaska Journal* 8 (winter 1978): 312–14.

20. Crane letter, July 9, 1897.

21. *Trade Register* (Seattle), 22 Jan. 1898, 30.

22. Ibid., 21 May 1898, 36; 8 Jan. 1897.

23. Harvey A. Levenstein, *Revolution at the Table: The Transformation of the American Diet* (New York: Oxford University Press, 1988), 36–37, 41–42.

24. *Trade Register* (Seattle), 11 Sept. 1897.

25. Levenstein, *Revolution at the Table,* 37, 23–26.

26. Boorstin, *The Americans,* 322.

27. Margaret Archibald, *Grubstake to Grocery Store: The Klondike Emporium, 1897–1907,* rev. ed. (Ottawa: Parks Canada, Dept. of Indian and Northern Affairs, 1973), 26.

28. *Trade Register* (Seattle), 22 Jan. 1898.

29. John C. Callbreath letter, March 28, 1898, Callbreath, Grant, & Cook Papers, Charles Hubbell Collection, Letterpress Copy Books, vol. 6, UW.

30. Levenstein, *Revolution at the Table,* 22, 30, 32.

31. Boorstin, *The Americans,* 309–16; Levenstein, *Revolution at the Table,* 31, 34–35.

32. Archibald, *Grubstake to Grocery,* 153; Levenstein, *Revolution at the Table,* 31; *Trade Register* (Seattle), 11 Sept. 1897; 1 Jan. 1898; 8 Jan. 1898; 6 Jan. 1900, 29.

33. *Trade Register* (Seattle), 14 Aug. 1897, 17.

34. Ibid., 8 Sept. 1900.

35. William Cronon, *Nature's Metropolis: Chicago and the Great West* (New York: W. W. Norton, 1991), 146–47.

36. Ibid., 145, 150, 212–14, 221–23.

37. *Trade Register* (Seattle), 4 Sept. 1897, 11, 15; 11 Sept. 1897, 9. In 1898 and 1899, Washington apple growers in Wenatchee and on Orcas Island shipped apples not only to Seattle, but also to Chicago by railroad, and from there to eastern markets. In 1898, the Seattle Commission Co., a fruit dealer, shipped over fifteen thousand boxes of apples to eastern cities; the state as a whole shipped a thousand railroad carloads east, at two hundred bushels per car. *Trade Register,* Dec. 1898 Trade Summary; 10 Dec. 1898, 20. If so many apples reached national markets, plenty reached Seattle outfitters and wholesalers, and thus the Alaska-Yukon market as well.

38. *Trade Register* (Seattle), 11 Sept. 1897, 24.

39. Ibid., 31 Dec. 1898.

40. Ibid., 14 August 1897; 28 August 1897; 6 April 1898.

41. Ibid., 15 Jan. 1898, 11.

42. Ibid., 9 April 1898, 37.

43. Ibid., 14 August 1897, 20; 8 Jan. 1898.

44. Dorothy O. Johansen, *Empire of the Columbia: A History of the Pacific Northwest,* 2nd ed. (New York: Harper & Row, 1967), 626. Seattle's *Trade Register* listed outbound cargo each week. In 1898, it listed regular shipments of wheat to the U.K. and San Francisco, and more sporadic shipments to Chile, Peru, and even Russia. In December 1898, twenty-two deep-water vessels were in port, preparing to take wheat around the world. *Trade Register,* 3 Dec. 1898. According to *Trade Register* figures for December 1898, both railroads delivered 1,777 carloads of wheat, of 400 bushels each, to Seattle in 1897. In 1898, the figure jumped to 3,679 carloads.

45. *Trade Register* (Seattle), 22 Jan. 1898, 19. James J. Hill's Great Northern Railroad invested heavily in Seattle's grain and flour facilities in the 1890s. In 1898 Hill funded a million-dollar steel grain elevator, complete with docks and warehouses, at Smith Cove, just north of the main harbor at Elliott Bay. With Hill's railroad in place, Northwest farmers could ship Big Bend wheat east to mills in Minneapolis. Likewise, Seattle's wholesalers and retailers could offer miners and other consumers the best of midwestern grains. In July 1898, one of the city's leading grain and feed dealers, Lilly Bogardus, advertised stocks of Minnesota buckwheat and rye flour, and Dakota and Minnesota hard wheat flour. *Trade Register* (Seattle), 12 Nov. 22, 1898, 21; 18 Sept. 1897, 24; 27 August 1898; 30 July 1898, 13. In 1897 and 1898, trade reports regularly reported shipments of wheat by rail to Minneapolis, and by ship to Hawaii, the U.K., Chile, and Peru. *Trade Register* (Seattle), 15 Jan. 1898; 23 April 1898, 31; 4 Sept. 1897.

46. *Seattle Post-Intelligencer,* 12 Sept. 1897. Not all of the miners' bacon came from the Midwest, either. Seattle's leading meatpacker, the Frye-Bruhn Co., packed its own brand of bacon, ham, and lard for the gold rush, building four new smokehouses for the Klondike trade in 1898. Early that year, Charles Bruhn won contracts to supply seventy-five thousand pounds of bacon to the U.S. government's relief expedition to the Klondike mines. See *Trade Register* (Seattle), 1 Jan. 1898; 15 Jan. 1898; 2 Oct. 1897. By 1898 Seattle butchers were killing a hundred hogs a day to keep up with the 16,380 hogs that arrived on the Northern Pacific and Great Northern Railroads in the eighteen months from January 1897 through June 1898. *Trade Register* (Seattle), 1898 Trade Summary, 31 Dec. 1898. Seattle also served as a market for local perishable foods—milk, eggs, and butter—by gathering, storing, preserving,

and shipping truck farmers' goods for consumption along the Yukon. Miners recognized and bought national brands of condensed milk, Borden's in the United States and Reindeer brand in Canada, but dairymen in Washington State recognized a local niche. In January 1898 the Washington Condensed Milk Company increased its capital and moved to Kent to be closer to supplies of fresh milk, citing large orders from Alaska and Japan. They ran advertisements in Seattle to compete with national brands like Borden's and Eagle—claiming that "Washington" and "Tillicum" milk were the favored items at Dawson City. See *Trade Register* (Seattle), 21 August 1897; 1 Jan. 1898. J. B. Agens, of Seattle and Tacoma, held the monopoly on vacuum-packed butter, a popular item among northern miners. Archibald, *Grubstake to Grocery,* 25. Agens moved into the modern new Colman Building on Western Avenue in Seattle in September 1897, and installed a cold storage plant with a capacity for five thousand tubs of butter and four thousand cases of eggs. See *Trade Register* (Seattle), 11 Sept. 1897; 1 Jan. 1898.

47. McMichael letter, August 6, 1898.

48. Archibald, *Grubstake to Grocery,* 28.

49. Levenstein, *Revolution at the Table,* 34–36; Boorstin, *The Americans,* 89–90.

50. Although my discussion here focuses on scurvy, dysentery and typhoid played a serious role as well, especially in Dawson City. Dawson's swampiness combined with the total lack of sewage facilities to foul the water supply in the hot weather in the summer of 1898, which led to typhoid fever and dysentery, as well as malaria. R. M. Courtnay wrote on September 28, 1898, "The town is also lately without sewage, and, being on marshy ground, the water is impure." Adney reported only two outhouses in town for over twenty thousand people. James Lynn Anderson suffered badly; after spending the entire winter frozen in at "Suckerville" on the lower Yukon, he arrived at Dawson in June and immediately "got the bloody flux," and remained ill until August. "I came out better than Hundreds of other poor Fellows who between Flux and Fever were laid away in Dawson burial place." Adney estimated three or four deaths a day from typhoid, malaria, and dysentery. It was definitely worst in the summer and fall of 1898. Courtnay continued in September that "There has been a large amount of malaria and typhoid fever this fall, but now it is turning cool and the sickness is disappearing." The U.S. Consul reported over two hundred cases of typhoid in Dawson in October 1898. By the following March, however, the city instituted cleaning rules for privies, pipes, and water closets, and forced everyone to take drinking water higher up on both the Yukon and the Klondike, above the heaviest areas of settlement. By spring, there were ditches draining the Dawson flats, and plans in place to pipe clean water to town from up the Klondike River. Although there were further cases of typhoid in 1899, Dawson became much healthier, and

had clean water that summer. See Marks, *Precious Dust*, 234; Adney, *Klondike Stampede*, 429; R. M. Courtnay diary, Sept. 28, 1898, TS, DCM; James Lynn Anderson diary, vol. 2, summer 1898, James Lynn Anderson Diaries, 1895–99, Vertical File MS, UAF; U.S. Consul letters, Oct. 20, 1898, March 1899, May 24, 1899, June 8, 1899, June 20, 1899, July 28, 1899, "Despatches from U.S. Consuls in Dawson City, Canada, 1898–1906," Microfilm no. 199, UAF. Thomas J. Kearney's letter of May 29, 1899, also describes draining and sewer systems in the spring of 1899, and enforcement of sanitary regulations. Thomas J. Kearney letter, Diaries File, File Collection, DCM. See also M. K. Lux, "Disease and the Growth of Dawson City: The Seamy Underside of a Legend," *Northern Review* 3/4 (summer-winter 1898): 97, 114–15.

51. Ballou letter, June 10, 1899.

52. U.S. Consul letter, August 2, 1898; Dec. 21, 1898. See also E. Hazard Wells, "Up and Down the Yukon," in U.S. Congress, Senate, Committee on Military Affairs, *Compilation of Narratives of Explorations in Alaska, 1869–1900*, 515. Wells wrote of Dawson in December 1897 that "There was more than a dozen cases of scurvy, well defined, in Dawson before I left there on December 20. Dr. Chambers, one of the most experienced physicians in the place, told me that he expected that several hundred of the disease, and possibly many more would develop in camp before next spring."

53. Barry C. Anderson, *Lifeline to the Yukon: A History of Yukon River Navigation* (Seattle: Superior Publishing, 1983), 47.

54. Karen B. Morehouse, "Alaska Native Diet and Nutrition: An Ethnohistorical View," (Master's thesis, University of Alaska, 1981), 7–8, 11–18. Morehouse cites only a few reports of scurvy among Indians. She also reports the vitamin C content of common native foods, as measured in the 1950s: moose: 4 mg/100g; smoked salmon: 3 mg/100g; fresh salmon: 5–13 mg/100g; ptarmigan: 7 mg/100g; willow leaves: 298 mg./100g; salmonberries: 115 mg/100g. A current nutrition text provides vitamin C contents for other foods: raw blackberries: 30 mg/cup; raw blueberries: 20 mg/cup; raw strawberries: 88 mg/cup. See Ioannis S. Scarpa and Helen Chilton Keifer, eds., *Sourcebook on Food and Nutrition* (Chicago: Marquis Academic Media, 1978), 73–101. The U.S. recommended daily allowance of vitamin C for adults is between 50 and 60 mg.

55. Josiah Edward Spurr, *Through the Yukon Gold Diggings: A Narrative of Personal Travel* (Boston: Eastern Publishing Co., 1900), 113.

56. Lux, "Disease and the Growth of Dawson City," 101; Adney, *Klondike Stampede*, 350–351. See also Michael Gates, *Gold at Fortymile Creek: Early Days in the Yukon* (Vancouver: University of British Columbia Press, 1994), 45–46. Among doctors and

others who cared for the sick, it became common knowledge that both raw potatoes and tea made from spruce leaves and bark, or poplar bark, cured scurvy.

57. Walter R. Curtin, *Unofficial Log of the Steamer Yukoner* (Caldwell, Idaho: Caxton Printers, Ltd., 1938), 98, 102; Archibald, *Grubstake to Grocery*, 29; Thomas W.
Moore Account, 1898, MSS 007, Acc. 82/121, YA; Archibald, *Grubstake to Grocery*,
29; Hiscock diary, Feb. 2, 1899; Smith letters, March 2, 16, 1899; McMichael letter,
August 27, 1898; Purdy diary, Jan. 25, 1899; McMichael letters, Oct. 27, 1898, Nov.
28, 1898, Dec. 1, 1898.

58. McMichael letter, August 27, 1898. Processed fruits, citrus products, and evaporated potatoes all had invisible drawbacks. Vitamin C is the most unstable of all
vitamins, and does not survive heating, processing, or dehydrating well. See Henrietta Fleck, *Introduction to Nutrition*, 4th ed. (New York: Macmillan, 1981), 187.
Prunes, raisins, cranberries, apricots, and peaches all lose all or most of their vitamin C when dried. If dried fruits are then cooked, they lose whatever ascorbic acid
remains. Fruits lose up to half of their vitamin C content when canned. Tomatoes
and potatoes, both crucial sources of vitamin C for gold miners in the 1890s, lose
over 70 percent of their vitamin C in the canning process. This loss of vitamin C
may explain why miners eating processed fruit still grew ill. It also explains why miners often turned to fresh food to cure scurvy. See Miloslav Rechcigl, Jr., ed., *Handbook of Nutritive Value of Processed Food*, Vol. 1, *Food for Human Use* (Boca Raton,
Fla.: CRC Press, 1982), 303–9; 353; 488. If dried fruit is sulfured in the process, the
vitamin C is retained. As much of potatoes' nutrient value is in their skins, miners
eating dehydrated peeled potatoes may well have done themselves little good with
regard to ascorbic acid.

59. Cronon, *Nature's Metropolis*, 234–35. The ideas in this discussion draw from
and are shaped by chapter 5 of *Nature's Metropolis*, "Annihilating Space: Meat."

60. Richard White, "Animals and Enterprise," in *The Oxford History of the Amer-
ican West*, ed. Clyde A. Milner II, Carol A. O'Connor, and Martha A. Sandweiss
(New York: Oxford University Press, 1994), 252, 256; Levenstein, *Revolution at the
Table*, 21.

61. There were supplies of fresh beef and other meats in Alaska and the Yukon
earlier, but they remained highly seasonal and quite expensive. In the mid-1890s,
Jack Dalton established the Dalton Trail over Chilkat Pass. This route led from the
Lynn Canal at Haines Mission, just south of Skagway, over the mountains to the
Yukon at Ft. Selkirk. The trail was far too long—over two hundred miles—for
prospectors on foot, but drovers took at least forty cattle across in 1896, loaded them
on scows, and took them downriver to be slaughtered at Fortymile. Allen A. Wright,

Prelude to Bonanza: The Discovery and Exploration of the Yukon (Sidney, B.C.: Gray's Publishing, Ltd.), 232–33, 275. Catharine McClellan, "Tutchone," in June Helm, ed., *Subarctic,* vol. 6 of *Handbook of North American Indians, Northwest Coast,* gen. ed. William C. Sturtevant (Washington, D.C.: Smithsonian Institution, 1990), 503 (hereafter referred to as *Handbook, Subarctic*). When the crowds arrived in 1897, other entrepreneurs took stock over the Dalton Trail in even greater numbers. Sam Dunham reported 350 cattle and 1,550 sheep arriving in the fall of 1897, and 2,000 cattle came across the Chilkat route in the summer of 1898. See Archibald, *Grub-stake to Grocery,* 148. In the fall, drovers would hold the animals at the end of the trail on the Yukon until the freeze. James Cooper's party passed the place where the Dalton Trail met the Yukon, below Five Fingers Rapids, as they raced toward Dawson in October 1897. "See four men who have just butchered about 20 head of cattle, they came over the Dalton Trail and are freezing them to take to the mines." Cooper diary, Oct. 9, 1897. This was a risky business. Cattlemen had to bring expensive feed over the passes as well, and then face the risks of losing the entire investment on the river. Tappan Adney ran into some men on the Yukon who asked if he had seen a missing raft of beef. The owner had driven seventy head of cattle over the Dalton Trail and butchered them below Five Fingers Rapids, only to lose them on the river. Adney, *Klondike Stampede,* 168–69. Samuel C. Dunham, *The Alaskan Gold Fields* (1898; reprint Anchorage: Alaska Northwest Pub. Co., 1983), 59. Dunham recorded the perils of livestock drives. One drover, crossing the Chilkat, had eighty-five cattle sink in quicksand, but sixty of them pulled out and made it to Dawson. As steamer service improved on the upper and lower Yukon, meat dealers barged live herds safely down from Ft. Selkirk, or up the river from St. Michael's, and then slaughtered them right in town at Dawson. When Mary Hitchcock, an upper-class tourist, visited Dawson in 1898, she visited a butcher to purchase veal, mutton, and brains for a dinner party. See Mary E. Hitchcock, *Two Women in the Klondike: The Story of a Journey to the Gold Fields of Alaska* (New York: G. P. Putnam's Sons, 1899), 100–102, 118, 156, 166, 171, 174. In the summer of 1899, the Alaska Commercial Company and NAT&T brought cattle and sheep in for fresh meat, a practice which continued and grew thereafter. The animals themselves came from the interior Northwest and Montana. Seattle meatpacker Charles Bruhn bought cattle from Washington, Idaho, Oregon, and Montana in 1897, which indicates similar sources for cattle brokers shipping animals to Alaska. An August 1897 article spoke of five thousand sheep en route to Seattle from Ellensburg, Washington, and other articles throughout the gold rush reported cattle arriving in Seattle from Walla Walla and Montana for shipment to the Klondike and Nome. Some shipments of live cattle and hogs, however, came from as far away as Kansas City. In 1899 Frye-Bruhn received a substantial shipment for the Alaska trade—seventeen carloads of live cattle from California. *Trade Register* (Seattle), 14 August 1897; 2 Oct. 1897, 1; 22 Feb. 1899; 20 May 1899; 28 April 1900, 9.

62. *Trade Register* (Seattle), 20 May 1899, 29.

63. John C. Cantwell, *Report of the Operations of the U.S. Revenue Steamer "Nunivak" on the Yukon River Station, Alaska, 1899–1901* (Washington, D.C.: GPO, 1902), 72.

64. *Trade Register* (Seattle), 8 June 1901, 33.

65. Robert G. McCandless, *Yukon Wildlife: A Social History* (Edmonton: University of Alberta Press, 1985), 46.

66. *Trade Register* (Seattle), 4 Feb. 1899, 9.

67. Archibald, *Grubstake to Grocery*, 148.

68. Ibid., 147.

69. Numerous references to small game occur in miners' diaries, ranging in place from the headwater lakes of the Yukon to the mining camps, to the trails to and from mining towns. In May 1898 at the lakes, McMichael reported that "Last night for supper we had the bird and squirrel that Knapp shot. They were stewed and very good." McMichael letter, May 16, 1898. Stewart Campbell's diary between April and August 1898 refers consistently to small game. At Tagish Lake in April, Campbell "shot 4 squirrels and had a feed of fresh meat."

70. Fitzhugh letter, May 5, 1898.

71. Hiscock diary, June 14, 1898. In early July 1898, poling up the Indian River, Stewart Campbell and his party gathered "a lot" of mushrooms to eat later. Charles Mosier "gathered some wild onions" along the Yukon. See Mosier diary, June 9, 1898.

72. Tom Boldrick Diary, June 14, 1898, Vertical File MS, Klondike Miners, UAF.

73. Archibald, *Grubstake to Grocery*, 150.

74. Maud Case letter, July 3, 1903, George E. Case and Family Letters, MSS 172, Acc. 81/91, YA; Fitzhugh letter, May 19, 1899.

75. Smith letter, May 25, 1898; McMichael letters, July 29, 1898, Feb. 2, 1899.

76. McCandless, *Yukon Wildlife*, 31.

77. Purdy diary, Aug. 3, 1899, June 15, 1898; Boldrick diary, June 18, 1898, White River, July 2, June 18, 21, 1898.

78. Fitzhugh letter, August 1, 1900.

79. Anderson diary, vol. 1, May 24, 1896.

80. Adney, *Klondike Stampede*, 449.

81. McCrae diary, July 8, 11, 12, 1899.

82. Ballou letter, Sept. 18, 1898.

83. Archibald, *Grubstake to Grocery*, 141–42.

84. Tappan Adney, "The Indian Hunter of the Far Northwest: On the Trail to the Klondike," *Outside* 39 (March 1902): 624.

85. Ibid.

86. Smith letters, Nov. 29, 1898; April 30, 1899.

87. Ibid., Sept. 27, 1900.

88. Adney, "The Indian Hunter," 633.

89. Kenneth S. Coates, *Best Left as Indians: Native-White Relations in the Yukon Territory, 1840–1973* (Montreal: McGill-Queen's University Press, 1991), 35–37; Charlene Porsild, "Culture, Class, and Community: New Perspectives on the Klondike Gold Rush, 1896–1905" (Ph.D. diss., Carleton University, Ottawa, 1994), 106, 108–9.

90. Coates, *Best Left as Indians,* 38.

91. Porsild, "Culture, Class, and Community," 106, 108–9. Catharine McClellan writes that it is difficult to distinguish precontact and postcontact Indian ideas and practices, but that the peoples of the southern Yukon had a large capacity for dealing with and adopting new ideas and ways of life. See Catharine McClellan, *My Old People Say: An Ethnographic Survey of Southern Yukon Territory,* Part 1 (Ottawa: National Museum of Man, National Museums of Canada, 1975), 65.

92. John R. Crow and Philip R. Obley, "Han," in *Handbook, Subarctic,* 509.

93. Catharine McClellan, *Part of the Land, Part of the Water: A History of the Yukon Indians* (Vancouver/Toronto: Douglas & McIntyre, 1987), 166; Cornelius Osgood, *The Han Indians: A Compilation of Ethnographic and Historical Data on the Alaska-Yukon Boundary Area,* Yale University Publications in Anthropology No. 74 (New Haven: Yale University Department of Anthropology, 1971), 129. On caribou fences, see McClellan, *Part of the Land,* 116.

94. Osgood, *Han Indians,* 130. Hunter Fitzhugh wrote of the constant presence of salmon: "But I am sick of it. Fish don't do for a steady diet with me. . . . I am drying them for dog feed next winter." Fitzhugh letter, August 1, 1900.

95. Letter, Capt. P. H. Ray, Ft. Yukon, Alaska, Dec. 20, 1897, to Adjutant General, United States Army, in U.S. Congress, Senate, Committee on Military Affairs, *Compilation of Narratives of Explorations,* 549–50.

96. Adney, *Klondike Stampede,* 450–54; Edward H. Hosley, "Intercultural Relations and Cultural Change in the Alaska Plateau," *Handbook, Subarctic,* 549. McClellan, *My Old People Say,* 96, writes that toward the end of the nineteenth century, the caribou began to move north while moose increased. It is difficult to document such patterns, however. The caribou population declined after 1900, due both to shifting migrations as well as increased hunting pressure. See Edward H. Hosley, "Environment and Culture in the Alaska Plateau," *Handbook, Subarctic,* 545. The migration pattern was probably the more crucial factor. There were clearly major shifts in the

caribou population of the southern Yukon after 1900, but the causes are unclear. Toward the end of the nineteenth century, greater numbers of moose moved into the southern Yukon, which may have pushed caribou into other regions. Julie Cruik-shank, *Life Lived Like a Story: Life Stories of Three Yukon Native Elders* (Lincoln: University of Nebraska Press, 1990), 277; and McClellan, *My Old People Say,* 108.

97. Smith letter, Sept. 24, 1901; Campbell diary, March 22, 27, 1899; Smith letter, Sept. 24, 1901; Case letter, July 16, 1903.

98. Adney, *Klondike Stampede,* 99. Miners bought salmon and trout to eat along the Dyea Trail.

99. Spurr, *Through the Yukon Gold Diggings,* 215.

100. Cooper diary, Oct. 6–7, 1897. Cooper also traded at a village at the Little Salmon, exchanging tobacco for moose meat. "They are a miserable lot, they have a great quantity of furs, hides and bear grease."

101. Purdy diary, July 9, 1898.

102. Kimball letter, Feb. 8, 1900.

103. Curtin, *Unofficial Log,* 55–57, 66, 102.

104. Ibid., 165.

105. Cantwell, *Nunivak,* 80.

106. Ibid., 224–25.

107. Osgood, *Han Indians,* 156. Thomas Moore, for example, found "game of any sort scarce" around Lake Labarge in the spring of 1898. He saw "only squirrels." Moore account, 1898.

108. McCandless, *Yukon Wildlife,* 47.

109. Cantwell, *Nunivak,* 90.

110. McCandless, *Yukon Wildlife,* 32. See also Porsild, "Culture, Class, and Community," 117–18.

111. McCandless, *Yukon Wildlife,* 32.

112. Ibid. The Yukon territory set up game ordinances, which included bag limits and seasons, but they were not always enforced. The 1901 game ordinance limited hunters to six caribou, two moose, two sheep, and two goats in a year, with no hunting of female game. Such prohibitions made no sense to Native hunters and were widely ignored by both Indians and whites. In Alaska, the 1902 game law regulated only market and recreational hunting. There were no restrictions on Indians hunting for food or clothing, or miners hunting for food or clothing, or travelers on a journey. The law set up a two-month fall season for caribou and moose, and limited all hunting to two moose, four each of caribou, sheep, and goats, and eight deer, with no killing of female moose, caribou, deer, or sheep. McCandless, *Yukon Wildlife,* 33–34; 1902 Alaska Game Law, as reported in *Rampart Miner,* 22 July 1902.

113. Osgood, *Han Indians*, 1. Osgood used the term "disoriented." The net result, according to Osgood, when thirty thousand newcomers descended on three thousand total Native peoples in the upper Yukon basin, was that the miners "almost completely disoriented the normal activities of the Han." Osgood, *Han Indians*, 13, 138, 157.

114. McCandless, *Yukon Wildlife*, 32; Coates, *Best Left as Indians*, 42; and Kenneth S. Coates, "Furs Along the Yukon: Hudson's Bay Company–Native Trade in the Yukon River Basin, 1890–1893," *BC Studies* 55 (autumn 1982): 78. Hunter Fitzhugh was a prime, and thus perhaps unique, example of a miner who hunted for his own food supply. In July 1899 Fitzhugh wrote his grandmother that he had just returned from a ten-day hunt. "We killed about 50 squirrels, and caught 100 mountain trout and grayling. . . . And we always had a string of squirrels, grouse and trout hanging up in plain view." Good hunters clearly had little trouble taking great amounts of game. "I killed a great many Ptarmigan this Fall . . . 27 birds with my 22 calibre rifle." Fitzhugh letter, Oct. 29, 1900.

115. Letter, Comm. Z. T. Wood, NWMP, to T. Stewart, Fish Inspector, Dawson, July 2, 1902, Fisheries, Govt. no. 1888, Series 3, File 2019, YA.

116. Spurr, *Through the Yukon Gold Diggings*, 105.

117. Adney, *Klondike Stampede*, 449.

118. Crow and Obley, "Han," 507; Osgood, *Han Indians*, 115, 154.

119. Coates, *Best Kept as Indians*, 84–85. The Moosehide band often came to the Alaska Commercial Company store in Dawson to exchange furs, firewood, and meat for goods or vouchers for goods. See Margaret Archibald, *A Substantial Expression of Confidence: The Northern Commercial Company Store, Dawson, 1897–1951* (Ottawa: Parks Canada and Environment Canada, National Historic Parks and Sites Branch, 1982), 42.

120. Charlene Porsild, "Culture, Class, and Community," 105–6.

121. Fitzhugh letters, July 5, 1900; August 1, 1900. See also Porsild, "Culture, Class, and Community," 117–18.

122. Coates, "Furs Along the Yukon," 75–77.

123. Osgood, *Han Indians*, 139.

124. Moore account, 1898; Osgood, *Han Indians*, 139–140.

125. The work that Indians did supplying miners with food was only one part of the larger story of the effects of the Alaska-Yukon gold rush on Native peoples along the Yukon. But it was a significant part of the story. This supply work reshaped the Natives' patterns of subsistence in several ways. Catharine McClellan argues that the 1898 rush "radically changed" the lives of many Yukon peoples and "virtually destroyed" the Han. See McClellan, "Intercultural Relations and Cultural Change in the

Cordillera," *Handbook, Subarctic,* 394–95. McClellan writes of the "cataclysmic" nature of the gold rush in which "Yukon Indians confronted . . . an overwhelming mass of new knowledge and new ways of doing things." McClellan, *My Old People Say,* 65.

126. Quoted in Osgood, *Han Indians,* 134.

127. Coates, *Best Left as Indians,* 9. Hudson's Bay Company boat crews brought scarlet fever in 1855, and up to two hundred Indians died at Fort Yukon. The Upper Stikine Tahltan population fell by as much as three quarters in the early nineteenth century, through contact with coastal Indians. Information is thin at best, but there are indications of epidemics among the Chilkoot Tlingit, Tagish, and Han in the fur trade period as well. See Coates, "Furs Along the Yukon," 69; Bruce B. MacLachlan, "Tahltan," *Handbook, Subarctic,* 460; Crow and Obley, "Han," *Handbook, Subarctic,* 510–11.

128. Research on the Han, who worked closely with whites, especially at Dawson, mentions diphtheria in particular. Crow and Obley, "Han," *Handbook, Subarctic,* 510–11.

129. Cruikshank, *Life Lived Like a Story,* 21, 52, 58, 150.

130. Ibid., 161, 166, 176.

131. Cantwell, *Nunivak,* 87. On late winter lean times, see Hosley, "Environment and Culture in the Alaska Plateau," *Handbook, Subarctic,* 544.

132. Smith letter, Dec. 17, 1903.

133. Cantwell, *Nunivak,* 67–69.

134. Ibid., 70.

135. Terrence M. Cole, "A History of the Nome Gold Rush: The Poor Man's Paradise" (Ph.D. diss., University of Washington, 1983), 87–88, 111–12. See also E. M. Rininger, M.D. "Scourge of the Mining Camps: Typhoid Fever in Alaska," *Alaska Journal* 15 (winter 1985): 29–32.

136. William H. Wilson, "To Make a Stake: Fred G. Kimball in Alaska, 1899–1909," *Alaska Journal* 13 (winter 1983): 109–10.

137. Richard Frederick and Jeanne Engerman, *Asahel Curtis: Photographs of the Great Northwest* (Tacoma, Wash.: Washington State Historical Society, 1986), 65.

7 / THE NATURE AND CULTURE OF SEATTLE

1. O.S. Johnson records, in author's possession, on loan from Kathryn Utter.

2. William Cronon, *Nature's Metropolis: Chicago and the Great West* (New York: W. W. Norton, 1990), 339.

3. This discussion of Seattle as a gateway city relies heavily on Cronon, *Nature's Metropolis,* particularly chapter 7, and pp. 339–40.

4. *Seattle Post-Intelligencer,* 17 July 1897, 9 o'clock edition; *Trade Register* (Seattle), 31 July 1897, 26.

5. *Trade Register* (Seattle), 25 December 1897, 1; Margaret Archibald, *Grubstake to Grocery Store: The Klondike Emporium, 1897–1907,* rev. ed. (Ottawa: Parks Canada, Dept. of Indian and Northern Affairs, 1973), 35; Richard Ralph Still, "Historical and Competitive Aspects of Grocery Wholesaling in Seattle, Washington" (Doctor of Commercial Science thesis, University of Washington, 1953), 48–49; Charles M. Gates, "Human Interest Notes on Seattle and the Alaska Gold Rush," *Pacific Northwest Quarterly* 34 (April 1943): 207–9.

6. *Seattle Post-Intelligencer,* 18 July 1897.

7. Ibid., 24 July 1897.

8. *Trade Register* (Seattle), 21 August 1897, 19, 22.

9. William B. Ballou letter, April 1, 1898, William B. Ballou Papers, 1889–1918, UAF.

10. *Trade Register* (Seattle), 8, 15, 22 January 1898.

11. Ibid., 21 May 1898, 21; 26 March 1898; Erastus Brainerd letter, April 26, 1898, Erastus Brainerd Scrapbooks, 1897–98, Microform Collections and M-Series Microfiche, UW. Between January and March, 15,000 total left from Seattle, and 7,500 from other Pacific ports.

12. *Seattle Post-Intelligencer,* 24 July 1897.

13. *Trade Register* (Seattle), 1898 Trade Summary, 31 December 1898, 26, 35.

14. Robert Hunter Fitzhugh letter, January 7, 1898, Robert Hunter Fitzhugh Collection, UAF.

15. Diary of Stewart L. Campbell, February 7, 1898, MSS 122, Acc. 81/129, YA.

16. Ballou letter, March 29, 1898.

17. Alfred "Mac" McMichael letter, March 1898, Alfred McMichael Diary and Letters, Juliette Reinicker Papers, MSS 100, Acc. 79/68, YA.

18. Ibid., March 24, 1898.

19. Ballou letter, April 1, 1898.

20. Seattle Trading Company form, April 5, 1898, in O. G. Herning Diaries, UAF; *Trade Register* (Seattle), 31 July 1897, front cover, 2, 27; Archibald, *Grubstake to Grocery,* 36.

21. *Trade Register* (Seattle), 19 March 1898, 39.

22. Josiah Edward Spurr, *Through the Yukon Gold Diggings: A Narrative of Personal Travel* (Boston: Eastern Publishing Company, 1900), 215.

23. Cronon, *Nature's Metropolis,* 307.

24. On gateway cities in general, see ibid., ch. 6.

25. *Trade Register* (Seattle), 2 July 1898, 5.

26. Ibid., 30 June 1900, 11.

27. Ibid., 29 Dec. 1900, 27–29.

28. Ibid., 21 August 1897, 22.

29. *The Argus* (Seattle), "The Klondike Year," 18 Dec. 1897.

30. *Seattle Post-Intelligencer,* 28 July 1897, as quoted in Norbert MacDonald, "Seattle, Vancouver, and the Klondike," *Canadian Historical Review* 49 (September 1986): 234–46.

31. *Seattle Post-Intelligencer,* 21 July 1898.

32. *The Argus* (Seattle), 18 Dec. 1897, 17.

33. *Trade Register* (Seattle), 13 July 1901, 17.

34. Ibid., 16 June 1900, 26–27.

35. *Seattle Post-Intelligencer,* 3 June 1900.

36. Ibid., 3 Oct. 1897; 27 March 1898; 30 Jan. 1898.

37. Ibid., 21 July 1898.

38. Ibid., 29 Nov. 1897; 24 Jan. 1898.

39. Eugene Higgins letter, New York to Seattle, Jan. 22, 1898, Erastus Brainerd Scrapbooks.

40. *Daily News* (Tacoma), 14 Dec. 1897; *Seattle Post-Intelligencer,* 13 Oct. 1897.

41. Seattle Chamber of Commerce, "Seattle 'The Queen City': Klondike—Alaska," and "SEATTLE," Erastus Brainerd Scrapbooks.

42. *Trade Register* (Seattle), 1898 Trade Summary, 31 Dec. 1898, 28–29. Mapmakers themselves capitalized on the competition as rival cities struggled to naturalize their geographic linkages to Alaska and the Yukon. J. J. Millroy, a map publisher in Salt Lake City, offered Brainerd "a proposition to make Seattle the chief starting point on my new map." For reasons not revealed, Brainerd refused the deal. See Letter, Millroy to Brainerd, San Francisco, Dec. 14, 1897, Erastus Brainerd Scrapbooks.

43. "Report of the Klondike Advertising Committee," Brainerd Collection. Brainerd also directed his colleagues in the Chamber and around Seattle to pen letters to relatives, friends, and newspapers in eastern cities and towns, extolling Seattle's virtues as "the best Alaskan outfitting point." Other cities were spending more money than Seattle, he noted, but "the letter to the trade paper, the religious papers, the society papers . . . coming from you and your clients, congregations, subordinates, employees or friends will be apt to receive more careful attention than one coming from an organization." Brainerd letter, Nov. 20, 1897, Erastus Brainerd Scrapbooks. Brainerd sent questionnaires to thousands of mayors in small towns and cities across the country, asking for information on how many town citizens planned to leave for the Klondike, and whether those adventurers were well prepared, had proper supplies and information, and planned to travel via Seattle. In letters, he asked the

governors and mayors to publish the Chamber's statement as to the true dangers, distances, and expenses involved in a Yukon journey. Most gold seekers did not realize what they were getting into, he explained, and he wished all to be adequately prepared. "Seattle can outfit all BONA FIDE intending prospectors," he wrote, but did not seek anyone likely to become a public burden. Brainerd circular, Oct. 1, 1897, Erastus Brainerd Scrapbooks. This show of concern, no matter how self-interested, proved to be an impressive source of contact between Seattle and community leaders across the nation. If mayors provided names of prospective gold seekers, Brainerd gave the miners' names to Seattle merchants, who contacted them to solicit their business. He also sent copies of Seattle newspapers, full of Klondike information, to each one, in an attempt to make personal contact with every potential outfitting customer. Brainerd, "List of the members of Watertown, S.D., Organization going to Alaska." In handwriting: "Argus to checks," with check marks next to names. Brainerd Scrapbooks.

44. John C. Callbreath Journal/Order Book, 1878–1879, Box 3, John C. Callbreath Diaries, Callbreath, Grant, & Cook Papers, Charles Hubbell Collection, UW.

45. U.S. Department of Commerce and Labor, Bureau of Statistics, *Commercial Alaska, 1867–1903* (Washington, D.C.: GPO, 1903), 114.

46. Still, "Grocery Wholesaling in Seattle," 21–22, 26. Two other large wholesalers, Seattle Hardware and Stewart and Holmes Drug Co., appeared in 1888.

47. Ibid., 5–7, 17, 26.

48. Ibid., 203.

49. Ibid., 42–44; MacDonald, "Seattle, Vancouver, and the Klondike," 236–37.

50. Still, "Grocery Wholesaling in Seattle," 45.

51. Ibid., 42; MacDonald, "Seattle, Vancouver, and the Klondike," 236–37.

52. Callbreath letter, March 27, 1896.

53. Still, "Grocery Wholesaling in Seattle," 48.

54. *Seattle Post-Intelligencer,* 8 March 1896.

55. *Trade Register* (Seattle), 18 June 1898.

56. *Seattle Post-Intelligencer,* 8, 9, 13, 16–17, 29–31 March 1896, 3 Jan. 1897; Still, "Grocery Wholesaling in Seattle," 48.

57. Nora Crane letter, June 1897, Kepner-Crane Collection, Microfiche, UAF.

58. Callbreath letter, May 6, 1898.

59. *Trade Register* (Seattle), 25 Sept. 1897, 19, 26.

60. Ibid., 18 Sept. 1897, 26; 1 Jan. 1898; 19 March 1898; 1, 9 April 1898; 12 August 1899.

61. Gates, "Human Interest Notes," 209.

62. *Trade Register* (Seattle), 1 Jan. 1898, 13.

63. Ibid., 1 Jan. 1898; 8 Jan. 1898, 31; 19, 23 April 1898; 14 May 1898, 14.

64. Ibid., 4 Dec. 1897, 9.

65. Ibid., 25 Dec. 1897, 30.

66. Ibid., 28 April 1900, 31.

67. Ibid., 1 July 1899, 29.

68. Ibid., 25 Feb. 1899, 26.

69. Still, "Grocery Wholesaling in Seattle," 203; *Trade Register* (Seattle), 25 May 1900, 31.

70. Fitzhugh letter, Jan. 7, 1898.

71. *Trade Register* (Seattle), 1898 Trade Summary, 31 Dec. 1898; 2 Oct. 1897; 8 Oct. 1897, 17.

72. Schwabacher Hardware ledger, 1898, Schwabacher Brothers and Company Collection, UW.

73. *Trade Register* (Seattle), 4 Dec. 1897; 9 Oct. 1897.

74. *Trade Register* (Seattle), 8 April 1898.

75. A. S. Allen, comp., *The City of Seattle, 1900* (Seattle: Chamber of Commerce, 1900).

76. *Trade Register* (Seattle), 21 July 1897, 26.

77. Ibid., 1898 Seattle Commerce Edition, 30D, 47; 31 March 1900, 22.

78. Ibid., 22 July 1899, 29.

79. Ibid., 10 March 1900.

80. Terrence Cole, "Home of the Arctic Club: The Alaska and Arctic Buildings in Seattle," *Alaska Journal* 15 (winter 1985): 8–12.

81. *Trade Register* (Seattle), 24 July 1897, 25.

82. *Seattle Post-Intelligencer,* 2 Jan. 1897.

83. *Trade Register* (Seattle), 24 July 1897, 22.

84. Ibid., 9 July 1898, 34.

85. Ibid., 30 July 1898, 19.

86. Ballou letter, July 20, 1901.

87. Archibald, *Grubstake to Grocery Store,* 82.

88. U.S. Mint, *Report of the Director of the Mint Upon The Production of Precious Metals in the United States During the Calendar Year 1898* (Washington, D.C.: GPO, 1899), 56, 222; U.S. Mint, *Report of the Director of the Mint Upon The Production of Precious Metals in the United States During the Calendar Year 1899* (Washington, D.C.: GPO, 1900), 51, 55, 193, 356–357; U.S. Mint, *Report of the Director of the Mint Upon the Production of Precious Metals in the United States During the Calendar Year 1900* (Washington, D.C.: GPO, 1901). Bullion of Alaskan Production received at U.S. Mints and Assay Offices and private smelters: 1900: $8,166,187 (p. 55); Bullion of NW Pro-

duction received at U.S. Mints and Assay Offices and private smelters, 1900: $22,419,626.85 (p. 57). Total gold received at U.S. Mints and Assay Offices and private smelters, from Alaska and NWT: 1900: $30,585,813 (p. 305). Deposits and purchases of gold and silver by value during the calendar year ending Dec. 31, 1900: Seattle Assay Office: Domestic Bullion, unrefined: $4,375, 366; Foreign Bullion, unrefined: $17,346,884. Total incoming, unrefined: $21,722,250. In 1899, with gold from the Nome rush beginning to pour in, the total was $12.8 million; in 1900, $22 million; and in 1901, $14 million. In total, between 1898 and 1901, the Seattle U.S. Assay Office received over $54 million in gold from the Klondike, the Alaskan Yukon, Nome, and other regions. *Trade Register* (Seattle), 26 May 1900, 3; 7 Dec. 1901, 22.

89. Tappan Adney, *The Klondike Stampede* (1900; reprint, Vancouver, B.C.: University of British Columbia Press, 1994), 87.

90. John A. Gould and Richard C. Stuart, "Permafrost Gold: A Treatise on Early Klondike Mining History, Methods and Technology," Microfiche Report Series No. 11 (Ottawa: Parks Canada, 1980), Microfiche, 57, DCM.

91. "Statement of gold assayed by Selby of San Francisco for the Alaska Commercial Company" in "Banking in Yukon Territory," Govt. no. 1629, File 3429, YA.

92. James A. McRae Diary, June 9, 1899, "Bound for the Klondyke," MSS 104, Acc. 80/1, YA.

93. Gould and Stuart, "Permafrost Gold," 56–57.

94. David Doig, "Opening of the First Bank in Dawson in May 1898: How the Bank of British North America Pioneered the Way to the Heart of the Gold Country," MSS 006, Acc. 82/103, YA; Canadian Bank of Commerce correspondence, Feb. 5, 1898, "Banking in Yukon Territory," Govt. no. 1629, File 3429, YA. See also Victor Ross, *A History of the Canadian Bank of Commerce*, vol. 2 (Toronto: Oxford University Press, 1922), 137–39. In 1897, the Klondike royalty was 10 percent of the output of placer mines up to $500 per week, and then 20 percent; in 1898, it was 10 percent of output with an exemption of $2,500 per year; in 1899 the exemption rose to $5,000; in 1901 the royalty was reduced to 5 percent; in 1902 to 2.5 percent. See Ross, *Canadian Bank of Commerce*, 174.

95. Letter, July 7, 1900, "Banking in Yukon Territory."

96. Brainerd to Hill, Erastus Brainerd Scrapbooks.

97. Charles P. Mosier Diary, July 20, 1899, MSS 012, Acc. 82/168, YA.

98. Director of the Mint to U.S. Assay Office, Seattle, Sept. 27, 1910, Records of the Assay Office, Seattle, Records of the U.S. Mint, Record Group 104, Box 11, Folder 5-4-2, National Archives and Records Administration, Pacific Northwest Region, Seattle, Washington.

99. Cronon, *Nature's Metropolis*, 266–67. Cronon writes of Chicago, "In Chicago,

the exchange of merchandise became an exercise in regional transmutation. Whether one turned dried apples into nails, or salted hams into lumber, or bushels of wheat into bolts of printed cotton, the net effect was to link West with East, rural with urban, farm with factory. City streets became places where the products of different ecosystems, different economies, and different ways of life came together and exchanged places." *Nature's Metropolis,* 61.

100. Ibid., 340.

CONCLUSION: NATURE, CULTURE, AND VALUE

1. Jack London, "The Economics of the Klondike," *American Monthly Review of Reviews* 21 (January 1900): 71, 72.

2. Ibid., 73.

3. Ibid., 74.

4. Frederick Jackson Turner, *The Frontier in American History* (New York: Henry Holt and Company, 1920), 1–38; London, "Economics," 74.

5. Given the tenor of many of London's Klondike stories, it is fair to say that he himself understood and captured the very negative consequences of the gold rush for many individual miners. His stories are generally quite scary and negative as he looks at the cruelties and dangers of Alaska and the Yukon.

6. Herbert N. Casson, "The Call of Gold," *Munsey's Magazine* 39 (July 1908): 457.

7. *High Country News* (Paonia, Colo.), 28 Sept. 1998, 22 Dec. 1997; David James Duncan, *My Story As Told By Water* (San Francisco: Sierra Club Books, 2001), 148. In November 2001, a state judge upheld the 1998 anti-cyanide mining law as constitutional. See *Missoulian,* 2 Nov. 2001, *Missoulian.com News Online.*

8. *High Country News* (Paonia, Colo.), 22 Dec. 1997, 7, 9; Duncan, *My Story,* 138–39.

9. Duncan, *My Story,* 142–43.

10. John Edward Crane letter, June 23, 1898, Kepner-Crane Collection, Microfiche, UAF.

SELECTED BIBLIOGRAPHY

MANUSCRIPT SOURCES

Dawson City Museum and Historical Society, Dawson City, Yukon Territory

Cooper, James S. and Associates. Diary. TS.
Courtnay, R. M. Diary. TS.
Hiscock, F. Wm. Diary, "The Youkon Trail of Year 1898." TS.
Kearney, Thomas J. Letters, Dawson, 1899.

National Archives and Records Administration,
Pacific Northwest Region, Seattle, Washington

Records of the Assay Office, Seattle. Records of the U.S. Mint, Record Group 104.

Elmer E. Rasmuson Library, University of Alaska, Fairbanks, Alaska,
and Polar Regions Department, Manuscripts, Historical Photographs,
and University Archives, Fairbanks, Alaska

Adams, Edward C. "Dairy [*sic*] of the Tripp from Seattle to Dawson City and also
    for the whole year of 1900."
Anderson, Eskil. Collection.
Anderson, James Lynn. Diaries, 1895–99. 2 vols.
Ballou, William B. Papers, 1889–1918. Letters.
Boldrick, Tom. Diary.

Boston-Alaska Transportation Co. Letter, July 18, 1898.

Cavanagh, Joseph H. Diary, "Journey to Alaska-Yukon 1898–1900."

"Chapter 10." Untitled Klondike manuscript.

"Despatches from U.S. Consuls in Dawson City, Canada, 1898–1906." Microfilm
    no. 199.

"Dredges."

"Dyea and the Dyea Trail."

Fitzhugh, Robert Hunter. Collection.

Gibson, Sarah Ellen. Collection, Correspondence, 1884–1903.

Haldeman, Bruce. Papers, Folder 1. Alaska-Yukon Transportation Co.

Hamil, James H. Letters, 1897.

Heller, Herbert. Collection.

Herning, O.G. Collection, Diaries.

Houck, Jonas B. Papers.

Hulse, Hamlin. Diary.

Kepner-Crane Collection. Microfiche.

Kimball, Fred G. Letters, 1899–1909.

Makinson, Paul. "Alaska, My Second Home."

Michaels, William. Collection. Iowa-Alaska Mining Company.

Nagley, H. Willard. Collection. Alaska Commercial Company Journal.

Petersen, Harold. "Diary of Mr. Harold Petersen."

Pilz, George G. TS, "Mining Experiences in Alaska."

Purdy, Frank. Diary.

Rampart City, Alaska. Minutes of Citizens Meeting, 1898–1902.

Rasmuson, Elmer E. "History of Early Banking in Alaska."

Record of Arrivals by Small Boat or Sled. United States National Archives. Microfilm
    Publications, Microfilm no. T1189.

Records of Alaskan Customhouses, 1867–1939. Microfilm, rolls 115, 116.

Smith, Robert Lynn. Correspondence and Diaries. Herbert Heller Collection, Box 1.

Steiner, C. O. Diary, "A Journey to Dawson in 1898."

"St. Michael, July 1898."

*University of Washington Libraries, Manuscripts, Special Collections,
University Archives Division, Seattle, Washington*

Ballaine, John Edmund. Papers, 1889–1940.

Brainerd, Erastus. Papers, 1880–1919.

Callbreath, Grant, & Cook. Papers, Letterpress Copy Books, 1878–98, vols. 1–6, and
     John C. Callbreath Diaries, Charles Hubbell Collection.
Cooper-Levy Family Collection.
Curtis, Asahel. Collection. Diary, 1898.
Dulien, Louis. Oral History.
Nelson, Albert Jr. Diaries, 1867–1901.
Perkins, William T. Collection.
Rosene, John. Collection.
Schwabacher Brothers and Company Collection.
Schwabacher Family. Interviews and tapes.
Schwabacher Hardware Company Collection.
Schwartz, Louis. Oral history.
Shucklin, Gerald. Oral history.

University of Washington Libraries,
Microfilm Collections and M-Series Microfiche

"Alaska and the Klondike: The New Gold Fields and How to Reach Them." Port-
     land: Harry L. Wells, 1897. M-2501, no. 16437.
Ballou, Maturin. *The New Eldorado: A Summer Journey to Alaska.* Boston: Houghton
     Mifflin, 1890. M-2501, no. 14084.
Blethen, A. J. "Nature's Doorway to the Land of Gold." *Illustrated American* (5 March
     1898). M-2501, no. 14279.
Brainerd, Erastus. Scrapbooks, 1897–98, vol. 1.
Hayne, M. H. E. *The Pioneers of the Klondyke.* London: Sampson, Low, Marston
     and Co., 1897. M-2501, no. 05522.
"Ho! for Alaska: How to Go, What to take, What It Costs, What You Find." New
     York: Republic Press, 1897. M-2501, no. 14011.
"Klondyke: A Guide to the New Eldorado." London, Victoria, Dawson City:
     Klondyke & Columbian Passenger Agency, 1898(?). M-2501, no. 15379.
"Klondyke and Yukon Guide: Alaska and Northwest Territory Gold Fields." Seat-
     tle: Alaska Illustrators, 1898. M-2501, no. 15371.
"Klondyke Gold Fields, Yukon District." Vancouver, 1898. M-2501, no. 15380.
Ladue, Joseph. *Klondyke Nuggets: A Brief Description of the Great Gold Regions in
     the Northwest Territories and Alaska.* Montreal, 1897. M-2501, no. 15405.
Scarth, W. H. "Report of Trip to the Yukon, 1897." Ottawa: GPO, 1898. M-2501,
     no. 13255.

Tacoma–Port Orchard Navigation Co. "Stikine River Route to the Klondike: Shortest, Safest, Quickest, and Best." Tacoma, Wash., 1898. M-2501, no. 15918.

"To the Klondike and Alaska Gold Fields via The Alaska Commercial Company." San Francisco: Alaska Commercial Company, 1898. M-2501, no. 16260.

"To the Land of Gold." Vancouver, 1898. M-2501, no. 16319

Yukon Archive, Department of Education,
The Government of Yukon, Whitehorse, Yukon Territory

Manuscripts

Banks, Henry Dow. "Account of Voyage, ca. 1898." MSS 40, Acc. 82/240.

Beatty, James E. Papers. MSS 122, Acc. 82/390.

Bolton, W. W. Account, 1914. MSS 5, Acc. 82/99.

Calam, John. Account of Student Summer Employment, 1947. MSS 095, Acc. 70/79.

Campbell, Stewart L. Diary. MSS 122, Acc. 81/129.

Case, George E., and Family. Letters. MSS 172, Acc. 81/91.

Cautley, R. W. "Highlights of Memory. Incidents in the life of a Canadian Surveyor." MSS 005, Acc. 82/97.

Childs, Will. Letters. MSS 166, Acc. 84/65.

Davies, John D. Diary, 1898–1900. MSS 160, Acc. 81/137.

Doig, David, "Opening of the First Bank in Dawson in May 1898: How the Bank of British North America Pioneered the Way to the Heart of Gold Country." MSS 006, Acc. 82/103.

"Dredging, Thawing, and Prospecting Placer Ground in the Klondike District—Y.T.," ca. 1918. MSS 169, Acc. 84/80.

Greene, Joseph J. Journal. MSS 004, Acc. 82/52.

Kingsley, James E. "Reminiscences of Grand Forks." MSS 145, Acc. 80/86.

Lindsay, John H. Diary and Letters, Lindsay Family Papers. MSS 12, Acc. 82/173.

McMichael, Alfred. Diary and Letters, Folders 2–10, Juliette Reinicker Papers. MSS 100, Acc. 79/68.

McRae, James A. Diary, "Bound for the Klondyke." MSS 104, Acc. 80/1.

Moore, Thomas W. Account. MSS 007, Acc. 82/121.

Mosier, Charles P. Diary. MSS 012, Acc. 82/168.

Park, William John. Diary, 1897. MSS 166, Acc. 84/55.

Schuldenfrei, Rebecca. Letters, Schuldenfrei Family Papers. MSS 166, Acc. 84/47.

Ledgers

Daily Recordings: Steamers Arriving and Departing from or to Dawson, Season of 1902 (May 18, 1902–Nov. 1, 1902). Acc. No. 991R-1–67.

Mining Recorder Records. Record Books for Placer Mining Claims. Eldorado Creek. Govt. Series 10, vols. 30–31.

Unidentified Ledger. Account Book, Sept. 21–Nov. 30, 1903. Daily recordings of customers and their purchases. Acc. No. 991R-1–50.

Government Records

Application for Timber Berths, Yukon Territory. Govt. no. 2099, vol. 21.

Banking and Gold. Govt. no. 1626, Files 3429, 3720.

Banking in Yukon Territory. Govt. no. 1629, File 3429.

Dredging Regulations, 1898. Govt. no. 1984, vol. 8, File 2–0–33.

Fisheries. Govt. no. 1888, File 2019.

George, Arnold F. Alaska-Yukon-Pacific Exposition Address. Govt. no. 1641, File 16721.

Gold Commissioner. Govt. no. 1619, File 1432.

Gold Commissioner. Gold Production. Govt. no. 1642, File 18387.

Gold Commissioner's Office Letter Book, 1899. Govt. no. 1695, vol. 85.

Gold Commissioner's Records. Govt. no. 1619, File 1477 (1).

Hay and Grazing Regulations. Govt. no. 1950, File 328.

Labor in Yukon Territory, 1909. Govt. no. 1646, File 25254.

Mining Regulations, 1904. Govt. no. 1985, vol. 2, File 2–0–1.

Report on Wood, 1898. Govt. no. 1078, vol. 8A, File 3.

Robinson, J. Lewis. "Agriculture and Forests of Yukon Territory," ca. 1946. Govt. no. 2078, vol. 8A.

Steamer Fuel Reports, British Yukon Navigation Company, 1901. Govt. no. 1684, File 65.

Steamer Fuel Reports, British Yukon Navigation Company, 1902. Trips 1–18. Govt. no. 1683, File 47, 1(2).

Sulphur Creek, Record of Work Done. Govt. no. 2130, Series 8, vol. 52.

Timber Agent Reports, 1899–1900. Govt. no. 1683, File 43, 1(2).

Timber and Fuel Records; Log Boom Reports. Govt. no. 1625, File 3230, File 3530.

Timber Berths, 1898. Govt. no. 1684, File 68, 1(2).

Timber Permits, 1897–1905. Govt. no. 2090, Series 8, vol. 12.

Timber Resources of Yukon Territory, 1910–1914. Govt. no. 1649, File 26747, vol. 39.

Water Regulations. Govt. no. 1643, File 20347.

Wood Cutting, Adams Gulch. Govt. no. 1684, File 69 1(1), File 70, 2(2).

Woodcutting Royalties. Govt. no 1078, vol. 8A, File 8.

Wood Permits, Gold Commissioner. Govt. no. 1622, File 2518 2(2); File 2549 (1/1).

GOVERNMENT REPORTS AND DOCUMENTS

Archibald, Margaret. *Grubstake to Grocery Store: The Klondike Emporium, 1897–1907.* Rev. ed. Ottawa: Parks Canada, Dept. of Indian and Northern Affairs, 1973.

————. *A Substantial Expression of Confidence: The Northern Commercial Company Store, Dawson, 1897–1951.* Ottawa: Parks Canada and Environment Canada, National Historic Parks and Sites Branch, 1982.

Blake, William P. *Geographical Notes Upon Russian America and the Stickeen River, Being A Report Addressed to the Hon. W. H. Seward, Secretary of State, with a Map of the Stickeen River.* Washington, D.C.: GPO, 1868.

Cantwell, John C. *Report of the Operations of the U.S. Revenue Steamer "Nunivak" on the Yukon River Station, Alaska, 1899–1901.* Washington, D.C.: GPO, 1904.

Carter, Margaret. "A History of the Use of Wood in the Yukon to 1903." Ottawa: National Historic Sites Service, 1973. Dawson City Museum and Historical Society.

Dunham, Samuel C. *The Alaskan Gold Fields.* Reprint, Anchorage: Alaska Northwest Pub. Co., 1983. Orig. pub. as "The Alaskan Gold Fields and the Opportunities They Offer for Capital and Labor," in *Bulletin of the Department of Labor,* no. 16 (May 1898): 297–425.

Gould, John A., and Richard C. Stuart. "Permafrost Gold: A Treatise on Early Klondike Mining History, Methods and Technology." Microfiche Report Series No. 11. Ottawa: Parks Canada, December 1980. Dawson City Museum and Historical Society.

Hunt, William R. *Golden Places: The History of Alaska-Yukon Mining.* Anchorage: National Park Service, Alaska Region, 1990.

Kemmerer, Edwin Walter. "Seasonal Variations in the Relative Demand for Money and Capital in the United States: A Statistical Study." Senate Doc. 588. Washington, D.C.: National Monetary Commission, 1910.

Lloyd, Denby L. "Turbidity in Freshwater Habitats of Alaska: A Review of Published and Unpublished Literature Relevant to the Use of Turbidity as a Water Quality Standard." Juneau, Alaska: Alaska Dept. of Fish and Game, Habitat Division, January 1985.

Lutz, Harold John. *Early Forest Conditions in the Alaska Interior: An Historical Account with Original Sources.* Juneau, Alaska: U.S. Department of Agriculture, U.S. Forest Service, Northern Forest Experiment Station, June 1963.

Madison, R. J. "Effects of Placer Mining on Hydrologic Systems in Alaska—Status of Knowledge." USGS Open-File Report 81–217. Anchorage, Alaska: U.S. Dept. of Interior, U.S. Geological Survey and Bureau of Land Management, 1981.

Neufeld, David. *An Annotated Bibliography of Placer Gold Mining, 1896–1966.* Ottawa: Parks Canada, September 1994.

Northern Design Consultants. "A History of Logging in the Yukon, 1896–1970." Vol. I. Whitehorse, Yukon Territory: Northern Design Consultants, 1993. Logging File, Dawson City Museum and Historical Society.

Richardson, Capt. W. P., Eighth Infantry, U.S. Army. "The Mighty Yukon as Seen and Explored." In U.S. Congress, Senate, Committee on Military Affairs, *Compilation of Narratives of Explorations in Alaska, 1869–1900.* Washington, D.C.: GPO, 1900.

———. "Report of an Expedition into Alaska." In U.S. Congress, Senate, Committee on Military Affairs, *Compilation of Narratives of Explorations in Alaska, 1869–1900.* Washington, D.C.: GPO, 1900.

Smith, Richard C. *Potential Economic Development of Forest Resources in Interior Alaska.* Portland: Pacific Northwest Forest and Range Experiment Station, U.S. Department of Agriculture, U.S. Forest Service, November 1980.

Soroka, I. K., and G. Mackenzie-Grieve. "A Biological and Water Quality Assessment at A Placer Mine on Barlow Creek, Yukon Territory." Environment Canada, Environmental Protection Service, Pacific Region, Yukon Branch, Regional Program Report 84–16. Whitehorse, Yukon Territory: Environment Canada, 1984.

U.S. Congress. Senate. Committee on Military Affairs. *Compilation of Narratives of Explorations in Alaska, 1869–1900.* Washington, D.C.: GPO, 1900.

U.S. Department of Commerce and Labor, Bureau of Statistics. *Commercial Alaska, 1867–1903.* Washington, D.C.: GPO, 1903.

U.S. Department of Interior. Federal Water Pollution Administration, Northwest Region, Alaska Water Laboratory. "Effects of Placer Mining on Water Quality in Alaska." College, Alaska: Alaska Water Laboratory, 1969.

U.S. Department of the Interior. National Park Service. *Final Environmental Impact Statement.* Vol. 1, *Mining in Yukon-Charley Rivers National Preserve, Alaska.* Washington, D.C.: GPO, 1990.

U.S. Mint. *Report of the Director of the Mint upon the Production of the Precious Metals in the United States During the Calendar Year 1898, 1899, 1900.* Washington, D.C.: GPO, 1899, 1900, 1901.

Ward, Henry Baldwin. "Placer Mining on the Rogue River, Oregon, in Its Relation to the Fish and Fishing in that Stream." Portland: Oregon Dept. of Geology and Mineral Industries, 1938, 4–31.

BOOKS, CHAPTERS, ARTICLES,
DISSERTATIONS, AND THESES

Adams, George Edward. "Where the Klondike Gold is Valued." *Cosmopolitan,* February 1900, 425–34.

Adney, Tappan. *The Klondike Stampede.* 1900. Reprint, Vancouver, B.C.: University of British Columbia Press, 1994.

———. "The Indian Hunter of the Far Northwest: On the Trail to the Klondike." *Outside* 39 (March 1902): 623–33.

Agricola, Georgius. *De Re Metallica.* 1556. Trans. by Herbert C. Hoover and Lou Henry Hoover, 1912. Reprint, New York: Dover Publications, 1950.

Aitchison, Leslie. *A History of Metals.* 2 vols. London: Macdonald & Evans, 1960.

Alberts, Laurie. "Petticoats and Pickaxes." *Alaska Journal* 7 (summer 1977): 146–59.

Allen, A. S., comp. *The City of Seattle, 1900.* Seattle: Chamber of Commerce, 1900.

Alley, William. "Yakutat Bound: A Prospector's Letter and Photographs." *Pacific Northwest Quarterly* 83 (January 1992): 2–8.

Anderson, Barry C. *Lifeline to the Yukon: A History of Yukon River Navigation.* Seattle: Superior Publishing, 1983.

Andrews, Clarence L. *Wrangell and the Gold of the Cassiar: A Tale of Fur and Gold in Alaska.* Seattle: L. Tinker, 1937.

Angell, Norman. *The Story of Money.* New York: Frederick A. Stokes, 1929.

Appleby, Joyce Oldham. "Locke, Liberalism, and the Natural Law of Money." *Past and Present* 71 (May 1976): 43–69.

Arno Press, comp. *Gold and Silver in the Presidential Campaign of 1896.* New York: Arno Press, 1974.

Arnold, David. "'Putting Up Fish': Environment, Work, and Culture in Tlingit Society, 1780s–1940s." Ph.D. diss., University of California, Los Angeles, 1997.

———. "Work, Culture, and Environment: Tlingit Fishing and Economic Change, 1890s–1940s." Paper presented at the annual conference of the Western History Association, Lincoln, Nebraska, October 5, 1996.

Barbour, David. *The Standard of Value.* London: Macmillan & Co., 1912.

Barnes, James A. "Myths of the Bryan Campaign." *Mississippi Valley Historical Review* 34 (December 1947): 367–404.

Bensel, Richard Franklin. *Yankee Leviathan: The Origins of Central State Authority in America, 1859–1877.* New York: Cambridge University Press, 1990.

Berner, Richard C. *Seattle 1900–1920: From Boomtown, Urban Turbulence, to Restoration.* Seattle: Charles Press, 1991.

Berton, Pierre. *Klondike: The Last Great Gold Rush, 1896–1899*. Toronto: McClelland & Stewart, 1958; rev. ed. 1972.

———, ed. *The Klondike Quest: A Photographic Essay*. Boston: Little Brown, 1983.

Bjerklie, David M., and Jacqueline D. LaPerriere. "Gold-Mining Effects on Stream Hydrology and Water Quality, Circle Quadrangle, Alaska." *Water Resources Bulletin* 21 (April 1995): 235–43.

Bolotin, Norm. "A Spendable History of Alaska." *Alaska Journal* 8 (summer 1978): 214–16.

———. "Klondike Lost: Tales from a Forgotten Gold Rush Boom Town." *Alaska Journal* 10 (spring 1980): 65–72.

———, ed. *Klondike Lost: A Decade of Photography by Kinsey & Kinsey*. Anchorage: Alaska Northwest, 1980.

Boorstin, Daniel J. *The Americans: The Democratic Experience*. New York: Vintage Books, 1973.

Braudel, Fernand. *Civilization and Capitalism*. 3 vols. Trans. by Sian Reynolds, 1979. Reprint, Berkeley: University of California Press, 1992.

Braverman, Harry. *Labor and Monopoly Capital: The Degradation of Work in the Twentieth Century*. New York: Monthly Review Press, 1974.

Burlingame, Virginia S. "John J. Healy's Alaskan Adventure." *Alaska Journal* 8 (winter 1978): 310–19.

Bush, Sam Stone. "The Rush to the Klondike." *American Monthly Review of Reviews* 17 (March 1898): 299–300.

Cantwell, John C. *Report of the Operations of the U.S. Revenue Steamer "Nunivak" on the Yukon River Station, Alaska, 1899–1901*. Washington, D.C: GPO, 1902.

Carlson, Phyllis D. "Alaska's First Census: 1880." *Alaska Journal* 1 (winter 1971): 48–53.

Carmichael, Ann Carlisle, ed. *Hunter: The Yukon Gold Rush Letters of Robert Hunter Fitzhugh, Jr., 1897–1900*. Montgomery, Ala.: Black Belt Press, 1999.

Carstensen, Vernon, ed. *Farmer Discontent, 1865–1900*. New York: Wiley, 1974.

Casson, Herbert N. "The Call of Gold." *Munsey's Magazine* 39 (July 1908): 457–61.

Chandler, Alfred D., Jr. *The Visible Hand: The Managerial Revolution in American Business*. Cambridge, Mass.: Belknap Press, 1977.

Chicago Record. Klondike: The Chicago Record's Book for Gold Seekers. Chicago: Chicago Record Co., 1897.

Clanton, Gene. *Populism: The Humane Preference in America, 1890–1900*. Boston: Twayne Publishers, 1991.

Coates, Kenneth S. *Best Left as Indians: Native-White Relations in the Yukon Territory, 1840–1973*. Montreal: McGill-Queen's University Press, 1991.

————. "Furs Along the Yukon: Hudson's Bay Company–Native Trade in the Yukon River Basin, 1890–1893." *BC Studies* 55 (autumn 1982): 51–79.

Cohen, Stan. *Yukon River Steamboats: A Pictorial History.* Missoula, Mont.: Pictorial Histories Co., 1982.

Cole, Terrence M. "A History of the Nome Gold Rush: The Poor Man's Paradise." Ph.D. diss., University of Washington, 1983.

————. "Home of the Arctic Club: The Alaska and Arctic Buildings in Seattle." *Alaska Journal* 15 (winter 1985): 8–12.

————. "Klondike Visions: Dreams of a Promised Land." *Alaska Journal* 16 (1986): 82–93.

————. "Promoting the Pacific Rim: The AYP Exposition of 1909." *Alaska History* 6 (spring 1991): 18–34.

Coletta, Paolo E. *William Jennings Bryan.* Vol. 1, *Political Evangelist.* Lincoln: University of Nebraska Press, 1964.

Cordone, Almo J., and Don W. Kelley. "The Influences of Inorganic Sediment on the Aquatic Life of Streams." *California Fish and Game* 47:2 (1961): 189–228.

Cronon, William. *Nature's Metropolis: Chicago and the Great West.* New York: W.W. Norton, 1991.

————. "Kennecott Journey: The Paths Out of Town." In *Under an Open Sky: Rethinking America's Western Past,* ed. by William Cronon, George Miles, and Jay Gitlin. New York: W.W. Norton, 1992.

————, ed. *Uncommon Ground: Toward Reinventing Nature.* New York: W. W. Norton, 1995.

Cruikshank, Julie. *Life Lived Like a Story: Life Stories of Three Yukon Native Elders.* Lincoln: University of Nebraska Press, 1990.

————. "Images of Society in Klondike Gold Rush Narratives: Skookum Jim and the Discovery of Gold." *Ethnohistory* 39 (winter 1992): 21–41.

————. "Discovery of Gold on the Klondike: Perspectives from Oral Tradition." In *Reading Beyond Words: Contexts for Native History,* ed. by Jennifer S. H. Brown and Elizabeth Vibert. Peterborough, Ontario: Broadview Press, 1996.

Curtin, Walter R. *Unofficial Log of the Steamer Yukoner.* Caldwell, Idaho: Caxton Printers, Ltd., 1938.

Curtis, Edward S. "The Rush to the Klondike Over the Mountain Passes." *Century Magazine* 55 (February 1898): 692–93.

Dall, William H., et al. *Alaska.* Vol. 2, *History, Geography, Resources.* New York: Harriman Alaska Expedition and Doubleday, Page, & Co., 1902.

Davies, Glyn. *A History of Money: From Ancient Times to the Present.* Cardiff: University of Wales, 1994.

DeArmond, R. N. "A Letter to Jack McQuesten: 'Gold on the Fortymile.'" *Alaska Journal* 3 (winter 1973): 114–21.

———. "Riverboating on the Stikine." *Alaska Journal* 9 (autumn 1979): 68–81.

Degen, Robert A. *The American Monetary System: A Concise Survey of Its Evolution Since 1896.* Lexington, Mass.: Lexington Books, 1987.

Donnelly, Ignatius. *The American People's Money.* Chicago, 1896. Reprint, Hartford, Conn.: Hyperion, 1976.

Ducker, James H. "Gold Rushers North: A Census Study of the Yukon and Alaskan Gold Rushes, 1896–1900." *Pacific Northwest Quarterly* 85 (July 1994): 80–93.

Duncan, David James. *My Story As Told By Water.* San Francisco: Sierra Club Books, 2001.

Egan, Douglas. "A Young Man's Adventures in Gold Rush Days." *Alaska Journal* 10 (winter 1980): 86–87.

Emerson, Harrington. "The Rail Route to the Klondike." *American Monthly Review of Reviews* 20 (September 1899): 350.

Fabian, Ann Vincent. "Rascals and Gentlemen: The Meaning of American Gambling." Ph.D. diss., Yale University, 1982.

Faragher, John Mack, et al., eds. *Out of Many: A History of the American People.* 3rd combined ed. Upper Saddle River, N.J.: Prentice Hall, 2000.

Findlay, John M. *People of Chance: Gambling in American Society from Jamestown to Las Vegas.* New York: Oxford University Press, 1986.

Fleck, Henrietta. *Introduction to Nutrition.* 4th ed. New York: Macmillan, 1981.

Frederick, Richard. "Asahel Curtis and the Klondike Stampede." *Alaska Journal* 13 (spring 1983): 113–21.

Frederick, Richard, and Jeanne Engerman. *Asahel Curtis: Photographs of the Great Northwest.* Tacoma, Wash.: Washington State Historical Society, 1986.

Friedman, Milton, and Anna Jacobson Schwartz. *A Monetary History of the United States.* Princeton: Princeton University Press, 1963.

Gates, Charles M. "Human Interest Notes on Seattle and the Alaskan Gold Rush." *Pacific Northwest Quarterly* 34 (April 1943): 205–11.

Gates, Michael. *Gold at Fortymile Creek: Early Days in the Yukon.* Vancouver: University of British Columbia Press, 1994.

Gies, Joseph, and Francis Gies. *Merchants and Moneymen: The Commercial Revolution, 1000–1500.* New York: Crowell, 1972.

Glad, Paul W. *McKinley, Bryan, & The People.* Philadelphia: Lippincott, 1964.

Goodman, David. *Gold Seeking: Victoria and California in the 1850s.* Stanford: Stanford University Press, 1994.

Goodwyn, Lawrence. *Democratic Promise: The Populist Moment in America.* New York: Oxford University Press, 1976.

Goudie, Andrew. *The Human Impact: Man's Role in Environmental Change.* Cambridge: MIT Press, 1981.

Green, Timothy. *The World of Gold.* New York: Walker and Co., 1968.

Gutman, Herbert. *Work, Culture, and Society in Industrializing America: Essays in American Working-Class and Social History.* New York: Vintage Books, 1976.

Hanable, William S. "Floating Palaces on the Yukon." *Alaska Journal* 15 (winter 1985): 33–38.

Hansen, R. Gaurth, et al. *Nutritional Quality Index of Foods.* Westport, Conn.: AVI Publishing Co., 1979.

Harris, A. C. *Alaska and the Klondike Gold Fields.* Chicago: Monroe Book Co., 1897.

Harris, R. Cole. "Moving Amid the Mountains, 1870–1930." *BC Studies* 58 (summer 1983): 3–39.

———. *The Resettlement of British Columbia: Essays on Colonialism and Geographical Change.* Vancouver, B.C.: University of British Columbia Press, 1997.

Harvey, David. *Consciousness and the Urban Experience: Studies in the History and Theory of Capitalist Urbanization.* Baltimore: Johns Hopkins University Press, 1985.

———. *Justice, Nature, and the Geography of Difference.* Cambridge, Mass.: Blackwell, 1996.

Harvey, William H. *Coin's Financial School.* 1894. Reprint, ed. by Richard Hoftstader, Cambridge, Mass.: Belknap Press, 1963.

Haughland, Marylou McMahon. "A History of Alaska Steamship Company, 1895–1954." Master's thesis, University of Washington, 1968.

Heilprin, Angelo. *Alaska and the Klondike: A Journey to the New Eldorado with Hints to the Traveler.* London: C. Arthur Pearson, 1899.

Heller, Herbert L., ed. *Sourdough Sagas.* Cleveland: World Publishing, 1967.

Helms, Andrea R. C., and Mary Childers Mangusso. "The Nome Gold Conspiracy." *Pacific Northwest Quarterly* 73 (January 1982): 10–19.

Herron, John P., and Andrew G. Kirk, eds. *Human/Nature: Biology, Culture, and Environmental History.* Albuquerque: University of New Mexico Press, 1999.

Higham, John. "The Reorientation of American Culture in the 1890s." In *The Origins of Modern Consciousness,* ed. by John Weiss. Detroit: Wayne State University Press, 1965.

Hill, A. A. "The Klondike." *Munsey's Magazine* 20 (February 1899): 704–37.

Hitchock, Mary E. *Two Women in the Klondike: The Story of a Journey to the Gold Fields of Alaska.* New York: G.P. Putnam's Sons, 1899.

Howson, Embrey Bernard. "Jacob Sechler Coxey: A Biography of a Monetary Reformer, 1854–1951." Ph.D. diss., Ohio State University, 1973.

Hunt, John Clark, ed. "The Adventures of the Iowa Goldseekers." *Alaska Journal* 3 (winter 1973): 2–11.

Hunt, William R. "Judge Ballou of Rampart." *Alaska Journal* 2 (winter 1972): 41–47.

———. *Whiskey Peddler: Johnny Healy, North Frontier Trader*. Missoula, Mont.: Mountain Press Pub. Co., 1993.

Johansen, Dorothy O. *Empire of the Columbia: A History of the Pacific Northwest*. 2nd ed. New York: Harper & Row, 1967.

Johnson, Susan Lee. "'The gold she gathered': Difference, Domination, and California's Southern Miners, 1848–1853." Ph.D. diss., Yale University, 1993.

———. *Roaring Camp: The Social World of the California Gold Rush*. New York: W. W. Norton, 2000.

Johnston, Samuel P., ed. *Alaska Commercial Company, 1868–1940*. San Francisco: E. E. Wachter, 1940.

Jones, Stanley L. *The Presidential Election of 1896*. Madison: University of Wisconsin Press, 1964.

Kelley, Robert L. *Gold vs. Grain: The Hydraulic Mining Controversy in California's Sacramento Valley*. Glendale, Calif.: A. H. Clark Co., 1959.

Kemmerer, Edwin Walter. *Gold and the Gold Standard*. 1944. Reprint, New York: Arno Press, 1979.

Kern, Stephen. *The Culture of Time and Space: 1880–1918*. Cambridge: Harvard University Press, 1986.

Kinley, David. *Money: A Study of the Theory of the Medium of Exchange*. New York: Macmillan, 1904.

Kitchener, Lois D. *Flag Over the North: The Story of the Northern Commercial Company*. Seattle: Superior Pub. Co., 1954.

Knutson, Arthur E. *Sternwheelers on the Yukon*. Kirkland, Wash.: Knutson Enterprises, 1979.

Krooss, Herman E., ed. *Documentary History of Banking and Currency in the United States*. 4 vols. New York: Chelsea House, 1969.

Lane, Charles D. "The Gold Miner and the Silver Question." *Overland Monthly* 28 (November 1896): 585–88.

LaPerriere, Jacqueline D., Stephen M. Wagener, and David M. Bjerklie. "Gold-Mining Effects of Heavy Metals in Streams, Circle Quadrangle, Alaska." *Water Resources Bulletin* 21 (April 1985): 245–52.

Larson, Robert W. *Populism in the Mountain West*. Albuquerque: University of New Mexico Press, 1986.

Laughlin, J. Laurence. *The History of Bimetallism in the United States.* New York: D. Appleton and Company, 1896.

Lauzen, Elizabeth. "Marketing the Image of the Last Frontier: The AYP Exposition of 1909." *Alaska Journal* 12 (spring 1982): 13–19.

Lears, T. J. Jackson. *No Place of Grace: Antimodernism and the Transformation of American Culture, 1880–1920.* New York: Pantheon Books, 1981.

———. "The Concept of Cultural Hegemony: Problems and Possibilities." *American Historical Review* 90 (June 1985): 567–93.

Levenstein, Harvey A. *Revolution at the Table: The Transformation of the American Diet.* New York: Oxford University Press, 1988.

Livingston, Victoria Hartwell. "Erastus Brainerd: The Bankruptcy of Brilliance." Master's thesis, University of Washington, 1967.

Lloyd, Denby S. "Turbidity as a Water Quality Standard for Salmonid Habitats in Alaska." *North American Journal of Fisheries Management* 7 (1987): 34–45.

London, Jack. "The Economics of the Klondike." *American Monthly Review of Reviews* 21 (January 1900): 71–74.

———. "The One Thousand Dozen." In *The Bodley Head Jack London.* Vol. 4, *The Klondike Dream,* ed. by Arthur Calder-Marshall. London: Bodley Head, 1963–66.

———. *Novels & Stories.* New York: Library of America, 1982.

Lorant, Stefan. *The Presidency: A Pictorial History of Presidential Elections.* New York: The Macmillan Company, 1951.

Lux, M. K. "Disease and the Growth of Dawson City: The Seamy Underside of a Legend." *Northern Review* 3/4 (summer/winter 1989): 96–120.

MacDonald, Norbert. "Seattle, Vancouver and the Klondike." *Canadian Historical Review* 49 (September 1986): 234–46.

———. *Distant Neighbors: A Comparative History of Seattle & Vancouver.* Lincoln: University of Nebraska Press, 1987.

Map-Guide Seattle to Dawson: Over the Chilkoot, Through the Lakes and Down the Yukon. Seattle: Humes, Lysons and Sallee, 1897.

Marcuzzo, Maria Cristina, and Annalisa Rosselli. *Ricardo and the Gold Standard: The Foundations of the International Monetary Order.* Trans. by Joan Hall. New York: St. Martin's Press, 1991.

Marks, Paula Mitchell. *Precious Dust: The American Gold Rush Era, 1848–1900.* New York: William Morrow, 1994.

Marshall, Robert. *Arctic Village: A 1930s Portrait of Wiseman, Alaska.* 1933. Reprint, Fairbanks: University of Alaska Press, 1993.

Marx, Jennifer. *The Magic of Gold.* New York: Doubleday, 1978.

Marx, Karl. *Capital: A Critique of Political Economy.* Vol. 1. Trans. by Ben Fowkes. New York: Random House, 1977.

McCandless, Robert G. *Yukon Wildlife: A Social History.* Edmonton: University of Alberta Press, 1985.

McClellan, Catharine. *My Old People Say: An Ethnographic Survey of Southern Yukon Territory.* Part 1. Ottawa: National Museum of Man, National Museums of Canada, 1975.

————. *Part of the Land, Part of the Water: A History of the Yukon Indians.* Vancouver/Toronto: Douglas & McIntyre, 1987.

McLeay, D. J., G. L. Ennis, I. K. Birtwell, and G. F. Hartman. "Effects on Arctic Grayling of Prolonged Exposure to Yukon Placer Mining Sediment: A Laboratory Study." *Canadian Technical Report of Fisheries and Aquatic Sciences,* no. 1241 (January 1984): 1–96.

Meijer, Fik, and Onno van Nijf. *Trade, Transport, and Society in the Ancient World: A Sourcebook.* New York: Routledge, 1992.

Michaels, Walter Benn. *The Gold Standard and the Logic of Naturalism: American Literature at the Turn of the Century.* Berkeley: University of California Press, 1987.

Mill, John Stuart. *Principles of Political Economy.* Ed. by W. J. Ashley. 1848. Reprint, London: Longmans, 1940.

Minter, Roy. *The White Pass: Gateway to the Klondike.* Fairbanks: University of Alaska Press, 1987.

Monroe, Arthur Eli. *Monetary Theory Before Adam Smith.* Cambridge: Harvard University Press, 1923.

Morehouse, Karen B. "Alaska Native Diet and Nutrition: An Ethnohistorical View." Master's thesis, University of Alaska, 1981.

Morrow, James E. "The Effects of Extreme Floods and Placer Mining on the Basic Productivity of Sub Arctic Streams." Report No. IWR-14. Fairbanks, University of Alaska Institute of Water Resources, 1971.

Mouat, Jeremy. *Roaring Days: Rossland's Mines and the History of British Columbia.* Vancouver: University of British Columbia Press, 1995.

Nackenoff, Carol. *The Fictional Republic: Horatio Alger and American Political Discourse.* New York: Oxford University Press, 1994.

Nichols, Jeannette Paddock. "Advertising and the Klondike." *Washington Historical Quarterly* 13 (January 1922): 20–26.

"The Northern Gold Fields." *The Nation,* 29 July 1897, 83.

Nugent, Walter T. K. *Money and American Society, 1865–1880.* New York: Free Press, 1968.

Nussbaum, Arthur. *A History of the Dollar.* New York: Columbia University Press, 1957.

O'Malley, Michael. "Specie and Species: Race and the Money Question in Nineteenth-Century America." *American Historical Review* 99 (April 1994): 369–408.

Osborne, Alice. "Rails Across the Tundra." *Alaska Journal* 2 (summer 1972): 2–12.

Osgood, Cornelius. *The Han Indians: A Compilation of Ethnographic and Historical Data on the Alaska-Yukon Boundary Area.* Yale University Publications in Anthropology No. 74. New Haven: Yale University Department of Anthropology, 1971.

Parker, Genevieve Alice. "The Evolution of Placer Mining Methods in Alaska." B.S. thesis, Alaska Agricultural College and School of Mines, College, Alaska, 1929.

Paul, Rodman. *California Gold: The Beginning of Mining in the Far West.* Lincoln: University of Nebraska Press, 1947.

Poor, Henry V. *Money and Its Laws.* London: Keegan Paul, 1877.

Porsild, Charlene. "Culture, Class, and Community: New Perspectives on the Klondike Gold Rush, 1896–1905." Ph.D. diss., Carleton University, Ottawa, 1994.

———. *Gamblers and Dreamers: Women, Men, and Community in the Klondike.* Vancouver: University of British Columbia Press, 1998.

Price, Jennifer. *Flight Maps: Adventures with Nature in Modern America.* New York: Basic Books, 1999.

Rechcigl, Miloslav, Jr., ed. *Handbook of Nutritive Value of Processed Food.* Vol. 1, *Food For Human Use.* Boca Raton, Fla.: CRC Press, 1982.

Reinicker, Juliette C., ed. *Klondike Letters: The Correspondence of a Gold Seeker in 1898.* Anchorage: Alaska Northwest Publishing Co., 1984.

Republican Congressional Committee. *Republican Campaign Textbook, 1896.* Washington, D.C.: Republican Congressional Committee, 1896.

Republican National Convention. *Official Proceedings of the Eleventh Republican National Convention.* Pittsburgh: James Francis Burke, 1896.

Reynolds, James B., Rodney C. Simmons, and Alan R. Burkholder. "Effects of Placer Mining Discharge on Health and Food of Arctic Grayling." *Water Resources Bulletin* 25 (June 1989): 625–35.

Rickard, T. A. *Man and Metals: A History of Mining in Relation to the Development of Civilization.* Vol. 1. New York: McGraw Hill, 1932.

Rininger, E. M., M.D. "Scourge of the Mining Camps: Typhoid Fever in Alaska." *Alaska Journal* 15 (winter 1985): 29–32.

Ritter, Gretchen. *Goldbugs and Greenbacks: The Antimonopoly Tradition and the Politics of Finance in America.* New York: Cambridge University Press, 1997.

Robbins, William G. *Colony & Empire: The Capitalist Transformation of the American West*. Lawrence: University Press of Kansas, 1994.

Rockoff, Hugh. "The 'Wizard of Oz' as a Monetary Allegory." *Journal of Political Economy* 98 (August 1990): 739–60.

Rodgers, Daniel T. *The Work Ethic in Industrial America, 1850–1920*. Chicago: University of Chicago Press, 1974.

Rodney, William. "Pioneer Dredging in the Klondike." *Alaska Journal* 6 (winter 1976): 50–53.

Roll, Eric. *A History of Economic Thought*. 4th ed. London: Faber, 1973.

Ross, Victor. *A History of the Canadian Bank of Commerce*. Vol. 2. Toronto: Oxford University Press, 1922.

Rust, Clara Hickman. "To Fairbanks by Steamboat." *Alaska Journal* 1 (winter 1971): 20–26.

Sale, Roger. *Seattle: Past to Present*. Seattle: University of Washington Press, 1976.

Scarpa, Ioannis S., and Helen Chilton, eds. *Sourcebook on Food and Nutrition*. Chicago: Marquis Academic Media, 1978.

Schlesinger, Arthur M. Jr., ed. *History of American Presidential Elections, 1789–1968*. 4 vols. New York: Chelsea House, 1971.

Schwantes, Carlos A. *The Pacific Northwest: An Interpretive History*. Lincoln: University of Nebraska Press, 1989.

Schwartz, Anna J., ed. *Money in Historical Perspective*. Chicago: University of Chicago Press, 1987.

Schwatka, Lt. Frederick. *Along Alaska's Great River, Together with the Latest Information on the Klondike Country*. Chicago: G. M. Hill Co., 1898.

Sherwood, Morgan. *Exploration of Alaska, 1865–1900*. New Haven: Yale University Press, 1965; Fairbanks: University of Alaska Press, 1988.

Simmel, Georg. *The Philosophy of Money*. Berlin, 1907. Reprint, trans. by Tom Bottomore and David Frisby, London: Routledge & Kegan Paul, 1978.

Slobodin, Richard. "'The Dawson Boys'—Peel River Indians and the Klondike Gold Rush." *Polar Notes* 5 (June 1963): 24–36.

Sloss, Frank H. "Who Owned the Alaska Commercial Company?" *Pacific Northwest Quarterly* 68 (July 1977): 120–30.

Smith, Adam. *An Inquiry into the Nature and Causes of the Wealth of Nations*. 2 vols. Ed. by R. H. Campbell and A. S. Skinner. Oxford: Clarendon Press, 1976.

Smith, Duane. *Mining America: The Industry and the Environment, 1800–1980*. Lawrence: University Press of Kansas, 1987.

Sokla, Paul J. "'Wrong Foot' Thompson." *Alaska Journal* 4 (winter 1984): 66–81.

Spence, Clark. *The Northern Gold Fleet: Twentieth-Century Gold Dredging in Alaska.* Urbana: University of Illinois Press, 1996.

Spurr, Josiah Edward. *Through the Yukon Gold Diggings: A Narrative of Personal Travel.* Boston: Eastern Publishing Company, 1900.

Still, Richard Ralph. "Historical and Competitive Aspects of Grocery Wholesaling in Seattle, Washington." Doctor of Commercial Science thesis, University of Washington, 1953.

Stone, Thomas. *Miners' Justice: Migration, Law and Order on the Alaska-Yukon Frontier, 1873–1902.* New York: Peter Lang, 1988.

Sturtevant, William C., gen. ed. *Handbook of North American Indians.* Vol. 6, *Subarctic,* ed. by June Helm. Washington, D.C.: Smithsonian Institution, 1981.

———, gen. ed. *Handbook of North American Indians.* Vol. 7, *Northwest Coast,* ed. by Wayne Suttles. Washington, D.C.: Smithsonian Institution, 1990.

Sumner, Francis H., and Osgood R. Smith. "Hydraulic Mining and Debris Dams in Relation to Fish Life in the American and Yuba Rivers of California." *California Fish and Game* 26 (January 1940): 2–22.

Timberlake, Richard. *Monetary Policy in the United States: An Intellectual and Institutional History.* 2d ed. Chicago: University of Chicago Press, 1993.

Tindall, George Brown, ed. *A Populist Reader: Selections from the Works of American Populist Leaders.* New York: Harper & Row, 1966.

Trachtenberg, Alan. *The Incorporation of America: Culture and Society in the Gilded Age.* New York: Hill & Wang, 1982.

Turner, Frederick Jackson. *The Frontier in American History.* New York: Henry Holt and Company, 1920.

Unger, Irwin. *The Greenback Era: A Social and Political History of American Finance, 1865–1879.* Princeton: Princeton University Press, 1964.

Van Nieuwenhuyse, Erwin E., and Jacqueline D. LaPerriere. "Effects of Placer Gold Mining on Primary Production in Subarctic Streams of Alaska." *Water Resources Bulletin* 22 (February 1986): 91–99.

Vilar, Pierre. *A History of Gold and Money, 1450–1920.* Translated by Judith White. London: Verso, 1991.

Wagener, Stephen M, .and Jacqueline D. LaPerriere. "Effects of Placer Mining on the Invertebrate Communities of Interior Alaska Streams." *Freshwater Invertebrate Biology* 4 (November 1985): 208–14.

Walker, Amasa. *The Science of Wealth: Manual of Political Economy.* Philadelphia: Lippincott, 1872.

Walker, Franklin. *Jack London & The Klondike: The Genesis of an American Writer.* San Marino, Calif.: Huntington Library, 1966.

Warner, Iris. "Pioneer Banking at Dawson." *Alaska Journal* 1 (spring 1971): 41–48.

———. "Taylor & Drury, Ltd., Yukon Merchant." *Alaska Journal* 5 (spring 1975): 74–80.

Webb, John Sidney. "The River Trip to the Klondike." *Century Magazine* 55 (February 1898): 685–86.

Webb, Melody. *The Last Frontier: A History of the Yukon Basin of Canada and Alaska.* Albuquerque: University of New Mexico Press, 1985.

Weinstein, Allen. *Prelude to Populism: Origins of the Silver Issue, 1867–1878.* New Haven: Yale University Press, 1970.

Wells, David A. *The Silver Question: The Dollar of the Fathers versus The Dollar of the Sons.* New York: G. P. Putnam's Sons, 1877.

———. *Robinson Crusoe's Money.* Rev. ed. New York: Harper, 1896.

White, Richard. *Land Use, Environment, and Social Change: The Shaping of Island County, Washington.* Seattle: University of Washington Press, 1980.

———. *"It's Your Misfortune and None of My Own": A History of the American West.* Norman: University of Oklahoma Press, 1991.

———. "Animals and Enterprise." In *The Oxford History of the American West,* ed. by Clyde A. Milner II, Carol A. O'Connor, and Martha A. Sandweiss. New York: Oxford University Press, 1994.

———. *The Organic Machine: The Remaking of the Columbia River.* New York: Hill & Wang, 1995.

———. "'Are You an Environmentalist or Do You Work for a Living?': Work and Nature." In *Uncommon Ground: Toward Reinventing Nature,* ed. by William Cronon. New York: W. W. Norton, 1995.

Willis, Bruce L. "The Environmental Effects of the Yukon Gold Rush 1896–1906: Alterations to Land, Destruction of Wildlife, and Disease." Master's thesis, University of Western Ontario, 1997.

Wilson, William H. "To Make a Stake: Fred G. Kimball in Alaska, 1899–1909." *Alaska Journal* 13 (winter 1983): 108–13.

Woodman, Lyman L. "Nome Harbor." *Alaska Journal* 6 (autumn 1976): 199–209.

Worster, Donald. *Dust Bowl: The Southern Plains in the 1930s.* New York: Oxford University Press, 1979.

Wright, Allen A. *Prelude to Bonanza: The Discovery and Exploration of the Yukon.* Sidney, B.C.: Gray's Publishing, Ltd., 1976.

NEWSPAPERS, MAGAZINES, AND TRADE JOURNALS

Alaska Forum (Rampart)

Alaska-Yukon Mining Journal, 1901–1902.

American Monthly Review of Reviews
Argus (Seattle)
Century Magazine
Cosmopolitan
Dawson Daily News, Golden Clean-Up Edition, 1902
Dawson Daily News, Summer Mining Edition, 1899
Harper's Weekly
High Country News (Paonia, Colo.)
Missoulian Online
Munsey's Magazine
The Nation
Overland Monthly
Puck
Rampart (Alaska) *Miner*
San Francisco Examiner
Seattle Post-Intelligencer
Tacoma Daily News
Trade Register (Seattle)
Whitehorse Star

INDEX

Pages with illustrations are indicated in boldface type.

LIBRARY OF CONGRESS CATALOGING-IN-PUBLICATION DATA

Morse, Kathryn Taylor.
The nature of gold : an environmental history of the Klondike gold rush /
Kathryn Morse ; foreword by William Cronon.
p. cm.—(Weyerhaeuser environmental books)
Includes bibliographical references and index.
ISBN 0-295-98329-9 (cloth : alk. paper)

1. Klondike River Valley (Yukon)—Gold discoveries.
2. Alaska—Gold discoveries.
3. Frontier and pioneer life—Yukon Territory—Klondike River Valley.
4. Frontier and pioneer life—Alaska.
5. Klondike River Valley (Yukon)—Environmental conditions.
6. Alaska—Environmental conditions.
7. Gold mines and mining—Environmental aspects—
Yukon Territory—Klondike River Valley.
8. Gold mines and mining—Environmental aspects—Alaska.
9. Gold miners—Yukon Territory—Klondike River Valley—
History—19th century.
10. Gold miners—Alaska—History—19th century.
I. Title.
II. Weyerhaeuser environmental book.
F1095.K5M67 2003   971.9'1—dc21   2003048411